Complete Panjabi

Surjit Singh Kalra
and
Navtej Kaur Purewal
with
Sue Tyson-Ward

The publisher has used its best endeavours to ensure that the
URLs for external websites referred to in this book are correct and
active at the time of going to press. However, the publisher has no
responsibility for the websites and can give no guarantee that a site
will remain live or that the content is or will remain appropriate.

For UK order enquiries: please contact Bookpoint Ltd,
130 Milton Park, Abingdon, Oxon OX14 4SB.
Telephone: + 44 (0) 1235 827720. Fax: + 44 (0) 1235 400454.
Lines are open 09.00–17.00, Monday to Saturday, with a 24-hour
message answering service. Details about our titles and how to
order are available at www.teachyourself.com

For USA order enquiries: please contact McGraw-Hill
Customer Services, PO Box 545, Blacklick, OH 43004-0545, USA.
Telephone: 1-800-722-4726. Fax: 1-614-755-5645.

For Canada order enquiries: please contact McGraw-Hill
Ryerson Ltd, 300 Water St, Whitby, Ontario L1N 9B6, Canada.
Telephone: 905 430 5000. Fax: 905 430 5020.

Long renowned as the authoritative source for self-guided learning –
with more than 50 million copies sold worldwide – the **Teach Yourself**
series includes over 500 titles in the fields of languages, crafts, hobbies,
business, computing and education.

British Library Cataloguing in Publication Data: a catalogue record
for this title is available from the British Library.

Library of Congress Catalog Card Number: on file.

First published in UK 2007 as *Teach Yourself Panjabi* by Hodder Education,
part of Hachette UK, 338 Euston Road, London NW1 3BH.

First published in US 2007 by The McGraw-Hill Companies, Inc.

This edition published 2010.

The **Teach Yourself** name is a registered trademark of Hodder
Headline.

Typeset by MPS Limited, a Macmillan Company.

Printed in Great Britain for Hodder Education, an Hachette UK
Company, 338 Euston Road, London NW1 3BH.

Hachette UK's policy is to use papers that are natural, renewable
and recyclable products and made from wood grown in sustainable
forests. The logging and manufacturing processes are expected to
conform to the environmental regulations of the country of origin.

Impression number 10 9 8 7 6 5 4 3 2 1

Year 2014 2013 2012 2011 2010

Contents

iv

Credits

Meet the authors

Panjabi is my mother tongue, acquired as a first language at home, though in school I studied Urdu along with English in pre-partition India. Later on, I gained qualifications in Hindi and Panjabi, being the national and regional languages respectively. My interest in Panjabi was kindled after migrating to England where I worked as a full-time teacher and part-time lecturer in a training college, as well as gaining experience as a translator and interpreter. I founded and directed the Panjabi Language Development Board in Birmingham, a voluntary organization dedicated to the promotion and development of the Panjabi language. I was integrally involved with various examination bodies in Britain, acting as an examiner, moderator and assessor of different programmes. Ultimately, I retired as Head of South Asian Languages in Birmingham. I have produced copious teaching and learning material in the form of dictionaries, posters, CDs and primers. I am a regular contributor to the internationally read Panjabi newspaper, *Des Pardes*, and have written and published a number of collections of short stories. I served a successful term as the Sikh representative on the Inner Cities Religious Council in the UK.

Surjit S. Kalra

I was born and raised in the US and learned Panjabi as a second language. Ironically, my learning of Panjabi took place largely in the UK where I not only studied and became interested in Panjabi history, culture and literature, but also where I have many relatives and friends, for whom Panjabi is an integral part of everyday life and communication. I studied Hindi during my postgraduate studies at the School of Oriental and African Studies, University of London and then went on to do doctoral research on Panjab (on which my thesis was published), spending extended time in Amritsar. I have continued to do research on social issues in Panjab, spending extensive time in both East Panjab (India) and West Panjab (Pakistan) where the ability to converse in Panjabi was an essential part of both living and doing research. I have a keen interest in Panjabi music, culture and history, not only with respect to Panjabis in Panjab but also to those who are scattered around the globe. Being myself a learner of Panjabi as a second language, I appreciate the different techniques and methods of learning Panjabi which I hope gives this course a user-friendly approach. I currently teach at the University of Manchester in the Department of Sociology.

Navtej K. Purewal

I am a former Subject Officer for Community Language examinations at a National Exam Board. I have extensive experience of teaching, examining and writing foreign language courses and have been delighted to work with Surjit and Navtej on aspects of this course.

Sue Tyson-Ward

....

Acknowledgements

The authors would like to thank a number of people who were involved in different capacities throughout the inception and production of this book. Thanks first go to Dr Virinder S. Kalra, (Manchester University, UK), who gave invaluable guidance, moral and technical support and advice each step of the way. To Balbir K. Kalra, Jas, Nurpreet, Eesher, Gursymrun, Gurtej and Amarjit K. Purewal for their patience and understanding during the entire process. Also, Neelu Kalsi, G. S. Bhogal and Jaswinder Kaur for their vocal contributions in recording the text.

Only got a minute?

The Panjabi language

Panjabi is one of sixteen recognized languages of India and is an official language of the state of Panjab. Panjabi is not only spoken in India and Pakistan but also globally due to the worldwide Panjabi diaspora.

The literal meaning of Panjab is 'land of five rivers'. According to various sources, Panjabi has no fewer than 100 million native speakers throughout the world, making it the 11th most widely-spoken language globally today.

The history of the Panjabi language is significantly old, and the records of Sheikh Farid's poetry of the 12th century have been preserved in the sacred book of the Sikhs, the *Guru Granth Saahib*.

There are many different ways to access Panjabi learning besides educational institutions. In the UK, there are Panjabi settlements which offer good opportunities to learn and practise your spoken Panjabi. Visiting a gurdwara, attending a Panjabi wedding, shopping in a South Asian grocery shop or dining in an Indian restaurant are good opportunities to learn new vocabulary and discover Panjabi culture. Visiting Panjab is another excellent way to improve your Panjabi spoken skills.

The Panjabi sound and script system

Gurmukhi is the most suitable and accurate script to convey the sounds of spoken Panjabi. In this book we have used the Gurmukhi script and for transliteration purposes the Roman script is used. Unlike English, the Gurmukhi script follows a 'one sound – one symbol' principle, though there are some exceptions to this rule.

Colloquial Panjabi

Dialects are offshoots of the main language. There are 12 well-known recognized dialects of Panjab. Majhi dialect of both Indian and Pakistani Panjabs represents the standard Panjabi language.

Panjabi grammar

As you become acquainted with grammar and vocabulary in this course, you will come to understand how the Panjabi language works.

10 Only got ten minutes?

The Panjabi language

Panjabi is one of the sixteen recognized languages of India and is an official language of the state of Panjab. It enjoys a mixed status: it is a means of instruction to informal household speech and extends to academic and literary language. Panjabi is a second language in the adjoining states and union territories like Chandigarh, Himachal Pradesh, Haryana and Delhi. Delhi, the capital of India, is the only city where Panjabi is widely spoken outside Panjab. Even in Ganga Nagar, a neighbouring state of Rajasthan, Panjabi flourishes and is popularly spoken. Globally, India ranks second and Pakistan first as far as population of Panjabi-speakers is concerned. Outside South Asia, Panjabi enjoys second and fourth place among the spoken languages of England and Canada respectively. Though Panjabi is a secular language spoken by Hindus, Sikhs, Muslims and Christians, the Sikh community has a unique association with the Panjabi language because their sacred book is written in Gurmukhi script. Both Panjabi University in Patiala and Guru Nanak Dev University in Amritsar, situated in Panjab have contributed significantly to the development and status of the Panjabi language.

The literal meaning of Panjab is 'land of five rivers' (*panj-* five, *aab-* water). In 1947 Panjab was divided and since then three of the five rivers are in Pakistan and two, namely the Sutlej and Beas, are in India. Panjabi literally means 'belonging to Panjab' whether it is language, people, food, origins, culture or dress. Both spellings, Panjab and Punjab, are acceptable. According to various sources, Panjabi has no fewer than 100 million native speakers worldwide, making it the 11th most widely-spoken language in the world. There are about 60 million speakers of Panjabi in Pakistan, which is nearly half of the population of the country. In Pakistan, Panjabi is written in Persian/Nastaleeq script, also known as Shahmukhi, whereas in India it is written in Gurmukhi script (used in this course). However, in Western countries some people have started using Roman script for the sake of convenience. Lahore is the cultural and political capital of Pakistani Panjab and is the most populous city of native Panjabi speakers in the world. Despite the fact that Panjabi is neither an official nor a religious language of Pakistan, Panjabi remains a popular and vibrant language of the region largely because it is the colloquial language of the masses. The present Indian Panjab, which has 20 districts, is only one-ninth of the area of the 18th century boundaries of Panjab.

Panjabi is not only spoken in East Panjab (India) and West Panjab (Pakistan) but also in many parts of the world where Panjabis have settled. There are many areas where the Panjabi language has become well established, such as the UK, USA, Canada, Kenya, Singapore, and Australia. In these places Panjabi is not only spoken, but is also taught in schools, colleges, community centres and gurdwaras (Sikh places of worship).

Panjabi is a well-known international language because of the Panjabi diaspora throughout the world. Stereotypically, Panjabis are known to be good farmers in peace, excellent soldiers in wartime and have an enthusiasm for migration. The history of the Panjabi language is significantly old, and the records of Sheikh Farid's poetry of the 12th century have been preserved in the sacred book of the Sikhs. Other writings in Panjabi in the form of romantic tales in poetry and verse, idioms, sayings, moral stories, folk songs and religious episodes are passed verbally from one generation to another. Prior to the advent of the Gurmukhi script, early Panjabi literature was written in the Persian/Nastaleeq script. The *Guru Granth Saahib*, the sacred book of the Sikhs, is considered to be the first major book written in Gurmukhi script. At present in India the Panjabi language is making tremendous progress compared with other regional languages in every respect such as production of books, the music industry, media, research and information technology. Panjab is commonly associated with vibrant culture, hearty living and generous hospitality, which accompanies the state of Panjab's performance in India as a state of high agricultural production and relatively high per capita income.

There are many different ways to access Panjabi learning. The internet is an indispensable resource where many websites can be visited. Panjabi media such as satellite, radio stations, cable channels, live entertainment shows and Panjabi newspapers are good sources of learning. If you visit Panjab, you will not only learn Panjabi through everyday interactions and observations but you will also become acquainted with Panjabi culture, as language and culture go together.

If you live in the UK, there are many Panjabi settlements which offer good opportunities to learn and practise your spoken Panjabi. In Birmingham, Bradford, Manchester and London, there are many Indian restaurants, South Asian grocery and sweet shops which can be visited for this purpose. Shopping and tasting food would be quite an enjoyable way of enhancing your vocabulary.

Sometimes it is difficult to translate religious terminology, so if you are interested in learning more about Sikhism, it would be a good idea to pay a visit to a gurdwara to learn the meanings of some of the related Panjabi words. Your visit can serve three purposes: learn new vocabulary; learn about the Sikh religion; and taste Panjabi food. In gurdwaras, Langar (free vegetarian community kitchen cuisine) is served to all visitors irrespective of class, creed, colour, caste, status and religion, and this in itself is a cultural encounter.

Attending a Panjabi wedding is a wonderful experience which provides musical entertainment, an abundance of food, plenty of drink, lively company and an opportunity to learn Panjabi and to find out about wedding ceremonies.

The Panjabi sound and script system

It is ideal to learn a language through its own native script. Gurmukhi is the most suitable and accurate script to convey the sounds of the spoken Panjabi language. In this book we have used the Gurmukhi script and for transliteration purposes, the Roman script. Originally, there were 35 letters in the Panjabi alphabet but subsequently five more were added in order to accommodate the Urdu vocabulary. The present-day Panjabi alphabet has 40 letters, 10 clear pure vowels and three auxiliary signs. Unlike English, the Gurmukhi script follows a 'one sound – one symbol' principle, though there are a few exceptions to this rule. The Panjabi language is read and written from left to right. Moreover, it has neither capitals nor articles such as 'a', 'an' and 'the'. It has no silent letters like 'k' in knife but it has some silent vowels which generally occur in the sacred language. There are a number of Panjabi fonts available to use on the computer which have differing typefaces, some of which are very clear, attractive and decorative. One of the unique features of Panjabi in the variety of modern South Asian languages is the presence of pitch contours. These change the meaning of the word depending on how it sounds. In technical terms, these are called tones and there are three types: low, high and level.

Colloquial Panjabi

Dialects are offshoots of the main language. The difference between a dialect and a standard language is that a dialect is spoken in a small district by the local community which originates from a certain area. There are 12 well-known recognized dialects of Panjab - five of East Panjab (India) and seven of West Panjab (Pakistan). Majhi dialect of both Panjabs is considered to be a prestigious dialect and has the status of representing the standard Panjabi language.

South Asian greetings generally vary according to the religion of the speaker or the religious social context. As India is a vast multi-ethnic country, a variety of greetings from touching the feet of seniors to waving of hands can be observed. Exchanging greetings is not only a part of social etiquette but also a religious obligation. Men shaking hands with ladies is not always socially acceptable. 'Sat̲ sree akaal', 'Namast̲e' and 'Asslaam alekam' are the most common Sikh, Hindu and Muslim greetings respectively.

Both boys and girls of the Sikh faith can have common first names. The second name, however, is gendered, with *Singh* designated for men and *Kaur* for women.

The English language is very popular in India to the extent that common words like bus, station, computer, telephone, etc. have no equivalent words in the vernacular. Panjabis are generally multilingual, so whenever you are stuck for a Panjabi word you can use an English one and take it for granted that others will get a sense of what you are trying to say. This would be quite acceptable.

All languages borrow words from other languages. There are numerous English words which have been adopted by the Indian languages, including Panjabi, such as 'college', 'school', 'platform', 'doctor', 'nurse' and so on. In Panjabi, the word 'ticket' is used in different expressions as in English but it also means a postage stamp. Similarly the English language has also been corrupted by Indian words like khaki, dhobi, guru, samosa and sari. There are some words which have been taken from English but have been modified according to Panjabi pronunciation e.g. police, officer, manager and hospital.

In Panjabi the word 'jee' is often used in different ways. It shows respect and good manners to elders and superiors. It is a sign of formality, politeness and social etiquette. 'Saahib' is another honorific particle like 'jee', which is most commonly used in conversation.

The word 'achchaa' is another common colloquial word used in different situations and contexts. It could mean 'OK', 'fine', 'all right', 'yes', 'nice' and 'good'. It also shows confirmation, acknowledgement, agreement, surprise, anxiety or disbelief.

In Panjabi there is only one word, 'gaddee', which means both 'car' and 'train'. Similarly the word 'kallh' means both 'yesterday' and 'tomorrow'. To get a sense of whether it is being used to refer to the past or future, one can gauge from the tense and context of the sentence.

Panjabi society is religion- and kinship-orientated, and this affects the vast vocabulary associated with relations. For example, Sikhs/Hindus address their mother and father as 'pitaa' and 'maataa', and Muslims address them as 'abbaa' and 'ammee'. The English word 'uncle' signifies five different possible relations in Panjabi. Panjabi is a rich language with a vast vocabulary of specific terms describing the exact nature of extended family relations. It is quite common to address people with whom you wish to express closeness or affection with such terms ordinarily associated with kinship. Examples:

bhaaee saahib (brother), chaachaa jee (uncle), bhainh jee (sister) and bhaabee jee (brother's wife). To address someone senior to you by his/her first name is not considered good social etiquette.

Panjabi grammar: some basics

As you become acquainted with the grammar of Panjabi in this course, you will come to learn a number of different aspects of the language. Here are some general language points which might be helpful to understand the working of the Panjabi language:

A. When the Panjabi word 'vaalaa' is added to nouns, it expresses a relationship between the noun and the object. Examples: sabzee vaalaa = vegetable seller, saarh-h-ee vaalee = the lady wearing a saarh-h-ee, Birmingham vaale = people from Birmingham, London vaaleeaa<u>n</u> = ladies from London.

B. Politeness in Panjabi is expressed in different ways. There are specific words like 'miharbaanee' and 'kirpaa' to represent the words 'thank you' and 'please' but these are not used as frequently as they are in English. In fact the sense of 'please' can also be built into a structure of a Panjabi formal sentence. Politeness is expressed through the mode of address. The quality of language, tone or form of address ranges from very polite to inferior or rude.

C. The Indian calendar is based on the lunar system, and the 12 months of a year have their own equivalent Panjabi names which are reference points for religious days and festivals. Among the Sikh community, the first day of the lunar month is considered to be very auspicious, and more religious-minded people go to gurdwaras (Sikh places of worship) to get blessings for the forthcoming month. In daily speech English month names are commonly used.

D. The word order in Panjabi is quite flexible because of colloquial and stylistic expressions. Usually a Panjabi sentence begins with the subject and ends with a verb, with the object coming in between.

E. There is a clear distinction between formal and informal speech in Panjabi. Plural forms of address are used to show respect even to one addressee.

F. The habitual use of repetitive and echo words is one of the many special characteristics of Panjabi which makes it such an expressive language.

G. The Panjabi words 'utte' (on, at) and 'ate' (and) have the same abbreviation, i.e. te.

H. Names of places, persons and concrete or abstract objects are called nouns. Every noun in Panjabi, even an inanimate object, is assigned a masculine or feminine gender. In logical terms all nouns which represent something seen as male are masculine and those which are seen as female are feminine. But the process of assignment of a gender, especially to inanimate objects, is quite arbitrary. There are many nouns in Panjabi like adhiapak (teacher) and samaaj sevak (social worker) which are grammatically masculine but represent both males and females. The female counterparts of adhiapak and samaaj sevak are adhiaapakaa (lady teacher) and samaaj sevakaa (lady social worker) respectively but are seldom used because of a gender consciousness which generally does not see the need to distinguish.

I. Panjabi nouns can be used in three different cases: direct, oblique and vocative. Let us illustrate this as follows: a. Masculine (mundaa – boy). b. Feminine (kurhee – girl).

	Direct	Oblique	Vocative
Masculine singular	mundaa	munde	mundiaa
Masculine plural	munde	mundiaan	mundio
Feminine singular	kurhee	kurhee	kurhee-e
Feminine plural	kurheeaan	kurheeaan	kurhee-o

The oblique case refers to the changes that some nouns undergo when affected by a proposition. There is no oblique case for the feminine nouns. The vocative case reflects when someone is being addressed.

J. In Panjabi, nouns are affected by both gender and number. Variable nouns are those which change from the singular form when they are plural. Invariable nouns are those which do not change forms ordinarily from the singular to the plural.

K. Singular nouns ending in the masculine gender suffix 'aa' would change to the plural form by replacing 'aa' with 'e', e.g. larhkaa (boy, son) would change to larhke (boys, sons). Singular nouns ending in the feminine gender suffix 'ee' would become plural by adding 'aan', e.g. larhkee (girl, daughter) would change to larhkeeaan (girls, daughters).

L. There are some rules of changing nouns from singular to plural forms but there are also exceptions. Some words like 'hair' (vaal) and 'rice' (chaaval) remain grammatically in the plural form in Panjabi. However, second-language speakers of any language usually follow the rules of their first language to change singular to plural. Note that the plural of 'samosa' in Panjabi is 'samose' but 'samosas' in English.

M. Similar to nouns, adjectives are also either masculine or feminine and are used in singular and plural forms, reflecting the gender and numerical traits of the noun they are describing. There are two types of adjectives, variable and invariable. Variable adjectives change their form according to number and gender but invariable adjectives do not change their form.

N. Sometimes inanimate nouns are used in their colloquial form: e.g. 1. ghar vich = ghare (in the house); 2. pind ton = pindo (from a village); 3. haththaan naal = haththeen (with hands).

O. Prepositions are words such as 'to', 'by', 'on,' 'for' and 'of', which usually have a noun or nouns as their object (e.g. 'to him', 'for the girl'). The Panjabi equivalents of the English preposition are placed *after* nouns and pronouns rather than before. Hence Panjabi has postpositions instead of prepositions: e.g. 1. saver noon = in the morning; 2. tuhaade vaaste = for you.

P. Just as in point N. where inanimate objects can have a colloquial form, the postposition can be omitted from the following words but they would be slightly modified: 1. saver noon = savere (in the morning); 2. dupahir noon = dupahiree (at midday); 3. shaam noon = shaameen (in the evening); 4. raat noon = raateen (at night).

Q. There is no gender distinction in Panjabi pronouns so there is no special word conveying the gender sense of 'him' or 'her' in Panjabi. Only the verb endings give information about the gender of the subject.

The literal meanings of 'ih' and 'uh' are 'he', 'she', 'it' and 'this'/'that' in the singular and 'they', 'these' and 'those' in the plural. 'Uh' refers to a person or persons who are absent or at a distance, whereas 'ih' is used when the person or persons are present or in close proximity.

R. The possessive adjectives in Panjabi change according to what is being possessed: e.g. meraa larhkaa (my son), meree larhkee (my daughter), mere larhke (my sons), mereeaan larhkeeaan (my daughters).

S. Indirect speech in Panjabi is expressed with the particle 'ki' (that) to denote what was actually said or done.

T. The infinitive form of every verb consists of two parts - the root and the ending. The infinitive form of 'likhnhaa' (to write) has two parts: 'likh' is the root and 'nhaa' is the ending. You will come across a variety of endings of Panjabi verbs, depending upon the tense and the subject.

U. The infinitive form of the verb 'to be' is 'honhaa' (ho + nhaa). The auxiliary form of 'to be' (is, am, are) is 'hai', 'han', 'haan' and 'ho' in the present, 'see' and 'san' (was, were) in the past, and 'gaa', 'gee', 'geeaan' and 'ge' (will, would) in the future tense.

Introduction

Geographically, the present-day area of Panjab is divided between the nation states of India and Pakistan (see Map 1 below). This division took place in 1947 upon the departure of the British from colonial rule of the sub-continent. While the language and culture of East and West Panjab are similar, there are religious differences, with Muslims being the predominant group in Pakistan Panjab, Hindus and Sikhs in Indian Panjab, and a substantial Christian minority in both parts. Panjab has come to some prominence in the West because of the long history of migration from the region to the four corners of the world.

1. Panjab (Map 2, p. xxi)
2. Pakistan
3. India
4. Nepal
5. Bhutan
6. Sri Lanka
7. Bangladesh

Map 1 Indian sub-continent

There are, therefore, mainly three areas of the world where Panjabi is spoken; in East Panjab (India) where it is a state language, in West Panjab (Pakistan) where it is most widely spoken and in the diaspora, particularly Britain, North America, East Africa and Australasia. This wide geographic spread of the language is ironic given the fact that the word Panjabi – also spelt Punjabi – designates the language of the 'Panj – ab', the 'Five Rivers'. These are the Jhelum, Chenab, Ravi, Beas and the Satluj (see Map 2).

No accurate figures are available on the number of Panjabi speakers, either as a first or second language, but if the three Panjabs and various dialects are taken into account an approximation of 100 million would not be too far from the truth. One of the main problems with designating the exact number of Panjabi speakers is the presence of a large number of distinct dialects that are spoken across the large geographical area of East and West Panjab. There are many recognized dialects of Panjabi: Majhi, Doabi, Powadhi, Malwi, Multani (Siraiki), Putohari and Hindko. The last three can arguably call Panjabi a dialect of themselves and are all spoken in the Pakistan part of Panjab. In the diaspora the most spoken form of Panjabi is the Doabi, and encompasses those speakers from the Jalandhar area of East Panjab.

Given the great variety of Panjabi there is some debate as to what is standard. This book is based upon the Majhi dialect which is the everyday form used in Lahore and Amritsar. The most important point is that once you have mastered the language using this book you will be understood across Panjab. The language used here is neither the colloquial rural nor the urban literary, as the focus of this course has been on developing an ability to communicate in as many different situations as possible.

One of the more interesting facts about the Panjabi language is that where it is numerically the most widely spoken, in Pakistani Panjab, it is hardly written at all. Panjabi is most often written in East Panjab in the Gurmukhi script. It is also possible to write the language in the Persian script often referred to as Shahmukhi in this context. However, in the last 100 years or so, Panjabi has become closely associated with Sikhs and Sikhism, thus Gurmukhi has also become associated with Panjabi. Gurmukhi literally means 'proceeding from

Map 2 Panjab and the 'Five Rivers'
Source: Mawi and Tiwana, 1990

the mouth of the Guru', and it is widely acknowledged that Guru Angad, the second Sikh Guru (AD 1504–1552), began the process of modifying existing scripts of the time, laying the basis for the modern Panjabi alphabet that is used in this book.

Despite the modern day usage of Gurmukhi, the first Panjabi literature was written in Shahmukhi, and popular history associates this writing with Shaikh Farid and Goraknath. However, the literary period of the language begins with the sacred scriptures of the Sikhs, the *Guru Granth Saahib*. This collection of writings by the Sikh Gurus is probably the first manuscript of the Panjabi language. After the period of the Gurus, it was the Sufi poets who developed the Panjabi language. In fact it is the folk literature developed by the Sufis, and particularly the Quissa – love ballad form – which has had a long and lasting impact on the development of Panjabi literature. The stories of Heer-Ranjha and Mirza Saahiba are deeply embedded in the everyday life and culture of Panjab.

During the period of British colonial rule, the advent of the printing press saw the proliferation of the Panjabi language in the Gurmukhi script. Pamphlets, journals, novels and short stories all began to appear at the beginning of the 20th century using the Panjabi typewriter. However, the official language of the time was either English or Urdu. The division of Panjab in 1947 between East (India) and West (Pakistan) and subsequently of East Panjab in 1966 led to the formation of the State of Panjab in the Indian Union. Panjabi is the official language of communication in East Panjab and the modern development of the language has been greatly accelerated by state patronage. Indeed, the development of Panjabi University in Patiala is one such example of state sponsorship.

Language may be the basis of culture, but there are many other aspects of Panjabi society and everyday life that impinge on the use of language. We have included a Commentary section in each unit which will introduce various aspects of the social and cultural life of the three Panjabs, although these are by no means exhaustive discussions of the rich culture of Panjab and the Panjabi diaspora.

How to use this course

Who is this course for?

This course in Panjabi has been designed for the absolute beginner who may or may not have studied a language before. The course will be useful for people who want to learn Panjabi in order to speak with their Panjabi friends and relatives, to communicate with Panjabi communities in relation to their work, to learn about aspects of Panjabi culture and society or to travel to Panjab itself. The course will also be useful for those who already know a little Panjabi but who may not have the confidence to speak and even for those fluent in spoken Panjabi but who wish to learn to read and write the Gurmukhi script. Throughout the course you will come across a number of different situations in which you will learn how to make requests, ask and give information and to express your feelings. The units include dialogues, language points and background information about Panjab and Panjabi people both in the region of Panjab as well as in other parts of the world where Panjabi communities have settled.

The course is divided into two parts. The first part (Units 1–10) is specifically designed for those who want to learn the basics of grammar and vocabulary in order to communicate in a simple manner and also enable you to read and write simple sentences. The second part (Units 11–16) will help you to expand your knowledge of spoken Panjabi further and is designed for those who are committed to becoming proficient in the Gurmukhi script.

Overall, the course introduces you to a wide range of vocabulary and covers the basic grammar of Panjabi. By the end of the course, you will be able to understand the spoken language, communicate in Panjabi in a number of everyday situations while also having a sufficient level of understanding of the written language to begin to read newspapers and to write letters. We hope that this course will be the beginning of your journey into the world of the Panjabi language.

How to use this course

The structure of the book is outlined in the contents pages. It is recommended that you read the introductory chapters before proceeding with the course. The Panjabi script and sound system follows this section and it is advisable to work through this section regardless of whether you intend to learn the script or not. Through this section you will gain practice of listening, speaking and reading which will help you for the rest of the course. After the script chapter, the book is divided into 16 units. The pattern of each unit is as follows:

- First there is an outline in English of what you will learn in the unit.
- ਗੱਲ ਬਾਤ gall baat (Dialogue): Each unit has two or three dialogue passages containing situations and commonly used speech which include the vocabulary and grammar to be covered in that unit. In the first part (Units 1–10) the dialogues use Gurmukhi, Roman script and English translations. In the remainder of the book (Units 11–16) the dialogues are only in Gurmukhi and English. However, Roman script is maintained in the vocabulary sections throughout the book.
- ਸ਼ਬਦਾਵਲੀ shabdaavalee (Vocabulary): The vocabulary sections follow each Dialogue and include all new words, and sometimes key expressions, which appear in the dialogue text. All nouns are denoted according to their masculine or feminine (m./f.) gender in parentheses and all adjectives which vary according to gender and number are identified with a (v.).
- ਅਭਿਆਸ abhiaas (Exercises): These follow the vocabulary and often make reference to the dialogues that they follow. There is a range of different exercises including true/false, matching, comprehension, 'fill in the blanks' and crosswords.
- ਬੋਲੀ ਬਾਰੇ bolee baare (Language points): These sections cover the main grammar points which appear in the dialogues. Each new grammar point is explained clearly using examples to illustrate. Often, English equivalents to the Panjabi are given alongside the explanations.

- ਵਿਆਖਿਆ viaakhiaa (Commentary): These sections introduce you to various aspects of Panjabi culture which have been touched upon in the content of the dialogues. These will help you to become acquainted with colloquial speech, social etiquette and Panjabi history, traditions and customs.
- ਅਭਿਆਸ abhiaas (Exercises): Further exercises come at the end of each unit and review some of the main vocabulary, content and grammatical elements that were introduced in that unit. While the exercises that come after the dialogues in the units do not contain references to grammar, the exercises at the end of the units may test you on your ability to use the grammar you have learned.

At the end of the book there is a key to the exercises so that you can check your answers. There is also a Panjabi–English glossary which will be of use to you throughout the course in referring to the English definitions of Panjabi words which appear in the units.

How to study each unit

- Read the summary at the beginning of each unit to learn about what will be covered.
- Study the dialogues using the vocabulary lists for words that you do not understand and then read the dialogues out loud.
- Read the Commentary section which will give you the relevant background to the dialogues.
- Complete the exercises which follow the dialogues and vocabulary. Check your answers with the key to the exercises at the end of the book.
- Go through the grammar sections to understand the new grammar points introduced.
- After learning the grammar, read the dialogue again to make sure that you fully understood the content.
- Go back to the dialogue and repeat it as often as you can, acting out the roles of the different characters.
- Complete the exercises at the end of the unit, checking your answers with the key to the exercises at the end of the book.

How to use the course with the recording

The book is accompanied by a recording which will help you to recognize and distinguish the Panjabi sound system and also to improve your listening and speaking abilities. While the book is in itself a complete course, the recording will be an added advantage for all Panjabi learners as it contains pronunciation exercises, dialogues from the units and oral comprehension activities based on the ਅਭਿਆਸ abhiaas (Exercises).

As you begin to go through the first part of the book (Units 1–10), you should listen to the recording of each ਗੱਲ ਬਾਤ gall baat (Dialogue) as you read it. Listen to it again without looking at the book once you have understood the general meaning. This will allow you to pay attention to the pronunciation and intonation of the speakers. Imitating the speakers in the dialogues is a useful way of picking up the language quickly. As you progress through the course to the second part (Units 11–16), you should try to listen to the dialogue on the recording without reading it in the book.

Symbols and abbreviations

◄⟩	recording
m.	masculine
f.	feminine
v.	variable adjective
sing.	singular
plu.	plural
lit.	literally
form.	formal
inform.	informal

The Panjabi script and sound system

Introduction

Panjabi is most commonly written in the Gurmukhi script, which is the most complete and accurate way to represent Panjabi sounds. Unlike English, the Gurmukhi script follows a 'one sound–one symbol' principle. There are a few exceptions to this rule and these will become apparent throughout the book. However, with some practice you will be able to recognize the characters and know their names and sounds. Ultimately, with even a basic knowledge of the sound system, you will be able to read and write Panjabi in the Gurmukhi script.

The Gurmukhi alphabet has 40 letters including 37 consonants and three basic vowel sign bearers. There are ten clear pure vowels and three auxiliary signs. The most striking characteristic of the Gurmukhi script, in comparison with English, is that, with the exception of five, all letters are joined by a line across the top. Like English and other European, Latin-based languages, it is written and read from left to right. However, there are neither capital letters in Panjabi nor articles such as 'a' and 'the'. Panjabi spellings are, for the most part, regular and relatively simple to learn, though you may come across variations in spellings of some words, since Panjabi spellings are not fully standardized.

Handwritten Panjabi, as with any script, differs from person to person in style. Some people prefer to write Panjabi without lifting a pen, making curves and having an irregular top line. It is up to the individual as to what sort of style he or she wants to adopt. Our advice to new learners is to follow the simple, clear style of lettering. There are a number of Panjabi fonts available online, some of which are very clear, attractive and decorative.

Equivalent sounds which have been given in Romanized (English) script are only approximate since the Gurmukhi alphabet has many unfamiliar sounds to the English speaker which often may not be exactly represented by the English alphabet. It is hoped that you will use the recording, attend classes, or seek help from a native speaker so as to perfect your pronunciation and to familiarize yourself with the sounds. In order to learn any language it is important to follow these basic rules: listen carefully, repeat out loud and distinctly, and do not worry about making mistakes. Apart from unfamiliar sounds, there are nasal and double sounds, intonation, stress and different dialects which might initially dishearten the student. However, with a little practice, you will begin to enjoy learning Panjabi.

Transliteration

The standard modern system of transliteration (the writing of Panjabi in the Roman alphabet) is used in this book with some modifications. As there are 40 letters, ten vowel sounds and three auxiliary signs in Panjabi, it is necessary to adapt the standard English alphabet. You will note two ways of distinguishing letters:

1 by a combination of two English letters such as rh, kh, bh, nh, etc. In those few cases where these letters appear together but *not* in combination, for instance, a 'r' and 'h' appear together, a '-' is shown between those letters.

2 by underlining, for example, the letter n (n) indicates nasalization or underlining ch (ch) indicates an aspirated sound.

However, you will come across some words in this book which are so commonly written and recognized in English that we have used their conventional spellings, such as *gurdwara*, *Amritsar* and *kebab*.

Consonants

The Panjabi alphabet

South Asian languages are richly endowed with sounds and consonants. Sanskrit may have been one of the first languages to group the letters according to their sounds. At one time there were only 35 letters in the Panjabi script, but later five more letters were added in order to accommodate Urdu sounds correctly. This need arose because of the many loan words from Urdu used in Panjabi. More recently, an extra character (.ਲ਼ l) was introduced, though it has not become popular and hence will not be included in this book. The complete Panjabi alphabet is given in Table A.

Table A   Panjabi alphabet

ੳ	ਅ	ੲ	ਸ	ਹ
—	a	—	s	h
ਕ	ਖ	ਗ	ਘ	ਙ
k	kh	g	gh	ng
ਚ	ਛ	ਜ	ਝ	ਞ
ch	<u>ch</u>	j	jh	nj
ਟ	ਠ	ਡ	ਢ	ਣ
t	th	d	dh	nh
ਤ	ਥ	ਦ	ਧ	ਨ
t	<u>th</u>	<u>d</u>	<u>dh</u>	n
ਪ	ਫ	ਬ	ਭ	ਮ
p	ph	b	bh	m
ਯ	ਰ	ਲ	ਵ	ੜ
y	r	l	w/v	rh
ਸ਼	ਖ਼	.ਗ	ਜ਼	ਫ਼
sh	<u>kh</u>	<u>gh</u>	z	f

It is quite possible to learn the characters of the Gurmukhi script (ਗੁਰਮੁਖੀ ਲਿਪੀ gurmukhee lipee) and sounds of the language at the same time as, by and large, Panjabi is a phonetic language. It is more accurate to call the Panjabi writing system a syllabary because each character represents a syllable. It is important to note that two phonetic features of all North Indian languages are the system of contrasts between aspirated and unaspirated consonants and the contrast between retroflex and dental consonants. These do not occur in English. Aspirated consonants are accompanied by an audible expulsion of breath, whereas non-aspirated consonants are those produced with minimal breath. The letter 'k' in the word 'kit' and 't' in the word 'top' come close to Panjabi aspirated consonants. The problem for English speakers arises with non-aspirated consonants. To get an idea of the difference between the two, try saying the words 'kit' and 'top' while holding your breath. In dental consonants the tongue touches the upper front teeth, whereas with the retroflex consonants the tip of the tongue curls upwards against the palate (see diagrams in Appendix 2). The nearest approximations to English are the 't' sound in the word 'eighth' which is dental-like and the 'd' in the word 'breadth' which is retroflex-like.

There is a range of technical terms used to describe the pronunciation of Panjabi consonants. For those who are interested in technical and linguistic matters these can be found in Appendix 1. The important thing is to be able to distinguish between the different consonants. The recording or the help of a native speaker are invaluable tools in this process.

Panjabi syllabary

The syllabary in Table B gives the Panjabi letters in groups, according to pronunciation.

Table B   Panjabi syllabary

Gurmukhi	Transliteration	Pronunciation
ਸ	s	as 's' in 'sun'.
ਹ	h	this 'h' sound as in 'ahead' is the simplest form, although there is considerable variety, which will be discussed later.
ਕ	k	as 'k' in 'sky', but with less release of breath.
ਖ	kh	as 'k' in 'kit' but with stronger release of breath. No English equivalent.
ਗ	g	as 'g' in 'go' but with less release of breath.
ਘ	gh	as 'gh' in 'ghost' said quickly. No English equivalent.

ਙ	ng	as 'ng' in 'sing'. No English equivalent.
ਚ	ch	as 'ch' as in 'cheese' but with less release of breath.
ਛ	<u>ch</u>	strongly aspirated form of 'ch'. No English equivalent.
ਜ	j	as 'j' in 'jeer' but with less release of breath and with the tongue against the lower teeth.
ਝ	jh	the stronger aspirated counterpart of the above, somewhat like 'bridge'. No English equivalent.
ਞ	nj	representing the palatal nasal sound. No English equivalent.
ਟ	t	as 't' in 'train' but with the tongue further back and with less release of breath.
ਠ	th	the strongly aspirated counterpart of the above. No English equivalent.
ਡ	d	as 'd' in 'drum' but with tongue further back and with less release of breath.
ਢ	dh	strongly aspirated form of the above. No English equivalent.
ਣ	nh	representing the retroflex nasal sound. No English equivalent.
ਤ	<u>t</u>	unaspirated soft 't'. No English equivalent.
ਥ	<u>th</u>	as 'th' in 'thermos', strongly aspirated form of the above.
ਦ	<u>d</u>	as 'th' in 'then' with less release of breath.
ਧ	<u>dh</u>	strongly aspirated form of the above. No English equivalent.
ਨ	n	as 'n' in 'nice' but with the tongue flatter against the front teeth.
ਪ	p	as 'p' in 'spin' but with less release of breath.
ਫ	ph	as 'f' in 'fund', aspirated form of the above, though many Panjabi speakers pronounce 'ph' as 'f'.

ਬ	b	as 'b' in 'bin' but with less release of breath.
ਭ	bh	as 'bh' in 'club-house' spoken quickly. No English equivalent.
ਮ	m	as 'm' in 'mother'.
ਯ	y	as 'y' in 'yet'.
ਰ	r	as 'r' in 'motor'. This sound is always fully voiced and never lost like the English 'r'.
ਲ	l	as 'l' in 'life'.
ਵ	v/w	this sound lies between the English sounds 'v' and 'w'. However, unlike the English 'v' the lower lip hardly touches the upper teeth; unlike the English 'w' there is no lip-rounding. For transliteration purposes we only use 'v'.
ੜ	rh	no English equivalent.
ਸ਼	sh	as 'sh' in 'ship'.
ਖ਼	<u>kh</u>	similar to 'ch' in Scottish 'loch'. No English equivalent.
ਗ਼	<u>gh</u>	no English equivalent.
ਜ਼	z	as 'z' in 'zip'.
ਫ਼	f	as 'f' in 'find'.

Consonants with a dot

It is also important to note the distinction between plain consonants and those consonants which are marked by a dot, as shown in Table C.

Table C Consonants with dots

ਸ	ਸ਼	ਖ	ਖ਼	ਗ	ਗ਼	ਜ	ਜ਼	ਫ	ਫ਼
s	sh	kh	<u>kh</u>	g	<u>gh</u>	j	z	ph	f

These letters are named by adding the words ਪੈਰੀਂ ਬਿੰਦੀ **paireen bindee** to the name of the letter, so ਸ਼ is called ਸੱਸੇ ਪੈਰੀਂ ਬਿੰਦੀ **sasse paireen bindee,** which literally means sassa with a dot in its foot. Many Panjabi speakers do not make a distinction between ਖ ਖ਼, ਗ ਗ਼, and ਫ ਫ਼. There are two main reasons for this: first, their pronunciation is quite similar and second, they are used to differentiate borrowed words from Urdu, the knowledge of which is decreasing in East Panjab. You may come across written texts in which writers have not used the dot. In this book, however, we have maintained its use.

Subjoined consonants

Some Panjabi words require consonants to be written in a conjunct form, which takes the shape of a subscript to the main letter. The second consonant is written under the first as a subscript. The reason for this is discussed after we have looked at Panjabi vowels. There are only three commonly used subjoined letters (see Table D) and to distinguish them from their normal forms the word ਪੈਰੀਂ **paireen**, which means *belonging to the foot*, is attached under the letter.

Table D   Subjoined consonants

Full letter	Name of full letter	Subjoined letter	Name of subjoined letter	Transliteration
ਹ	ਹਾਹਾ haa-haa	੍ਹ	ਪੈਰੀਂ ਹਾਹਾ paireen haahaa	h
ਰ	ਰਾਰਾ raaraa	੍ਰ	ਪੈਰੀਂ ਰਾਰਾ paireen raaraa	r
ਵ	ਵੱਵਾ vavvaa	੍ਵ	ਪੈਰੀਂ ਵੱਵਾ paireen vavvaa	v

For the purposes of transliteration there is no special sign for the subjoined character so you will have to pay careful attention to the Panjabi spelling.

Nasalization

There are five nasal consonants in Panjabi:

• ਙ ng   • ਞ nj   • ਣ nh   • ਨ n   • ਮ m

As shown in the syllabary, the nasal consonants belong to the five different classes of consonants. Nasalization is produced by directing a substantial part of the breath towards the nasal cavity as the letter is being uttered. In addition there are two nasalization signs in Panjabi which accompany consonants:

- ਬਿੰਦੀ bindee •   • ਟਿੱਪੀ tippee ੰ

These will be dealt with in detail later.

Pronunciation of consonants

Most letters in Panjabi have a fixed pronunciation, however some are variable and this depends on their position in a word. Consider the letters in Table E.

Table E   Pronunciation of consonants

	ਘ	ਝ	ਢ	ਧ	ਭ
	gh	jh	dh	dh	bh
Sound at beginning of word	ਕ	ਚ	ਟ	ਤ	ਪ
	k	ch	t	t	p
Sound in middle or at end of word	ਗ	ਜ	ੜ	ਦ	ਬ
	g	j	d	d	b

Perhaps the most variable pronunciation of a single consonant in Panjabi is that of the letter ਹ *h*. Words beginning with ਹ *h* and those where no vowel precedes or affects it, carry the *h* sound as it would be used in English. For instance:

ਹਕੂਮਤ hakoomt *government*   ਹਕੀਮ hakeem *doctor*

However, when ਹ *h* is used in the middle of a word following consonants and vowels its pronunciation is varied. We will return to this point after considering the vowel symbols and sounds.

Vowels

There are ten vowels in Panjabi in contrast to the English five (*a, e, i, o, u*). Panjabi vowels are generally pronounced as they are written, following the one sign – one sound rule. They are pure vowels making only one sound. However, there are two forms that vowels can take.

The independent vowel form which does not require a consonant and the dependent form which is attached to a consonant. All consonants use the dependent form of the vowel. Tables F and G show the dependent vowels on their own and combined with the letter ਸ *s*.

◀) CD 1, TR 1, 03:02

Table F   Dependent vowels on their own

	Vowel sign		Name of vowel	
1	invisible	a	ਮੁਕਤਾ	muktaa
2	ਾ	aa	ਕੰਨਾ	kannaa
3	ਿ	i	ਸਿਹਾਰੀ	sihaaree
4	ੀ	ee	ਬਿਹਾਰੀ	bihaaree
5	ੁ	u	ਔਂਕੜ	aunkarh
6	ੂ	oo	ਦੁਲੈਂਕੜੇ	dulainkarhe
7	ੇ	e	ਲਾਂਵ	laanv
8	ੈ	ai	ਦੁਲਾਂਵਾਂ	dulaanvaan
9	ੋ	o	ਹੋੜਾ	horhaa
10	ੌ	au	ਕਨੌੜਾ	kanaurhaa

◀) CD 1, TR 1, 03:18

Table G   Dependent vowels in combination with *s*

Consonant and vowel sign		Pronunciation
ਸ	sa	*a* in ahead
ਸਾ	saa	*a* in part
ਸਿ	si	*i* in it
ਸੀ	see	*ee* in see
ਸੁ	su	*u* in put
ਸੂ	soo	*oo* in food
ਸੇ	se	*a* in cake
ਸੈ	sai	*a* in man
ਸੋ	so	*o* in show
ਸੌ	sau	*o* in bought

You may note that the vowels are divided into five pairs. In the first three, the distinction is between a short and long sound, for example between *u* and *oo*. In the last two pairs the distinction is between closed and open sounds so *e* is closed and *ai* is open sounding.

Short *a* sound – 'muk̲taa'

We have seen that in Panjabi there are ten vowels and they are represented by nine symbols. The vowel **muk̲taa** has no equivalent sign to be used with consonants. The individual consonant expresses its own sound and also implies an *a* sound with it. This means that, unlike English, words can be formed with consonants only without using any visible vowel. Each consonant has an inherent sound, making it a syllable on its own. However, there is no symbol for this sound in Panjabi, though we have chosen to represent **muk̲taa** with the letter *a* for purposes of transliteration. Examples of the use of **muk̲taa** can be found in many borrowed words from English, for example: ਕਪ **kap**, *cup*, and ਮਗ **mag**, *mug*.

The inherent *a* is not pronounced in three main positions:

- at the end of a word, e.g. ਕਾਰ **kaar**
- with a subjoined consonant, e.g. ਸ੍ਰੀ **sree**
- at a syllable break, e.g. ਗਰਦਨ ਗਰ-ਦਨ **gar–d̲an**

Independent vowels

The independent form can occur in three ways. First, when the vowel comes at the beginning of a word or a syllable; second, in those instances where two vowel sounds are required, as a consonant cannot support two vowels; and third, in a diphthong – when two vowels are present in one syllable. In fact one of the features of Panjabi is the presence of many diphthongs, sometimes with three vowel sounds in one word with no consonants, for instance ਆਇਆ **aaiaa** (*he*) *came*.

Independent vowels are represented by dependent vowels carried by the first three letters of the Panjabi alphabet:

◀» CD 1, TR 1, 03:50

ੳ ਉੜਾ oorhaa	ਅ ਐੜਾ airhaa	ੲ ਈੜੀ eerhee

They are never used on their own and do not represent any consonant sounds. They *must* be accompanied by their allocated vowel signs. Their main function is to denote their own respective vowel sounds. They are founder, basic or parent vowel bearers representing the ten sounds.

However, the pronunciation of both independent and dependent vowels is the same (see Table H).

◀) CD 1, TR 1, 4:00

Table H   Independent vowel

	Formula	Example word	Trans-literation	Meaning
̶	u is added to ੳ to give ਉ	ਉਪਜ	upaj	*production*
̤	oo is added to ੳ to give ਊ	ਊਠ	ooth	*camel*
̖	o is added to ੳ to give ਓ	ਓਟ	ot	*shelter*
	Invisible sign 'a' is added to ਅ	ਅਮਰ	amar	*immortal*
ਾ	aa is added to ਅ to give ਆ	ਆਟਾ	aataa	*flour*
ੈ	ai is added to ਅ to give ਐ	ਐਨਕ	ainak	*spectacles*
ੌ	au is added to ਅ to give ਔ	ਔਰਤ	aura<u>t</u>	*woman*
ਿ	i is added to ੲ to give ਇ	ਇਨਾਮ	inaam	*prize*
ੀ	ee is added to ੲ to give ਈ	ਈਸਾ	eesaa	*Jesus*
ੇ	e is added to ੲ to give ਏ	ਏਕਤਾ	ek<u>t</u>aa	*unity*

Silent vowel signs

In English there are some silent or soft spoken consonants, for example *r* and *k*. There are no such consonants in Panjabi; however, there are silent vowels. These are not often found in modern Panjabi but occur often in the sacred language of Sikh religious texts. Silent vowels give special meaning to the word they are referring to. The most common use of the silent vowel you will come across is in the Sikh greeting ਸਤਿ ਸ੍ਰੀ ਅਕਾਲ **sat**(i) **sree akaal**. Note that the **sihaaree** in the word ਸਤਿ has no effect on the pronunciation, however its presence does alter the meaning:

• ਸਤ sa<u>t</u>   *extract*   • ਸੱਤ sa<u>tt</u>   *seven*   • ਸਤਿ sa<u>t</u>(i)   *true*

In this example we have included the silent vowel in brackets for purposes of illustration; however, throughout the rest of the book the silent vowel is not included in the transliterated text.

Tones

One of the unique features of Panjabi, in the variety of modern South Asian languages, is the presence of pitch contours. These change the meaning of the word depending on the way it sounds. In technical terms these are called 'tones' and there are three types: low, high and level. The Panjabi tone system is far less complex than Chinese, the best known tone language. The low tone is characterized by lowering the voice below the normal pitch and then rising back in the following syllable. In the high tone the pitch of the voice rises above its normal level, falling back at the following symbol. The level tone is carried by the remaining words. Tones are not represented by any letters or symbols in the Gurmukhi script. In this course we are not marking words with tone signs, as we believe this will create confusion. The best manner to learn tonality is from repetition from the recording or listening and imitating native speakers.

Table I illustrates how tone can change the meaning of a word.

Table I Tone illustrations

◄◙ CD 1, TR 1, 04:34

Low tone			Level tone			High tone		
ਝਾ	jhaa	*peep*	ਚਾਅ	chaa-a	*desire*	ਚਾਹ	chaah	*tea*
ਘੋੜਾ	ghorhaa	*horse*	ਕੋੜਾ	korhaa	*whip*	ਕੋਹੜਾ	kohrhaa	*leper*
ਘੜੀ	gharhee	*watch*	ਕੜੀ	karhee	*link of a chain*	ਕੜ੍ਹੀ	karhhee	*turmeric curry*

Return of ਹ 'haahaa'

We have already noted the variable pronunciation of the consonant ਹ *h*. Now that we have covered vowels and tones, we can return to look at some of the other varieties of **haahaa's** pronunciation.

1 When ਹ is preceded by a **sihaaree** the pronunciation of the vowel changes to resemble **dulaanvaan**. For instance the word ਸ਼ਹਿਰ

shahir is pronounced ਸ਼ੈਹਰ **shair**. The pronunciation of the word is therefore converted into a high tone.

2 When ਹ is accompanied by **auṇkarh**, the pronunciation of the word changes to resemble **kanaurhaa**. For instance the word ਬਹੁਤ **bahut** is pronounced ਬੌਹਤ **bauht**, once again changing the word to a high tone.

3 In a similar manner, when the letter preceding the ਹ has either the **auṇkarh** or **sihaaree** vowel attached, then the pronunciation of the word changes so as to produce the **horhaa** and **laaṇv** vowels respectively. For example: ਸੁਹਣਾ **suhnhaa** is pronounced as ਸੋਹਣਾ **sohnhaa** and ਸਿਹਤ **sihat** is pronounced as ਸੇਹਤ **sehat**.

Subjoined consonants revisited

As we previously noted, a few Panjabi words require consonants to be written in a subjoined form, which takes the shape of a subscript to the main letter. The reason for this is to indicate that the inherent **muktaa** vowel is not present. Where vowels are present on the first letter, these are meant to be applied to the subjoined consonant. Therefore, in the word ਪ੍ਰੇਮ **prem**, there is no *a* symbol in the transliteration indicating the absence of the **muktaa**. The **laaṇv** vowel is applied to the *r* in the foot of the *p*. Note that the pronunciation of the subjoined consonant is the same as the normal consonant.

Auxiliary signs

The double sound ਅਧਕ 'adhak' ੱ

◄) CD 1, TR 1, 04:53

The function of the ਅਧਕ **adhak** ੱ is to allocate a double sound to the particular letter that it is assigned to. It should be placed above the preceding letter that is to be read twice; however, in practice it is placed between the two letters. Therefore, when the **adhak** occurs between two letters, it is the second of the two that is to be repeated. For example, in the Panjabi word for **thigh**, ਪੱਟ **patt**, the **adhak** affects the letter ਟ *t* changing the sound of the word from **pat** to **patt**. In some cases another vowel sound may come in between the two letters, but the adhak still affects the second letter, for example in the word ਬੱਚਿਓ bachchio, the adhak comes before the sihaaree vowel but still affects the letter ਚ ch, so it is pronounced chch. The adhak is a very important, though subtle device, as two letters without an adhak give rise to completely different meanings. For example ਪਗ pag means *foot*, whereas ਪੱਗ pagg means *turban*. A similar effect can be seen in English with the words *super* and *supper*.

Nasal sounds: ਬਿੰਦੀ 'bindee' ਂ and ਟਿੱਪੀ 'tippee' ੰ

◀)) CD 1, TR 1, 05:10

The bindee and the tippee both serve to add a nasal sound to a particular vowel. The bindee is used with kannaa, laanv, dulaan-vaan, bihaaree, horhaa and kanaurhaa and the independent forms of vowels where ੳ is the bearer. For example: ਗਾਂ gaan *cow*.

The tippee is used with the muktaa, sihaaree, aunkarh and dulainkarhe. For example: ਖੰਡ khand *sugar*.

The sound of the tippee and bindee is almost equivalent to the *n* in *pound* or *bangle*. However, their sound varies from the almost totally nasalized to a more fully pronounced *n* sound. For transliteration purposes the letter *n* is used for both the tippee and bindee.

Panjabi loan words

The Panjabi language has a substantial number of words which have been borrowed from the English language, for example *school*, *college*, *telephone*, *bus*, *pen*, *pencil*, *chalk*, *ticket* and *computer*. Moreover, some Panjabi words have been adopted by English, including *chutney*, *pandit*, *kebab*, *samosa*, *saree*, *dhobi* and *guru*. Some English words borrowed by Panjabi have also been altered by Panjabi pronunciation and you will notice in the transliteration that English words and names have been written with this in mind.

Dictionary order

The letters in Panjabi dictionaries are arranged in the order of Table A, reading left to right, as are the order of words within each letter. The exceptions to this rule are those letters which are distinguished by a dot, that is ਸ਼, ਖ਼, ਗ਼, ਜ਼ and ਫ਼, as these letters occur within the non-dotted form. Subjoined letters are not differentiated from the full form. Dictionary order in the Gurmukhi script is based upon phonology as vowels precede consonants. Therefore, the vowel signs follow muktaa, kannaa, sihaaree, bihaaree, aunkarh, dulainkarhe, laanv, dulaanvaan, horhaa, kanaurhaa.

Writing

Panjabi words are made up partly of consonants and partly of vowel signs. Letters are written first and then the sound symbols. Panjabi punctuation is similar to that used in English. However, one distinct difference is that in Panjabi a vertical stroke is used at the end of a sentence to mark a full stop. For example: *My name is Ritu.* ਮੇਰਾ ਨਾਮ ਰਿਤੂ ਹੈ ।

There are ten vowels represented by nine signs. Their positions relating to consonants are as follows ‑ ⹀ are written beneath the letter; ੇ ੈ ੍ are written above the letter; ਿ is written on the left of the letter, while ਾ and ੀ are written on the right. The three auxiliary signs ੱ ੰ ੑ are written above the letter. Panjabi is best written on lined paper initially. In English the letters rest on the line, whereas in Panjabi the horizontal headstroke is written upon the line, the characters then hang from the line, in much the same way as clothes hang from a washing line.

Panjabi alphabet ਪੰਜਾਬੀ ਵਰਣਮਾਲਾ ਗੁਰਮੁਖੀ ਲਿਪੀ
panjaabee varanhmaalaa gurmukhee lipee

Letter	Name of letter		Sign of letter
ੳ	ਉੜਾ	oorhaa	—
ਅ	ਐੜਾ	airhaa	a
ੲ	ਈੜੀ	eerhee	—
ਸ	ਸੱਸਾ	sassaa	s
ਹ	ਹਾਹਾ	haahaa	h
ਕ	ਕੱਕਾ	kakkaa	k

ਖ	ਖੱਖਾ	khakhkhaa	kh
ਗ	ਗੱਗਾ	gaggaa	g
ਘ	ਘੱਗਾ	ghaggaa	gh
ਙ	ਙੰਙਾ	nganngaa	ng
ਚ	ਚੱਚਾ	chachchaa	ch
ਛ	ਛੱਛਾ	<u>ch</u>a<u>ch</u>chaa	<u>ch</u>
ਜ	ਜੱਜਾ	jajjaa	j
ਝ	ਝੱਜਾ	jhajjaa	jh
ਞ	ਞੰਞਾ	nja<u>n</u>njaa	nj
ਟ	ਟੈਂਕਾ	tai<u>n</u>kaa	t
ਠ	ਠੱਠਾ	thaththaa	th
ਡ	ਡੱਡਾ	daddaa	d
ਢ	ਢੱਡਾ	dhaddaa	dh
ਣ	ਣਾਣਾ	nhaanhaa	nh
ਤ	ਤੱਤਾ	<u>t</u>a<u>tt</u>aa	<u>t</u>
ਥ	ਥੱਥਾ	<u>th</u>a<u>th</u>thaa	<u>th</u>
ਦ	ਦੱਦਾ	<u>d</u>a<u>dd</u>aa	<u>d</u>
ਧ	ਧੱਦਾ	<u>dh</u>a<u>dd</u>aa	<u>dh</u>
ਨ	ਨੱਨਾ	nannaa	n
ਪ	ਪੱਪਾ	pappaa	p
ਫ	ਫੱਫਾ	phaphphaa	ph
ਬ	ਬੱਬਾ	babbaa	b
ਭ	ਭੱਬਾ	bhabbaa	bh
ਮ	ਮੱਮਾ	mammaa	m
ਯ	ਯੱਯਾ	yayyaa	y
ਰ	ਰਾਰਾ	raaraa	r
ਲ	ਲੱਲਾ	lallaa	l
ਵ	ਵੱਵਾ	vavvaa	v
ੜ	ੜਾੜਾ	rhaarhaa	rh
ਸ਼	ਸ਼ੱਸ਼ਾ	shashshaa	sh
ਖ਼	ਖ਼ੱਖ਼ਾ	<u>kh</u>a<u>kh</u>khaa	<u>kh</u>
ਗ਼	ਗ਼ੰ ਗ਼ਾ	<u>gh</u>a<u>ghgh</u>aa	<u>gh</u>
ਜ਼	ਜ਼ੱਜ਼ਾ	zazzaa	z
ਫ਼	ਫ਼ੱਫ਼ਾ	faffaa	f

Script diagrams

Relationship between independent and dependent vowels:

Independent	ਅ	ਆ	ਇ	ਈ	ਉ	ਊ	ਏ	ਐ	ਓ	ਔ
Dependent		–	ਾ	ਿ	ੀ	ੁ	ੂ	ੇ	ੈ	ੋ	ੌ
Transliteration	a	aa	i	ee	u	oo	e	ai	o	au

Sample reading and writing lessons

Section 1 ਮੁਕਤਾ ਅ 'mukṯaa a'

The vowel **mukṯaa** has no visible symbol in the Gurmukhi script. For transliteration purposes it is represented by the letter *a*.

Reading

1 ਕਰਮ, ਕਪ, ਕਮਰ
  karam, kap, kamar
  Karam, cup, Kamar

2 ਕਮਲ ਮਗ ਭਰ
  kamal, mag bhar
  Kamal, fill the mug.

3 ਅਮਰ, ਚਰਚ ਚਲ
  amar, charach chal
  Amar, go to church.

4 ਮਲਕ, ਜਗ ਭਰ
  malak, jag bhar
  Malik, fill the jug.

Writing pattern

Exercises

◀) CD 1, TR 1, 05;45

1 Read the following sentences out loud and check your pronunciation with the recording.

a	ਕਪ ਭਰ ਕਰਮ	c	ਭਰ ਜਗ ਮਲਕ
b	ਮਗਾ ਭਰ ਕਮਲ	d	ਚਰਚ ਚਲ ਕਮਰ

2 Copy out the following words:

a ਕਮਲ   **b** ਚਰਚ   **c** ਜਗ

Section 2 ਕੰਨਾ ਆ ा 'kannaa aa'

The dependent form of the ka<u>nn</u>aa vowel is placed to the right of the letter that is affected. For transliteration purposes it is represented by the symbol *aa*.

Reading

1 ਸ਼ਾਮ ਕਾਕਾ, ਵਾਲ ਵਾਹ
shaam kaakaa, vaal vaah
Sham little boy comb hair.

2 ਰਾਮ, ਬਸ ਫੜ
raam, bas pharh
Ram, catch the bus.

3 ਚਾਚਾ, ਘਰ ਆ
chaachaa, ghar aa
Uncle, come home.

4 ਨਾਨਾ, ਅਨਾਰ ਖਾ
naanaa anaar khaa
Grandfather, eat the pomegranate.

Writing pattern

Exercises

🔊 **CD 1, TR 1, 06:00**

1 Read the following sentences out loud and check your pronunciation with the recording.

a ਨਾਨਾ ਬਸ ਫੜ	c ਕਾਕਾ ਘਰ ਆ
b ਸ਼ਾਮ ਵਾਲ ਵਾਹ	d ਚਾਚਾ ਅਨਾਰ ਖਾ

2 Copy out the following words:

a ਬਸ   b ਸ਼ਾਮ   c ਨਾਨਾ

Section 3 ਅਧਕ 'adhak' ੱ

The ਅਧਕ 'adhak' ੱ should be placed above the preceding letter that is to be read twice; in practice, however, it is placed in between the two letters. Therefore, when the **adhak** occurs between two letters it is the second letter of the two that is to be repeated. For transliteration purposes the **adhak** has the effect of doubling the consonant affected.

Reading

1 ਅੱਖ, ਪੱਟ, ਲੱਤ
akhkh, patt, la<u>tt</u>
eye, thigh, leg

2 ਸ਼ਾਮ, ਪੱਗ ਰੱਖ
shaam, pagg rakhkh
Sham, put on the turban.

3 ਅੱਠ ਹੱਥ
athth ha<u>thth</u>
eight hands

4 ਸੱਤ ਨੱਕ
sa<u>tt</u> nakk
seven noses

Writing pattern

Exercises

🔊 **CD 1, 06;20**

1 Read the following words out loud and check your pronunciation with the recording.

a ਸ਼ਾਮ ਪੱਗ ਰੱਖ	c ਸੱਤ ਹੱਥ
b ਅੱਠ ਨੱਕ	d ਅੱਖ, ਲੱਤ, ਪੱਟ

2 Copy out the following words:

a ਪੱਟ   **b** ਅੱਠ   **c** ਹੱਥ

Section 4 ਸਿਹਾਰੀ ਇ ਿ 'sihaaree i'

The dependent form of the **sihaaree** vowel is placed to the left of the letter being affected. For transliteration purposes it is represented by the letter *i*.

Reading

1 ਕਿਰਨ, ਇੱਟ, ਇੱਕ, ਕਿੱਲ
kiran, itt, ikk, kill
Kiran, brick, one, nail

2 ਜਿੱਲ, ਸਿੱਧਾ ਲਿਖ
jill, si<u>dhdh</u>aa likh
Jill, write straight.

3 ਦਿਲਬਰ, ਰਿੱਛ ਗਿਣ
<u>dilbar</u>, <u>richch</u> ginh
Dilbar, count the bears.

4 ਇਹ ਚਾਰ ਹਿਰਨ ਹਨ
ih chaar hiran han
These are four deer.

Writing pattern

ੲ → ੨ ੲ ੲ   ਛ → ੨ ੲ ੲ

ਪ → ੯ ੲ ਪ   ੲ → ੫ ੲ ੲ

ਦ → ੨ ੲ

Exercises

◀) CD 1, TR 1, 06:33

1 Read the following sentences out loud and check your pronunciation with the recording.

a ਇੱਕ ਇੱਟ   **c** ਦਿਲਬਰ ਕਿੱਲ ਗਿਣ
b ਕਿਰਨ ਸਿੱਧਾ ਲਿਖ   **d** ਇਹ ਚਾਰ ਰਿੱਛ ਹਨ

2 Write the names in Gurmukhi of the items in the pictures:

a ri<u>chch</u>   **b** kill   **c** hiran

Section 5 ਬਿਹਾਰੀ ਈ ੀ 'bihaaree ee'

The dependent form of the **bihaaree** vowel is placed to the right of the letter that is being affected. For transliteration purposes it is represented by the letter *ee*.

Reading

1 ਸੀਟੀ, ਡੱਬੀ, ਵਾਲੀ, ਸੀਤਾ
seetee, dabbee, vaalee, seetaa
whistle, small box, earring, Sita

2 ਰੀਟਾ, ਗਲੀਚਾ ਸਾਫ਼ ਕਰ
reetaa, ghaleechaa saaf kar
Rita, clean the rug.

3 ਚਾਚੀ ਖ਼ਤਾਈ ਲਿਆਈ
chaachee <u>kh</u>ataaee liaaee
Aunty has bought a biscuit.

4 ਈਸ਼ਰ ਦੀ ਬਿੱਲੀ ਕਾਲੀ ਸੀ
eeshar <u>d</u>ee billee kaalee see
Eesher's cat was black.

Writing pattern

Exercises

◄) CD 1, TR 1, 06:49

1 Read the following sentences out loud and check your pronunciation with the recording.

a ਰੀਟਾ ਬਿੱਲੀ ਲਿਆਈ   **c** ਚਾਚੀ ਗਲੀਚਾ ਲਿਆਈ

b ਸੀਤਾ ਖ਼ਤਾਈ ਲਿਆਈ   **d** ਈਸ਼ਰ ਸੀਟੀ ਲਿਆਈ

2 Write the names in Gurmukhi of the items in the pictures:

     a seetee   **b** billee   **c** vaalee

Section 6 ਔਂਕੜ ੁ 'au<u>n</u>karh u'

The dependent form of the vowel **au<u>n</u>karh** is placed under the letter to be affected. For transliteration purposes it is represented by the letter *u*.

Reading

1 ਦੁੱਧ, ਢੱਕਣ, ਸੁਖ, ਪੀ
<u>dudhdh</u>, dhakkanh, sukh, pee
milk, lid, Sukh, drink

3 ਯੁਵਕ, ਜ਼ਬਾਨ ਨਾ ਕੱਢ
yuvak, zabaan naa kadhdh
Young boy! Do not stick out your tongue.

2 ਉਪਕਾਰ, ਉੱਨ ਲਿਆ
upkaar, unn liaa
Upkar, bring the wool.

4 ਗੁਲਾਬ, ਚੁੱਪ ਕਰ
gulaab, chupp kar
Gulab, keep quiet.

Writing pattern

Exercises

1 Read the following sentences out loud and check your pronunciation with the recording.

1

a ਸੁਖ ਢੱਕਣ ਲਿਆ	**c** ਯੁਵਕ ਦੁੱਧ ਪੀ
b ਗੁਲਾਬ ਉੱਨ ਲਿਆ	**d** ਉਪਕਾਰ ਚੁੱਪ ਕਰ

2 Write the name in Gurmukhi of the items in the pictures:

a dhakkanh	**b** zabaan	**c** unn

Section 7 ਦੁਲੈਂਕੜੇ ◌ੂ = '<u>d</u>ulain<u>k</u>arhe oo'

The dependent form of the vowel <u>d</u>ulain<u>k</u>arhe appears under the letter being affected. For purposes of transliteration the symbol *oo* is used to represent the <u>d</u>ulain<u>k</u>arhe.

Reading

1 ਸੂਰ, ਫੜ, ਝਾੜੂ, ਭੂਪ
soor, pharh, jhaarhoo, bhoop
pig, hold, broom, Bhup

2 ਰੂਪ, ਆੜੂ ਖਾ
Roop, aarhoo khaa
Rup, eat the peach.

3 ਸਰੂਪ ਦਾ ਊਠ
Saroop <u>d</u>aa ooth
Sarup's camel

4 ਅਨੂਪ, ਮੂਰਤ ਬਣਾ
Anoop, moora<u>t</u> banhaa
Anup, draw a picture.

Writing pattern

Exercises

◀) CD 1, TR 1, 07:26

1 Read the following sentences out loud and check your pronunciation with the recording.

a ਸਰੂਪ ਦਾ ਊਠ	**c** ਅਨੂਪ ਆੜੂ ਖਾ
b ਰੂਪ ਮੂਰਤ ਬਣਾ	**d** ਭੂਪ ਝਾੜੂ ਫੜ

2. Write the names in Gurmukhi of the items in the pictures:

a ooth   **b** soor   **c** jhaarhoo

Section 8 ਲਾਂਵ ਏੇ 'laanv e'

The dependent form of the vowel **laanv** is placed on top of the affected letter. For transliteration purposes the letter *e* will be used to symbolize the **laanv**.

Reading

1 ਲੇਲੇ, ਪਿਆਰੇ, ਭੇਡ, ਮੇਰਾ
lele, piaare, bhed, meraa
lambs, beloved, sheep, my

2 ਇਹ ਛੇ ਮੇਜ਼ ਹਨ
ih che mez han
These are six tables.

3 ਉਹ ਜੇਨ ਦਾ ਸੇਬ ਏ
uh jen daa seb e
That is Jane's apple.

4 ਡੇਵਿਡ, ਸ਼ੇਰ ਦੇਖ
devid, sher dekh
David, look at the lion.

Exercises

◀) CD 1, TR 1, 07:43

1 Read the following sentences out loud and check your pronunciation with the recording.

   a ਇਹ ਛੇ ਲੇਲੇ ਹਨ   **c** ਇਹ ਮੇਰਾ ਸੇਬ ਏ
   b ਲੇਲੇ ਪਿਆਰੇ ਹਨ   **d** ਉਹ ਭੇਡ ਏ

2 Fill in the blanks by writing the correct words in Gurmukhi:

   a _____ lele   **b** _____ bhed   **c** _____ seb

Section 9 ਦੁਲਾਂਵਾਂ ਐ `' 'dulaanvaan ai'

The dependent form of the vowel <u>dulaanvaan</u> is written on top of the affected letter. For transliteration purposes the symbol *ai* is used to represent <u>dulaanvaan</u>.

Reading

1 ਸਵੈਟਰ, ਬੈਗ, ਜਰਨੈਲ, ਪੈਰ
svaitar, baig, jarnail, pair
sweater, bag, Jarnail, foot

2 ਇਹ ਐਨਕ ਲੈ
ih ainak lai
Have these spectacles.

3 ਅੱਜ ਐਤਵਾਰ ਹੈ
ajj ai<u>t</u>vaar hai
Today is Sunday.

4 ਇਹ ਕੈਮਰਾ ਮੇਰੀ ਭੈਣ ਦਾ ਹੈ
ih kaimraa meree bhainh <u>d</u>aa hai
This is my sister's camera.

Exercises

◀) CD 1, TR 1, 08:00

1 Read the following sentences out loud and check your pronunciation with the recording.

a ਇਹ ਕੈਮਰਾ ਜਰਨੈਲ ਦਾ ਹੈ   **c** ਇਹ ਬੈਗ ਮੇਰੀ ਭੈਣ ਦਾ ਹੈ
b ਇਹ ਮੇਰਾ ਸਵੈਟਰ ਹੈ   **d** ਇਹ ਐਨਕ ਲੈ

2 Fill in the blanks by writing the correct words in Gurmukhi:

a _____ bhainh   **b** _____ ai<u>t</u>vaar   **c** _____ ainak

Section 10 ਹੋੜਾ ਓ ` 'horhaa o'

The dependent form of the vowel **horhaa** appears above the affected letter. For transliteration purposes the letter *o* is used to represent **horhaa**.

Reading

1 ਖੋਤਾ, ਮੋਟਾ, ਘੋੜਾ, ਸੋਟੀ
kho<u>t</u>aa, mo<u>t</u>aa, ghorhaa, sotee
donkey, fat, horse, stick

2 ਸੋਹਣ ਕੋਲ ਤੋਤਾ ਹੈ
sohanh kol <u>t</u>o<u>t</u>aa hai
Sohan has a parrot.

3 ਰੋਟੀ ਖਾ ਮੋਹਨ
rotee khaa mohan
Eat your food Mohan.

4 ਆਓ ਬੱਚਿਓ ਮੋਰ ਦੇਖੋ
aao bachchio mor <u>d</u>ekho
Come on children, look at the peacock.

Exercises

◄) CD 1, TR 1, 08:25

1 Read the following sentences out loud and check your pronunciation with the recording.

a ਸੋਹਣ ਰੋਟੀ ਖਾ   c ਮੋਹਨ ਕੋਲ ਘੋੜਾ ਹੈ
b ਥੋਤਾ ਮੋਟਾ ਹੈ   d ਆਓ ਬਾੱਚਿਓ ਤੋਤਾ ਦੇਖੋ

2 Fill in the missing letters in Gurmukhi:

a _____ ਤਾ khoṭaa   b _____ ਟਾ motaa   c _____ ੜਾ ghorhaa

Section 11 ਕਨੌੜਾ ਔ ` 'kanaurhaa au'

The dependent form of the **kanaurhaa** vowel appears above the affected letter. For transliteration purposes the symbol *au* is used to represent **kanaurhaa**.

Reading

1 ਫੌਜੀ, ਪੌੜੀ, ਬਲੌਰ, ਦੌੜ
faujee, paurhee, balaur, ḍaurh
soldier, ladder, playing marbles, run

2 ਸ਼ਰਨ ਕੌਰ, ਚੌਲ ਉਬਾਲ
sharan kaur, chaul ubaal
Sharan Kaur, boil the rice.

3 ਉਹ ਔਰਤ ਕੌਣ ਹੈ
uh aurat kaunh hai?
Who is that woman?

4 ਇਹ ਮੇਰੇ ਖਿਡੌਣੇ ਹਨ
ih mere khidaunhe han
These are my toys.

Exercises

◄) CD 1, TR 1, 08:43

1 Read the following sentences out loud and check your pronunciation with the recording.

a ਚੌਲ ਉਬਾਲ   c ਉਹ ਫੌਜੀ ਹੈ
b ਉਹ ਕੌਣ ਹੈ ?   d ਇਹ ਮੇਰੇ ਬਲੌਰ ਹਨ

2 Fill in the missing letters and vowels in Gurmukhi:

a _____ ਲ chaul   b ਖਿ _____ ਣੇ khidaunhe   c _____ ਜੀ faujee

Section 12 ਬਿੰਦੀ 'bindee' ˙ and ਟਿੱਪੀ 'tippee' ˚ 'n'

The **bindee** and the **tippee** both serve to add a nasal sound to a particular vowel. For transliteration purposes, the letter _n_ is used for both the **tippee** and **bindee**.

Reading

1 ਸਿੰਘ, ਚੁੰਜ, ਮੂੰਹ
singh, chunj, moonh
lion, beak, mouth

2 ਅੰਬ, ਜੰਞ, ਲੰਙਾ
anb, jannj, lanngaa
*mango, marriage party,
    lame person*

3 ਕਾਂ, ਗੇਂਦ, ਕੈਂਚੀ, ਮੀਂਹ
kaan, gend, kainchee, meenh
crow, ball, scissors, rain

4 ਹੋਠ, ਪੌਂਡ, ਉਂਗਲੀ, ਵਤਾਊਂ
honth, paund, unglee, vataaoon
lips, pound, finger, aubergine

Writing pattern

Exercises

🔊 **CD 1, TR 1, 09:01**

1 Read the following words out loud and check your pronunciation with the recording.

   a ਸਿੰਘ, ਜੰਞ, ਕੈਂਚੀ   **c** ਮੂੰਹ, ਅੰਬ, ਮੀਂਹ
   b ਚੁੰਜ, ਲੰਙਾ, ਉਂਗਲੀ   **d** ਕਾਂ, ਗੇਂਦ, ਵਤਾਊਂ

2 Fill in the missing letters and vowels in Gurmukhi:

   a ਜ＿＿＿jannj   **b** ਲ＿＿＿lanngaa   **c** ਵ＿＿＿vataaoon

1

ਤੁਹਾਡਾ ਕੀ ਹਾਲ ਹੈ ?

ṯuhaadaa kee haal hai?

How are you?

In this unit you will learn:

- How to use simple greetings
- How to introduce yourself
- How to ask how people are

1 *What is your name?*

ਗੱਲ ਬਾਤ ੧ ਤੁਹਾਡਾ ਕੀ ਨਾਮ ਹੈ ?

gall baaṯ 1 ṯuhaadaa kee naam hai?

🔊 **CD 1, TR 2, 00:15**

It is the first day of the new Panjabi class at Heywood College. Mr Charan Singh is the teacher and Jane, Henry and David are students.

ਚਰਨ ਸਿੰਘ **Charan Singh**	ਸਤਿ ਸ੍ਰੀ ਅਕਾਲ ਜੀ ! saṯ sree akaal jee! *Hello!* (see Commentary section)
ਜੇਨ **Jane**	ਸਤਿ ਸ੍ਰੀ ਅਕਾਲ ਜੀ ! saṯ sree akaal jee! *Hello!*
ਚਰਨ ਸਿੰਘ **Charan Singh**	ਮੇਰਾ ਨਾਮ ਚਰਨ ਸਿੰਘ ਹੈ । ਤੁਹਾਡਾ ਕੀ ਨਾਮ ਹੈ ? meraa naam charan singh hai. ṯuhaadaa kee naam hai? *My name is Charan Singh. What's your name?* (to Jane)

ਜੇਨ	ਜੀ ਮੇਰਾ ਨਾਮ ਜੇਨ ਹੈ ।
Jane	jee meraa naam jen hai.
	My name is Jane.
ਚਰਨ ਸਿੰਘ	ਅੱਛਾ! ਤੁਹਾਡਾ ਕੀ ਨਾਮ ਹੈ ?
Charan Singh	a<u>chch</u>aa. <u>t</u>uhaadaa kee naam hai?
	OK! What's your name? (to Henry)
ਹੈਨਰੀ	ਜੀ ਮੇਰਾ ਨਾਮ ਹੈਨਰੀ ਹੈ ।
Henry	jee meraa naam hainree hai.
	My name is Henry.
ਚਰਨ ਸਿੰਘ	ਸ਼ਾਬਾਸ਼!
Charan Singh	shaabaash!
	Well done!

David and Jane exchange greetings in an informal manner.

ਜੇਨ	ਸਤਿ ਸ੍ਰੀ ਅਕਾਲ । ਮੇਰਾ ਨਾਂ ਜੇਨ ਏ । ਤੇਰਾ ਕੀ ਨਾਂ ਏ ?
Jane	sa<u>t</u> sree akaal. meraa naa<u>n</u> jen e. <u>t</u>eraa kee naa<u>n</u> e?
	Hello. My name is Jane. What's your name?
ਡੇਵਿਡ	ਸਤਿ ਸ੍ਰੀ ਅਕਾਲ । ਮੇਰਾ ਨਾਂ ਡੇਵਿਡ ਏ ।
David	sa<u>t</u> sree akaal. meraa naa<u>n</u> devid e.
	Hello. My name is David.

ਸ਼ਬਦਾਵਲੀ	**shab<u>d</u>aavalee**	*Vocabulary*
ਤੁਹਾਡਾ	<u>t</u>uhaadaa	*your* (formal)
ਕੀ	kee	*what*
ਨਾਮ	naam	*name* (m.) (formal)
ਹੈ	hai	*is* (formal)*
ਸਤਿ ਸ੍ਰੀ ਅਕਾਲ	sa<u>t</u> sree akaal	Sikh greeting (lit. God is truth)
ਜੀ	jee	honorific particle signifying respect (see Commentary)
ਮੇਰਾ	meraa	*my*
ਅੱਛਾ	a<u>chch</u>aa	*OK, all right*
ਸ਼ਾਬਾਸ਼	shaabaash	*well done*
ਤੇਰਾ	<u>t</u>eraa	*your* (informal)
ਨਾਂ	naa<u>n</u>	*name* (m.) (informal)
ਏ	e	*is* (informal)*

*The ways in which *is*, *am* and *are* are formed in Panjabi will be referred to in Unit 2.

Insight

'*Shaabaash*' '**ਸ਼ਾਬਾਸ਼**' is a colloquial word, most often used to praise and encourage children or students. Normally it is a compliment given by elders to younger people and not vice versa.

ਅਭਿਆਸ abhiaas *Exercises*

After reading the dialogue and/or listening to the recording, try to do the following exercises.

1 True or false?

◀) CD 1, TR 2, 01:32

a	ਤੁਹਾਡਾ	<u>t</u>uhaadaa	means *your*	True/False
b	ਮੇਰਾ	meraa	means *my*	True/False
c	ਅੱਛਾ	a<u>chch</u>aa	means *well done*	True/False

2 Arrange in correct word order

a	ਮੇਰਾ ਹੈ ਡੇਵਿਡ ਨਾਂ	meraa-hai-devid-naa<u>n</u>	*My name is David.*
b	ਤੁਹਾਡਾ ਹੈ ਨਾਮ ਕੀ ?	<u>t</u>uhaadaa-hai-naam-kee?	*What is your name?*
c	ਨਾਂ ਏ ਕੀ ਤੇਰਾ ?	naa<u>n</u>-e-kee-<u>t</u>eraa?	*What is your name?*

---

2 *How are you?*
ਗੱਲ ਬਾਤ ੨ ਤੁਹਾਡਾ ਕੀ ਹਾਲ ਹੈ ?
gall baa<u>t</u> 2 <u>t</u>uhaadaa kee haal hai?

◀) CD 1, TR 2, 02:01

Parveen and Talat meet each other in the city centre. Parveen is with her brother Rahim and sister Salma.

ਪਰਵੀਨ	ਅੱਸਲਾਮ ਅਲੈਕਮ । ਤੁਹਾਡਾ ਕੀ ਹਾਲ ਹੈ ?
Parveen	asslaam alaikam. <u>t</u>uhaadaa kee haal hai?
	Hello. How are you?

ਤਲਤ **Talat**	ਵਾਲੈਕਮ ਅੱਸਲਾਮ। ਮੇਰਾ ਹਾਲ ਠੀਕ ਹੈ। vaalaikam asslaam. meraa haal theek hai. *Hello. I'm fine.*
ਪਰਵੀਨ **Parveen**	ਇਹ ਮੇਰਾ ਭਰਾ ਹੈ ਅਤੇ ਇਹ ਮੇਰੀ ਭੈਣ ਹੈ। ih meraa bharaa hai ate ih meree bhainh hai. *This is my brother and this is my sister.*
ਤਲਤ **Talat**	ਕੀ ਤੁਹਾਡਾ ਪਰਵਾਰ ਠੀਕ ਹੈ? kee <u>t</u>uhaadaa parvaar theek hai? *Is your family all right?*
ਸਲਮਾ ਤੇ ਰਹੀਮ **Salma and Rahim**	ਸ਼ੁਕਰੀਆ। ਸਾਡਾ ਪਰਵਾਰ ਠੀਕ ਹੈ। shukreeaa. saadaa parvaar theek hai. *Thank you. Our family is fine.*
ਤਲਤ **Talat**	ਖ਼ੁਦਾ ਹਾਫ਼ਿਜ਼। <u>kh</u>u<u>d</u>aa haafiz. *Goodbye.*
ਰਹੀਮ, ਸਲਮਾ ਤੇ ਪਰਵੀਨ **Rahim, Salma and Parveen**	ਖ਼ੁਦਾ ਹਾਫ਼ਿਜ਼। <u>kh</u>u<u>d</u>aa haafiz. *Goodbye.*

ਸ਼ਬਦਾਵਲੀ	**shab<u>d</u>aavalee**	*Vocabulary*
ਹਾਲ	haal	*condition* (lit.) (m.)
ਹੈ	hai	*is*

ਤੁਹਾਡਾ ਕੀ ਹਾਲ ਹੈ?	<u>t</u>uhaadaa kee
	    haal hai?
		How are you?
		    (see Commentary)

ਅੱਸਲਾਮ ਅਲੈਕਮ	asslaam alaikam	Muslim greeting

ਵਾਲੈਕਮ ਅੱਸਲਾਮ	vaalaikam
	    asslaam
		response to Muslim
		    greeting

ਠੀਕ	theek	*fine/OK/all right*
ਇਹ	ih	*this*
ਭਰਾ	bharaa	*brother* (m.)
ਅਤੇ	a<u>t</u>e	*and*
ਭੈਣ	bhainh	*sister* (f.)
ਪਰਵਾਰ	parvaar	*family* (m.)
ਸ਼ੁਕਰੀਆ	shukreeaa	*thank you* (m.)
ਸਾਡਾ	saadaa	*our*
ਖ਼ੁਦਾ ਹਾਫ਼ਿਜ਼	<u>kh</u>u<u>d</u>aa haafiz	Muslim departing phrase

Insight

Across South Asia, many greetings have a religious connotation, such as '*namaste*' 'ਨਮਸਤੇ', '*saṯ sree akaal*' 'ਸਤਿ ਸ੍ਰੀ ਅਕਾਲ' and '*aslaam alaikam*' 'ਅੱਸਲਾਮ ਅਲੈਕਮ'. After the independence of India, a new greeting was coined – '*jai hind*' 'ਜੈ ਹਿੰਦ'(victory to India) – which is secular in nature but did not gain popularity. The other greetings continue to be used most widely.

ਅਭਿਆਸ abhiaas *Exercises*

After reading the dialogue and/or listening to the recording, try to do the following exercises.

1 Begin the conversation

◀) CD 1, TR 2, 02:52

a ਵਾਲੈਕਮ ਅੱਸਲਾਮ।
vaalaikam asslaam.
Hello.

b ਮੇਰਾ ਹਾਲ ਠੀਕ ਏ।
meraa haal theek e.
I am fine.

c ਜੀ, ਪਰਵਾਰ ਠੀਕ ਹੈ।
Jee, parvaar theek hai.
The family is fine.

2 Match the expressions

a ਮੇਰਾ ਭਰਾ	meraa bharaa	**1**	*our family*
b ਮੇਰੀ ਭੈਣ	meree bhainh	**2**	*my brother*
c ਸਾਡਾ ਪਰਵਾਰ	saadaa parvaar	**3**	*my sister*

ਬੋਲੀ ਬਾਰੇ   bolee baare   *Language points*

Possessive adjectives

1 Adjectives are words which describe people, places and objects. The words *my*, *your* and *his/her* are possessive adjectives. Unlike in English, the possessive adjective in Panjabi changes according to what is being possessed. In Dialogues 1 and 2 the word ਹਾਲ **haal** (*condition*) is grammatically masculine and therefore requires a masculine possessive adjective. Similarly, a woman talking about her children will use two forms of the word *my*, distinguishing between her son and daughter. ਮੇਰਾ **meraa** would apply to the male and ਮੇਰੀ **meree** for the female. Note that it is the ending which changes. This distinction is the same even if the father were talking about his son and daughter.

Examples:

Mother talking about her children:

ਮੇਰਾ ਲੜਕਾ ਠੀਕ ਹੈ।	meraa larhkaa theek hai.	*My son is fine.*
ਮੇਰੀ ਲੜਕੀ ਠੀਕ ਹੈ।	meree larhkee theek hai.	*My daughter is fine.*

Father talking about his children:

ਮੇਰਾ ਲੜਕਾ ਠੀਕ ਹੈ।	meraa larhkaa theek hai.	*My son is fine.*
ਮੇਰੀ ਲੜਕੀ ਠੀਕ ਹੈ।	meree larhkee theek hai.	*My daughter is fine.*

You will have noticed that there is no difference between the sentences spoken by the mother and the father. The form of the possessive adjective does not depend on the gender of the possessor (i.e. whether male or female) but on the gender of what is being possessed. In addition to gender, possessive adjectives also change according to whether the possessed object is singular or plural. As both parents are talking about one person, the possessive adjective is in the *singular* form.

There are, therefore, three factors which need to be taken into account when selecting the appropriate possessive adjective:

- whether the object is masculine or feminine
- whether the object is singular or plural
- whether the situation is formal or informal

2 In addition to describing objects, possessive adjectives are also used to describe different states of being, i.e. how you are, how you are feeling or other personal descriptions such as your name. You will remember from Dialogue 2 that Parveen uses the possessive adjective *your* when asking her friend Talat *How are you?* The literal meaning of this question in Panjabi is *How is your condition?* Talat responds by saying *I'm fine*, literally *My condition is fine* with the possessive adjective *my*.

The following tables illustrate the way in which possessive adjectives are formed with singular, masculine and feminine objects. Note that the plural forms given here (*their*, *our*) refer only to the nature of the possessor, not of the object being possessed.

Possessive adjectives with singular masculine objects

1st person

| ਮੇਰਾ | meraa | *my* |
| ਸਾਡਾ | saadaa | *our* |

2nd person

| ਤੇਰਾ | teraa | *your* (informal) |
| ਤੁਹਾਡਾ | tuhaadaa | *your* (formal) |

3rd person

ਇਹ ਦਾ/ਇਸ ਦਾ	ih daa/is daa	*his/her*
ਇਹਨਾਂ ਦਾ	ihnaan daa	*his/her* (formal) *their*
ਉਹ ਦਾ/ਉਸ ਦਾ	uh daa/us daa	*his/her*
ਉਹਨਾਂ ਦਾ	uhnaan daa	*his/her* (formal) *their*

Possessive adjectives with singular feminine objects

1st person

| ਮੇਰੀ | meree | *my* |
| ਸਾਡੀ | saadee | *our* |

2nd person

| ਤੇਰੀ | teree | *your* (informal) |
| ਤੁਹਾਡੀ | tuhaadee | *your* (formal) |

3rd person

ਇਹ ਦੀ / ਇਸ ਦੀ	ih dee/is dee	*his/her*
ਇਹਨਾਂ ਦੀ	ihnaan dee	*his/her* (formal) *their*
ਉਹ ਦੀ / ਉਸ ਦੀ	uh dee/us dee	*his/her*
ਉਹਨਾਂ ਦੀ	uhnaan dee	*his/her* (formal) *their*

Further examples of possessive adjectives with plural objects will be illustrated in Unit 3.

Formal and informal speech

◀) CD 1, TR 2, 03:17

There is a clear distinction between formal and informal speech in Panjabi. For instance, two sisters talking over the phone will use significantly different speech from two strangers meeting for the first time. Let us consider the example of a telephone conversation between Surinder and Mohinder who are sisters.

| Surinder | ਕਿੱਦਾਂ ਮੋਹਿੰਦਰ ? | kiddaan Mohindar? *How are you, Mohinder?* |
| Mohinder | ਠੀਕ ਹਾਂ । ਤੇਰਾ ਕੀ ਹਾਲ ਏ ? | theek haan. teraa kee haal e? *I'm fine. How are you?* |

Now let's contrast this situation with two strangers meeting in an office.

| Mr Sandhu | ਤੁਹਾਡਾ ਕੀ ਹਾਲ ਹੈ ਜੀ ? | tuhaadaa kee haal hai jee? *How are you?* |
| Mr Johal | ਧੰਨਵਾਦ । ਮੇਰਾ ਹਾਲ ਠੀਕ ਹੈ । | dhannvaad meraa haal theek hai. *Thank you. I am fine.* |

If you compare these two example situations, you will notice that there are two Panjabi words for the same English word *your*. In the first meeting between Mr Singh and the Panjabi class at Heywood College, the words ਤੇਰਾ *teraa* and ਤੁਹਾਡਾ *tuhaadaa* are used for *your*. Either word is used depending on who is being addressed. The word ਤੁਹਾਡਾ *tuhaadaa* is used normally when addressing more than one person (plural) or when addressing one person, male or female, formally as a sign of respect. Therefore, the word ਤੁਹਾਡਾ *tuhaadaa* serves two purposes:

- to address a singular male/female in a formal manner
- to address more than one person, male or female, in an informal or formal manner

Conversely, the word ਤੇਰਾ *teraa* is used only in an informal manner to address a single person, male or female.

Here are two common examples of the formal and informal:

ਤੁਹਾਡਾ ਕੀ ਨਾਮ ਹੈ?	<u>t</u>uhaadaa kee naam hai?	*What is your name?* (formal)
ਤੇਰਾ ਕੀ ਨਾਂ ਹੈ/ਏ?	<u>t</u>eraa kee naa<u>n</u> hai/e?	*What is your name?* (informal)

Insight

In the initial stages of learning Panjabi, it is a good idea to learn the formal mode of speech. This form shows politeness and can be used in a variety of different situations.

Asking questions in Panjabi

In Dialogue 1 the word ਕੀ *kee* is used to turn a statement into a question. For example:

Statement	ਤੁਹਾਡਾ ਪਰਵਾਰ ਠੀਕ ਹੈ।	<u>t</u>uhaadaa parvaar theek hai.	*Your family is fine.*
Question	ਕੀ ਤੁਹਾਡਾ ਪਰਵਾਰ ਠੀਕ ਹੈ?	kee <u>t</u>uhaadaa parvaar theek hai?	*Is your family fine?*

However, you do not always need to use a question word, or interrogative, to turn a statement into a question. The use of intonation (rise and fall of the voice in speech) and emphasis can serve the same purpose. Raising your voice at the end of a sentence or using a questioning tone are equally effective. To ask the question *What is your name?* you can simply say:

ਜੀ ਤੁਹਾਡਾ ਨਾਮ ?   jee ṯuhaadaa naam?   *Your name, please?*

The use of any question depends on the context of the conversation, the relationship between the speakers, and the number of people involved. You may have noted that the question *How are you?* is given as ਤੁਹਾਡਾ ਕੀ ਹਾਲ ਹੈ ? ṯuhaadaa kee haal hai? There are three literal meanings of this sentence: *What is your condition?, How are you getting on?* and *How are you feeling?* The various forms of *How are you?* will be used throughout the rest of the book. So look out for them!

There are many ways of asking and responding to the question *How are you?* in Panjabi. Some of the possibilities are listed in the Commentary section. You do not have to learn all of these, but they are useful to know when trying to understand the speech of other Panjabi speakers.

ਵਿਆਖਿਆ viaakhiaa *Commentary*

1 How are you?

There are various ways of saying *How are you?* in Panjabi. Here are some examples:

- ਤੂੰ ਕਿਵੇਂ ਹੈਂ ?   ṯoon kiven hain? (informal)
- ਤੇਰਾ ਕੀ ਹਾਲ ਹੈ ?   ṯeraa kee haal hai? (informal)
- ਕਿੱਦਾਂ ?   kiddaan? (colloquial)

Now let's have a look at the variety of responses to the question *How are you?*

- ਠੀਕ ਏ   theek e   *Fine.* (informal)
- ਤੁਹਾਡੀ ਕਿਰਪਾ ਹੈ   ṯuhaadee kirpaa   *By your blessings.*
                    hai   *(I am fine)* (formal)
- ਵਾਹਿਗੁਰੂ ਦਾ   vaahiguroo daa   *By the grace of God.*
  ਸ਼ੁਕਰ ਹੈ   shukar hai   *(I am fine)* (formal)

It is common for Panjabi speakers to respond to *How are you?* reciprocally by asking the same of the enquirer:

| • ਤੂੰ ਸੁਣਾ | <u>t</u>oon sunhaa | *You tell (how you are).* (informal) |
| • ਤੁਸੀਂ ਸੁਣਾਓ | <u>t</u>usee<u>n</u> sunhaao | *You tell (how you are).* (formal) |

As in English when asked the question *How are you?* many people say *thank you* after replying with such responses as *I'm fine*. There are a few common ways of expressing *thank you* in Panjabi:

• ਧੰਨਵਾਦ	<u>dh</u>annvaad
• ਸ਼ੁਕਰੀਆ	shukreeaa
• ਮਿਹਰਬਾਨੀ	miharbaanee
• ਤੁਹਾਡੀ ਕਿਰਪਾ ਹੈ ।	<u>t</u>uhaadee kirpaa hai

2 Panjabi greetings

◀)) **CD 1, TR 2, 04:02**

Panjabi greetings are chosen, not according to the time of day – as in cases such as *Good morning* or *Good evening* – but according to the religion of the speakers. All the world's main faiths are represented in Panjab. However, after the partition of the region, the main religious group in West Panjab (Pakistan) is Muslim, with a sizeable Christian minority, and in East Panjab there is a mixture of Sikhs and Hindus with a Christian and Buddhist minority. Throughout the remainder of the book, we have focused on the Hindu, Sikh and Muslim religious groupings.

Sikhs greet each other by saying: ਸਤਿ ਸ੍ਰੀ ਅਕਾਲ ਜੀ **sa<u>t</u> sree akaal jee,** or simply ਸਤਿ ਸ੍ਰੀ ਅਕਾਲ **sa<u>t</u> sree akaal.** There is an associated body language with each greeting. When saying ਸਤਿ ਸ੍ਰੀ ਅਕਾਲ **sa<u>t</u> sree akaal** the hands are, usually, joined together in front of the chest, with the head slightly bowed. In formal and respectful circumstances the suffix ਜੀ **jee** is added. The reply to the greeting is the same, ਸਤਿ ਸ੍ਰੀ ਅਕਾਲ **sa<u>t</u> sree akaal.** This is also used on departure, and may be combined with other sayings such as ਫਿਰ ਮਿਲਾਂ ਗੇ **phir milaa<u>n</u> ge** (*See you again*) or ਰੱਬ ਰਾਖਾ **rabb raakhaa** (*May God protect you*).

The Muslim greeting is ਅੱਸਲਾਮ ਅਲੈਕਮ **asslaam alaikam,** which is taken from Arabic and means *Peace be upon you.* The reply to this is ਵਾਲੈਕਮ ਅੱਸਲਾਮ **vaalaikam asslaam,** which means *Peace be upon you also.* On departing, a Muslim may say ਖ਼ੁਦਾ ਹਾਫ਼ਿਜ਼ <u>kh</u>u<u>d</u>aa haafiz, which means *May God protect you*. Men will greet each other by a shake of the hand and an embrace or by the raising of the right hand. Women would greet one another with an embrace or a clasping of the hand.

ਨਮਸਤੇ namaste, ਨਮਸਤੇ ਜੀ namaste jee, or ਨਮਸਕਾਰ, namaskaar are different forms of Hindu greetings. The greeting is from Sanskrit and literally means *I greet you respectfully*. The reply to ਨਮਸਤੇ namaste is ਨਮਸਤੇ namaste. Men may shake hands in greeting. However, to and among women the folding of hands and a slight bowing of the head is considered a mark of respect. There is no specific departing phrase.

It is considered good practice to use the greeting of the other person's religion on first meeting. Therefore if Mr Singh, who is a Sikh teacher, had a Muslim student in his class, he would greet him by saying ਅੱਸਲਾਮ ਅਲੈਕਮ asslaam alaikam. The student could equally reply ਵਾਲੈਕਮ ਅੱਸਲਾਮ vaalaikam asslaam or say ਸਤਿ ਸ੍ਰੀ ਅਕਾਲ sat sree akaal as a sign of respect. However, if you are not certain of the other person's religious background, it is advisable to use the westernized, secular greeting *hello* or *hello jee*.

ਜੀ jee is an extra added word known as an honorific particle, signifying respect. The use of the word ਜੀ jee is very common in the Panjabi language. It can be added to the end (and sometimes before) almost any sentence as a sign of respect in a formal context. To some extent **jee** is the equivalent of *please* and also of *sir/madam* in English.

Insight

A word of caution: men shaking hands with or kissing women when greeting is not always socially acceptable as in the West.

ਅਭਿਆਸ abhiaas *Exercises*

1 Word search

Three words are hidden in the box. These words are ਅੱਛਾ achchaa, OK, ਸ਼ਾਬਾਸ਼ shaabaash, *well done*, and ਰੱਬ ਰਾਖਾ rabb raakhaa, *goodbye*. Find them by looking horizontally across each of the rows.

ੳ	ਰੱ	ਬ	ਗਾ	ਖਾ
ਮਾ	ਪਾ	ਰ	ਗ	ਚ
ਸ਼ਾ	ਬਾ	ਸ਼	ਕਾ	ਜ
ਜ	ੜ	ਖ	ਸ	ਬਾ
ਕੱ	ਲ	ਹਿ	ਅੱ	ਛਾ

2 Greeting response

How would you respond to someone who greets you with the following expressions?

a ਨਮਸਤੇ   namaste
b ਅੱਸਲਾਮ ਅਲੈਕਮ   asslaam alaikam
c ਸਤਿ ਸ੍ਰੀ ਅਕਾਲ   sat sree akaal

3 Use the appropriate formal and informal possessive adjectives in the following sentences

a _____ ਕੀ ਨਾਮ ਹੈ?   _____ kee naam hai?
     What is your name? (formal)

b _____ ਕੀ ਹਾਲ ਹੈ?   _____ kee haal hai?
     How are you? (informal)

c _____ ਕੀ ਨਾਂ ਏ?   _____ kee naan e?
     What is your name? (informal)

4 Complete the conversation

◀) CD 1, TR 2, 04:48

You have just met Kiran, a new student in the Panjabi class. Following the English prompts complete the following conversation in Panjabi.

Kiran	ਸਤਿ ਸ੍ਰੀ ਅਕਾਲ ਜੀ । ਤੁਹਾਡਾ ਕੀ ਨਾਮ ਹੈ?
	sat sree akaal jee. tuhaadaa kee naam hai?
	Hello. What is your name?
You	**Say hello, tell her your name and ask what her name is.**

Kiran	ਮੇਰਾ ਨਾਮ ਕਿਰਨ ਹੈ । ਤੁਹਾਡਾ ਕੀ ਹਾਲ ਹੈ ?
	meraa naam Kiran hai. tuhaadaa kee haal hai?
	My name is Kiran. How are you?
You	**Tell her you are fine and then ask her how she is.**
Kiran	ਮੇਰਾ ਹਾਲ ਵੀ ਠੀਕ ਹੈ ।
	meraa haal vee theek hai.
	I am fine too.
You	**Say goodbye.**

Ten important things to remember

1 The words that Panjabi speakers use depend on the formality of the situation.
2 Possessive adjectives (words like 'my', 'your', etc.) change in Panjabi according to the gender and number of what is being described and also according to the formality of the context.
3 Questions are formed in Panjabi by the addition of the word 'kee' 'ਕੀ' at the beginning of the sentence.
4 Panjabi greetings depend on the religion of the speakers.
5 The Sikh greeting *sat sree akaal* ਸਤਿ ਸ੍ਰੀ ਅਕਾਲ means 'God is truth'.
6 The Sikh greeting is accompanied by a slight bow of the head with the hands joined together in front of the chest.
7 The Muslim greeting *asslaam alaikam* ਅੱਸਲਾਮ ਅਲੈਕਮ means 'Peace be upon you'.
8 The Muslim greeting is accompanied by a shake of the hand or an embrace or raising of the right hand (men) or an embrace or clasping of the hands (women).
9 The Hindu greeting *namaste* ਨਮਸਤੇ means 'I greet you respectfully'.
10 The Hindu greeting may be accompanied by a handshake (men); to and among women the folding of hands and a slight bow of the head is considered a mark of respect.

14

2

ਮੈਂ ਕਿਰਨ ਹਾਂ
main kiran haan
I'm Kiran

In this unit you will learn:

- How to say who you are
- How to ask about and describe ethnicity or nationality
- About Panjabi sentence word order

---

1   *Are you English too?*
ਗੱਲ ਬਾਤ ੧ ਕੀ ਤੁਸੀਂ ਵੀ ਅੰਗਰੇਜ਼ ਹੋ ?
gall baat 1 kee tuseen vee angrez ho?

🔊 **CD 1, TR 3, 00:21**

It is the second day of the Panjabi class at Heywood College. Mr Singh is the teacher and Henry, Jane, Ashok, Kiran and David are students attending the class.

ਚਰਨ ਸਿੰਘ **Charan Singh**	ਜੇਨ, ਕੀ ਤੂੰ ਜਰਮਨ ਹੈਂ ? jen, kee toon jarman hain? *Jane, are you German?*
ਜੇਨ **Jane**	ਨਹੀਂ ਜੀ, ਮੈਂ ਜਰਮਨ ਨਹੀਂ ਹਾਂ । ਮੈਂ ਅੰਗਰੇਜ਼ ਹਾਂ । naheen jee, main jarman naheen haan. main angrez haan. *No, I'm not German. I'm English.*

ਡੇਵਿਡ **David**	ਮੈਂ ਵੀ ਅੰਗਰੇਜ਼ ਹਾਂ ਅਤੇ ਮੈਂ ਵਿਦਿਆਰਥੀ ਹਾਂ। main vee angrez haan ate main vidiaarthee haan. *I'm also English and I am a student.*
ਚਰਨ ਸਿੰਘ **Charan Singh**	ਬਹੁਤ ਅੱਛਾ। ਅਸ਼ੋਕ, ਕੀ ਤੁਸੀ ਭਾਰਤੀ ਹੋ? bahut achchaa. ashok, kee tuseen bhaartee ho? *Very good. Ashok, are you Indian?*
ਅਸ਼ੋਕ **Ashok**	ਮੇਰਾ ਦੇਸ਼ ਭਾਰਤ ਹੈ ਅਤੇ ਮੇਰੀ ਬੋਲੀ ਗੁਜਰਾਤੀ ਹੈ। meraa desh bhaarat hai ate meree bolee gujraatee hai. *My country is India and my language is Gujarati.*
ਚਰਨ ਸਿੰਘ **Charan Singh**	ਸ਼ਾਬਾਸ਼! ਹੈਨਰੀ, ਕੀ ਕਿਰਨ ਗੁਜਰਾਤੀ ਹੈ? shaabaash! hainree, kee kiran gujraatee hai? *Well done! Henry, is Kiran Gujarati?*
ਹੈਨਰੀ **Henry**	ਨਹੀਂ, ਉਹ ਪੰਜਾਬੀ ਹੈ ਅਤੇ ਹਿੰਦੂ ਹੈ। naheen, uh panjaabee hai ate hindoo hai. *No, she is Panjabi and Hindu.*
ਚਰਨ ਸਿੰਘ **Charan Singh**	ਧੰਨਵਾਦ। dhannvaad. *Thank you.*

ਸ਼ਬਦਾਵਲੀ	shabdaavalee	*Vocabulary*
ਤੂੰ	toon	*you* (informal)
ਜਰਮਨ	jarman	*German* (m./f.)
ਅੰਗਰੇਜ਼	angrez	*English* (m./f.)
ਵਿਦਿਆਰਥੀ	vidiaarthee	*student* (m./f.)
ਤੁਸੀਂ	tuseen	*you* (formal)
ਭਾਰਤੀ	bhaartee	*Indian* (m./f.)
ਦੇਸ਼	desh	*country* (m.)
ਭਾਰਤ	bhaarat	*India* (m.)
ਬਹੁਤ ਅੱਛਾ	bahut achchaa	*very good*
ਬੋਲੀ	bolee	*language* (f.)
ਗੁਜਰਾਤੀ	gujraatee	a person from Gujarat or of Gujarati origin (m./f.)
ਵੀ	vee	*also*
ਹੋਣਾ	honhaa	*to be*
ਮੈਂ	main	*I*

ਨਹੀਂ	naheen	*no*
ਪੰਜਾਬੀ	panjaabee	a person from Panjab or of Panjabi origin (m./f.)
ਅਤੇ	ate	*and*
ਹਿੰਦੂ	hindoo	*Hindu* (m./f.)

Insight

You might have come across some words in Panjabi which have sounds unfamiliar to English speakers. Follow this simple rule to learn these new sounds: listen carefully, mimic the sound or word and repeat it as many times as you like.

ਅਭਿਆਸ abhiaas *Exercises*

After reading the dialogue and/or listening to the recording, try to do the following exercises.

1 True or false?

Say whether these statements about the students' ethnicities and nationalities are true or false.

a	ਕਿਰਨ ਗੁਜਰਾਤੀ ਹੈ	kiran gujraatee hai	True/False
b	ਜੇਨ ਜਰਮਨ ਹੈ	jen jarman hai	True/False
c	ਅਸ਼ੋਕ ਭਾਰਤੀ ਹੈ	ashok bhaartee hai	True/False

2 Listen to the recording and tick the correct box

◀) CD 1, TR 3, 01:24

	Panjabi	**English**	**Gujarati**
Jeevan			
John			
Ram			

2 I'm Kiran

ਗੱਲ ਬਾਤ ੨ ਮੈਂ ਕਿਰਨ ਹਾਂ
gall baat 2 main kiran haan

◀) CD 1, TR 3, 02:05

Kiran and Ashok meet at the Hindu temple. They have only met
once in the Panjabi class and are still unacquainted with one another.

ਕਿਰਨ	ਨਮਸਤੇ । ਮੈਂ ਕਿਰਨ ਹਾਂ । ਕੀ ਤੁਸੀਂ ਅਸ਼ੋਕ ਹੋ ?
Kiran	namaste. main kiran haan. kee tuseen ashok ho?
	Hello. I'm Kiran. Are you Ashok?
ਅਸ਼ੋਕ	ਨਮਸਤੇ । ਹਾਂ ਜੀ, ਮੈਂ ਅਸ਼ੋਕ ਹਾਂ । ਇਹ ਮੇਰੇ ਮਾਤਾ ਜੀ ਹਨ, ਮਿਸਜ਼ ਸ਼ਰਮਾ ।
Ashok	namaste. haan jee, main ashok haan. ih mere maataa jee han, misaz sharmaa.
	Hello. Yes, I'm Ashok. This is my mother, Mrs Sharma.
ਕਿਰਨ	ਨਮਸਤੇ ਮਿਸਜ਼ ਸ਼ਰਮਾ । ਤੁਹਾਡਾ ਕੀ ਹਾਲ ਹੈ ?
Kiran	namaste misaz sharmaa. tuhaadaa kee haal hai?
	Hello Mrs Sharma. How are you?
ਮਿਸਜ਼ ਸ਼ਰਮਾ	ਮੈਂ ਠੀਕ ਹਾਂ । ਕੀ ਤੁਹਾਡੇ ਮਾਤਾ ਜੀ ਇਥੇ ਹਨ ? ਅਸੀਂ ਦੋਨੋਂ ਸਹੇਲੀਆਂ ਹਾਂ ।
Mrs Sharma	main theek haan. kee tuhaade maataa jee iththe han? aseen donon saheleeaan haan.
	I'm fine. Is your mother here? We are both friends.
ਕਿਰਨ	ਨਹੀਂ ਜੀ, ਉਹ ਇਥੇ ਨਹੀਂ ਹਨ, ਉਹ ਘਰ ਹਨ ।
Kiran	naheen jee, uh iththe naheen han, uh ghar han.
	No, she's not here. She's at home.
ਅਸ਼ੋਕ	ਮਾਤਾ ਜੀ, ਕਿਰਨ ਤੇ ਮੈਂ ਦੋਨੋਂ ਇੱਕੋ ਕਲਾਸ ਵਿਚ ਹਾਂ ।
Ashok	maataa jee, kiran te main donon ikko kalaas vich haan.
	Mother, Kiran and I are both in the same class.

ਸ਼ਬਦਾਵਲੀ	shabdaavalee	*Vocabulary*
ਇਹ	ih	*he, she, it, this, they, these*
ਮਾਤਾ ਜੀ	maataa jee	*mother* (f.)
ਮੈਂ	main	*I*

ਇੱਥੇ	<u>i</u>ththe	*here*
ਅਸੀਂ	aseen	*we*
ਦੋਨੋਂ	<u>d</u>onon	*both*
ਸਹੇਲੀ	sahelee	*friend* (f.)
ਉਹ	uh	*he, she, that, they, those*
ਨਹੀਂ	naheen	*no*
ਘਰ	ghar	*house, home* (m.)
ਅਸੀਂ ਦੋਨੋਂ	aseen <u>d</u>onon	*both of us*
ਇੱਕੋ	ikko	*same*
ਕਲਾਸ	kalaas	*class* (f.)
ਵਿਚ	vich	*in*
ਤੇ	<u>t</u>e	*and*

Insight

The Panjabi words '*u<u>tt</u>e*' ਉੱਤੇ (on, at) and '*a<u>t</u>e*' ਅਤੇ (and) have the same abbreviation, i.e. *<u>t</u>e* ਤੇ.

ਅਭਿਆਸ abhiaas *Exercises*

After reading the dialogue and/or listening to the recording, try to do the following exercises.

1 Listen and give appropriate responses

◄⑴ CD 1, TR 3, 03:02

Kiran	Ashok
ਕੀ ਤੁਸੀਂ ਅਸ਼ੋਕ ਹੋ? kee <u>t</u>useen ashok ho?	
Kiran	Mrs Sharma
ਤੁਹਾਡਾ ਕੀ ਹਾਲ ਹੈ? <u>t</u>uhaadaa kee haal hai?	
Mrs Sharma	Kiran
ਕੀ ਤੇਰੇ ਮਾਤਾ ਜੀ ਇੱਥੇ ਹਨ? kee <u>t</u>ere maa<u>t</u>aa jee i<u>th</u>the han?	

2 Arrange in correct word order

a	ਹਾਂ ਮੈਂ ਕਿਰਨ	haan-main-kiran	*I am Kiran.*
b	ਹੋ ਅਸ਼ੋਕ ਕੀ ਤੁਸੀਂ?	ho-ashok-kee-<u>t</u>useen?	*Are you Ashok?*
c	ਨਹੀਂ ਇੱਥੇ ਉਹ ਹਨ	naheen-i<u>th</u>the-uh-han	*She is not here.*

3 Crossword

Complete the crossword in English using clues taken from Dialogues 1 and 2.

1 ਕਿਰਨ _____ ਹੈ kiran _____ hai
2 ਜੇਨ _____ ਹੈ jen _____ hai
3 ਕਿਰਨ ਤੇ ਅਸ਼ੋਕ ਦੋਨੋਂ ਇੱਕੋ _____ ਵਿਚ ਹਨ kiran ṯe ashok ḏonon ikko _____ vich han
4 ਅਸ਼ੋਕ ਦੇ ਮਾਤਾ ਜੀ ਦਾ ਨਾਮ _____ਹੈ ashok ḏe maaṯaa jee ḏaa naam _____ hai
5 ਕਿਰਨ ਦੇ ਮਾਤਾ ਜੀ _____ ਹਨ kiran ḏe maaṯaa jee _____ han

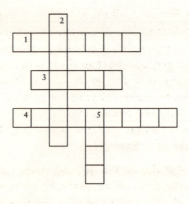

ਬੋਲੀ ਬਾਰੇ bolee baare *Language points*

Subject pronouns

Pronouns are words used in the place of nouns, or naming words, which are used to refer to persons, places or objects. In English the words *I*, *you*, *he*, *she*, *it*, *they* and *we* are called subject pronouns. In Panjabi they are very important as the endings of verbs change according to which subject pronoun is being used, as will be seen in subsequent units.

Singular subject pronouns

First person	ਮੈਂ	main	*I*
Second person	ਤੂੰ	toon	*you* (informal)
	ਤੁਸੀਂ	tuseen	*you* (formal)

| Third person | ਇਹ | ih | he/she/it/this |
| | ਉਹ | uh | he/she/it/that |

Plural subject pronouns

First person	ਅਸੀਂ	aseen	we
Second person	ਤੁਸੀਂ	tuseen	you
Third person	ਇਹ	ih	these, they (near)
	ਉਹ	uh	those, they (far)

Unlike in English, but as in all the Latin-based languages, persons, places and objects (nouns) are grammatically either male or female in Panjabi. Even though some objects have ambiguous status in the sense that some people may refer to them as masculine and others as feminine, generally all nouns, even those with ambiguous status, belong to either the masculine or feminine gender. Some nouns can be used for both male and female, such as doctor. You will note in the vocabulary sections that we have given (m.), (f.) and (m./f.) to represent the gender of a noun.

There is no gender distinction in the actual forms of subject pronouns, only in the verb endings that refer to the subject pronoun. For example, ਉਹ **uh** can refer to one man or woman or a group of either men or women. There is no way of distinguishing, by looking only at the subject pronoun, between *he*, *she* or *they* as the third person singular and plural forms are interchangeable. It is the verb ending which will enable you to recognize whether it is *he*, *she* or *they* being referred to. In Panjabi there is no equivalent to the word *it* which implies gender neutrality in English.

Use of subject pronouns

1 ਇਹ **ih** and ਉਹ **uh** literally mean *he/she/it* in the singular and *they* in the plural. There is however a recognizable distinction between the use of ਉਹ **uh** and ਇਹ **ih**. ਉਹ **uh** refers to a person or persons absent or at a distance, whereas ਇਹ **ih** is used when the person or persons are present or in close proximity.

2 In English the words *these* and *those* are called demonstrative pronouns. In Panjabi there are no specific equivalents. ਉਹ **uh** and

ਇਹ **ih**, however, often translate into *those* and *these,* respectively, in many situations.

3 When talking about a singular person who is deserving of respect, such as Kiran's mother in Dialogue 2, it is grammatically correct always to use the plural form:

ਉਹ ਇੱਥੇ ਨਹੀਂ ਹਨ, ਉਹ ਘਰ ਹਨ I uh ith<u>th</u>e nahee<u>n</u> han, uh ghar han. *She's not here, she's at home.*

ਉਹ **uh** and ਇਹ **ih** are used in the plural in this case, which is reflected in the use of the plural form of ਹੋਣਾ (ਹਨ) **honhaa** (**han**) instead of the singular ਹੈ **hai**, even though only one mother (she) is being talked about.

4 In a similar way, the word ਤੂੰ **<u>t</u>oon** *you* is used informally and ਤੁਸੀਂ **<u>t</u>usee<u>n</u>** is used in both formal speech as well as in the plural form. These two forms of *you* require discretion in their application. ਤੂੰ **<u>t</u>oon** is used between family members and close friends as well as when speaking to younger people. It is also used in public speech where a degree of informality is expected, such as when bargaining in the market or fixing the price of a taxi fare. ਤੁਸੀਂ **<u>t</u>usee<u>n</u>** is a more formal and polite form which is used between people of equal status and age as well as to people deserving respect due to age or social standing. However, when the distinction between the formal and informal use is not obvious, it is always safest to use the formal. Formal and informal speech is a crucial distinction in Panjabi and will crop up many times as you progress through the course. If you have some knowledge of French or Spanish, you will note the similarity here between the singular, informal use of *you, tu* and *tú* and the plural and singular formal forms of *you, vous* (French) and *usted* (Spanish).

The present tense of ਹੋਣਾ 'honhaa' *is, am* and *are*

Subject pronouns are assigned appropriate forms of the verb *to be.* This can similarly be compared with English: *I am, you are, we are, he is, they are.* In Panjabi *to be* is expressed in the verb ਹੋਣਾ **honhaa** which denotes states of being, conditions and existence. Note the following pairings of subject pronouns with their assigned forms of ਹੋਣਾ **honhaa**:

Singular

First person	ਮੈਂ ਹਾਂ	main haan	*I am*
Second person	ਤੂੰ ਹੈਂ	toon hain	*you are* (informal)
	ਤੁਸੀਂ ਹੋ	tuseen ho	*you are* (formal)
Third person	ਇਹ ਹੈ	ih hai	*he/she/it is*
	ਉਹ ਹੈ	uh hai	*he/she/it is*

Plural

First person	ਅਸੀਂ ਹਾਂ	aseen haan	*we are*
Second person	ਤੁਸੀਂ ਹੋ	tuseen ho	*you are*
Third person	ਇਹ ਹਨ	ih han	*they/these are*
	ਉਹ ਹਨ	uh han	*they/those are*

Formal uses of possessive adjectives

The formal uses of subject pronouns in Panjabi also extend to possessive adjectives. In Unit 1 we saw how possessive adjectives are formed with singular masculine and feminine objects. Possessive adjectives used to describe people with respect or in a formal situation always take the formal form, even when the person being described is in the singular. Note the following examples where the possessive adjectives and forms of ਹੋਣਾ **honhaa** *to be* change according to the formal and informal contexts in which they are used to describe singular people. In the following examples, note how ਮੇਰੀ **meree** (*my*) and ਤੇਰੀ **teree** (*your*) change into ਮੇਰੇ **mere** and ਤੁਹਾਡੇ **tuhaade**.

Formal   ਇਹ ਮੇਰੇ ਮਾਤਾ ਜੀ ਹਨ   ih mere maa<u>t</u>aa jee han   *This is my mother.*

Informal   ਇਹ ਮੇਰੀ ਮਾਤਾ ਹੈ   ih meree maa<u>t</u>aa hai   *This is my mother.*

Formal   ਕੀ ਤੁਹਾਡੇ ਮਾਤਾ ਜੀ ਇੱਥੇ ਹਨ?   kee <u>t</u>uhaade maa<u>t</u>aa jee ith<u>th</u>e han?   *Is your mother here?*

Informal   ਕੀ ਤੇਰੀ ਮਾਤਾ ਇੱਥੇ ਹੈ?   kee <u>t</u>eree maa<u>t</u>aa ith<u>th</u>e hai?   *Is your mother here?*

These examples illustrate how the plural in Panjabi can be used to make speech more formal. However, this is only one aspect of plural possessive adjectives. In these examples the object here is itself not in the plural (and the form of the adjective is being used in a formal situation). Unit 3 illustrates possessive adjectives with plural objects.

> ## Insight
> The words '*ṯuhaadaa*' 'ਤੁਹਾਡਾ' (your) and '*ṯuseen*' 'ਤੁਸੀਂ'(you) are grammatically plural forms but these can also be used to address a singular person in a formal way. Moreover, the English word 'your' has as many as 12 different forms in Panjabi.

Word order

Note the word order of a simple Panjabi sentence – subject (person carrying out the action) first, verb (the action) last and the rest in between. The sentence *I am fine* is written in Panjabi as *I fine am*, where *I* is the subject and *am* is the verb. For example: ਮੈਂ ਠੀਕ ਹਾਂ main theek haan *I am fine:*

ਮੈਂ	ਠੀਕ	ਹਾਂ
main	theek	haan
I	*fine*	*am*
subject		**verb**

Word order in Panjabi is generally more flexible than it is in English. Note how the meaning does not change though the word order does in the following sentences:

| ਤੁਹਾਡਾ ਨਾਮ ਕੀ ਹੈ? | tuhaadaa naam kee hai? |
| ਤੁਹਡਾ ਕੀ ਨਾਮ ਹੈ? | ṯuhaadaa kee naam hai? |

Both examples mean *What is your name?* However, this does not mean that any word order is allowed. The form of the verb ਹੋਣਾ honhaa (ਹੈ hai) is still at the end of the sentence in both examples.

> ## Insight
> Though there is flexibility in placing a question mark in a sentence, sometimes the meaning is affected by where the question mark is positioned.

ਵਿਆਖਿਆ viaakhiaa *Commentary*

1 Where are you from?

The question of where someone comes from depends on who is doing the asking and where the conversation is taking place. For example, a person born in Panjab living in London will respond that they are from India if the questioner is an English person. However, if the questioner is a fellow Panjabi they may say the district or the village they are from. This apparently simple question becomes even more complicated when asked to diaspora South Asians. The response to the question *Where are you from?* can give rise to replies such as *Birmingham* or *New Jersey* which are quite legitimate responses. Increasingly, the use of a religious identity tagged onto a national identity is a form of self-identification used in the diaspora. Therefore, a young person responding to the question *Who are you?* may reply a *British Muslim* or *Canadian Sikh*. It is important to remember that Panjabi speakers come from a huge variety of national, religious and social contexts and this is reflected in the many possibilities that the questions *Where do you come from?* and *Who are you?* can evoke.

If you meet a Panjabi in England or North America, they are likely to live, or at least have relatives, in three areas which are known as centres of Panjabi settlement: Southall in England, Yuba City in California and Vancouver in Canada. Each of these areas is often called *Little Panjab*. Early Panjabi immigrants settled here and these places are still icons on the global map of Panjabi travels, serving as temporary embarkation ports to would-be emigrants. These areas are distinctive for the range of shops selling South Asian goods such as groceries, sweets, music, jewellery, clothing and food. Apart from being a central shopping area they are the focus of social, religious, political and cultural activities.

2 Names

South Asian names can provide many clues about a person's sex, background, country of origin and religious affiliation. These are often very important pieces of information, particularly when engaging in formal conversation.

Sikh names

Most Sikhs have three names: a personal name, a second name and a surname. The second name, 'Singh' for men and 'Kaur' for women, is in fact a religious name and its addition is one of the main ways of distinguishing men from women. Otherwise first names can be the same for men and women. Surnames vary from representing someone's caste or the name of their village.

Hindu names

The Hindu naming system is similar to the English naming system, in that most individuals have one or two personal names followed by a common surname. First names are generally male and female specific. A middle name of Kumar or Chand is quite popular in North India and is a way of distinguishing a Hindu Panjabi from a Sikh.

Muslim names

Muslim names tend to be less fixed in the order of first and second name. There is also a tendency for women not to have the surnames of their husbands, but just to have the word **bibi** or **begum** attached, which means lady or woman. Muslim names tend to be a composite of Koranic names with some local flavour. Male and female names are distinguished.

Throughout the book you will come across a range of Sikh, Hindu and Muslim names. Try and see if you can distinguish them. It is worth remembering, however, that some names transcend religious boundaries, and also that you may come across a lot of nicknames.

ਅਭਿਆਸ abhiaas *Exercises*

1 Complete the box

ਹਨ	han	
ਹੈ		*is*
	ho	*are*

2 Say the sentences in Panjabi

a Are you Ashok?
b Are you Kiran?
c I am Kiran.
d He is Ashok.

3 Refer to the dialogue and choose the correct forms of *to be* from the options given

a ਕੀ ਤੂੰ ਜਰਮਨ _____ (ਹੋ, ਹੈਂ)? kee <u>t</u>oo<u>n</u> jarman _____ (ho, hai<u>n</u>)? *Are you German?*

b ਮੈਂ ਵੀ ਅੰਗਰੇਜ਼ _____ (ਹਾਂ, ਹੈ) mai<u>n</u> vee a<u>n</u>grez _____ (haa<u>n</u>, hai). *I'm also English.*

c ਕੀ ਅਸ਼ੋਕ ਤੇ ਕਿਰਨ ਪੰਜਾਬੀ _____ (ਹੈਂ, ਹਨ)? kee ashok <u>t</u>e kiran pa<u>n</u>jaabee _____ (hai<u>n</u>, han)? *Are Ashok and Kiran Panjabi?*

4 Word search

Three words are hidden in the box. These words are ਜਰਮਨ jarman *German*, ਪੰਜਾਬੀ pa<u>n</u>jaabee *Panjabi* and ਅੰਗਰੇਜ਼ a<u>n</u>grez *English*. Find them by looking horizontally across each of the rows.

ੳ	ਜ	ਰ	ਮ	ਨ
ਕ	ਖ	ਪ	ਰ	ਲ
ਪੰ	ਜਾ	ਬੀ	ਸੀ	ਸਿ
ਟ	ਅੰ	ਗ	ਰੇ	ਜ਼
ਕੇ	ਕਾ	ਕਿ	ਕੀ	ਕੋ

Ten important things to remember

1 The word '*a<u>chch</u>aa*' 'ਅੱਛਾ' is perhaps the most commonly used word in Panjabi.

2 The word '*a<u>chch</u>aa*' 'ਅੱਛਾ' has different meanings, depending upon the situation and the context. It can mean 'OK', 'fine', 'all right', 'nice' as well as other meanings.

3 The use of the word 'jee' 'ਜੀ' shows good manners and formality.
4 Ordinarily, a Panjabi sentence begins with a subject and ends with a verb, with an object appearing between them.
5 Both Panjabi words '_utte_' 'ਉੱਤੇ' (on, about, at) and '_ate_' 'ਅਤੇ' (and) have the same abbreviation, i.e. '_te_' 'ਤੇ'.
6 Names for both Sikh boys and girls are common for both genders.
7 It is not essential in Panjabi conversation to use complete sentences.
8 The formal use of subject pronouns in Panjabi also extends to possessive adjectives.
9 There is no gender distinction in Panjabi pronouns. It is only in the verb endings that refer to the subject pronoun that the gender is denoted.
10 Both Panjabi words _toon_ ਤੂੰ and _tuseen_ ਤੁਸੀਂ convey the meaning of 'you', and are grammatically singular and plural respectively.

3

ਇਸ ਦਾ ਸੁਆਦ ਕੀ ਹੈ ?
is daa suaad kee hai?
What does it taste like?

In this unit you will learn:

- The names of vegetables and Panjabi food
- How to ask questions
- How to describe people and things

1 *What is this?*
ਗੱਲ ਬਾਤ ੧ ਇਹ ਕੀ ਹੈ ?
gall baat 1 ih kee hai?

◀)) **CD 1, TR 4, 00:22**

Mr Singh has taken the Panjabi class to Southall in order to give the
students an opportunity to hear and speak Panjabi in a real situation.
They are in a grocery shop.

ਹੈਨਰੀ **Henry**	ਇਹ ਕੀ ਹੈ ? ih kee hai? *What is this?*
ਦੁਕਾਨਦਾਰ **dukaandaar Shopkeeper**	ਇਹ ਕਰੇਲਾ ਹੈ। ih karelaa hai. *It (this) is a bitter gourd.*

ਹੈਨਰੀ **Henry**	ਇਸ ਦਾ ਸੁਆਦ ਕੀ ਹੈ? is daa suaad kee hai? *What does it taste like?*
ਦੁਕਾਨਦਾਰ **Shopkeeper**	ਇਸ ਦਾ ਸੁਆਦ ਕੌੜਾ ਹੈ। is daa suaad kaurhaa hai. *It has a bitter taste.*
ਜੇਨ **Jane**	ਉਸ ਸਬਜ਼ੀ ਦਾ ਕੀ ਨਾਮ ਹੈ? us sabzee daa kee naam hai? *What is the name of that vegetable?*
ਦੁਕਾਨਦਾਰ **Shopkeeper**	ਛੋਟੀ ਸਬਜ਼ੀ ਭਿੰਡੀ ਹੈ ਤੇ ਵੱਡੇ ਸ਼ਲਗਮ ਹਨ। chotee sabzee bhindee hai te vadde shalgam han. *The small vegetable is okra and the large ones are turnips.*
ਜੇਨ **Jane**	ਕੀ ਸ਼ਲਗਮ ਮਿੱਠਾ ਹੈ ਜਾਂ ਕਸੈਲਾ? kee shalgam miththaa hai jaan kasailaa? *Are turnips sweet or bitter?*
ਦੁਕਾਨਦਾਰ **Shopkeeper**	ਉਹ ਮਿੱਠੇ ਹਨ ਤੇ ਬਹੁਤ ਸਸਤੇ ਵੀ ਹਨ। uh miththe han te bahut saste vee han. *They are sweet and also very cheap*

ਸ਼ਬਦਾਵਲੀ	shabdaavalee	*Vocabulary*
ਕਰੇਲਾ	karelaa	*bitter gourd* (type of vegetable) (m.)
ਇਸ	is	*it, this*
ਦਾ	daa	*of*
ਸੁਆਦ	suaad	*taste* (m.)
ਕੌੜਾ/ਕਸੈਲਾ	kaurhaa/kasailaa	*bitter* (v.)
ਉਸ	us	*that*
ਸਬਜ਼ੀ	sabzee	*vegetable* (f.)
ਛੋਟਾ	chotaa	*small* (v.)
ਭਿੰਡੀ	bhindee	*okra* (type of vegetable) (f.)
ਵੱਡਾ	vaddaa	*big, large* (v.)
ਸ਼ਲਗਮ	shalgam	*turnip* (m.)
ਸਸਤਾ	sastaa	*cheap* (v.)
ਮਿੱਠਾ	miththaa	*sweet* (v.)

| ਜਾਂ | jaa<u>n</u> | *or* |
| ਬਹੁਤ | bahu<u>t</u> | *very* |

ਅਭਿਆਸ abhiaas *Exercises*

After reading the dialogue and/or listening to the recording, try to do
the following exercises.

1 True or false?

a	ਭਿੰਡੀ	bhi<u>n</u>dee means *bitter*	True/False
b	ਕਰੇਲਾ	karelaa means *okra*	True/False
c	ਸ਼ਲਗਮ	shalgam means *turnip*	True/False
d	ਸਸਤਾ	sas<u>t</u>aa means *expensive*	True/False
e	ਸੁਆਦ	suaa<u>d</u> means *taste*	True/False

2 Mr Khan's shopping list

◀) CD 1, TR 4, 01:07

Mr Khan is at the local grocery shop buying vegetables. Listen to the
recording to hear which items he has purchased from the shopping
list that Mrs Khan has given him. As the items are spoken on the
recording, tick them off the list. Don't worry if you can't recognize
all the words.

ਕਰੇਲਾ	karelaa	*bitter gourd*
ਸ਼ਲਗਮ	shalgam	*turnip*
ਭਿੰਡੀ	bhi<u>n</u>dee	*okra*
ਗਾਜਰ	gaajar	*carrot*
ਆਲੂ	aaloo	*potatoes*
ਗੋਭੀ	gobhee	*cauliflower*
ਟਮਾਟਰ	tamaatar	*tomatoes*
ਮਟਰ	matar	*peas*

2 Which sweets are good?
ਗੱਲ ਬਾਤ ੨ ਕਿਹੜੀਆਂ ਮਿਠਿਆਈਆਂ ਚੰਗੀਆਂ ਹਨ ?
gall baat 2 kihrheeaan mithiaaeeaan changeeaan han?

🔊 CD 1, TR 4, 01:42

After visiting the grocery shop, Mr Singh takes Jane and Henry to the Panjabi sweet shop (ਮਿਠਿਆਈ ਦੀ ਦੁਕਾਨ mithiaaee dee dukaan). Panjabi sweet shops are not like confectionery shops, because although they are most famous for the sweet dishes that they sell, they also provide a range of other dishes.

ਮਿਸਟਰ ਸਿੰਘ **Mr Singh**	ਇਹ ਬਹੁਤ ਚੰਗੀ ਮਿਠਿਆਈ ਦੀ ਦੁਕਾਨ ਹੈ । ih bahut changee mithiaaee dee dukaan hai. *This is a very good sweet shop.*
ਜੇਨ **Jane**	ਇੱਥੇ ਕਿਹੜੀਆਂ ਮਿਠਿਆਈਆਂ ਚੰਗੀਆਂ ਹਨ ? iththe kihrheeaan mithiaaeeaan changeeaan han? *Which sweets are good here?*
ਮਿਸਟਰ ਸਿੰਘ **Mr Singh**	ਸਾਰੀਆਂ ਮਿਠਿਆਈਆਂ ਚੰਗੀਆਂ ਹਨ ਪਰ ਲੱਡੂ ਖ਼ਾਸ ਸੁਆਦੀ ਹਨ । saareeaan mithiaaeeaan changeeaan han par laddoo khaas suaadee han. *All of them are good, but* ladoos *are especially tasty.*
ਹੈਨਰੀ **Henry**	ਪਰ ਲੱਡੂ ਮਹਿੰਗੇ ਹਨ । par laddoo mahinge han. *But* ladoos *are expensive.*
ਜੇਨ **Jane**	ਕੀ ਕੋਈ ਨਮਕੀਨ ਚੀਜ਼ ਹੈ ? kee koee namkeen cheez hai? *Is there anything salty?*
ਦੁਕਾਨਦਾਰ **Shopkeeper**	ਹਾਂ ਜੀ, ਪਕੌੜੇ ਤੇ ਸਮੋਸੇ ਹਨ । haan jee, pakaurhe te samose han. *Yes, there are* pakoras *and* samosas.
ਜੇਨ **Jane**	ਕੀ ਸਮੋਸੇ ਕਰਾਰੇ ਹਨ ? kee samose karaare han? *Are the* samosas *spicy?*

ਦੁਕਾਨਦਾਰ	ਹਾਂ ਜੀ, ਸਮੋਸੇ ਬਹੁਤ ਕਰਾਰੇ ਹਨ।
Shopkeeper	haan jee, samose bahut karaare han.
	Yes, the samosas are very spicy.

ਸ਼ਬਦਾਵਲੀ	shab<u>d</u>aavalee	*Vocabulary*
ਕਿਹੜੀ	kihrhee	*which, which one* (v.)
ਮਿਠਿਆਈ	mithiaaee	*Panjabi sweet* (f.)
ਚੰਗੀ	cha<u>n</u>gee	*good* (v.)
ਦੁਕਾਨ	<u>d</u>ukaan	*shop* (f.)
ਇੱਥੇ	ith<u>th</u>e	*here*
ਲੱਡੂ	laddoo	a type of Panjabi sweet (m.)
ਖ਼ਾਸ	<u>kh</u>aas	*especially*
ਸੁਆਦੀ	suaa<u>d</u>ee	*tasty*
ਪਰ	par	*but*
ਮਹਿੰਗਾ	mahi<u>n</u>gaa	*expensive, costly* (v.)
ਕੋਈ	koee	*any*
ਚੀਜ਼	cheez	*thing* (f.)
ਨਮਕੀਨ	namkeen	*salty*
ਹਾਂ ਜੀ	haa<u>n</u> jee	*yes* (polite)
ਪਕੋੜਾ	pakaurhaa	a type of deep-fried pastry similar to fritters (m.)
ਸਮੋਸਾ	samosaa	*triangular stuffed pastry* (m.)
ਕਰਾਰਾ	karaaraa	*spicy* (v.)

Insight

The best advice to students of Panjabi is that in the initial stages of learning, they should learn the full version of the sentence in a formal manner.

ਅਭਿਆਸ abhiaas *Exercises*

After reading the dialogue and/or listening to the recording, try to do the following exercises.

1 Complete the table

ਮਿੱਠਾ		sweet
ਕੋੜਾ	kaurhaa	
	suaa<u>d</u>	taste

2 Arrange in correct word order

a ਹੈ ਦੁਕਾਨ ਇਹ   hai-<u>d</u>ukaan-ih   *This is a shop.*

b ਹੈ ਚੰਗੀ ਦੁਕਾਨ ਇਹ   hai-changee-<u>d</u>ukaan-ih   *This is a good shop.*

c ਇਹ ਦੀ ਮਿਠਿਆਈ ਹੈ ਦੁਕਾਨ   ih-<u>d</u>ee-mithiaaee-hai-<u>d</u>ukaan   *This is a sweet shop.*

d ਹੈ ਦੁਕਾਨ ਦੀ ਮਿਠਿਆਈ ਚੰਗੀ ਇਹ   hai-<u>d</u>ukaan-<u>d</u>ee-mithiaaee-changee-ih   *This is a good sweet shop.*

---

3 *This is our sitting room*
ਗੱਲ ਬਾਤ 3 ਇਹ ਸਾਡੀ ਬੈਠਕ ਹੈ
gall baa<u>t</u> 3 ih saadee baithak hai

◄)) CD 1, TR 4, 02:50

Mr Singh has taken his students to visit his house and is showing them around.

ਚਰਨ ਸਿੰਘ	ਇਹ ਸਾਡੀ ਬੈਠਕ ਹੈ। ਮਾਫ਼ ਕਰਨਾ, ਹਰ ਪਾਸੇ ਮੇਰੀਆਂ ਕਿਤਾਬਾਂ ਹਨ।
Charan Singh	ih saadee baithak hai. maaf karnaa, har paase mereeaa<u>n</u> ki<u>t</u>aabaan han.
	This is our sitting room. Sorry, my books are everywhere.
ਹੈਨਰੀ	ਤੁਹਾਡਾ ਘਰ ਵੱਡਾ ਹੈ। ਪੌੜੀਆਂ ਚੌੜੀਆਂ ਹਨ।
Henry	<u>t</u>uhaadaa ghar vaddaa hai. paurheeaa<u>n</u> chaurheeaa<u>n</u> han.
	Your house is big. The stairs are wide.
ਜੇਨ	ਕਿੰਨੇ ਕਮਰੇ ਹਨ ?
Jane	ki<u>n</u>ne kamre han?
	How many rooms are there?
ਚਰਨ ਸਿੰਘ	ਚਾਰ ਕਮਰੇ ਹਨ ਅਤੇ ਦੋ ਗ਼ੁਸਲ ਖ਼ਾਨੇ ਹਨ।
Charan Singh	chaar kamre han a<u>t</u>e <u>d</u>o <u>gh</u>usal <u>kh</u>aane han.
	There are four rooms and two bathrooms.

34

ਅਸ਼ੋਕ	ਬਗੀਚਾ ਲੰਬਾ ਹੈ ਪਰ ਰਸੋਈ ਛੋਟੀ ਹੈ ।
Ashok	ba<u>gh</u>eechaa la<u>n</u>baa hai par rasoee <u>ch</u>otee hai.
	The garden is long but the kitchen is small.
ਚਰਨ ਸਿੰਘ	ਇਹ ਸੱਚ ਹੈ, ਪਰ ਮੇਰੇ ਬੱਚੇ ਅਤੇ ਮੇਰੀ ਪਤਨੀ ਇੱਥੇ ਖ਼ੁਸ਼ ਹਨ ।
Charan Singh	ih sachch hai, par mere bachche a<u>t</u>e meree pa<u>t</u>nee
	i<u>tth</u>e <u>kh</u>ush han.
	That's true, but my children and my wife are happy here.

ਸ਼ਬਦਾਵਲੀ	shab<u>d</u>aavalee	*Vocabulary*
ਬੈਠਕ	baithak	*sitting room* (f.)
ਮਾਫ਼ ਕਰਨਾ	maaf karnaa	*sorry*
ਹਰ ਪਾਸੇ	har paase	*everywhere*
ਪੌੜੀਆਂ	paurheeaa<u>n</u>	*stairs* (f.)
ਚੌੜਾ	chaurhaa	*wide* (v.)
ਕਮਰਾ	kamraa	*room (m.)*
ਕਿੰਨੇ	ki<u>nn</u>e	*how many*
ਗ਼ੁਸਲ ਖ਼ਾਨਾ	<u>gh</u>usal <u>kh</u>aanaa	*bathroom* (m.)
ਬਗੀਚਾ	ba<u>gh</u>eechaa	*garden* (m.)
ਲੰਬਾ	la<u>n</u>baa	*long* (v.)
ਰਸੋਈ	rasoee	*kitchen* (f.)
ਸੱਚ	sachch	*true, truth* (v.)
ਬੱਚੇ	bachche	*children* (m.)
ਪਤਨੀ	pa<u>t</u>nee	*wife* (f.)
ਖ਼ੁਸ਼	<u>kh</u>ush	*happy*

> **Insight**
> It is not essential in Panjabi conversation to use complete sentences.

ਬੋਲੀ ਬਾਰੇ bolee baare *Language points*

Interrogative words

Interrogative words change sentences into questions. In Panjabi, interrogative words generally begin with the letter ਕ **k** and may appear at the beginning of the sentence or within the sentence.

ਕੋਣ	kaunh	*who*
ਕੀ	kee	*what*
ਕਿੱਥੇ	kith̲h̲e	*where*
ਕਿਉਂ	kiun̲	*why*
ਕਿਵੇਂ	kiven̲	*how*
ਕਦੋਂ	kad̲on	*when*
ਕਿਹੜਾ	kihrhaa	*which**
ਕਿਹੜੀ	kihrhee	*which**

*Note that these two examples of 'which' only apply to singular objects.

The endings of ਕਿਹੜਾ **kihrhaa** and ਕਿਹੜੀ **kihrhee** change according to the nature of the noun to which it is referring: whether it is singular or plural, or masculine or feminine.

Examples:

ਉਹ ਕੋਣ ਹੈ?	uh kaunh hai?	*Who is he/she?*
ਉਹ ਕੀ ਹੈ?	uh kee hai?	*What is that?*
ਉਹ ਕਿੱਥੇ ਹੈ?	uh kith̲h̲e hai?	*Where is she/he?*
ਉਹ ਇੱਥੇ ਕਿਉਂ ਹੈ?	uh ith̲h̲e kiun̲ hai?	*Why is he/she here?*
ਉਹ ਕਿਵੇਂ ਹੈ?	uh kiven̲ hai?	*How is she/he?*
ਕਲਾਸ ਕਦੋਂ ਹੈ?	kalaas kad̲on hai?	*When is the class?*
ਕਿਹੜਾ ਫਲ? (m.)	kihrhaa phal? (m.)	*Which fruit?*
ਕਿਹੜੀ ਸਬਜ਼ੀ (f.)	kihrhee sabzee? (f.)	*Which vegetable?*

36

Insight

In spoken Panjabi, you can form a question by changing your intonation without using the interrogative marker (question mark).

Nouns

In Panjabi, nouns are affected by gender, either masculine or feminine, and number, either singular or plural. Every noun in Panjabi, even an inanimate object, is assigned a masculine or feminine gender and has a singular or plural numerical character. The process of assignment of gender to nouns is quite arbitrary. There are no obvious reasons, for example, why ਕੁਰਸੀ **kursee** *chair* is feminine and ਮੇਜ਼ **mez** *table* is masculine. However, in logical terms, all nouns which represent males are masculine and those which represent females are feminine. For example, ਮੁੰਡਾ **mundaa** *boy* is masculine and ਕੁੜੀ **kurhee** *girl* is feminine.

There are no steadfast rules about the distinction of the gender of inanimate objects. In Panjabi this is a matter of convention, whereby the gender of a noun is often simply understood. There is a general code that nouns ending in ਈ (**ee**) are feminine and nouns ending in ਆ (**aa**) are masculine, such as ਲੜਕਾ **larhkaa** *boy* and ਲੜਕੀ **larhkee** *girl*. Exceptions to this, however, are plentiful, with words such as ਹਾਥੀ **haathee** (*elephant*) masculine, ਮਾਂ **maan** (*mother*) feminine and ਮਾਲਾ **maalaa** (*necklace*) feminine, all having endings which counter this general code. So be careful! You will learn more about nouns as you go along.

Type 1: Variable nouns
Variable nouns are those which change from the singular form when they are plural.

Masculine

Singular	ਮੁੰਡਾ	mundaa	*boy*
Plural	ਮੁੰਡੇ	munde	*boys*
Singular	ਚਾਚਾ	chaachaa	*uncle*
Plural	ਚਾਚੇ	chaache	*uncles*

Feminine

Singular	ਕੁੜੀ	kurhee	*girl*
Plural	ਕੁੜੀਆਂ	kurhee<u>aan</u>	*girls*
Singular	ਦੁਕਾਨ	<u>d</u>ukaan	*shop*
Plural	ਦੁਕਾਨਾਂ	<u>d</u>ukaan<u>aan</u>	*shops*

Type 2: Invariable nouns

Invariable nouns are those which do not change forms from the singular to the plural.

Masculine

Singular	ਆਦਮੀ	aa<u>d</u>mee	*man*
Plural	ਆਦਮੀ	aa<u>d</u>mee	*men*
Singular	ਹੱਥ	ha<u>thth</u>	*hand*
Plural	ਹੱਥ	ha<u>thth</u>	*hands*

Some other examples of invariable nouns:

ਮੋਤੀ	mo<u>t</u>ee	*pearl*
ਹਾਰ	haar	*necklace*
ਨੱਕ	nakk	*nose*
ਦਰਿਆ	<u>d</u>ariaa	*river*

Note that generally all feminine nouns are variable, that is feminine nouns change from the singular to the plural form.

Adjustable nouns

In Panjabi the same noun can often be used to represent both genders by simply changing the ending to express their femininity or masculinity. These types of nouns are irregular, though the pattern of endings that they take can be distinctly identified.

		Masculine				Feminine	
ਚਾਚਾ	chaachaa	*uncle*	= ਚਾਚੀ	chaachee	*paternal aunt*
ਪੁੱਤਰ	puttar	*son*	= ਪੁੱਤਰੀ	puttaree	*daughter*
ਊਠ	ooth	*male camel*	= ਊਠਣੀ	oothnhee	*female camel*
ਨੋਕਰ	naukar	*male servant*	= ਨੋਕਰਾਣੀ	naukaraanhee	*maid*

ਬਾਲ	baal	*male child*	= ਬਾਲੜੀ	baalrhee	*female child*
ਰਾਜਾ	raajaa	*king*	= ਰਾਣੀ	raanhee	*queen*
ਮੋਚੀ	mochee	*male cobbler*	= ਮੋਚਣ	mochanh	*female cobbler*

Some nouns are significantly different from their masculine/feminine counterparts:

ਭਰਾ	bharaa	*brother*	= ਭੈਣ	bhainh	*sister*
ਮੁੰਡਾ	mundaa	*boy*	= ਕੁੜੀ	kurhee	*girl*
ਬੰਦਾ	bandaa	*man*	= ਜਨਾਨੀ	janaanee	*woman*

Nouns borrowed from English

Words borrowed from English are also classified in terms of gender and are pluralized according to the pattern of Panjabi nouns. For example:

Masculine

Singular			Plural		
ਕੈਮਰਾ	kaimraa	*camera*	ਕੈਮਰੇ	kaimre	*cameras*
ਟੈਲੀਫ਼ੋਨ	taileefon	*telephone*	ਟੈਲੀਫ਼ੋਨ	taileefon	*telephones*

Feminine

Singular			Plural		
ਪਲੇਟ	palet	*plate*	ਪਲੇਟਾਂ	paletaan	*plates*
ਪੈਂਸਲ	painsal	*pencil*	ਪੈਂਸਲਾਂ	painsalaan	*pencils*

Similarly, the plural of ਸਮੋਸਾ samosaa (*samosa*) is ਸਮੋਸੇ samose in Panjabi and *samosas* in English.

Adjectives

An adjective is a word that gives descriptive information about a noun, pronoun or another adjective. Generally, adjectives come before the noun and after the pronoun. Similar to nouns, adjectives are also either masculine or feminine and are used in singular and plural forms, reflecting the gender and numerical traits of the nouns that they are describing. There are two types of simple adjectives, variable and invariable.

Variable adjectives

Variable adjectives end in ਆ **aa** for the masculine and ਈ **ee** for the feminine such as ਵੱਡਾ **vaddaa** (masculine) and ਵੱਡੀ **vaddee** (feminine) *big*. They inflect (i.e. change their endings) with the number and the gender of the noun.

Masculine singular	ਵੱਡਾ ਲੜਕਾ	vaddaa larhkaa	*big boy*
Masculine plural	ਵੱਡੇ ਲੜਕੇ	vadde larhke	*big boys*
Feminine singular	ਵੱਡੀ ਲੜਕੀ	vaddee larhkee	*big girl*
Feminine plural	ਵੱਡੀਆਂ ਲੜਕੀਆਂ	vaddee<u>aan</u> larhkee<u>aan</u>	*big girls*

When the noun is the same for both genders and singular/plural forms, it is the variable adjective and/or the verb which will indicate the numerical and gender characteristics of the noun.

Examples:

Singular	ਇਹ ਵੱਡਾ ਮਕਾਨ ਹੈ	ih vaddaa makaan hai	*This is a big house.*
Plural	ਇਹ ਵੱਡੇ ਮਕਾਨ ਹਨ	ih vadde makaan han	*These are big houses.*

Variable adjectives also indicate the gender characteristic of the noun.

ਇਹ ਵੱਡਾ ਮੇਜ਼ ਹੈ	ih vaddaa mez (m.) hai	*This is a big table.* (m.)
ਇਹ ਵੱਡੀ ਕੁਰਸੀ ਹੈ	ih vaddee kursee (f.) hai	*This is a big chair.* (f.)

There are some exceptions regarding adjectives of this type. Some adjectives do not change their form according to the noun's gender and number associations, despite the fact that they end in ਈ **ee** or ਆ **aa** such as:

ਵਧੀਆ va<u>dh</u>eeaa *superior*   ਗੁਲਾਬੀ gulaabee *pink*

You need to learn such exceptions as you go along.

Invariable adjectives

Invariable adjectives do not change according to the nouns that they specify and do not end with ਆ **aa** or ਈ **ee**, such as:

ਲਾਲ	laal	*red*
ਖ਼ੁਸ਼	<u>kh</u>ush	*happy*
ਸਾਫ਼	saaf	*clean*

ਖ਼ੁਸ਼ ਲੜਕਾ	<u>kh</u>ush larhkaa	*happy boy*
ਖ਼ੁਸ਼ ਲੜਕੇ	<u>kh</u>ush larhke	*happy boys*
ਖ਼ੁਸ਼ ਲੜਕੀ	<u>kh</u>ush larhkee	*happy girl*
ਖ਼ੁਸ਼ ਲੜਕੀਆਂ	<u>kh</u>ush larhkeeaa<u>n</u>	*happy girls*

The simple verb

Verbs indicate activity and are also called action words. Throughout the book the Panjabi verb is referred to in the infinitive form (i.e. the form *to*). The root of the verb plus the ending -ਣਾ **nhaa** or the ending -ਨਾ **naa** form the infinitive. Here are some common examples of verbs in the infinitive, or simple form:

Infinitive form (= 'to _____')			Root		Ending	
ਲਿਖਣਾ	likhnhaa	*to write*	ਲਿਖ	likh	ਣਾ	nhaa
ਦੇਣਾ	<u>d</u>enhaa	*to give*	ਦੇ	<u>d</u>e	ਣਾ	nhaa
ਖਾਣਾ	khaanhaa	*to eat*	ਖਾ	khaa	ਣਾ	nhaa
ਆਉਣਾ	aaunhaa	*to come*	ਆਉ	aau	ਣਾ	nhaa
ਬੋਲਣਾ	bolnhaa	*to speak*	ਬੋਲ	bol	ਣਾ	nhaa
ਕਹਿਣਾ	kahinhaa	*to say*	ਕਹਿ	kahi	ਣਾ	nhaa
ਰਹਿਣਾ	rahinhaa	*to live, stay*	ਰਹਿ	rahi	ਣਾ	nhaa
ਕਰਨਾ	karnaa	*to do*	ਕਰ	kar	ਨਾ	naa

The simple verb is also used as a form of command particularly related to actions in the near future.

Examples:

ਜਲਦੀ ਆਉਣਾ	jal<u>d</u>ee aaunhaa	*come back quickly*
ਹੌਲੀ ਬੋਲਣਾ	haulee bolnhaa	*speak softly*
ਚਿੱਠੀ ਲਿਖਣਾ	chiththee likhnhaa	*write a letter*

The possessive particle ਦਾ '<u>d</u>aa' *of*

In Panjabi, possession is expressed through the particle ਦਾ. In English possession is not usually expressed using the word *of*; for example, *the pencil of the girl* would usually be written *the girl's pencil*. The particle ਦਾ <u>d</u>aa is therefore similar to the apostrophe *s* in English as it establishes the relationship between possessions. The particle ਦਾ <u>d</u>aa *of* should agree with the gender and number of the object being possessed. Generally, it takes the following forms:

ਦਾ	<u>d</u>aa	masculine singular
ਦੇ	<u>d</u>e	masculine plural
ਦੀ	<u>d</u>ee	feminine singular
ਦੀਆਂ	<u>d</u>eeaa<u>n</u>	feminine plural

Words such as *of, in, to* or *from* are called prepositions in English and signify place or position. These words come before the noun and are therefore called prepositions.

In Panjabi these kinds of words come after the noun and are therefore called postpositions. This is also the second function of ਦਾ <u>d</u>aa in that it dictates word order and acts as a grammatical point determining the endings of the nouns and adjectives associated with the possession.

Examples:

ਕੁੜੀ ਦੀਆਂ ਪੈਂਸਲਾਂ	kurhee <u>d</u>eeaa<u>n</u> painsalaan	*the girl's pencils*
ਆਦਮੀ ਦੀ ਦੁਕਾਨ	aa<u>d</u>mee <u>d</u>ee <u>d</u>ukaan	*the man's shop*
ਮੇਰੀ ਭੈਣ ਦਾ ਕਮਰਾ	meree bhainh <u>d</u>aa kamraa	*my sister's room*

Insight

The particle '<u>d</u>aa' 'ਦਾ' (of) and its different forms are used in a variety of ways to express possession.

Possessive adjectives with plural objects

In Unit 1 you learned about possessive adjectives with singular objects. When objects being possessed are plural, the endings of possessive adjectives change accordingly. The following tables illustrate the use of the possessive adjective with plural objects.

Possessive adjectives with plural masculine objects

1st person

| ਮੇਰੇ | mere | *my* |
| ਸਾਡੇ | saade | *our* |

2nd person

| ਤੇਰੇ | ṯere | *your* (informal) |
| ਤੁਹਾਡੇ | ṯuhaade | *your* (formal) |

3rd person

ਇਹ ਦੇ/ਇਸ ਦੇ	ih ḏe/is ḏe	*his/her*
ਇਹਨਾਂ ਦੇ	ihnaan ḏe	*his/her* (formal) *their*
ਉਹ ਦੇ/ਉਸ ਦੇ	uh ḏe/us ḏe	*his/her*
ਉਹਨਾਂ ਦੇ	uhnaan ḏe	*his/her* (formal) *their*

Possessive adjectives with plural feminine objects

1st person

| ਮੇਰੀਆਂ | mereeaan | *my* |
| ਸਾਡੀਆਂ | saadeeaan | *our* |

2nd person

| ਤੇਰੀਆਂ | ṯereeaan | *your* (informal) |
| ਤੁਹਾਡੀਆਂ | ṯuhaadeeaan | *your* (formal) |

3rd person

ਇਹ ਦੀਆਂ/ਇਸ ਦੀਆਂ	ih ḏeeaan/is ḏeeaan	*his/her*
ਇਹਨਾਂ ਦੀਆਂ	ihnaan ḏeeaan	*his/her* (formal) *their*
ਉਹ ਦੀਆਂ/ਉਸ ਦੀਆਂ	uh ḏeeaan/us ḏeeaan	*his/her*
ਉਹਨਾਂ ਦੀਆਂ	uhnaan ḏeeaan	*his/her* (formal) *their*

Examples:

ਮੇਰੇ ਬੱਚੇ	mere bachche	*my children*
ਤੁਹਾਡੀਆਂ ਕਿਤਾਬਾਂ	t̲uhaadeeaan kit̲aabaan	*your books*
ਉਹਨਾਂ ਦੀਆਂ	uhnaan d̲eeaan	*their sweets*
ਮਿਠਿਆਈਆਂ	mithiaaeeaan	
ਸਾਡੇ ਲੜਕੇ	saade larhke	*our sons*

Numbers

◄)) **CD 1, TR 4, 03:34**

In Dialogue 3, you were introduced to the numbers ਚਾਰ **chaar** and ਦੋ **d̲o**. The following is the list of numbers from 1–20. The topic vocabulary list at the end of the book gives the remaining numbers up to 100.

੧	1	ਇੱਕ	ikk	੧੧	11	ਗਿਆਰਾਂ	giaaraan
੨	2	ਦੋ	d̲o	੧੨	12	ਬਾਰਾਂ	baar-haan
੩	3	ਤਿੰਨ	t̲inn	੧੩	13	ਤੇਰਾਂ	t̲er-haan
੪	4	ਚਾਰ	chaar	੧੪	14	ਚੌਦਾਂ	chaud̲-haan
੫	5	ਪੰਜ	panj	੧੫	15	ਪੰਦਰਾਂ	pand̲araan
੬	6	ਛੇ	che	੧੬	16	ਸੋਲ੍ਹਾਂ	solhaan
੭	7	ਸੱਤ	satt	੧੭	17	ਸਤਾਰਾਂ	sataar-haan
੮	8	ਅੱਠ	athth	੧੮	18	ਅਠਾਰਾਂ	athaar-haan
੯	9	ਨੌਂ	naun	੧੯	19	ਉੱਨੀ	unnee
੧੦	10	ਦਸ	d̲as	੨੦	20	ਵੀਹ	veeh

ਵਿਆਖਿਆ viaakhiaa *Commentary*

1 *The vegetable seller* ਸਬਜ਼ੀ ਵਾਲਾ sabzee vaalaa

In Panjab, fresh seasonal vegetables are available in abundance. The land is rich and the climate is tropical. Vegetables can generally be bought from a variety of sources. A street hawker carrying vegetables in his hand-pulled cart will make his daily rounds in the streets, shouting the names of vegetables at the top of his lungs in a manner that signals his presence more than does the content of his wares. Vegetables can also be bought from the market (often called a ਮੰਡੀ ma<u>n</u>dee or even ਮਾਰਕੇਟ maarket) where dozens of greengrocery stalls and shops are situated next to each other. These stalls offer a wide variety of fresh vegetables (ਸਬਜ਼ੀਆਂ sabzeeaa<u>n</u>) according to the season. In Panjab, visiting the market, especially in the evenings, is more than just for shopping; it is also a social and entertaining experience. Prices are not displayed so that customers have to make enquiries to shopkeepers, comparing prices of different stalls and bargaining as they go along. An accepted and often time-consuming part of shopping in Panjab is bargaining. Once a bargain has been made, the shopkeeper uses his age-old technique of weighing the goods between two pans on his scale. Most shopkeepers are efficient in mentally calculating the price of the weighed goods and are keen to chat, pointing out the low prices of other vegetables on offer and generally to praise their goods. This is a contrast to shopping for vegetables in Western countries which is usually impersonal and mechanical.

2 *The Panjabi sweet shop* ਮਿਠਿਆਈ ਦੀ ਦੁਕਾਨ mithiaaee <u>d</u>ee <u>d</u>ukaan

Sweet shops are an integral part of shopping areas catering for South Asian communities in England, America, Canada and other parts of the world. These sweet shops are not like confectionery shops or bakeries, as they are often attached to take-away restaurants and also offer a range of spicy snacks and nibbles. It is customary for most South Asians to exchange boxes of sweets among friends and family on happy occasions. These can range from weddings and birthdays to festivals. Sweet shops, therefore, remain busy throughout the year. There is an enormous variety of sweets from different regions of the Indian sub-continent. Most sweet shops in the diaspora offer about 50 of the more common types of sweets and savoury dishes. Here is a list of some of the more popular items.

Sweets

ਲੱਡੂ laddoo	a sweet round ball, generally orange in colour, consisting of tiny particles made of gram flour
ਗੁਲਾਬ ਜਾਮਣ gulaab jaamanh	a round, soft brown ball made of milk powder soaked in a sweet syrup
ਬਰਫੀ barfee	a bar of milk powder, similar to fudge, which is cut into diamond and rectangular shapes and is also found in a variety of colours such as white, pink and green
ਜਲੇਬੀਆਂ jalebeeaa<u>n</u>	whirls of batter, yellow-orange in colour, which are soaked in a sweet syrup
ਰਸ ਗੁੱਲੇ ras gulle	sweet round balls made of cheese soaked in a clear sweet syrup
ਰਸ ਮਲਾਈ ras malaaee	sweet round balls made of cheese soaked in thick, sweet milk
ਗਜਰੇਲਾ gajrelaa	a sweet dish made from grated carrots
ਪਿੰਨੀਆਂ pi<u>nn</u>eeaa<u>n</u>	sweet round balls made from ground lentils and gram flour

Savouries

There are about a dozen salty dishes which are available from sweet shops. These are the most common ones:

ਪਕੌੜੇ pakaurhe	seasoned and spiced vegetables covered in a gram flour batter which are deep fried in oil

| ਸਮੋਸੇ | deep-fried triangular pastries filled with boiled |
| samose | peas, potatoes and sometimes minced meat |

Insight

Language and culture go together. You are suggested to visit a South Asian grocery shop, Panjabi sweet shop, a 'gurdwara' (Sikh place of worship) 'ਗੁਰਦਵਾਰਾ' and/or an Indian restaurant.

ਅਭਿਆਸ abhiaas *Exercises*

1 Choose the appropriate adjectives

Bitter gourd and turnip are masculine and okra is feminine.

small
ਛੋਟਾ   <u>ch</u>otaa   ਛੋਟੀ   <u>ch</u>otee

big
ਵੱਡਾ   vaddaa   ਵੱਡੀ   vaddee

a ਇਹ ਕਰੇਲਾ _____ ਹੈ।   ih karelaa _____ hai.
    This bitter gourd is small.
b ਇਹ ਕਰੇਲਾ _____ ਹੈ।   ih karelaa _____ hai.
    This bitter gourd is large.
c ਇਹ ਭਿੰਡੀ _____ ਹੈ।   ih bhi<u>n</u>dee _____ hai.
    This okra is small.
d ਇਹ ਭਿੰਡੀ _____ ਹੈ।   ih bhi<u>n</u>dee _____ hai.
    This okra is large.
e ਇਹ ਸ਼ਲਗਮ _____ ਹੈ।   ih shalgam _____ hai.
    This turnip is small.
f ਇਹ ਸ਼ਲਗਮ _____ ਹੈ।   ih shalgam _____ hai.
    This turnip is large.

ਕਰੇਲਾ   ਭਿੰਡੀ   ਸ਼ਲਗਮ

2 Who has ordered what?

◀》 CD 1, TR 4, 04:05

Mr Singh, Jane and Henry have each ordered several food items. Listen to the recording and tick the box to show who has ordered what.

	ਸਮੋਸਾ samosaa	ਲੱਡੂ laddoo	ਪਕੌੜੇ pakaurhe	ਰਸ ਮਲਾਈ ras malaaee	ਭਿੰਡੀ bhindee	ਗੋਭੀ gobhee
Mr Singh						
Jane						
Henry						

3 Who am I?

After reading the Commentary section, try to guess who I am from the descriptions given below.

a I am sweet, full of syrup, round and dark brown in colour.
b I am sweet like fudge, in diamond and rectangular shapes and come in a variety of different colours such as white, pink and green.
c I am a very popular savoury snack, triangular in shape, covered in pastry, filled with potatoes and peas, and deep fried.
d I am like a fritter, dipped in a batter of gram flour mixture, and deep fried. My core ingredients are usually cauliflower, potatoes and aubergine.

4 Insert the correct possessive adjectives

(Remember that the forms of possessive adjectives change not only in terms of who is in possession of the object, but also by the gender and number of the object being possessed.)

a _____	ਸਮੋਸੇ ਸੁਆਦੀ ਹਨ ।	samose suaadee han.	*Their samosas are tasty.*
b _____	ਲੜਕੇ ਕਿੱਥੇ ਹਨ ?	larhke kiththe han?	*Where are my sons?*

c _____	ਕਿਤਾਬਾਂ ਹਰ ਪਾਸੇ ਹਨ।	kitaabaan har paase han.	*Our books are everywhere.*
d _____	ਮਿਠਿਆਈਆਂ ਸਭ ਤੋਂ ਚੰਗੀਆਂ ਹਨ!	mithiaaeeaan sabh ton changeeaan han!	*Your (formal) sweets are the best!*

Ten important things to remember

1 Panjabi nouns are marked by both number (singular and plural) and gender (masculine and feminine).

2 Every noun in Panjabi, even an inanimate object, is assigned a masculine or feminine gender.

3 The process of assignment of gender, especially to an inanimate object, can be quite arbitrary.

4 Invariable nouns do not change their form from the singular to the plural.

5 Singular nouns ending in the masculine gender suffix 'aa' would change to the plural form by replacing 'aa' with 'e'.

6 Singular nouns ending in the feminine gender suffix 'ee' would become a plural by adding 'aan'. For example, *larhkee* ਲੜਕੀ (girl, daughter) would change to *larhkeeaan* ਲੜਕੀਆਂ (girls, daughters).

7 Adjectives are also either masculine or feminine and are used in singular and plural forms.

8 The particle '*daa*' 'ਦਾ' (of) should agree with the gender and number of the object being possessed.

9 The Panjabi equivalents of English prepositions are placed *after* nouns, hence they are known as postpositions.

10 Panjabi verbs have a variety of endings. Their forms change according to the tense and the subject.

4

ਬੜੀ ਖ਼ੁਸ਼ੀ ਦੀ ਗੱਲ ਹੈ!
barhee <u>kh</u>ushee <u>d</u>ee gall hai!
That's very good news!

In this unit you will learn:

- How to introduce yourself and others
- How to ask and answer questions about work
- How to ask and respond to questions about place of origin
- How to talk about your family
- How to describe actions and objects in the present

---

1 *What do you do?*
ਗੱਲ ਬਾਤ ੧ ਤੁਸੀਂ ਕੀ ਕਰਦੇ ਹੋ?
gall baa<u>t</u> 1 <u>t</u>usee<u>n</u> kee kar<u>d</u>e ho?

◀)) CD 1, TR 5, 00:21

Dr Singh and Mrs Sharma are travelling on a train going from Birmingham to London. They are meeting for the first time.

ਮਿਸਜ਼ ਸ਼ਰਮਾ **Mrs Sharma**	ਸਤਿ ਸ੍ਰੀ ਅਕਾਲ। ਕੀ ਇਹ ਸੀਟ ਖ਼ਾਲੀ ਹੈ? sa<u>t</u> sree akaal. kee ih seet <u>kh</u>aalee hai? *Hello. Is this seat vacant?*
ਡਾਕਟਰ ਸਿੰਘ **Dr Singh**	ਸਤਿ ਸ੍ਰੀ ਅਕਾਲ। ਹਾਂ ਜੀ, ਖ਼ਾਲੀ ਹੈ। ਬੈਠੋ ਜੀ। sa<u>t</u> sree akaal. haa<u>n</u> jee, <u>kh</u>aalee hai. baitho jee. *Hello. Yes, it's vacant. Please sit down.*

ਮਿਸਜ਼ ਸ਼ਰਮਾ	ਧੰਨਵਾਦ ਮੇਰਾ ਨਾਮ ਮਿਸਜ਼ ਸ਼ਰਮਾ ਹੈ। ਸਰਦਾਰ ਸਾਹਿਬ, ਤੁਹਾਡਾ ਕੀ ਨਾਮ ਹੈ?
Mrs Sharma	dhannvaad. meraa naam misaz sharmaa hai. sardaar saahib tuhaadaa kee naam hai?
	Thank you. My name is Mrs Sharma. Sardar Saahib, what is your name?
ਡਾਕਟਰ ਸਿੰਘ	ਮੇਰਾ ਨਾਮ ਅਜੀਤ ਸਿੰਘ ਹੈ। ਮੈਂ ਡਾਕਟਰ ਹਾਂ। ਤੁਸੀਂ ਕੀ ਕਰਦੇ ਹੋ, ਮਿਸਜ਼ ਸ਼ਰਮਾ?
Dr Singh	meraa naam ajeet singh hai. main daaktar haan. tuseen kee karde ho, misaz sharmaa?
	My name is Ajeet Singh. I'm a doctor. What do you do, Mrs Sharma?
ਮਿਸਜ਼ ਸ਼ਰਮਾ	ਮੈਂ ਅਧਿਆਪਕਾ ਹਾਂ ਅਤੇ ਮੈਂ ਬਰਮਿੰਘਮ ਵਿਚ ਰਹਿੰਦੀ ਹਾਂ। ਤੁਸੀਂ ਕਿੱਥੇ ਰਹਿੰਦੇ ਹੋ?
Mrs Sharma	main adhiaapkaa haan ate main barmingham vich rahindee haan. tuseen kiththe rahinde ho?
	I am a teacher and I live in Birmingham. Where do you live?
ਡਾਕਟਰ ਸਿੰਘ	ਮੈਂ ਵੀ ਬਰਮਿੰਘਮ ਵਿਚ ਰਹਿੰਦਾ ਹਾਂ। ਮੈਂ ਕੀਨੀਆ ਤੋਂ ਹਾਂ। ਕੀ ਤੁਸੀਂ ਪੰਜਾਬ ਤੋਂ ਹੋ?
Dr Singh	main vee barmingham vich rahindaa haan. main keeneeaa ton haan. kee tuseen panjaab ton ho?
	I live in Birmingham too. I am from Kenya. Are you from Panjab?
ਮਿਸਜ਼ ਸ਼ਰਮਾ	ਨਹੀਂ ਜੀ। ਮੈਂ ਦਿੱਲੀ ਤੋਂ ਹਾਂ।
Mrs Sharma	naheen jee. main dillee ton haan.
	No. I'm from Delhi.

ਸ਼ਬਦਾਵਲੀ	**shabdaavalee**	*Vocabulary*
ਸੀਟ	seet	*seat* (f.)
ਖ਼ਾਲੀ	khaalee	*empty, vacant*
ਬੈਠਣਾ	baithnhaa	*to sit*
ਬੈਠੋ ਜੀ	baitho jee	*please sit down* (formal)
ਸਰਦਾਰ ਸਾਹਿਬ	sardaar saahib	*Mr* (see Commentary)
ਡਾਕਟਰ	daaktar	*doctor* (m./f.)
ਅਧਿਆਪਕਾ	adhiaapkaa	*teacher* (f.)
ਬਰਮਿੰਘਮ	barmingham	*Birmingham* (m.)
ਰਹਿਣਾ	rahinhaa	*to stay, to live*

ਕੀਨੀਆ	keeneeaa	*Kenya* (m.)
ਤੋਂ	to<u>n</u>	*from*
ਪੰਜਾਬ	pa<u>n</u>jaab	*Panjab* (m.)
ਦਿੱਲੀ	<u>d</u>illee	*Delhi* (f.)

ਅਭਿਆਸ abhiaas *Exercises*

After reading the dialogue and/or listening to the recording, try to do the following exercises.

1 Fill in the blanks

Following the first example, fill in the blanks with the Panjabi phrases according to the English ones given to you. You may borrow phrases from the dialogue.

a	ਮੈਂ ਡਾਕਟਰ ਹਾਂ।	mai<u>n</u> daaktar haa<u>n</u>.	*I am a doctor.*
b	_____	*Is this seat vacant?*	_____ *Yes, it is.*
c	_____	*I'm a teacher.*	
d	_____	*What do you (formal) do?*	

2 Arrange in correct word order

a	ਵੀ ਮੈਂ ਬਰਮਿੰਘਮ ਰਹਿੰਦਾ ਹਾਂ।	vee mai<u>n</u> barmi<u>n</u>gham rahi<u>n</u>daa haa<u>n</u>.	*I live in Birmingham too.*
b	ਦਿੱਲੀ ਤੋਂ ਮੈਂ ਹਾਂ।	<u>d</u>illee to<u>n</u> mai<u>n</u> haa<u>n</u>.	*I am from Delhi.*
c	ਤੁਸੀਂ ਹੋ ਕਰਦੇ ਕੀ?	tusee<u>n</u> ho kar<u>d</u>e kee?	*What do you do?*

3 Remarks and responses

The following conversation is between two unacquainted passengers on a train. Put the responses of Passenger B into order according to Passenger A's remarks by using the correct corresponding number.

	Passenger A		Passenger B
1	ਕੀ ਇਹ ਟਰੇਨ ਲੰਡਨ ਜਾਂਦੀ ਹੈ? kee ih taren la<u>n</u>dan jaa<u>n</u>dee hai?	a	ਮੈਂ ਲੀਡਜ਼ ਰਹਿੰਦਾ ਹਾਂ mai<u>n</u> leedz rahi<u>n</u>daa haa<u>n</u>

2	ਤੁਸੀਂ ਕਿੱਥੇ ਰਹਿੰਦੇ ਹੋ ? tuseen kiththe rahinde ho?	b	ਮੈਂ ਅਧਿਆਪਕਾ ਹਾਂ main adhiaapkaa haan
3	ਤੁਸੀਂ ਕੀ ਕੰਮ ਕਰਦੇ ਹੋ ? tuseen kee kanm karde ho?	c	ਹਾਂ, ਇਹ ਟਰੇਨ ਲੰਡਨ ਜਾਂਦੀ ਹੈ haan, ih taren landan jaandee hai
4	ਕੀ ਤੁਸੀਂ ਹਿੰਦੀ ਬੋਲਦੇ ਹੋ ? kee tuseen hindee bolde ho?	d	ਮੈਂ ਪੰਜਾਬ ਤੋਂ ਹਾਂ main panjaab ton haan
5	ਕੀ ਤੁਸੀਂ ਪੰਜਾਬ ਤੋਂ ਹੋ ਜਾਂ ਦਿੱਲੀ ਤੋਂ ਹੋ ? kee tuseen panjaab ton ho jaan dillee ton ho?	e	ਮੈਂ ਹਿੰਦੀ ਅਤੇ ਪੰਜਾਬੀ ਬੋਲਦਾ ਹਾਂ main hindee ate panjaabee boldaa haan

Insight

The auxiliary forms of Panjabi verbs like *'hai, hain, han, haan and ho'* 'ਹੈ, ਹੈਂ, ਹਨ, ਹਾਂ ਅਤੇ ਹੋ' (*is, are, am*) belong to the present tense and operate at three levels.

2 *That's very good news!*
ਗੱਲ ਬਾਤ ੨ ਬੜੀ ਖ਼ੁਸ਼ੀ ਦੀ ਗੱਲ ਹੈ!
gall baat 2 barhee khushee dee gall hai!

◀) CD 1, TR 5, 01:24

While Dr Singh and Mrs Sharma chat on the train going from Birmingham to London, Fatima Khan boards the train at Coventry. Mrs Sharma and Fatima Khan know each other. Fatima Khan addresses Mrs Sharma by her first name, Sita.

ਫ਼ਾਤਿਮਾ ਖ਼ਾਨ **Fatima Khan**	ਨਮਸਤੇ ਸੀਤਾ। ਤੇਰੀ ਸਿਹਤ ਕਿਵੇਂ ਹੈ ? namaste seetaa. teree sihat kiven hai? *Hello Sita. How's your health?*
ਸੀਤਾ ਸ਼ਰਮਾ **Sita Sharma**	ਨਮਸਤੇ! ਮੇਰੀ ਸਿਹਤ ਹੁਣ ਬਿਲਕੁਲ ਠੀਕ ਹੈ। ਮਿਹਰਬਾਨੀ। namaste! meree sihat hunh bilkul theek hai. miharbaanee. *Hello! My health is perfectly fine now. Thank you.*

ਫ਼ਾਤਿਮਾ ਖ਼ਾਨ **Fatima Khan**	ਬੜੀ ਖ਼ੁਸ਼ੀ ਦੀ ਗੱਲ ਹੈ! barhee <u>kh</u>ushee <u>d</u>ee gall hai! *That's very good news!*
ਸੀਤਾ ਸ਼ਰਮਾ **Sita Sharma**	ਤੇਰੇ ਪਰਵਾਰ ਦਾ ਕੀ ਹਾਲ ਹੈ? tere parvaar <u>d</u>aa kee haal hai? *How is your family?*
ਫ਼ਾਤਿਮਾ ਖ਼ਾਨ **Fatima Khan**	ਸਾਰੇ ਠੀਕ ਹਨ। ਮਿਸਟਰ ਖ਼ਾਨ ਮੌਜਾਂ ਕਰਦੇ ਹਨ। ਸਾਡਾ ਬੇਟਾ ਅਤੇ ਬੇਟੀ ਕਾਲਜ ਵਿਚ ਪੜ੍ਹਦੇ ਹਨ। saare theek han. mistar <u>kh</u>aan maujaa<u>n</u> karde han. saadaa betaa ate betee kaalaj vich parhh<u>d</u>e han. *Everyone is fine. Mr Khan is enjoying life. Our son and daughter are studying at college.*

(Sita Sharma introduces Dr Singh and Fatima Khan to one another.)

ਸੀਤਾ ਸ਼ਰਮਾ **Sita Sharma**	ਡਾਕਟਰ ਸਿੰਘ, ਇਹ ਮੇਰੀ ਸਹੇਲੀ ਫ਼ਾਤਿਮਾ ਖ਼ਾਨ ਹੈ। ਫ਼ਾਤਿਮਾ, ਇਹ ਡਾਕਟਰ ਸਿੰਘ ਹਨ। daaktar si<u>ng</u>h, ih meree sahelee faa<u>t</u>imaa <u>kh</u>aan hai. faa<u>t</u>imaa, ih daaktar si<u>ng</u>h han. *Dr Singh, this is my friend Fatima Khan. Fatima, this is Dr Singh.*
ਡਾਕਟਰ ਸਿੰਘ **Dr Singh**	ਅੱਸਲਾਮ ਅਲੈਕਮ asslaam alaikam. *Hello.*
ਫ਼ਾਤਿਮਾ ਖ਼ਾਨ **Fatima Khan**	ਵਾਲੈਕਮ ਅੱਸਲਾਮ। vaalaikam asslaam. *Hello.*

(Sita addresses Fatima.)

ਸੀਤਾ ਸ਼ਰਮਾ **Sita Sharma**	ਫ਼ਾਤਿਮਾ। ਅਗਲੇ ਹਫ਼ਤੇ ਨੂੰ ਸਕੂਲ ਦੀਆਂ ਛੁੱਟੀਆਂ ਸ਼ੁਰੂ ਹੁੰਦੀਆਂ ਹਨ। ਬੱਚਿਆਂ ਨਾਲ ਬਰਮਿੰਘਮ ਆਉਣਾ। faa<u>t</u>imaa, agle haf<u>t</u>e noo<u>n</u> sakool <u>d</u>eeaa<u>n</u> <u>ch</u>utteeaa<u>n</u> shuroo hu<u>nd</u>eeaa<u>n</u> han. bachchiaa<u>n</u> naal barmingham aaunhaa. *School holidays start next week. Come with the children to Birmingham.*
ਫ਼ਾਤਿਮਾ ਖ਼ਾਨ **Fatima Khan**	ਇਨਸ਼ਾ ਅੱਲਾ। inshaa allaa. *We'll try. (lit. If God wishes.)*

ਸ਼ਬਦਾਵਲੀ	shab<u>d</u>aavalee	*Vocabulary*
ਬੜੀ	barhee	*very* (v.)
ਖ਼ੁਸ਼ੀ	<u>kh</u>ushee	*good* (f.) (lit. happiness)
ਗੱਲ	gall	*matter, news* (f.)
ਸਿਹਤ	siha<u>t</u>	*health* (f.)
ਹੁਣ	hunh	*now*
ਬਿਲਕੁਲ	bilkul	*absolutely, perfectly*
ਸਾਰੇ	saare	*everyone, all* (v.)
ਮੌਜਾਂ ਕਰਨਾ	maujaa<u>n</u> karnaa	*to enjoy*
ਬੇਟਾ	betaa	*son* (m.)
ਬੇਟੀ	betee	*daughter* (f.)
ਕਾਲਜ	kaalaj	*college* (m.)
ਪੜੂਨਾ	parh-h-naa	*to read, to study*
ਸਹੇਲੀ	sahelee	*friend* (f.)
ਅਗਲਾ	aglaa	*next*
ਹਫ਼ਤਾ	haf<u>t</u>aa	*week* (m.)
ਸ਼ੁਰੂ ਹੋਣਾ	shuroo honhaa	*to start, to begin*
ਸਕੂਲ	sakool	*school* (m.)
ਛੁੱਟੀਆਂ	<u>ch</u>utteeaan	*holidays* (f.)

Insight

You will have come across a variety of endings of Panjabi verbs which vary according to the tense and the subject.

ਅਭਿਆਸ abhiaas *Exercises*

After reading the dialogue and/or listening to the recording, try to do the following exercises.

1 True or false?

a ਮਿਸਜ਼ ਸ਼ਰਮਾ ਬਰਮਿੰਘਮ ਰਹਿੰਦੀ ਹੈ। misaz sharmaa barmi<u>ng</u>ham rahi<u>nd</u>ee hai.   True/False

b ਮਿਸਜ਼ ਸ਼ਰਮਾ ਅਧਿਆਪਕਾ ਹੈ। misaz sharmaa a<u>dh</u>iaapkaa hai.   True/False

c ਮਿਸਜ਼ ਸ਼ਰਮਾ ਡਾਕਟਰ ਹੈ। misaz sharmaa daaktar hai.   True/False

2 Talking about yourself

CD 1, TR 5, 03:05

You have just met someone for the first time. Listen to their questions on the recording and/or read them from the following list and respond with information about yourself.

a ਤੁਹਾਡਾ ਨਾਮ ਕੀ ਹੈ?   tuhaadaa naam kee hai?   _____
b ਤੁਸੀਂ ਕੀ ਕਰਦੇ ਹੋ?   tuseen kee karde ho?   _____
c ਕੀ ਤੁਸੀਂ ਇੰਗਲੈਂਡ ਤੋਂ ਹੋ?   kee tuseen inglaind ton ho?   _____
d ਤੁਸੀਂ ਕਿੱਥੇ ਰਹਿੰਦੇ ਹੋ?   tuseen kiththe rahinde ho?   _____

ਬੋਲੀ ਬਾਰੇ   bolee baare   *Language points*

The present tense

The simple present tense is used to describe either actions which are habitual (i.e. done on a regular basis) or objects which have permanent or fixed qualities. It is formed by adding the appropriate endings to the root of the main verb followed by a corresponding auxiliary verb. The 'ingredients' for constructing the present tense are, therefore, as follows:

subject + main verb (simple present) + auxiliary verb = present tense

ਦਾ daa, ਦੀ dee, ਦੇ de and ਦੀਆਂ deeaan are the endings which are added to the root of the main verb to reflect the gender, person and number of the subject.

The auxiliary is formed by use of the simple present of the verb ਹੋਣਾ honhaa *to be* (see Unit 2 where it is used for *is, am* and *are*). The auxiliary verb operates at three levels:

1 helping the main verb
   ਮੈਂ ਕਰਦੀ ਹਾਂ   main kardee haan   *I do*
2 functioning independently
   ਮੈਂ ਠੀਕ ਹਾਂ   main theek haan   *I'm fine*
3 showing the existence of the object or situation being described
   ਕੀ ਕੋਈ ਕਿਤਾਬਾਂ ਹਨ?   kee koee kitaabaan han?   *Are there any books?*

56

Now we can look at examples of the simple present tense. The verb ਕਰਨਾ karnaa (*to do*) is used here as an illustration. Verb root ਕਰ kar:

ਮੈਂ main *I* (1st person singular masculine) + ਕਰਦਾ kardaa *do* (present form of *to do*) + ਹਾਂ haan *am* (auxiliary, 1st person singular) = ਮੈਂ ਕਰਦਾ ਹਾਂ main kardaa haan *I do*:

Singular

Masculine	Feminine	
ਮੈਂ ਕਰਦਾ ਹਾਂ main kardaa haan	ਮੈਂ ਕਰਦੀ ਹਾਂ main kardee haan	*I do*
ਤੂੰ ਕਰਦਾ ਹੈਂ toon kardaa hain	ਤੂੰ ਕਰਦੀ ਹੈਂ toon kardee hain	*you do*
ਇਹ/ਉਹ ਕਰਦਾ ਹੈ ih/uh kardaa hai	ਇਹ/ਉਹ ਕਰਦੀ ਹੈ ih/uh kardee hai	*he, she, it does*

Plural

Masculine	Feminine	
ਅਸੀਂ ਕਰਦੇ ਹਾਂ aseen karde haan	ਅਸੀਂ ਕਰਦੀਆਂ ਹਾਂ aseen kardeeaan haan	*we do*
ਤੁਸੀਂ ਕਰਦੇ ਹੋ tuseen karde ho	ਤੁਸੀਂ ਕਰਦੀਆਂ ਹੋ tuseen kardeeaan ho	*you do*
ਇਹ/ਉਹ ਕਰਦੇ ਹਨ ih/uh karde han	ਇਹ/ਉਹ ਕਰਦੀਆਂ ਹਨ ih/uh kardeeaan han	*they/these/those do*

The example of ਕਰਨਾ shows the manner in which verb roots ending with consonants are formed in the simple present tense. However, those roots which end in vowels follow a slightly different pattern. The nasal consonant is placed between the root and the present tense endings. Here, the verb ਪੀਣਾ peenhaa (*to drink*) is used to illustrate. Note that the bindee · follows the bihaaree ੀ ee of ਪੀਣਾ peenhaa.

Simple verb: ਪੀਣਾ peenhaa *to drink*. Verb root: ਪੀ pee:

subject + (object, where appropriate) + simple present + auxiliary = present tense

ਮੈਂ main *I* (subject) (1st person, singular feminine) + ਪਾਣੀ paanhee *water* (object) + ਪੀਂਦੀ peendee *drink* (present of *to drink*) + ਹਾਂ haan *am* (auxiliary) (1st person singular) = ਮੈਂ ਪਾਣੀ ਪੀਂਦੀ ਹਾਂ main paanhee peendee haan *I drink water*:

Singular

Masculine	Feminine	

ਮੈਂ ਪਾਣੀ ਪੀਂਦਾ ਹਾਂ
main paanhee
    peendaa haan
	ਮੈਂ ਪਾਣੀ ਪੀਂਦੀ ਹਾਂ
	main paanhee
	    peendee haan
		I drink water

ਤੂੰ ਪਾਣੀ ਪੀਂਦਾ ਹੈਂ
toon paanhee
    peendaa hain
	ਤੂੰ ਪਾਣੀ ਪੀਂਦੀ ਹੈਂ
	toon paanhee
	    peendee hain
		you drink water

ਇਹ/ਉਹ ਪਾਣੀ ਪੀਂਦਾ ਹੈ
ih/uh paanhee
    peendaa hai
	ਇਹ/ਉਹ ਪਾਣੀ ਪੀਂਦੀ ਹੈ
	ih/uh paanhee
	    peendee hai
		he, she, it
		    drinks water

Plural

Masculine	Feminine	

ਅਸੀਂ ਪਾਣੀ ਪੀਂਦੇ ਹਾਂ
aseen paanhee
    peende haan
	ਅਸੀਂ ਪਾਣੀ ਪੀਂਦੀਆਂ ਹਾਂ
	aseen paanhee
	    peendeeaan haan
		we drink water

ਤੁਸੀਂ ਪਾਣੀ ਪੀਂਦੇ ਹੋ
tuseen paanhee
    peende ho
	ਤੁਸੀਂ ਪਾਣੀ ਪੀਂਦੀਆਂ ਹੋ
	tuseen paanhee
	    peendeeaan ho
		you drink water

ਇਹ/ਉਹ ਪਾਣੀ
    ਪੀਂਦੇ ਹਨ
ih/uh paanhee
    peende han
	ਇਹ/ਉਹ ਪਾਣੀ
	    ਪੀਂਦੀਆਂ ਹਨ
	ih/uh paanhee
	    peendeeaan han
		they drink water

Here are a few more examples of other verbs in the simple present:

ਮੈਂ ਸੋਚਦੀ ਹਾਂ	main sochdee haan	*I think*
ਬੱਚੇ ਖੇਡਦੇ ਹਨ	bachche khedde han	*the children play*
ਅਸੀਂ ਉਰਦੂ ਬੋਲਦੀਆਂ ਹਾਂ	aseen urdoo boldeeaan haan	*we speak Urdu*

Subject–verb agreement

The verb in a sentence must agree with the gender and number of its subject (with a few exceptions in the past tense, which will be discussed in Unit 10). If the subject is feminine and singular, then the verb must also be feminine and singular. As you should have noticed in the previous section on the simple present tense, there are two verbs: one is the main verb which indicates the action and the other is the auxiliary verb (a form of ਹੋਣਾ *to be*). The main verb changes according to the gender and number of the subject, and the auxiliary verb must also agree with the subject but only changes according to the person (1st – *I*, 2nd – *you*, 3rd – *they*) of the subject.

In the following examples note how the verbs (main and auxiliary) are in agreement with the subject:

ਮੈਂ	ਜਾਂਦੀ	ਹਾਂ	main	jaandee	haan
ਉਹ	ਜਾਂਦੇ	ਹਨ	uh	jaande	han
ਤੁਸੀਂ	ਜਾਂਦੇ	ਹੋ	tuseen	jaande	ho
ਮੁੰਡੇ	ਜਾਂਦੇ	ਹਨ	munde	jaande	han

Notice that the main verb and the auxiliary verb agree with one another in the singular and plural aspect of the subject. This is an essential element of forming sentences in Panjabi, and it should therefore be understood how verbs change accordingly.

Simple postpositions

You will recall from Unit 3 that the particle ਦਾ *daa*, in addition to showing possession, can be used as a postposition. Simple postpositions can be used to denote a number of different senses. In Panjabi the most common simple postpositions are as follows:

ਵਿਚ, ਦੇ ਵਿਚ	vich, de vich	*in, inside*
ਤੋਂ	ton	*from*
ਤੇ	te	*on*
ਤਕ	tak	*until, up to*
ਨਾਲ, ਦੇ ਨਾਲ	naal, de naal	*with*
ਨੂੰ	noon	*to*

Here are some simple examples of the uses of postpositions:

ਬਾਗ਼ ਵਿਚ	baagh vich	*in the garden*
ਪੰਜਾਬ ਤੋਂ	panjaab ton	*from Panjab*
ਮੇਜ਼ ਤੇ	mez te	*on the table*
ਅੱਜ ਤਕ	ajj tak	*until today*
ਇੱਥੇ ਤਕ	iththe tak	*up to here*

ਪਰਵਾਰ ਨਾਲ	parvaar naal	*with the family*
ਕਲਮ ਨਾਲ	kalam naal	*with a pen*
ਅਮਰੀਕਾ ਨੂੰ	amreekaa noo<u>n</u>	*to America*
ਸ਼ਾਮ ਨੂੰ	shaam noo<u>n</u>	*in the evening*

Insight

Sometimes inanimate nouns are used in their colloquial forms.

Example: *pi<u>n</u>d <u>t</u>on* ਪਿੰਡ ਤੋਂ – *pi<u>nd</u>o<u>n</u>* 'ਪਿੰਡੋ' – *from the village*.

Nouns in the oblique

Panjabi nouns can be used in three different cases (modes of expression): the vocative, direct, and oblique. Each has its own corresponding way of formation. The vocative case reflects direct speech and will be dealt with in Unit 8. Direct nouns only change according to gender and number, as has been explained in Unit 3, and are not affected by any postposition. In contrast, the oblique case refers to the changes that some nouns undergo when affected by postpositions. In the examples of nouns with postpositions, all of the nouns are in the oblique case, though their forms do not reveal this because they are either invariable or are feminine in gender (see Unit 3). All nouns before a postposition, whether or not in a changed form, take on the oblique case. Proper nouns such as names of people and places are commonly inflected in the colloquial form by the postposition which follows them. In addition, masculine and feminine nouns have noticeably different formations in the oblique. You will note that feminine nouns in the singular and plural do not change in the oblique. Only masculine nouns change form when followed by postpositions.

Masculine singular

Direct			Oblique		
ਮੁੰਡਾ	mu<u>n</u>daa	*boy*	ਮੁੰਡੇ ਨੂੰ	mu<u>n</u>de noo<u>n</u>	*to the boy*
ਘੋੜਾ	ghorhaa	*horse*	ਘੋੜੇ ਤੇ	ghorhe <u>t</u>e	*on the horse*
ਕਮਰਾ	kamraa	*room*	ਕਮਰੇ ਵਿਚ	kamre vich	*in the room*

Masculine plural

Direct			Oblique		
ਮੁੰਡੇ	munde	*boys*	ਮੁੰਡਿਆਂ ਨੂੰ	mundiaan noon	*to the boys*
ਘੋੜੇ	ghorhe	*horses*	ਘੋੜਿਆਂ ਤੇ	ghorhiaan te	*on the horses*
ਕਮਰੇ	kamre	*rooms*	ਕਮਰਿਆਂ ਵਿਚ	kamriaan vich	*in the rooms*

Feminine singular

Direct			Oblique		
ਤਸਵੀਰ	tasveer	*picture*	ਤਸਵੀਰ ਵਿਚ	tasveer vich	*in the picture*
ਕੁੜੀ	kurhee	*girl*	ਕੁੜੀ ਨੂੰ	kurhee noon	*to the girl*
ਜਨਾਨੀ	janaanee	*lady*	ਜਨਾਨੀ ਤੋਂ	janaanee ton	*from the lady*

Feminine plural

Direct			Oblique		
ਤਸਵੀਰਾਂ	tasveeraan	*pictures*	ਤਸਵੀਰਾਂ ਵਿਚ	tasveeraan vich	*in the pictures*
ਕੁੜੀਆਂ	kurheeaan	*girls*	ਕੁੜੀਆਂ ਨੂੰ	kurheeaan noon	*to the girls*
ਜਨਾਨੀਆਂ	janaanee-aan	*ladies*	ਜਨਾਨੀਆਂ ਤੋਂ	janaaneeaan ton	*from the ladies*

Insight

Superficially it appears difficult to understand when to use the oblique form and how to remember the long list of the oblique nouns. With practice this difficulty can be overcome.

Adjectives in the oblique

Adjectives must agree with the nouns they describe. Therefore, it is only logical that adjectives should also change form when attached to a noun followed by a postposition. In a similar manner to the oblique forms of nouns, adjectives are inflected in the oblique case, in addition to carrying the feminine or masculine, singular or plural nature of the nouns which they qualify. When adjectives are attached to oblique nouns, they also become oblique. Invariable adjectives, however, do not change. Notice the pattern of inflection of the adjectives in the following examples:

Direct		Oblique	
ਵੱਡਾ ਬੇਟਾ vaddaa betaa	*elder son*	ਵੱਡੇ ਬੇਟੇ ਨੂੰ vadde bete noo<u>n</u>	*to the elder son*
ਵੱਡੇ ਬੇਟੇ vadde bete	*elder sons*	ਵੱਡਿਆਂ ਬੇਟਿਆਂ ਨੂੰ vaddiaa<u>n</u> betiaa<u>n</u> noo<u>n</u>	*to the elder sons*
ਵੱਡੀ ਬੇਟੀ vaddee betee	*elder daughter*	ਵੱਡੀ ਬੇਟੀ ਨਾਲ vaddee betee naal	*with the elder daughter*
ਵੱਡੀਆਂ ਬੇਟੀਆਂ vaddeeaa<u>n</u> beteeaa<u>n</u>	*elder daughters*	ਵੱਡੀਆਂ ਬੇਟੀਆਂ ਨਾਲ vaddeeaa<u>n</u> beteeaa<u>n</u> naal	*with the elder daughters*
ਲਾਲ ਗੱਡੀ laal gaddee	*red car*	ਲਾਲ ਗੱਡੀ ਵਿਚ laal gaddee vich	*in the red car*
ਲਾਲ ਗੱਡੀਆਂ laal gaddeeaa<u>n</u>	*red cars*	ਲਾਲ ਗੱਡੀਆਂ ਵਿਚ laal gaddeeaa<u>n</u> vich	*in the red cars*

ਵਿਆਖਿਆ viaakhiaa *Commentary*

Employment and the Panjabi diaspora

There has been a long history of labour migration from Panjab to all parts of the world. The descendants of officers in the British Indian police force formed the core of the community in Malaysia and the Philippines, while political migrants at the beginning of the 20th century formed the core of the old community in Vancouver, Canada. In Britain, migration occurred after World War II and was primarily into the old industrial heartlands of the Midlands and the North, with a sizeable group also working in London. From a predominantly rural background to urban Britain, Panjabi men went from tilling the land to toiling on factory floors.

In the 1960s in Britain a Panjabi man would almost definitely be working in a factory or foundry in labouring or semi-skilled occupations. This is in contrast to migration to America in the 1960s where, due to the operation of quotas, only professionals such as doctors and engineers were allowed entry from the Indian sub-continent.

As communities have settled and the old industrial manufacturing sector has gone into decline, Panjabis are now found in all walks of life in Britain and North America. However, there is a concentration in certain parts of the economy, particularly in traditional professions such as law, medicine and engineering as well as self-employment. A large number of Panjabis are also involved in business ventures in textiles, food processing and retailing, the most popular niche markets. At the same time there is an increasing diversity of occupational and class profiles of Panjabis, from the long-term unemployed to multimillionaires.

ਅਭਿਆਸ abhiaas *Exercises*

1 True or false?

a ਸਿਹਤ	sihat	means *health*	True/False
b ਬਿਲਕੁਲ	bilkul	means *all right*	True/False
c ਅਧਿਆਪਕਾ	adhiaapakaa	means *doctor*	True/False
d .ਖੁਸ਼ੀ	khushee	means *fine*	True/False

2 Who made the statements?

Reread the dialogues, then look at the following:

a ਇਹ ਡਾਕਟਰ ਸਿੰਘ ਹਨ। ih daaktar singh han. *This is Doctor Singh.*

b ਮਿਸਟਰ ਖ਼ਾਨ ਮੌਜਾਂ ਕਰਦੇ ਹਨ। mistar khaan maujaan karde han. *Mr Khan is enjoying life.*

c ਮੈਂ ਵੀ ਬਰਮਿੰਘਮ ਰਹਿੰਦਾ ਹਾਂ। main vee barmingham rahindaa haan. *I live in Birmingham too.*

3 Oblique or direct?

The following sentences contain adjectives and nouns which have been underlined. Identify which ones are direct and which ones are oblique.

a ਕੀ ਇਹ <u>ਤੁਹਾਡੀ ਬੇਟੀ</u> ਹੈ?   kee ih <u>tuhaadee betee</u> hai?   *Is this your daughter?*

b <u>ਤੁਹਾਡੇ ਬੇਟੇ</u> ਦਾ ਨਾਮ ਕੀ ਹੈ?   <u>tuhaade bete</u> daa naam kee hai?   *What is your son's name?*

c <u>ਕਮਰਾ</u> ਸਾਫ਼ ਹੈ।   <u>kamraa</u> saaf hai.   *The room is clean.*

d ਕੁੜੀਆਂ <u>ਕਮਰੇ ਵਿਚ</u> ਹਨ।   kurheeaan <u>kamre</u> <u>vich</u> han.   *There are girls in the room.*

e <u>ਅਗਲੇ ਹਫ਼ਤੇ</u> ਨੂੰ ਆਉਣਾ।   <u>agle hafte</u> noon aaunhaa.   *Come next week.*

4 Subjects and verbs into plural forms

◀) CD 1, TR 5, 03:35

Listen to the following sentences and/or read them in the following list. The sentences are in the present tense. Change the subjects and verbs from the singular to the plural. Remember that the verbs (both main and auxiliary) must agree with the subject. The first one has been done for you.

a ਮੈਂ ਲੰਡਨ ਵਿਚ ਕੰਮ ਕਰਦੀ ਹਾਂ।   main landan vich kanm kardee haan.
I work in London.
ਅਸੀਂ ਲੰਡਨ ਵਿਚ ਕੰਮ ਕਰਦੀਆਂ ਹਾਂ।   aseen landan vich kanm kardeeaan haan.
We work in London.

b ਮੇਰੀ ਬੇਟੀ ਸਕੂਲ ਵਿਚ ਪੜ੍ਹਦੀ ਹੈ।   meree betee sakool vich parh-h-dee hai.

c ਤੁਹਾਡਾ ਲੜਕਾ ਕਿੱਥੇ ਰਹਿੰਦਾ ਹੈ?   tuhaadaa larhkaa kiththe rahindaa hai?

d ਕੀ ਉਹ ਮੁੰਡਾ ਪੰਜਾਬੀ ਬੋਲਦਾ ਹੈ?   kee uh mundaa panjaabee boldaa hai?

Ten important things to remember

1 The formula for constructing the present tense is:
Present tense = subject + main verb (simple present) + auxiliary verb.

2 The auxiliary verbs of the present tense are *haan* ਹਾਂ, *ho* ਹੋ, *hai* ਹੈ, *han* ਹਨ, and *hain* ਹੈਂ (is, am, are).

3 The infinitive form of the verb 'to do' *karnaa* has two parts: '*kar*' 'ਕਰ' is the root or stem and '*naa*' 'ਨਾ' is the ending.

4 In the present tense, the particle '*daa*' '**ਦਾ**' and its forms are the endings which are added to the root of the main verb.

5 The particle '*daa*' '**ਦਾ**' etc., in addition to showing possession, can also be used as postpositions.

6 The main verb and the auxiliary verb always agree with one another in both the singular and plural aspects of the subject.

7 Panjabi nouns can be used in three different cases: direct, oblique and vocative.

8 The oblique case refers to the changes that some nouns undergo when affected by the postpositions.

9 The vocative case reflects when somebody is addressed.

10 Sometimes inanimate nouns are used in their colloquial form. Example: *ghar vich* **ਘਰ ਵਿਚ** – *ghare* **ਘਰੇ** (at home).

5

ਕੀ ਗੱਲ ਸੀ?
kee gall see?
What was the matter?

In this unit you will learn:

- How to describe continuous actions in the present and past
- How to form commands and requests
- How to express *was* and *were*

---

1 *What are you doing?*
ਗੱਲ ਬਾਤ ੧ ਤੂੰ ਕੀ ਕਰ ਰਹੀ ਹੈਂ?
gall baat 1 toon kee kar rahee hain?

◄») **CD 1, TR 6, 00:19**

Geeta and Sita are two women working in a garments factory. They are sitting next to one another as they are sewing and have the following conversation.

ਗੀਤਾ	ਨਮਸਤੇ! ਤੂੰ ਕੀ ਕਰ ਰਹੀ ਹੈਂ?
Geeta	namaste! toon kee kar rahee hain?
	Hello! What are you doing?
ਸੀਤਾ	ਨਮਸਤੇ। ਮੈਂ ਜੇਬਾਂ ਲਗਾ ਰਹੀ ਹਾਂ। ਮੇਰੀ ਮਸ਼ੀਨ ਕੰਮ ਨਹੀਂ ਕਰ ਰਹੀ। ਮੈਂ ਸੂਈ ਵਰਤ ਰਹੀ ਹਾਂ।
Sita	namaste. main jebaan lagaa rahee haan. meree masheen kanm naheen kar rahee. main sooee vart rahee haan.
	Hello. I am stitching pockets. My machine is not working so I am using a needle.

ਗੀਤਾ	ਤੂੰ ਸਮਾਂ ਜ਼ਾਇਆ ਕਰ ਰਹੀ ਹੈਂ । ਸੁਣ! ਮੈਂ ਕੰਮ ਛੱਡ ਰਹੀ ਹਾਂ ।
Geeta	<u>toon</u> sam<u>aan</u> zaaiaa kar rahee hai<u>n</u>. sunh! main ka<u>n</u>m <u>chadd</u> rahee haa<u>n</u>.
	You are wasting your time. Listen! I am leaving work.
ਸੀਤਾ	ਤੂੰ ਕੰਮ ਕਿਉਂ ਛੱਡ ਰਹੀ ਹੈਂ ?
Sita	<u>toon</u> ka<u>n</u>m kiu<u>n</u> <u>chadd</u> rahee hai<u>n</u>?
	Why are you leaving work?
ਗੀਤਾ	ਮੈਨੇਜਰ ਸਾਡੀ ਤਨਖ਼ਾਹ ਨਹੀਂ ਵਧਾ ਰਿਹਾ । ਉਹ ਸਾਡੀਆਂ ਮੰਗਾਂ ਪੂਰੀਆਂ ਨਹੀਂ ਕਰ ਰਿਹਾ ਹੈ ।
Geeta	mainejar saadee <u>tankhaah</u> naheen va<u>dh</u>aa rihaa. uh saadeeaa<u>n</u> <u>mangaan</u> pooreeaa<u>n</u> naheen kar rihaa hai.
	The manager is not increasing our pay. He is not fulfilling our demands.
ਸੀਤਾ	ਤੂੰ ਠੀਕ ਕਹਿ ਰਹੀ ਹੈਂ!
Sita	<u>toon</u> theek kahi rahee hai<u>n</u>!
	You're right! (lit. *You are saying it right.*)

ਸ਼ਬਦਾਵਲੀ	shab<u>d</u>aavalee	*Vocabulary*
ਕਰਨਾ	karnaa	*to do*
ਜੇਬਾਂ	jeb<u>aan</u>	*pockets* (m./f.)
ਲਗਾਉਣਾ	lagaaunhaa	*to stitch, to apply, to put on*
ਮਸ਼ੀਨ	masheen	*machine* (f.)
ਕੰਮ ਕਰਨਾ	ka<u>n</u>m karnaa	*to work*
ਸੂਈ	sooee	*needle* (f.)
ਵਰਤਣਾ	vara<u>t</u>nhaa	*to use*
ਸਮਾਂ	sam<u>aan</u>	*time* (m.)
ਜ਼ਾਇਆ ਕਰਨਾ	zaaiaa karnaa	*to waste time*
ਸੁਣਨਾ	sunhnaa	*to listen*
ਕੰਮ	ka<u>n</u>m	*work* (m.)
ਛੱਡਣਾ	<u>chadd</u>nhaa	*to leave, to quit*
ਮੈਨੇਜਰ	mainejar	*manager* (m./f.)
ਤਨਖ਼ਾਹ	<u>tankhaah</u>	*pay, salary* (f.)
ਵਧਾਉਣਾ	va<u>dh</u>aaunhaa	*to increase*
ਮੰਗਾਂ	<u>mangaan</u>	*demands* (f.)
ਪੂਰੀਆਂ	pooreeaa<u>n</u>	*fulfilling*
ਠੀਕ	theek	*right, correct*
ਕਹਿਣਾ	kahinhaa	*to speak*

ਅਭਿਆਸ abhiaas *Exercises*

After reading the dialogue and/or listening to the recording, try to do the following exercises.

1 Arrange in correct word order

a ਨਮਸਤੇ ਹੈਂ ਰਹੀ ਕਰ ਕੀ ਤੂੰ? namaste-hain-rahee-kar-kee-toon?
   Hello. What are you doing?

b ਮੈਂ ਜੇਬਾਂ ਹਾਂ ਰਹੀ ਲਗਾ main-jebaan-haan-rahee-lagaa
   I am stitching pockets.

c ਨਹੀਂ ਵਧਾ ਰਿਹਾ ਤਨਖ਼ਾਹ ਮੈਨੇਜਰ ਸਾਡੀ naheen-vadhaa-rihaa tankhaah-mainejar-saadee *The manager is not increasing our pay.*

2 Crossword

Using the words given to you in Panjabi, complete the crossword with the English translations.

1	ਮਸ਼ੀਨ	masheen
2	ਕੰਮ	kanm
3	ਤਨਖ਼ਾਹ	tankhaah
4	ਜੇਬਾਂ	jebaan
5	ਸਮਾਂ	samaan
6	ਸੂਈ	sooee

---

2 *What was the matter?*
ਗੱਲ ਬਾਤ ੨ ਕੀ ਗੱਲ ਸੀ?
gall baat 2 kee gall see?

◄》 CD 1, TR 6, 01:15

Preet and Sumeet are close friends. They are meeting each other after the weekend.

ਪ੍ਰੀਤ **Preet**	ਤੁਸੀਂ ਕੱਲ੍ਹ ਕਿੱਥੇ ਸੀ? tuseen kallh kiththe see? *Where were you yesterday?*
ਸੁਮੀਤ **Sumeet**	ਅਸੀਂ ਘਰ ਸੀ। aseen ghar see. *We were at home.*
ਪ੍ਰੀਤ **Preet**	ਤੁਸੀਂ ਸਵੇਰੇ ਕੀ ਕਰ ਰਹੇ ਸੀ? tuseen savere kee kar rahe see? *What were you doing in the morning?*
ਸੁਮੀਤ **Sumeet**	ਮੈਂ ਫ਼ਿਲਮ ਦੇਖ ਰਹੀ ਸੀ। ਬੱਚੇ ਖੇਡ ਰਹੇ ਸਨ। main filam dekh rahee see. bachche khed rahe san. *I was watching a film. The children were playing.*
ਪ੍ਰੀਤ **Preet**	ਤੁਹਾਡੇ ਪਤੀ ਜੀ ਕੀ ਕਰ ਰਹੇ ਸਨ? tuhaade patee jee kee kar rahe san? *What was your husband doing?*
ਸੁਮੀਤ **Sumeet**	ਉਹ ਕਾਰ ਧੋ ਰਹੇ ਸਨ। uh kaar dho rahe san. *He was washing the car.*
	ਤੁਸੀਂ ਕਿਉਂ ਪੁੱਛ ਰਹੇ ਹੋ? ਕੀ ਗੱਲ ਸੀ? tuseen kiun puchch rahe ho? kee gall see? *Why are you asking? What was the matter?*
ਪ੍ਰੀਤ **Preet**	ਮੈਂ ਬੋਰ ਹੋ ਰਹੀ ਸੀ ਤੇ ਮੈਂ ਸਭ ਪਾਸੇ ਟੈਲੀਫ਼ੋਨ ਕਰ ਰਹੀ ਸੀ। ਮੈਂ ਤੁਹਾਡੇ ਬਾਰੇ ਸੋਚ ਰਹੀ ਸੀ। main bor ho rahee see te main sabh paase taileefon kar rahee see. main tuhaade baare soch rahee see. *I was feeling bored and I called [was calling] everywhere. I was thinking of you.*
ਸੁਮੀਤ **Sumeet**	ਪਰ ਸਾਡਾ ਟੈਲੀਫ਼ੋਨ ਕੰਮ ਨਹੀਂ ਕਰ ਰਿਹਾ ਸੀ। par saadaa taileefon kanm naheen kar rihaa see. *But our telephone was not working.*

Insight

The auxiliary verbs of the past tense are '*see*' 'ਸੀ' and '*san*' 'ਸਨ' (*was, were*). In some Panjabi dialects '*sain*' 'ਸੈਂ', '*so*' ਸੋ and '*saan*' 'ਸਾਂ' are also used but not in this course.

ਸ਼ਬਦਾਵਲੀ	shabdaavalee	*Vocabulary*
ਗੱਲ	gall	*matter* (f.) (lit. talk)
ਕੱਲੂ	kallh	*yesterday*
ਸਵੇਰੇ	savere	*morning*
ਫ਼ਿਲਮ	filam	*film* (f.)
ਦੇਖਣਾ	dekhnhaa	*to watch*
ਖੇਡਣਾ	khednhaa	*to play*
ਪਤੀ	patee	*husband* (m.)
ਕਾਰ	kaar	*car* (f.)
ਧੋਣਾ	dhonhaa	*to wash*
ਪੁੱਛਣਾ	puchchnhaa	*to ask*
ਬੋਰ ਹੋਣਾ	bor honhaa	*to be bored, to feel bored*
ਸਭ	sabh	*all, every*
ਸਭ ਪਾਸੇ	sabh paase	*everywhere*
ਪਾਸੇ	paase	*direction, way*
ਟੈਲੀਫ਼ੋਨ ਕਰਨਾ	taileefon karnaa	*to call by telephone*
ਤੁਹਾਡੇ ਬਾਰੇ	tuhaade baare	*about you*
ਸੋਚਣਾ	sochnhaa	*to think*

ਅਭਿਆਸ abhiaas *Exercises*

After reading the dialogue and/or listening to the recording, try to do the following exercises.

1 Word search

Four Panjabi words are hidden in the box. These words are **kaar**, **sumeet**, **kallh** and **ghar**. Find them by looking horizontally across each of the rows.

ਉ	ਸੁ	ਮੀ	ਤ
ਕੱ	ਲੂ	ਟ	ਤ
ਬ	ਭ	ਘ	ਰ
ਸ	ਕਾ	ਰ	ਮ

2 Answer the questions about the dialogue in Panjabi

a ਸੁਮੀਤ ਕੀ ਕਰ ਰਹੀ ਸੀ? sumeet kee kar rahee see?
b ਬੱਚੇ ਕੀ ਕਰ ਰਹੇ ਸਨ? bachche kee kar rahe san?
c ਸੁਮੀਤ ਦਾ ਪਤੀ ਕੀ ਕਰ ਰਿਹਾ ਸੀ? sumeet daa patee kee kar rihaa see?

ਬੋਲੀ ਬਾਰੇ bolee baare *Language points*

The present continuous tense (*-ing*)

The present continuous tense is generally used when an action is in progress. In English it is often signified by adding *-ing* to the end of a verb. In Panjabi, the stem, also known as the root, of the verb does not change its form. But the auxiliary verb and the progressive marker must agree with the subject. The progressive aspect of the verb, comparable with *-ing* in English, is expressed through ਰਹਿ **rahi** *the stem* of ਰਹਿਣਾ **rahinhaa**. It stands on its own as a separate word and should not be attached to either the main verb (*to . . .*) or the auxiliary verb. The progressive marker changes according to the gender and number of the subject.

For example: ਮੈਂ ਖਾ ਰਿਹਾ ਹਾਂ main khaa rihaa haan *I am eating*

ਮੈਂ **main** *I* (subject) (1st person singular, masculine) + ਖਾ **khaa** (stem of the verb ਖਾਣਾ (*to eat*)) + ਰਿਹਾ **rihaa** (= *-ing*) (progressive marker) (masculine/singular) + ਹਾਂ **haan** (auxiliary verb (*am*)).

The forms of ਰਹਿ **rahi** are as follows:

Masculine singular	Masculine plural	Feminine singular	Feminine plural
ਰਿਹਾ	ਰਹੇ	ਰਹੀ	ਰਹੀਆਂ
rihaa	rahe	rahee	raheeaan

The auxiliary verb also reflects the person, number and gender of the subject and takes on the present tense forms of ਹੋਣਾ **honhaa** as discussed in Unit 2.

1st person

Masculine singular	ਮੈਂ ਖਾ ਰਿਹਾ ਹਾਂ	*I am eating*
	main khaa rihaa haan	

Feminine singular	ਮੈਂ ਖਾ ਰਹੀ ਹਾਂ	I am eating
	main khaa rahee haan	
Masculine plural	ਅਸੀਂ ਖਾ ਰਹੇ ਹਾਂ	we are eating
	aseen khaa rahe haan	
Feminine plural	ਅਸੀਂ ਖਾ ਰਹੀਆਂ ਹਾਂ	we are eating
	aseen khaa raheeaan haan	

2nd person

Masculine singular	ਤੂੰ ਖਾ ਰਿਹਾਂ ਹੈਂ	you are eating
	toon khaa rihaa hain	
Feminine singular	ਤੂੰ ਖਾ ਰਹੀ ਹੈਂ	you are eating
	toon khaa rahee hain	
Masculine plural	ਤੁਸੀਂ ਖਾ ਰਹੇ ਹੋ	you are eating
	tuseen khaa rahe ho	
Feminine plural	ਤੁਸੀਂ ਖਾ ਰਹੀਆਂ ਹੋ	you are eating
	tuseen khaa raheeaan ho	

3rd person

Masculine singular	ਉਹ/ਇਹ ਖਾ ਰਿਹਾ ਹੈ	he is eating
	uh/ih khaa rihaa hai	
Feminine singular	ਉਹ/ਇਹ ਖਾ ਰਹੀ ਹੈ	she is eating
	uh/ih khaa rahee hai	
Masculine plural	ਉਹ/ਇਹ ਖਾ ਰਹੇ ਹਨ	they are eating
	uh/ih khaa rahe han	
Feminine plural	ਉਹ/ਇਹ ਖਾ ਰਹੀਆਂ ਹਨ	they are eating
	uh/ih khaa raheeaan han	

Uses of present continuous

Sometimes the simple present (see Unit 4) and present continuous tenses become interchangeable with one another when the action is on-going and habitual.

Simple present

| ਮੈਂ ਸਕੂਲ ਵਿਚ ਕੰਮ ਕਰਦਾ ਹਾਂ | main sakool vich kanm kardaa haan | I work in a school. |

Present continuous

| ਮੈਂ ਸਕੂਲ ਵਿਚ ਕੰਮ ਕਰ ਰਿਹਾ ਹਾਂ | main sakool vich kanm kar rihaa haan | I am working in a school. |

The present continuous tense may also be used in instances where an action in the immediate future is being denoted, though it may not be happening at the present time:

| ਉਹ ਸ਼ਾਮ ਨੂੰ | uh shaam noo<u>n</u> | *He is coming in* |
| ਆ ਰਿਹਾ ਹੈ | aa rihaa hai | *the evening.* |

A less formal but more common manner of this use of the present continuous occurs if we drop the auxiliary verb. The meaning of the sentence does not change. However, because the sense becomes slightly less formal a change of ਰਿਹਾ **rihaa** to ਰਿਹਾਂ **rihaa<u>n</u>** by nasalizing the ending is required.

Examples:

| ਉਹ ਜਾ ਰਿਹਾਂ | uh jaa rihaa<u>n</u> | *he's going* |
| ਮੈਂ ਪੜ੍ਹ ਰਿਹਾਂ | mai<u>n</u> parhh rihaa<u>n</u> | *I'm reading* |

The imperative

The imperative is a form of the verb which expresses request, command or suggestion. The imperative has two forms: formal and informal. The formal imperative adds the vowel sound 'o' to the stem of the verb and the informal uses the stem on its own. Here are two examples which illustrate the formal and informal aspects of the imperative using the verb ਸੁਣਨਾ **sunhnaa**, *to listen*:

| (ਤੂੰ) ਸੁਣ | (<u>too</u>n) sunh | *Listen!* (you, informal) |
| (ਤੁਸੀਂ) ਸੁਣੋ | (<u>tusee</u>n) sunho | *Listen!* (you, formal) |

ਤੂੰ **<u>too</u>n** (*you*) is generally used with children, close relatives, equals and intimate relations while ਤੁਸੀਂ **<u>tusee</u>n** (*you*) is used as a respectful address with elders or formal acquaintances or in references to more than one person. The person and the tone of voice used to express imperative situations determine the nature of the order or request. For example, an imperative form in the 2nd person ਤੁਸੀਂ **<u>tusee</u>n** would denote a more polite, formal request while an imperative using the 2nd person ਤੂੰ **<u>too</u>n** would reflect a more informal although authoritative order.

Was and *were*

The past tense of the verb *to be* ਹੋਣਾ **honhaa** is *was* and *were*. You have already learned that the auxiliary verb is formed with the verb *to be.* Just as the present tense of *to be* becomes *is*, *am* and *are*, the past tense of *to be* becomes *was* and *were*.

Here is the past tense of the verb **honhaa ਹੋਣਾ** *to be*:

Singular		Plural	
ਮੈਂ ਸੀ maiṉ see	*I was*	ਅਸੀਂ ਸੀ aseeṉ see	*we were*
ਤੂੰ ਸੀ tooṉ see	*you were*	ਤੁਸੀਂ ਸੀ tuseeṉ see	*you were*
ਇਹ ਸੀ ih see	*he /she/it was*	ਇਹ ਸਨ/ਸੀ ih san/see	*they were*
ਉਹ ਸੀ uh see	*he/she/that was*	ਉਹ ਸਨ/ਸੀ uh san/see	*they were*

Note that **ਸੀ see** can be used with any number, person or gender.

The past continuous tense

The past continuous tense describes actions which had continued to happen before and after a particular time (in English *was . . . -ing* and *were . . . -ing*). The past continuous tense follows the same pattern as the present continuous except that the auxiliary verb takes the past form. The progressive marker (*-ing*) is followed by the appropriate forms of *was* and *were*. **ਸੀ see** is the most commonly used past auxiliary, although **ਸਨ san** is also used for the plural. Both are neutral of gender and number.

Masculine singular	Masculine plural	Feminine singular	Feminine plural
ਰਿਹਾ ਸੀ	ਰਹੇ ਸਨ	ਰਹੀ ਸੀ	ਰਹੀਆਂ ਸਨ
rihaa see	rahe san	rahee see	raheeaaṉ san

ਮੈਂ **main** *I* (subject) (1st person singular, masculine) + ਖਾ **khaa** (stem of the verb ਖਾਣਾ (*to eat*)) + ਰਿਹਾ **rihaa** (= *-ing*) (progressive marker) (masculine singular) + ਸੀ **see** (auxiliary verb) (*was*) =

ਮੈਂ ਖਾ ਰਿਹਾ ਸੀ   maiṉ khaa rihaa see   *I was eating*

1st person

Masculine singular	ਮੈਂ ਜਾ ਰਿਹਾ ਸੀ	*I was going*
	maiṉ jaa rihaa see	

Feminine singular	ਮੈਂ ਜਾ ਰਹੀ ਸੀ	I was going
	main jaa rahee see	
Masculine plural	ਅਸੀਂ ਜਾ ਰਹੇ ਸੀ	we were going
	aseen jaa rahe see	
Feminine plural	ਅਸੀਂ ਜਾ ਰਹੀਆਂ ਸੀ	we were going
	aseen jaa raheeaan see	

2nd person

Masculine singular	ਤੂੰ ਜਾ ਰਿਹਾ ਸੀ	you were going
	toon jaa rihaa see	
Feminine singular	ਤੂੰ ਜਾ ਰਹੀ ਸੀ	you were going
	toon jaa rahee see	
Masculine plural	ਤੁਸੀਂ ਜਾ ਰਹੇ ਸੀ	you were going
	tuseen jaa rahe see	
Feminine plural	ਤੁਸੀਂ ਜਾ ਰਹੀਆਂ ਸੀ	you were going
	tuseen jaa raheeaan see	

3rd person

Masculine singular	ਉਹ/ਇਹ ਜਾ ਰਿਹਾ ਸੀ	he was going
	uh/ih jaa rihaa see	
Feminine singular	ਉਹ/ਇਹ ਜਾ ਰਹੀ ਸੀ	she was going
	uh/ih jaa rahee see	
Masculine plural	ਉਹ/ਇਹ ਜਾ ਰਹੇ ਸਨ/ਸੀ	they were going
	uh/ih jaa rahe san/see	
Feminine Plural	ਉਹ/ਇਹ ਜਾ ਰਹੀਆਂ ਸਨ/ਸੀ	they were going
	uh/ih jaa raheeaan san/see	

Negative sentences

Generally, sentences are made negative by inserting ਨਹੀਂ **naheen** (*not*) between the verb stem and the progressive marker:

| Statement | ਮੈਂ ਖਾ ਰਿਹਾ ਹਾਂ | main khaa rihaa haan | I am eating |
| Negative | ਮੈਂ ਖਾ ਨਹੀਂ ਰਿਹਾ ਹਾਂ | main khaa naheen rihaa haan | I am not eating |

In colloquial speech the auxiliary verb is often dropped in positive and negative statements. A native Panjabi speaker may instead say: ਮੈਂ ਖਾ ਨਹੀਂ ਰਿਹਾ **main khaa naheen rihaa.**

Making interrogative sentences

An interrogative sentence is made simply by adding ਕੀ **kee** at the beginning of the sentence. The literal definition of ਕੀ **kee** is 'what' which can turn a statement into a question.

| Statement | ਤੂੰ ਖਾ ਰਿਹਾ ਹੈਂ | toon khaa rihaa hain | *You are eating.* |
| Interrogative | ਕੀ ਤੂੰ ਖਾ ਰਿਹਾ ਹੈਂ? | kee toon khaa rihaa hain? | *Are you eating?* |

If ਕੀ **kee** is inserted between the subject and the verb, the meaning of the sentence will change. Note and compare the following sentences:

ਤੂੰ ਖਾ ਰਿਹਾ ਹੈਂ	toon khaa rihaa hain	*You are eating.*
ਕੀ ਤੂੰ ਖਾ ਰਿਹਾ ਹੈਂ?	kee toon khaa rihaa hain?	*Are you eating?*
ਤੂੰ ਕੀ ਖਾ ਰਿਹਾ ਹੈਂ?	toon kee khaa rihaa hain?	*What are you eating?*

Similarly, other interrogative pronouns can be used in turning statements into questions such as ਕਿਉਂ **kiun** (*why*), ਕਿਵੇਂ **kiven** (*how*) and ਕਿੱਥੇ **kiththe** (*where*).

ਵਿਆਖਿਆ viaakhiaa *Commentary*

1 ਕੱਲ੍ਹ kallh (*yesterday* and *tomorrow*)

In Panjabi there is one word which means both *yesterday* and *tomorrow* ਕੱਲ੍ਹ **kallh**. This may at first seem quite confusing, but the sense in which ਕੱਲ੍ਹ **kallh** is used in a conversation can be gauged from the tense of the verbs and the sense of the context. For example:

| ਮੈਂ ਕੱਲ੍ਹ ਘਰ ਸੀ | main kallh ghar see | *I was (at) home yesterday.* |
| ਮੈਂ ਕੱਲ੍ਹ ਆ ਰਹੀ ਹਾਂ | main kallh aa rahee haan | *I am coming tomorrow.* |

There is, however, a specific word for *tomorrow* – ਭਲਕ **bhalak** – but it is rarely used. The most common forms of signifying time are:

ਅੱਜ	ajj	*today*
ਕੱਲ੍ਹ	kallh	*yesterday/tomorrow*
ਭਲਕ/ਭਲਕੇ	bhalak/bhalke	*tomorrow*
ਪਰਸੋਂ	parson	*day before yesterday/ day after tomorrow*

You will see all of these forms used in later units.

> ### Insight
> Like '*kallh*' 'ਕੱਲ੍ਹ' (*yesterday* and *tomorrow*) there is only one
> word in Panjabi for *train* and *car* i.e. '*gaddee*' 'ਗੱਡੀ'

2 Panjabi women at work

In rural Panjab, women play a significant part in the contribution
to the household economy. From helping in the fields to animal
husbandry, women play a central role in the rural economy. This has
continued in the diaspora, where Panjabi women have worked in
factories in a similar way to their male counterparts. The factories of
the Midlands in Britain and more recently Silicon Valley in California
have employed Panjabi women. In Britain these women have been
at the forefront of industrial struggles, the most well-known being
'Imperial Typewriters', Grunwick photo processing factory, Burnsall
metal finishing company and Gate Gourmet airline catering. The
contemporary concentration of Panjabi women in the textiles sector
in sewing and stitching garments is a continuation of the jobs they
had on arrival in Britain. The daughters of these migrants are now
forging new paths in a wide variety of occupations and businesses, a
selection of which can be found in the book, *The Golden Thread*, by
Zerbanoo Gifford.

> ### Insight
> There are hundreds of English words which have been adopted
> by the Panjabi language. With this flexibility in mind, you are
> welcome to use English words whenever you are stuck for
> want of vocabulary. An inflection of an attempted Panjabi
> accent would make this seem even more natural!

ਅਭਿਆਸ abhiaas *Exercises*

1 Change the informal sentences into formal sentences

Complete this exercise by replacing the subject pronoun ਤੂੰ (**too̱n**)
with ਤੁਸੀਂ (**tusee̱n**).

a ਤੂੰ ਸਮਾਂ ਜ਼ਾਇਆ ਕਰ ਰਹੀ ਹੈਂ। <u>toon</u> samaa<u>n</u> zaaiaa kar rahee hai<u>n</u>.
You are wasting your time.

b ਤੂੰ ਕੰਮ ਕਿਉਂ ਛੱਡ ਰਹੀ ਹੈਂ? <u>toon</u> ka<u>n</u>m kiu<u>n</u> <u>ch</u>add rahee hai<u>n</u>?
Why are you leaving work?

c ਤੂੰ ਠੀਕ ਕਹਿ ਰਹੀ ਹੈਂ। <u>toon</u> theek kahi rahee hai<u>n</u>. *You are (saying) right.*

2 Complete the table

ਪਤੀ		husband
ਘਰ	ghar	
	kallh	yesterday

3 Change present continuous to past continuous

◀) CD 1, TR 6, 02:11

Listen to the recording. Phrases have been given to you in the present continuous (i.e. *am/is/are* ___ *-ing*). Change them to the past continuous (i.e. *was/were* ___ *-ing*). The first one has been done for you.

a ਮੈਂ ਕੰਮ ਕਰ ਰਹੀ ਹਾਂ। mai<u>n</u> ka<u>n</u>m kar rahee haa<u>n</u>. *I am working.*

ਮੈਂ ਕੰਮ ਕਰ ਰਹੀ ਸੀ। mai<u>n</u> ka<u>n</u>m kar rahee see. *I was working.*

b ਤੁਸੀਂ ਕੀ ਪੁੱਛ ਰਹੇ ਹੋ? <u>tuseen</u> kee pu<u>chch</u> rahe ho? *What are you asking?*

c ਉਹ ਕੀ ਕਰ ਰਹੇ ਹਨ? uh kee kar rahe han? *What are they doing?*

d ਉਹ ਕਾਰ ਧੋ ਰਿਹਾ ਹੈ। uh kaar <u>dho</u> rihaa hai. *He is washing the car.*

4 Fill in the blanks

Using the pictorial clues given, fill in the blanks with the main verb stem of the continuous actions being done.

a ਗੀਤਾ ਟੈਨਸ _____
geetaa tainas (tennis) _____

b ਅਵਤਾਰ ਖਾਣਾ
avtaar khaanhaa _____

c ਸੀਤਾ ਤੇ ਗੀਤਾ ਪੰਜਾਬੀ _____
seetaa te geetaa _____
panjaabee _____

Main haan theek

Kee haal hai?

d ਮੁੰਡਾ ਕਿਤਾਬ _____
mundaa kitaab _____

Insight

Unlike English, the Gurmukhi script follows a 'one sound–one symbol' principle, though there are a few exceptions to this rule.

Ten important things to remember

1 The formula for constructing the present continuous tense is: Subject + stem of the verb + progressive marker + auxiliary verb.
2 Please note that the stem of a verb does not change its form but the auxiliary verb and the progressive marker must agree with the subject.
3 The progressive marker changes according to the gender and number of the subject.

4 Sometimes the simple present and present continuous tenses become interchangeable when the action is on-going and habitual.

5 The present continuous tense may also be used in instances where an action in the immediate future is being denoted, though it may not be happening at the present time.

6 The past continuous tense follows the same pattern as the present continuous except that the auxiliary verb takes the past form.

7 The auxiliary verbs of the past tense are '*see*' 'ਸੀ' and '*san*' 'ਸਨ' (was, were) whereas '*hai, ho, hain, han and haan*' 'ਹੈ, ਹੋ, ਹੈਂ, ਹਨ; ਹਾਂ' (is, am and are) belong to the present tense.

8 The construction of imperative sentences has two forms, formal and informal.

9 Generally sentences are made negative by inserting '*naheen*' 'ਨਹੀਂ' (not) at the appropriate place.

10 An interrogative sentence is made by adding '*kee*' 'ਕੀ' (what) at the beginning of the sentence. However, by using an inquisitive intonation, you can omit the word '*kee*' 'ਕੀ'.

6

की तुसीं जलंधर पड़े सी?
kee tuseen jalandhar parh-h-e see?
Did you study in Jalandhar?

In this unit you will learn:

- How to express actions in the immediate past
- How to express habitual actions in the past
- About Sikh wedding customs
- About kinship and relations

1 *We went to London*
ਗੱਲ ਬਾਤ ੧ ਅਸੀਂ ਲੰਡਨ ਗਏ ਸੀ
gall baat 1 aseen landan gae see

◀) CD 1, TR 7, 00:20

Surjit Singh and Pavan Singh are friends and both belong to the Sikh religion. They are having a conversation on the phone.

ਸੁਰਜੀਤ ਸਿੰਘ	ਸਤਿ ਸ੍ਰੀ ਅਕਾਲ। ਤੁਸੀਂ ਐਤਵਾਰ ਕਿੱਥੇ ਸੀ? ਮੈਂ ਤੁਹਾਡੇ ਘਰ ਆਇਆ ਸੀ।
Surjit Singh	sat sree akaal. tuseen aitvaar kiththe see? main tuhaade ghar aaiaa see.
	Hello. Where were you on Sunday? I came to your house.

ਪਵਨ ਸਿੰਘ **Pavan Singh**	ਅਸੀਂ ਇੱਥੇ ਨਹੀਂ ਸੀ। ਅਸੀਂ ਹਫ਼ਤੇ ਦੇ ਅਖ਼ੀਰ ਲੰਡਨ ਗਏ ਸੀ। aseen *iththe* naheen see. aseen haf<u>t</u>e <u>d</u>e a<u>kh</u>eer la<u>nd</u>an gae see. *We were not here. We went to London over the weekend.*
ਸੁਰਜੀਤ ਸਿੰਘ **Surjit Singh**	ਕੀ ਕੋਈ ਖ਼ਾਸ ਮੌਕਾ ਸੀ? kee koee <u>kh</u>aas maukaa see? *Was there any special occasion?*
ਪਵਨ ਸਿੰਘ **Pavan Singh**	ਹਾਂ! ਮੇਰੀ ਭਤੀਜੀ ਦਾ ਵਿਆਹ ਸੀ। haan! meree bha<u>t</u>eejee <u>d</u>aa viaah see. *Yes! It was my niece's wedding.*
ਸੁਰਜੀਤ ਸਿੰਘ **Surjit Singh**	ਵਧਾਈਆਂ। ਕਿਹੜੇ ਸ਼ਹਿਰ ਤੋਂ ਬਰਾਤ ਆਈ ਸੀ? va<u>dh</u>aaeeaan. kihrhe shahir <u>t</u>on baraat aaee see? *Congratulations. Which city did the marriage party come from?*
ਪਵਨ ਸਿੰਘ **Pavan Singh**	ਉਹ ਮਾਨਚੈਸਟਰ ਤੋਂ ਆਈ ਸੀ। ਤਕਰੀਬਨ ੧੦੦ ਬੰਦੇ ਸਨ। uh maanchaistar <u>t</u>on aaee see. <u>t</u>akreeban 100 ba<u>nd</u>e san. *They came from Manchester. There were about 100 people.*
ਸੁਰਜੀਤ ਸਿੰਘ **Surjit Singh**	ਵਿਆਹ ਕਿਵੇਂ ਰਿਹਾ? viaah kiven rihaa? *How did the wedding go?*
ਪਵਨ ਸਿੰਘ **Pavan Singh**	ਬਹੁਤ ਸੁਹਣਾ। ਤੁਸੀਂ ਕਦੀ ਆਓ ਤੇ ਵਿਆਹ ਦੀਆਂ ਫ਼ੋਟੋ ਦੇਖੋ। bahu<u>t</u> suhnhaa. <u>t</u>useen ka<u>d</u>ee aao <u>t</u>e viaah <u>d</u>eeaan foto <u>d</u>ekho. *Excellent. Come over sometime and see the wedding photographs.*

ਸ਼ਬਦਾਵਲੀ	**shab<u>d</u>aavalee**	*Vocabulary*
ਲੰਡਨ	la<u>nd</u>an	*London* (m.)
ਐਤਵਾਰ	ai<u>t</u>vaar	*Sunday* (m.)
ਹਫ਼ਤੇ	haf<u>t</u>e	*week* (m.)
ਅਖ਼ੀਰ	a<u>kh</u>eer	*end*
ਹਫ਼ਤੇ ਦੇ ਅਖ਼ੀਰ	haf<u>t</u>e <u>d</u>e a<u>kh</u>eer	*weekend* (m.)
ਕੋਈ	koee	*any*
ਖ਼ਾਸ	<u>kh</u>aas	*special*
ਮੌਕਾ	maukaa	*occasion* (m.)
ਭਤੀਜੀ	bha<u>t</u>eejee	*niece* (f.)
ਵਿਆਹ	viaah	*wedding* (m.)
ਵਧਾਈਆਂ	va<u>dh</u>aaeeaan	*congratulations*

ਸ਼ਹਿਰ	shahir	*city* (m.)
ਮਾਨਚੈਸਟਰ	maanchaistar	*Manchester* (m.)
ਤਕਰੀਬਨ	takreeban	*about, approximately*
ਬੰਦੇ	bande	*people* (m.)
ਕਿਵੇਂ ਰਿਹਾ	kiven rihaa	*how did it go?*
ਬਹੁਤ ਸੁਹਣਾ	bahut suhnhaa	*very nice, excellent* (v.)
ਫ਼ੋਟੋ	foto	*photograph* (f.)
ਕਦੀ	kadee	*sometime*
ਆਓ	aao	*come* (formal)

ਅਭਿਆਸ abhiaas *Exercises*

After reading the dialogue and/or listening to the recording, try to do the following exercises.

1 Answer the following questions about Dialogue 1 in either short or long form

a ਪਵਨ ਹਫ਼ਤੇ ਦੇ ਅਖ਼ੀਰ ਕਿੱਥੇ ਸੀ ?

  pavan hafte de akheer kiththe see?

b ਖ਼ਾਸ ਮੌਕਾ ਕੀ ਸੀ ?

  khaas maukaa kee see?

c ਕਿਹੜੇ ਸ਼ਹਿਰ ਤੋਂ ਬਰਾਤ ਆਈ ਸੀ ?

  kihrhe shahir ton baraat aaee see?

d ਵਿਆਹ ਤੇ ਤਕਰੀਬਨ ਕਿੰਨੇ ਬੰਦੇ ਸਨ ?

  viaah te takreeban kinne bande san?

2 Translate the following into formal Panjabi

a Where were you on Sunday?
b Where were you yesterday?
c Where were you over the weekend?

---

2 *Did you study in Jalandhar?*
ਗੱਲ ਬਾਤ ੨ ਕੀ ਤੁਸੀਂ ਜਲੰਧਰ ਪੜ੍ਹੇ ਸੀ ?
gall baat 2 kee tuseen jalandhar parh-h-e see?

◀) CD 1, TR 7, 01:26

Surjit Singh visits Pavan Singh in order to see the photographs of Pavan's niece's wedding.

ਸੁਰਜੀਤ ਸਿੰਘ Surjit Singh	ਸਤਿ ਸ੍ਰੀ ਅਕਾਲ ਜੀ। ਕੀ ਹਾਲ ਹੈ?
	sat sree akaal jee. kee haal hai?
	Hello. How are you?

ਪਵਨ ਸਿੰਘ Pavan Singh	ਸਤਿ ਸ੍ਰੀ ਅਕਾਲ। ਵਾਹਿਗੁਰੂ ਦੀ ਕਿਰਪਾ ਨਾਲ ਸਭ ਕੁਝ ਠੀਕ ਠਾਕ ਹੈ।
	sat sree akaal. vaahiguroo dee kirpaa naal sabh kujh theek thaak hai.
	Hello. By the grace of God, everything is fine.

(Pavan hands the wedding album over to Surjit.)
(pointing to one of the photographs)

ਸੁਰਜੀਤ ਸਿੰਘ Surjit Singh	ਇਹ ਪੁਰਸ਼ ਤੇ ਇਸਤਰੀ ਕੌਣ ਹਨ?
	ih pursh te istaree kaunh han?
	Who are this gentleman and lady?

ਪਵਨ ਸਿੰਘ Pavan Singh	ਇਹ ਮੇਰਾ ਭਰਾ ਹੈ ਅਤੇ ਇਹ ਮੇਰੀ ਭਾਬੀ ਹੈ। ਅਸੀਂ ਇੱਕੇ ਮਕਾਨ ਵਿਚ ਰਹਿੰਦੇ ਸੀ।
	ih meraa bharaa hai ate ih meree bhaabee hai. aseen ikko makaan vich rahinde see.
	He is my brother, and she is my sister-in-law. We used to live in one house.

(looking at another photograph)

ਸੁਰਜੀਤ ਸਿੰਘ Surjit Singh	ਕੀ ਇਹ ਤੁਹਾਡੇ ਚਾਚਾ ਜੀ ਹਨ?
	kee ih tuhaade chaachaa jee han?
	Is this your uncle?

ਪਵਨ ਸਿੰਘ Pavan Singh	ਹਾਂ ਜੀ। ਅਸੀਂ ਕਾਲਜ ਵਿਚ ਹਾਕੀ ਇਕੱਠੇ ਖੇਡਦੇ ਸੀ।
	haan jee. aseen kaalaj vich haakee ikaththe khedde see.
	Yes. We used to play hockey together in college.

ਸੁਰਜੀਤ ਸਿੰਘ Surjit Singh	ਕੀ ਤੁਸੀਂ ਜਲੰਧਰ ਪੜ੍ਹੇ ਸੀ?
	kee tuseen jalandhar parh-h-e see?
	Did you study in Jalandhar?

ਪਵਨ ਸਿੰਘ Pavan Singh	ਨਹੀਂ ਜੀ। ਮੈਂ ਹੁਸ਼ਿਆਰਪੁਰ ਪੜ੍ਹਦਾ ਸੀ।
	naheen jee. main hushiaarpur parh-h-daa see.
	No. I used to study in Hoshiarpur.

ਸੁਰਜੀਤ ਸਿੰਘ Surjit Singh	ਕੀ ਵਿਆਹ ਵਿਚ ਬਹੁਤ ਪ੍ਰਾਹੁਣੇ ਸਨ?
	kee viaah vich bahut praahunhe san?
	Were there a lot of guests at the wedding?

ਪਵਨ ਸਿੰਘ Pavan Singh	ਹਾਂ, ਇਹ ਇੱਕ ਚੰਗਾ ਇਕੱਠ ਸੀ।
	haan, ih ikk changaa ikathth see.
	Yes, it was a good gathering.

ਸ਼ਬਦਾਵਲੀ	shabdaavalee	Vocabulary
ਰਹਿਣਾ	rahinhaa	to live, to stay
ਕਿਰਪਾ	kirpaa	blessings (f.)
ਸਭ ਕੁਝ	sabh kujh	everything
ਠੀਕ ਠਾਕ	theek thaak	OK, fine
ਪੁਰਸ਼	purash	gentleman (m.)
ਇਸਤਰੀ	istaree	lady (f.)
ਭਾਬੀ	bhaabee	sister-in-law (f.) (brother's wife)
ਚਾਚਾ ਜੀ	chaachaa jee	uncle (m.) (father's brother)
ਕਾਲਜ	kaalaj	college (m.)
ਖੇਡਣਾ	khednhaa	to play
ਪ੍ਰਾਹੁਣੇ	praahunhe	guests (m.)
ਇੱਕ	ikk	one, a
ਇਕੱਠ	ikaththh	gathering (m.)

Insight

Attending a Panjabi wedding is an enriching experience which provides an opportunity to learn about different customs and new vocabulary related to marriage and kinship.

ਅਭਿਆਸ abhiaas *Exercises*

After reading the dialogue and/or listening to the recording, try to do the following exercises.

1 Complete the table

The first one has been done for you.

ਪੁਰਸ਼	purash	man
	istaree	
ਇਕੱਠ		
		guests
	kaalaj	
		sister-in-law

2 Identify whether the statements are formal or informal

Tick the appropriate box.

	Formal	Informal
a ਇਹ ਮੇਰਾ ਭਰਾ ਹੈ। ih meraa bharaa hai. *This is my brother.*	☐	☐
b ਇਹ ਮੇਰੀ ਭਾਬੀ ਹੈ। ih meree bhaabee hai. *This is my sister-in-law.*	☐	☐
c ਇਹ ਮੇਰੇ ਚਾਚਾ ਜੀ ਹਨ। ih mere chaachaa jee han. *This is my uncle.*	☐	☐

ਬੋਲੀ ਬਾਰੇ bolee baare *Language points*

The past tense

The past tense in Panjabi describes actions or states of condition which have taken place at a particular time before the present one. Here we will discuss three different constructions of the past tense: the simple past, the remote past and the past habitual. As was shown in Unit 5, *was* and *were* in Panjabi are expressed through the past tense of the auxiliary verb *to be* ਹੋਣਾ **honhaa**. The more common forms for the past tense, however, are ਸੀ **see** and ਸਨ **san**. The appropriate form of the past of *to be* is determined by person, number and mode of address (formal or informal). Here are some examples to refresh your memory:

| ਮੁੰਡਾ ਚੰਗਾ ਸੀ | mundaa changaa see | *The boy was good.* |
| ਮੁੰਡੇ ਚੰਗੇ ਸਨ | munde change san | *The boys were good.* |

The simple past tense

The simple past tense is used when expressing actions or conditions completed in the past. The simple past is formed by adding appropriate endings to the stem of the main verb. The endings added to the stem reflect the gender and number of the subject. To determine if the subject is 1st/2nd or 3rd person, you need to refer to the subject pronoun. Here, the verb 'to speak' ਬੋਲਣਾ bolnhaa, will be used to illustrate the various past tenses:

Verb	Stem
ਬੋਲਣਾ bolnhaa (to speak)	ਬੋਲ - bol

Now note the endings added to the stem:

ਮੈਂ	main	I (subject) (1st person masculine)
ਬੋਲਿਆ	boliaa	spoke (simple past form of the verb to speak ਬੋਲਣਾ)

1st person

Masculine singular	ਮੈਂ ਬੋਲਿਆ	main boliaa	I spoke
Feminine singular	ਮੈਂ ਬੋਲੀ	main bolee	I spoke
Masculine plural	ਅਸੀਂ ਬੋਲੇ	aseen bole	we spoke
Feminine plural	ਅਸੀਂ ਬੋਲੀਆਂ	aseen boleeaan	we spoke

2nd person

Masculine singular informal	ਤੂੰ ਬੋਲਿਆ	toon boliaa	you spoke
Feminine singular informal	ਤੂੰ ਬੋਲੀ	toon bolee	you spoke
Masculine plural/formal	ਤੁਸੀਂ ਬੋਲੇ	tuseen bole	you spoke
Feminine plural	ਤੁਸੀਂ ਬੋਲੀਆਂ	tuseen boleeaan	you spoke

3rd person

Masculine singular	ਉਹ/ਇਹ ਬੋਲਿਆ	uh/ih boliaa	he spoke
Feminine singular	ਉਹ/ਇਹ ਬੋਲੀ	uh/ih bolee	she spoke
Masc. plural/formal	ਉਹ/ਇਹ ਬੋਲੇ	uh/ih bole	they spoke
Feminine plural	ਉਹ/ਇਹ ਬੋਲੀਆਂ	uh/ih boleeaan	they spoke

Some verbs change in a more irregular manner in the past tense. You will have to learn and watch out for them. Verbs such as ਜਾਣਾ jaanhaa to go, ਕਰਨਾ karnaa to do and ਦੇਣਾ denhaa to give take on irregular forms in the past tense which do not derive from the root. Here we give the example of how ਜਾਣਾ jaanhaa to go is formed in the simple past tense. Note that the forms are not affected by person, only by gender and number.

ਜਾਣਾ jaanhaa – *to go* (*went*)

Masculine singular	Feminine singular	Masculine plural	Feminine plural
ਗਿਆ	ਗਈ	ਗਏ	ਗਈਆਂ
giaa	gaee	gae	gaeeaa<u>n</u>

The remote past

The remote past in Panjabi expresses actions which occurred prior to the present or the immediate past. The main verb used in the simple past is combined with the auxiliary verb in the past to form the remote past. The remote past tense is used when one is:

- being definitive in a statement
- emphasizing a particular point
- conveying the completion of an action
- referring to the remote past

The form of the main verb follows the pattern of the simple past just shown while the auxiliary verb reflects the appropriate forms of *was* and *were*. For example:

1st person

Masculine singular	ਮੈਂ ਬੋਲਿਆ ਸੀ	mai<u>n</u> boliaa see	*I spoke, had spoken*
Feminine singular	ਮੈਂ ਬੋਲੀ ਸੀ	mai<u>n</u> bolee see	*I spoke, had spoken*
Masculine plural	ਅਸੀਂ ਬੋਲੇ ਸੀ	asee<u>n</u> bole see	*we spoke, had spoken*
Feminine plural	ਅਸੀਂ ਬੋਲੀਆਂ ਸੀ	asee<u>n</u> boleeaa<u>n</u> see	*we spoke, had spoken*

2nd person

Masculine singular informal	ਤੂੰ ਬੋਲਿਆ ਸੀ	<u>t</u>oon boliaa see	*you spoke, had spoken*
Feminine singular informal	ਤੂੰ ਬੋਲੀ ਸੀ	<u>t</u>oon bolee see	*you spoke, had spoken*
Masculine plural/ formal	ਤੁਸੀਂ ਬੋਲੇ ਸੀ	<u>t</u>usee<u>n</u> bole see	*you spoke, had spoken*
Feminine plural	ਤੁਸੀਂ ਬੋਲੀਆਂ ਸੀ	<u>t</u>usee<u>n</u> boleeaan see	*you spoke, had spoken*

3rd person

Masculine singular	ਇਹ/ਉਹ ਬੋਲਿਆ ਸੀ	ih/uh boliaa see	*he spoke, had spoken*
Feminine singular	ਇਹ/ਉਹ ਬੋਲੀ ਸੀ	ih/uh bolee see	*she spoke, had spoken*
Masculine plural/ formal	ਇਹ/ਉਹ ਬੋਲੇ ਸਨ/ਸੀ	ih/uh bole san/see	*they spoke, had spoken*
Feminine plural	ਇਹ/ਉਹ ਬੋਲੀਆਂ ਸਨ/ਸੀ	ih/uh boleeaa<u>n</u> san/see	*they spoke, had spoken*

The remote past of ਜਾਣਾ jaanhaa *to go* follows the same pattern using the simple past form with the appropriate form of *was* and *were*.

ਜਾਣਾ jaanhaa – *to go*

Masculine singular	Feminine singular	Masculine plural	Feminine plural
ਗਿਆ ਸੀ	ਗਈ ਸੀ	ਗਏ ਸੀ/ਸਨ	ਗਈਆਂ ਸੀ/ਸਨ
giaa see	gaee see	gae see/san	gaeeaa<u>n</u> see/san

Past habitual tense – *used to*

In English *used to* expresses actions which occurred regularly in the past but which no longer exist in the present. In Panjabi the past habitual tense is used in the same manner. For example:

ਮੈਂ ਬੋਲਦਾ ਸੀ mai<u>n</u> bol<u>d</u>aa see *I used to speak*

The components of this example can be broken down as follows:

ਮੈਂ	mai<u>n</u>	*I* (subject) (1st person masculine)
ਬੋਲਦਾ	bol<u>d</u>aa	*speak* (simple present form of *to speak* ਬੋਲਣਾ **bolnhaa**)
ਸੀ	see	*was* (simple past of *to be* ਹੋਣਾ **honhaa**)

Note from the example that the past habitual tense is formed with the main verb, which takes on the same form as in the simple present tense, and the past tense of *to be* ਹੋਣਾ **honhaa**. Some examples follow.

1st person

Masculine singular	ਮੈਂ ਬੋਲਦਾ ਸੀ	mai<u>n</u> bol<u>d</u>aa see	*I used to speak*

Feminine singular	ਮੈਂ ਬੋਲਦੀ ਸੀ	main boldee see	I used to speak
Masculine plural	ਅਸੀਂ ਬੋਲਦੇ ਸੀ	aseen bolde see	we used to speak
Feminine plural	ਅਸੀਂ ਬੋਲਦੀਆਂ ਸੀ	aseen boldeeaan see	we used to speak

2nd person

Masculine singular informal	ਤੂੰ ਬੋਲਦਾ ਸੀ	toon boldaa see	you used to speak
Feminine singular informal	ਤੂੰ ਬੋਲਦੀ ਸੀ	toon boldee see	you used to speak
Masculine plural/ formal	ਤੁਸੀਂ ਬੋਲਦੇ ਸੀ	tuseen bolde see	you used to speak
Feminine plural	ਤੁਸੀਂ ਬੋਲਦੀਆਂ ਸੀ	tuseen boldeeaan see	you used to speak

3rd person

Masculine singular	ਇਹ/ਉਹ ਬੋਲਦਾ ਸੀ	ih/uh boldaa see	he used to speak
Feminine singular	ਇਹ/ਉਹ ਬੋਲਦੀ ਸੀ	ih/uh boldee see	she used to speak
Masculine plural/ formal	ਇਹ/ਉਹ ਬੋਲਦੇ ਸਨ/ਸੀ	ih/uh bolde san/see	they used to speak
Feminine plural	ਇਹ/ਉਹ ਬੋਲਦੀਆਂ ਸਨ/ਸੀ	ih/uh boldeeaan san/see	they used to speak

Another form of the past habitual uses the verb expressing the action in the habitual and the habitual forms of ਹੋਣਾ **honhaa** with the past auxiliary. *I used to go* in this form is expressed in the following ways:

1st person

ਮੈਂ ਜਾਂਦਾ ਹੁੰਦਾ ਸੀ	main jaandaa hundaa see	I used to go
ਮੈਂ ਜਾਂਦੀ ਹੁੰਦੀ ਸੀ	main jaandee hundee see	I used to go
ਅਸੀਂ ਜਾਂਦੇ ਹੁੰਦੇ ਸੀ	aseen jaande hunde see	we used to go
ਅਸੀਂ ਜਾਂਦੀਆਂ ਹੁੰਦੀਆਂ ਸੀ	aseen jaandeeaan hundeeaan see	we used to go

2nd person

ਤੂੰ ਜਾਂਦਾ ਹੁੰਦਾ ਸੀ	<u>t</u>oon jaa<u>n</u>daa hu<u>n</u>daa see	*you used to go*
ਤੂੰ ਜਾਂਦੀ ਹੁੰਦੀ ਸੀ	<u>t</u>oon jaa<u>n</u>dee hu<u>n</u>dee see	*you used to go*
ਤੁਸੀਂ ਜਾਂਦੇ ਹੁੰਦੇ ਸੀ	<u>t</u>useen jaa<u>n</u>de hu<u>n</u>de see	*you used to go*
ਤੁਸੀਂ ਜਾਂਦੀਆਂ	<u>t</u>useen jaa<u>n</u>deeaan	*you used to go*
ਹੁੰਦੀਆਂ ਸੀ	hu<u>n</u>deeaa<u>n</u> see	

3rd person

ਇਹ/ਉਹ ਜਾਂਦਾ ਹੁੰਦਾ ਸੀ	ih/uh jaa<u>n</u>daa hu<u>n</u>daa see	*he used to go*
ਇਹ/ਉਹ ਜਾਂਦੀ ਹੁੰਦੀ ਸੀ	ih/uh jaa<u>n</u>dee hu<u>n</u>dee see	*she used to go*
ਇਹ/ਉਹ ਜਾਂਦੇ ਹੁੰਦੇ	ih/uh jaa<u>n</u>de hu<u>n</u>de	*he/she/they used*
ਸੀ/ਸਨ	see/san	*to go*
ਇਹ/ਉਹ ਜਾਂਦੀਆਂ	ih/uh jaa<u>n</u>deeaan	*they used to go*
ਹੁੰਦੀਆਂ ਸੀ/ਸਨ	hu<u>n</u>deeaa<u>n</u> see/san	

You will come across these various forms of the past tense in subsequent units and there will therefore be plenty of opportunity to practise all of these constructions.

Negative sentences

Negative sentences in the various past tenses are formed by adding ਨਹੀਂ <u>naheen</u> either before or after the main verb.

Simple past

ਮੈਂ ਬੋਲਿਆ	ਮੈਂ ਨਹੀਂ ਬੋਲਿਆ	ਮੈਂ ਬੋਲਿਆ ਨਹੀਂ
main boliaa	main <u>naheen</u> boliaa	main boliaa <u>naheen</u>
I spoke	*I did not speak*	*I did not speak*

Remote past

ਮੈਂ ਬੋਲਿਆ ਸੀ	ਮੈਂ ਨਹੀਂ ਬੋਲਿਆ ਸੀ	ਮੈਂ ਬੋਲਿਆ ਨਹੀਂ ਸੀ
main boliaa see	main <u>naheen</u> boliaa see	main boliaa <u>naheen</u> see
I spoke/had spoken	*I did not speak/had not spoken*	*I did not speak/had not spoken*

Habitual past

ਮੈਂ ਬੋਲਦਾ ਸੀ	ਮੈਂ ਨਹੀਂ ਬੋਲਦਾ ਸੀ	ਮੈਂ ਬੋਲਦਾ ਨਹੀਂ ਸੀ
main boldaa see	main <u>naheen</u> boldaa see	main bol<u>d</u>aa naheen see
I used to speak	*I did not use to speak*	*I did not use to speak*

Interrogative sentences

As with the other verb tenses in Panjabi, interrogative (question) sentences are formed in the past by adding the question word ਕੀ **kee** at the beginning of the sentence. Here are some examples of how questions are made out of statements in the past:

Simple past

Statement		Question	
ਮੈਂ ਬੋਲਿਆ	main boliaa	ਕੀ ਮੈਂ ਬੋਲਿਆ?	kee main boliaa?
I spoke		*Did I speak?*	

Remote past

Statement		Question	
ਮੈਂ ਬੋਲਿਆ ਸੀ	main boliaa see	ਕੀ ਮੈਂ ਬੋਲਿਆ ਸੀ?	kee main boliaa see?
I spoke/had spoken		*Did I speak/Had I spoken?*	

Habitual past

Statement		Question	
ਮੈਂ ਬੋਲਦਾ ਸੀ	main boldaa see	ਕੀ ਮੈਂ ਬੋਲਦਾ ਸੀ?	kee main boldaa see?
I used to speak		*Did I use to speak?*	

Insight

You already know that the main verb changes with gender, number, person and tense. Sometimes the main verb in Panjabi is used metaphorically. In such instances you should forget its literal meaning. Example: *raam noon panjaabee aaundee hai* - ਰਾਮ ਨੂੰ ਪੰਜਾਬੀ ਆਉਂਦੀ ਹੈ - (Ram knows Panjabi). Normally the infinitive verb *'aaunhaa'* 'ਆਉਣਾ' means *to come*, which does not apply here.

ਵਿਆਖਿਆ viaakhiaa *Commentary*

Panjabi families

Panjabi weddings are seen as social occasions and signify the coming together of two families rather than of two individuals, as is traditionally the case in modern Western marriages. Kinship relations form a central part of Panjabi society. Often families live in extended units with three or more generations all living under one roof. In contrast to English-speaking cultures, Panjabi has very specific terms for members of the nuclear and extended family. Most kinship terms are determined by the paternal and maternal nature of the relationship and whether or not it is a relationship by marriage. Beware . . . these are only half of the possible kin names you may come across in conversation with Panjabis!

Paternal		Maternal	
ਦਾਦਾ	daadaa *father's father*	ਨਾਨਾ	naanaa *mother's father*
ਦਾਦੀ	daadee *father's mother*	ਨਾਨੀ	naanee *mother's mother*
ਪਿਤਾ	pitaa *father*	ਮਾਤਾ	maataa *mother*
ਅੱਬਾ	abbaa *papa (father)*	ਅੱਮੀ	ammee *mama (mother)*
ਪਤੀ	patee *husband*	ਪਤਨੀ	patnee *wife*
ਭਰਾ	bharaa *brother*	ਭੈਣ	bhainh *sister*
ਜੀਜਾ	jeejaa *sister's husband*	ਭਾਬੀ	bhaabee *brother's wife*
ਚਾਚਾ	chaachaa *father's younger brother*	ਮਾਸੀ	maasee *mother's sister*
ਚਾਚੀ	chaachee *father's younger brother's wife*	ਮਾਸੜ	maasarh *mother's sister's husband*
ਤਾਇਆ	taaiaa *father's elder brother*	ਮਾਮਾ	maamaa *mother's brother*
ਤਾਈ	taaee *father's elder brother's wife*	ਮਾਮੀ	maamee *mother's brother's wife*
ਭੂਆ	bhooaa *father's sister*	ਪੁੱਤਰੀ	puttaree *daughter*
ਫੁਫੜ	phupharh *father's sister's husband*	ਭਾਂਜਾ	bhaanjaa *nephew (sister's son)*

ਪੁੱਤਰ	puttar *son*	ਭਾਂਜੀ bhaa<u>n</u>jee *niece* (*sister's daughter*)
ਭਤੀਜਾ	bha<u>t</u>eejaa *nephew* (*brother's son*)	
ਭਤੀਜੀ	bha<u>t</u>eejee *niece* (*brother's daughter*)	

Insight

The English word 'uncle' signifies five different possible relations in Panjabi: a. **chaachaa** ਚਾਚਾ (*father's younger brother*) b. **taaiaa** ਤਾਇਆ (*father's elder brother*) c. **maamaa** ਮਾਮਾ (*mother's brother*) d. **phupharh** ਫੁਫੜ (*father's sister's husband*) e. **maasarh** ਮਾਸੜ (*mother's sister's husband*).

ਅਭਿਆਸ abhiaas *Exercises*

1 The family tree

◄) CD 1, TR 7, 03:06

Pavan is showing his family photos to Surjit. Read and/or listen to the following passage on the recording. Then try to complete Pavan's family tree (ਕੁਰਸੀ ਨਾਮਾ kursee naamaa).

ਇਹ ਹੈ ਮੇਰਾ ਕੁਰਸੀ ਨਾਮਾ:

ਮੇਰੇ ਪਿਤਾ ਜੀ ਦਾ ਨਾਮ ਜੋਗਿੰਦਰ ਸਿੰਘ ਹੈ ਅਤੇ ਮੇਰੇ ਮਾਤਾ ਜੀ ਦਾ ਨਾਮ ਗੁਰਮੀਤ ਕੋਰ ਹੈ। ਉਹਨਾਂ ਦੇ ਤਿੰਨ ਬੱਚੇ ਹਨ। ਮੈਂ, ਮੇਰਾ ਭਰਾ ਸੁਖਜੀਤ ਸਿੰਘ ਤੇ ਮੇਰੀ ਭੈਣ ਕੁਲਦੀਪ ਕੋਰ। ਮੇਰੀ ਭਾਬੀ ਦਾ ਨਾਮ ਜਗਜੀਤ ਕੋਰ ਹੈ ਤੇ ਮੇਰੇ ਭਤੀਜੇ ਦਾ ਨਾਮ ਗੁਰਤੇਜ ਸਿੰਘ ਹੈ।

ਮੇਰੀ ਪਤਨੀ ਦਾ ਨਾਮ ਹਰਲੀਨ ਕੋਰ ਹੈ ਅਤੇ ਸਾਡੇ ਦੋ ਬੱਚੇ ਹਨ, ਇੱਕ ਪੁੱਤਰ, ਮਨਜੀਤ ਸਿੰਘ ਤੇ ਇੱਕ ਪੁੱਤਰੀ, ਬਲਦੇਵ ਕੋਰ।

ih hai meraa kursee naamaa:

mere piṯaa jee ḏaa naam joginḏar singh hai aṯe mere maaṯaa jee ḏaa naam gurmeeṯ kaur hai. uhnaan ḏe ṯinn bachche han. main, meraa bharaa sukhjeeṯ singh ṯe meree bhainh kulḏeep kaur. meree bhaabee ḏaa naam jagjeeṯ kaur hai ṯe mere bhaṯeeje ḏaa naam gurṯej singh hai. meree paṯnee ḏaa naam harleen kaur hai aṯe saade ḏo bachche han, ikk puṯṯar, manjeeṯ singh ṯe ikk puṯṯree, balḏev kaur.

2 Matching

Match the questions with their correct responses.

a ਮੈਂ ਹਫ਼ਤੇ ਦੇ ਅਖ਼ੀਰ ਮਾਨਚੈਸਟਰ ਸੀ।
main hafṯe ḏe akheer maanchaistar see.

b ਮੈਂ ਐਤਵਾਰ ਘਰ ਸੀ।
main aiṯvaar ghar see.

c ਮੈਂ ਕੱਲੂ ਲੰਡਨ ਸੀ।
main kallh lanḏan see.

i ਤੁਸੀਂ ਕੱਲੂ ਕਿੱਥੇ ਸੀ?
ṯuseen kallh kiththe see?

ii ਤੁਸੀਂ ਹਫ਼ਤੇ ਦੇ ਅਖ਼ੀਰ ਕਿੱਥੇ ਸੀ?
ṯuseen hafṯe ḏe akheer kiththe see?

iii ਤੁਸੀਂ ਐਤਵਾਰ ਕਿੱਥੇ ਸੀ?
ṯuseen aiṯvaar kiththe see?

3 True or false?

Indicate whether the following statements from the dialogues in the unit are true or false.

a ਪਵਨ ਸਿੰਘ ਹਾਕੀ ਖੇਡਦਾ ਸੀ।	pavan singh haakee kheddaa see.	True/False
b ਪਵਨ ਸਿੰਘ ਜਲੰਧਰ ਪੜ੍ਹਦਾ ਸੀ।	pavan singh jalandhar parh-h-daa see.	True/False
c ਵਿਆਹ ਵਿਚ ਬਹੁਤ ਪ੍ਰਾਹੁਣੇ ਸਨ।	viaah vich bahut praahunhe san.	True/False

4 Construct negative and interrogative sentences

The first example is given.

a ਰਾਮ ਲੰਡਨ ਰਹਿੰਦਾ ਸੀ।
Raam landan rahindaa see.
Ram used to live in London.

Negative:	ਰਾਮ ਲੰਡਨ ਨਹੀਂ ਰਹਿੰਦਾ ਸੀ। raam landan naheen rahindaa see. *Ram did not use to live in London.*
Interrogative:	ਕੀ ਰਾਮ ਲੰਡਨ ਰਹਿੰਦਾ ਸੀ? kee raam landan rahindaa see? *Did Ram use to live in London?*

b ਉਹ ਹਫ਼ਤੇ ਦੇ ਅਖ਼ੀਰ ਲੰਡਨ ਗਏ ਸਨ।
uh hafte de akheer landan gae san.
They went to London over the weekend.

c ਅਸੀਂ ਇੱਕਠੇ ਟੈਨਸ ਖੇਡਦੇ ਸੀ।
aseen ikaththe tainas khedde see.
We used to play tennis together.

d ਉਹ ਪੰਜਾਬੀ ਬੋਲਦੀ ਹੁੰਦੀ ਸੀ।
uh panjaabee boldee hundee see.
She used to speak Panjabi.

Ten important things to remember

1 The simple past tense is formed by adding appropriate endings to the stem of the main verb without an auxiliary verb.

2 Remote past tense = simple past tense + appropriate forms of 'was' and 'were'.

3 Past habitual tense = simple present tense form + appropriate form of 'was' and 'were'.

4 Negative sentences in the various past tenses are formed by adding '*naheen*' 'ਨਹੀਂ' before or after the main verb.

5 Interrogative sentences are formed in the past tense by adding a question word '*kee*' 'ਕੀ'.

6 Though word order is not rigid in Panjabi, we should be careful when using the word '*kee*' 'ਕੀ' as its positioning would change the meaning of the sentence.

7 Similarly other interrogative pronouns can be used in turning statements into questions by replacing '*kee*' 'ਕੀ' with other interrogative words.

8 Some words designating kinship relations vary according to the religious background of the community.

9 The English word 'uncle' signifies five different relations in Panjabi.

10 In the Panjabi language there is a vast vocabulary of specific terms describing the exact nature of extended family relations.

7

ਤੁਸੀਂ ਕੀ ਪੀਓ ਗੇ?
tuseen kee peeo ge?
What will you (have to) drink?

In this unit you will learn:

- How to express actions in the future
- Days of the week
- How to tell the time
- About repetitive and rhyming words

1 *I'll wait*
ਗੱਲ ਬਾਤ ੧ ਮੈਂ ਉਡੀਕਾਂ ਗਾ
gall baat 1 main udeekaan gaa

◀)) **CD 1, TR 8, 00:20**

Mr Ali and Mr Malik are old friends. Mr Ali is standing outside his house as Mr Malik happens to pass by.

ਮਿਸਟਰ ਅਲੀ **Mr Ali**	ਅੱਸਲਾਮ ਅਲੈਕਮ। ਕੀ ਹਾਲ ਚਾਲ ਏ? asslaam alaikam. kee haal chaal e?
ਮਿਸਟਰ ਮਲਿਕ **Mr Malik**	ਵਾਲੈਕਮ ਅੱਸਲਾਮ। ਮੈਂ ਠੀਕ ਠਾਕ ਹਾਂ। vaalaikam asslaam. main theek thaak haan.
ਮਿਸਟਰ ਅਲੀ **Mr Ali**	ਅੰਦਰ ਆ ਜਾ। ਚਾਹ ਚੂ ਪੀ। andar aa jaa. chaah choo pee.
ਮਿਸਟਰ ਮਲਿਕ **Mr Malik**	ਅੱਜ ਮੈਂ ਨਹੀਂ ਠਹਿਰਾਂ ਗਾ। ਮੈਂ ਕਾਹਲ ਵਿਚ ਹਾਂ। ajj main naheen thahiraan gaa. main kaahal vich haan.

ਮਿਸਟਰ ਅਲੀ **Mr Ali**	ਕੀ ਤੂੰ ਕੱਲੂ ਆਵੇਂ ਗਾ ? kee <u>t</u>oon kallh aaven gaa?
ਮਿਸਟਰ ਮਲਿਕ **Mr Malik**	ਇਨਸ਼ਾ ਅੱਲਾ। ਮੈਂ ਜ਼ਰੂਰ ਆਵਾਂ ਗਾ। ਕੱਲੂ ਐਤਵਾਰ ਹੈ। ਵਕਤ ਖੁੱਲ੍ਹਾ ਹੋਵੇ ਗਾ। inshaa alla. main zaroor aavaan gaa. kallh ai<u>t</u>vaar hai. vaka<u>t</u> khullhaa hove gaa.
ਮਿਸਟਰ ਅਲੀ **Mr Ali**	ਸੁਣ! ਤੂੰ ਕਿੰਨੇ ਵਜੇ ਆਵੇਂ ਗਾ ? sunh! <u>t</u>oon ki<u>nn</u>e vaje aaven gaa?
ਮਿਸਟਰ ਮਲਿਕ **Mr Malik**	ਅਸੀਂ ਸਾਰੇ ਕੱਲੂ ਪੰਜ ਵਜੇ ਆਵਾਂ ਗੇ। asee<u>n</u> saare kallh panj vaje aavaa<u>n</u> ge.
ਮਿਸਟਰ ਅਲੀ **Mr Ali**	ਚੰਗਾ ਫਿਰ। ਮੈਂ ਉਡੀਕਾਂ ਗਾ। cha<u>n</u>gaa phir. main udeekaan gaa.

Mr Ali	*Hello! How are you?*
Mr Malik	*Hello! I'm fine.*
Mr Ali	*Come inside. Have some tea.*
Mr Malik	*I'm sorry. I won't stop today. I'm in a hurry.*
Mr Ali	*Will you come tomorrow?*
Mr Malik	*Hopefully [lit. If God wishes]. I'll definitely come.* *Tomorrow is Sunday. There will be plenty of time.*
Mr Ali	*Listen! What time will you come round?*
Mr Malik	*We'll all come tomorrow, at 5 o'clock.*
Mr Ali	*Fine then. I'll wait.*

ਸ਼ਬਦਾਵਲੀ	**shab<u>d</u>aavalee**	*Vocabulary*
ਉਡੀਕਣਾ	udeeknhaa	*to wait*
ਅੰਦਰ	<u>and</u>ar	*inside*
ਆ ਜਾ	aa jaa	*come* (informal request)
ਅੱਜ	ajj	*today*
ਠਹਿਰਨਾ	thahirnaa	*to stay*
ਕਾਹਲ ਵਿਚ	kaahal vich	*in a hurry*
ਇਨਸ਼ਾ ਅੱਲਾ	inshaa allaa	*hopefully* (lit. *if God wishes*)
ਜ਼ਰੂਰ	zaroor	*definitely*
ਵਕਤ	vaka<u>t</u>	*time* (m.)
ਖੁੱਲ੍ਹਾ	khullhaa	*open, plenty* (v.)
ਕਿੰਨੇ ਵਜੇ	ki<u>nn</u>e vaje	*what time*
ਅਸੀਂ ਸਾਰੇ	asee<u>n</u> saare	*all of us, we all*
ਪੰਜ ਵਜੇ	pa<u>n</u>j vaje	*5 o'clock*

ਅਭਿਆਸ abhiaas *Exercises*

After reading the dialogue and/or listening to the recording, try to do the following exercises.

1 Fill in the blanks

Complete the sentences by filling in the blank with the correct Panjabi word.

a ਮੈਂ _____ ਆਵਾਂ ਗਾ।   *I'll definitely come.*
b ਕੀ ਤੂੰ _____ ਆਵੇਂ ਗਾ?   *Will you come tomorrow?*
c ਤੂੰ _____ ਆਵੇਂ ਗਾ?   *What time will you come?*

2 Arrange the sentences in the correct order

The order of the following sentences from the dialogue is mixed up. Can you unscramble them by numbering them in the correct order?

1	ਮਿਸਟਰ ਮਲਿਕ	ਅਸੀਂ ਸਾਰੇ ਕੱਲ੍ਹ ਪੰਜ ਵਜੇ ਆਵਾਂ ਗੇ।
	Mr Malik	aseen saare kallh panj vaje aavaan ge.
2	ਮਿਸਟਰ ਮਲਿਕ	ਵਾਲੈਕਮ ਅੱਸਲਾਮ, ਮੈਂ ਠੀਕ ਠਾਕ ਹਾਂ।
	Mr Malik	vaalaikam asslaam, main theek thaak haan.
3	ਮਿਸਟਰ ਅਲੀ	ਸੁਣ! ਤੂੰ ਕਿੰਨੇ ਵਜੇ ਆਵੇਂ ਗਾ?
	Mr Ali	sunh! toon kinne vaje aaven gaa?
4	ਮਿਸਟਰ ਅਲੀ	ਅੱਸਲਾਮ ਅਲੈਕਮ। ਕੀ ਹਾਲ ਚਾਲ ਏ?
	Mr Ali	asslaam alaikam. kee haal chaal e?

---

2 *What will you (have to) drink?*
ਗੱਲ ਬਾਤ ੨ ਤੁਸੀਂ ਕੀ ਪੀਓ ਗੇ?
gall baat 2 tuseen kee peeo ge?

🔊 CD 1, TR 8, 01:14

Mr and Mrs Malik visit Mr Ali's home. Mr Malik knocks on the door and Mr Ali opens it.

ਮਿਸਟਰ ਅਲੀ	ਜੀ ਆਇਆਂ ਨੂੰ ਭਾਈ ਸਾਹਿਬ ਤੇ ਭਾਬੀ ਜੀ।
Mr Ali	jee aaiaan noon bhaaee saahib te bhaabee jee.

(Mr and Mrs Ali exchange greetings with Mr and Mrs Malik.)

ਮਿਸੜ੍ਹ ਅਲੀ **Mrs Ali**	ਤਸ਼ਰੀਫ਼ ਰੱਖੋ ਜੀ । ਤੁਸੀਂ ਕੀ ਪੀਓ ਗੇ ? tashreef rakhkho jee. tuseen kee peeo ge?
ਮਿਸਟਰ ਮਲਿਕ **Mr Malik**	ਸ਼ੁਕਰੀਆ । ਮੈਂ ਚਾਹ ਪੀਵਾਂ ਗਾ । shukreeaa. main chaah peevaan gaa.
ਮਿਸੜ੍ਹ ਮਲਿਕ **Mrs Malik**	ਮੈਂ ਰਸ ਲਵਾਂ ਗੀ । main ras lavaan gee.

(Mrs Ali serves the drinks and then begins talking to Mrs Malik.)

ਮਿਸੜ੍ਹ ਅਲੀ **Mrs Ali**	ਬੱਚੇ ਕਦੋਂ ਆਉਣ ਗੇ ? bachche kadon aaunh ge?
ਮਿਸੜ੍ਹ ਮਲਿਕ **Mrs Malik**	ਉਹ ੧੫ ਮਿੰਟਾਂ ਵਿਚ ਆਉਣ ਗੇ । uh 15 mintaan vich aaunh ge.
ਮਿਸੜ੍ਹ ਅਲੀ **Mrs Ali**	ਕੀ ਤੂੰ ਮੇਰੇ ਨਾਲ ਉਰਦੂ ਫ਼ਿਲਮ ਦੇਖੇਂ ਗੀ ? kee toon mere naal urdoo filam dekhen gee?
ਮਿਸੜ੍ਹ ਮਲਿਕ **Mrs Malik**	ਕਿਹੜੀ ਫ਼ਿਲਮ ? kihrhee filam?
ਮਿਸੜ੍ਹ ਮਲਿਕ **Mrs Ali**	'ਅਨਾਰਕਲੀ' ੮ ਵਜੇ ਟੀ ਵੀ ਤੇ ਆ ਰਹੀ ਹੈ । 'anaarkalee' 8 vaje tee vee te aa rahee hai.
ਮਿਸੜ੍ਹ ਮਲਿਕ **Mrs Malik**	ਹਾਂ ਜੀ । ਮੈਂ ਜ਼ਰੂਰ ਦੇਖਾਂ ਗੀ! haan jee. main zaroor dekhaan gee!

Mr Ali	*Welcome brother and sister-in-law.*

(Mr and Mrs Ali exchange greetings with Mr and Mrs Malik.)

Mrs Ali	*Please have a seat. What will you drink?*
Mr Malik	*I'll have [drink] tea.*
Mrs Malik	*I'll have juice.*

(Mrs Ali serves the drinks and then begins talking to Mrs Malik.)

Mrs Ali	*When will the children arrive?*
Mrs Malik	*They'll be here in 15 minutes.*
Mrs Ali	*Will you [would you like to] watch an Urdu film with me?*
Mrs Malik	*Which film?*
Mrs Ali	*Anarkali [name of a film] is on television at 8 o'clock.*
Mrs Malik	*Yes. I'll definitely watch it!*

ਸ਼ਬਦਾਵਲੀ	shabdaavalee	Vocabulary
ਜੀ ਆਇਆਂ ਨੂੰ	jee aaiaan noon	welcome
ਭਾਈ ਸਾਹਿਬ	bhaaee saahib	brother (m.)
ਭਾਬੀ ਜੀ	bhaabee jee	sister-in-law (f.)
ਤਸ਼ਰੀਫ਼ ਰੱਖੋ ਜੀ	tashreef rakhkho jee	please have a seat
ਪੀਣਾ	peenhaa	to drink
ਰਸ	ras	(fruit) juice (m.)
ਲੈਣਾ	lainhaa	to take, to have
ਕਦੋਂ	kadon	when
ਮਿੰਟਾਂ	mintaan	minutes (m.)
ਮੇਰੇ ਨਾਲ	mere naal	with me
ਦੇਖਣਾ	dekhnhaa	to see, to watch
ਉਰਦੂ	urdoo	Urdu (m./f.)
ਅਨਾਰਕਲੀ	anaarkalee	name of a classic Urdu film (f.)
੮ ਵਜੇ	8 vaje	8 o'clock
ਟੀ ਵੀ	tee vee	TV (television) (m.)

ਅਭਿਆਸ abhiaas *Exercises*

After reading the dialogue and/or listening to the recording, try to do the following exercises.

1 Questions to ask guests

◀) CD 1, TR 8, 02:04

Two guests, Mr and Mrs Malik, have come to your house for tea. Ask them the following questions.

a What will you have to drink?
b Would you like to watch television?
c Would you like to have juice or tea?

2 Word search

Three words *children*, *Urdu* and *sister-in-law* are hidden in Panjabi in the box. Find them by reading horizontally across each of the rows.

ਬੱ	ਚੇ	ਓ	ਪ	ਓ
ਸਾਂ	ਸ	ਕ	ਨ	ਹੀਂ
ਕਾ	ਕਿ	ਉ	ਰ	ਦੂ
ਸੋ	ਸਿ	ਕੁ	ਚ	ਨ
ਇ	ਭਾ	ਬੀ	ਹਾ	ਕੈ

ਬੋਲੀ ਬਾਰੇ bolee baare *Language points*

The future tense

In Panjabi, as in English, the future tense is used when one is making predictions about the future or referring to intentions, offers, or promises in the future. The Panjabi ending -ਗਾ **gaa** is used to denote actions or conditions in the future and means *will, shall* or *would*. As has been explained with other verb tenses in Panjabi, the form of the future tense varies according to the number and gender of the subject. Here are the ways in which -ਗਾ **gaa** is formed (notice that the forms of -ਗਾ **gaa** do not change according to the person of the subject):

-ਗਾ	gaa	masculine singular
-ਗੀ	gee	feminine singular
-ਗੇ	ge	masculine plural
-ਗੀਆਂ	geeaa<u>n</u>	feminine plural

The future tense therefore, as is also the case with the present tenses, is constructed by combining the main verb with the auxiliary ending, -ਗਾ **gaa**. The main verb in the future tense, however, does vary according to the person as well as the number of the subject. In the first dialogue in this unit, the verb ਉਡੀਕਣਾ **udeeknhaa** *to wait* was used in the future tense ਮੈਂ ਉਡੀਕਾਂ ਗਾ **mai<u>n</u> udeekaa<u>n</u> gaa** *I will wait*. The example of ਕਰਨਾ **karnaa** *to do* is now illustrated to show how verbs with stems ending in consonants are formed in the future.

ਕਰਨਾ – infinitive form of *to do* ਕਰ – stem

1st person

Masc. sing.	ਮੈਂ ਕਰਾਂ ਗਾ	main karaan gaa	*I shall/will do*
Fem. sing.	ਮੈਂ ਕਰਾਂ ਗੀ	main karaan gee	*I shall/will do*
Masc. pl.	ਅਸੀਂ ਕਰਾਂ ਗੇ	aseen karaan ge	*we shall/will do*
Fem. pl.	ਅਸੀਂ ਕਰਾਂ ਗੀਆਂ	aseen karaan geeaan	*we shall/will do*

2nd person

Masc. sing. informal	ਤੂੰ ਕਰੇਂ ਗਾ	toon karen gaa	*you will do*
Fem. sing. informal	ਤੂੰ ਕਰੇਂ ਗੀ	toon karen gee	*you will do*
Masc. pl./formal	ਤੁਸੀਂ ਕਰੋ ਗੇ	tuseen karo ge	*you will do*
Fem. pl.	ਤੁਸੀਂ ਕਰੋ ਗੀਆਂ	tuseen karo geeaan	*you will do*

3rd person

Masc. sing.	ਉਹ/ਇਹ ਕਰੇ ਗਾ	uh/ih kare gaa	*he will do*
Fem. sing.	ਉਹ/ਇਹ ਕਰੇ ਗੀ	uh/ih kare gee	*she will do*
Masc. pl./formal	ਉਹ/ਇਹ ਕਰਨ ਗੇ	uh/ih karan ge	*they will do*
Fem. pl.	ਉਹ/ਇਹ ਕਰਨ ਗੀਆਂ	uh/ih karan geeaan	*they will do*

Another construction of the future tense occurs when the stem of the main verb ends in a vowel such as ਜਾ-ਣਾ jaa-nhaa *to go*, ਆਉ-ਣਾ aau-nhaa *to come*, ਪੀ-ਣਾ pee-nhaa *to drink*, and ਲੈ-ਣਾ lai-nhaa *to have*. There are generally two acceptable ways of forming the future tense with such vowel-ending stems. The first manner follows the pattern as given for consonant-ending verb stems. The second manner in which the future tense is often formed is by inserting ਵ vavvaa after the vowel. There is no significant difference between the two, although the ਵ vavvaa forms often have a slightly more formal tone. Note these examples of the two commonly used main verb formations in the future tense:

Example: ਜਾਣਾ   **jaanhaa**   *to go*   [ਜਾ is the stem of the verb ਜਾਣਾ]

sing./masc.	ਮੈਂ ਜਾਵਾਂ ਗਾ	main jaavaan gaa	*I will go*
sing./fem.	ਮੈਂ ਜਾਵਾਂ ਗੀ	main jaavaan gee	*I will go*
pl./masc.	ਅਸੀਂ ਜਾਵਾਂ ਗੇ	aseen jaavaan ge	*we will go*
pl./fem.	ਅਸੀਂ ਜਾਵਾਂ ਗੀਆਂ	aseen jaavaan geeaan	*we will go*
sing./masc./ informal	ਤੂੰ ਜਾਏਂ/ਜਾਵੇਂ ਗਾ	toon jaaen/jaaven gaa	*you will go*

sing./fem./ informal	ਤੂੰ ਜਾਏਂ/ਜਾਵੇਂ ਗੀ	<u>t</u>oon jaae<u>n</u>/jaave<u>n</u> gee	*you will go*
pl./formal	ਤੁਸੀਂ ਜਾਓ/ਜਾਵੋ ਗੇ	<u>t</u>usee<u>n</u> jaao/jaavo ge	*you will go*
fem. pl.	ਤੁਸੀਂ ਜਾਓ/ਜਾਵੋ ਗੀਆਂ	<u>t</u>usee<u>n</u> jaao/jaavo geeaa<u>n</u>	*you will go*
masc. sing. informal	ਉਹ/ਇਹ ਜਾਏ/ ਜਾਵੇ ਗਾ	uh/ih jaae/jaave gaa	*he will go*
fem. sing.	ਉਹ/ਇਹ ਜਾਏ/ ਜਾਵੇ ਗੀ	uh/ih jaae/jaave gee	*she will go*
masc. pl./ formal	ਉਹ/ਇਹ ਜਾਣ/ ਜਾਵਣ ਗੇ	uh/ih jaanh/ jaavanh ge	*they will go*
fem. pl.	ਉਹ/ਇਹ ਜਾਣ/ ਜਾਵਣ ਗੀਆਂ	uh/ih jaanh/jaavanh geeaa<u>n</u>	*they will go*

More forms of the imperative

In Unit 5 the imperative was briefly introduced as a means of expressing a request, order or command. The formal and informal uses of the imperative were illustrated through the verb ਸੁਣਨਾ **sunhnaa** *to listen*:

ਤੂੰ ਸੁਣ	<u>t</u>oon sunh	*listen* (you, informal)
ਤੁਸੀਂ ਸੁਣੋ	<u>t</u>usee<u>n</u> sunho	*listen* (you, formal/plural)

The plural form of the imperative is used to denote a respectful tone when addressed to a single person. To make the request yet more formal and respectful, the English equivalent of *please* can also be added by use of the honorific particle ਜੀ **jee**.

ਸੁਣੋ ਜੀ	sunho jee	*please listen* (you, formal)

Please in Panjabi is expressed in the phrase ਕਿਰਪਾ ਕਰ ਕੇ **kirpaa kar ke**. By using this phrase, a formal request can be made more polite:

ਅੰਦਰ ਆਓ	<u>an</u>dar aao	*come in*
ਕਿਰਪਾ ਕਰ ਕੇ ਅੰਦਰ ਆਓ	kirpaa kar ke <u>an</u>dar aao	*please come in*

Politeness is also expressed by forming the imperative in the future tense:

ਕੀ ਤੁਸੀਂ ਸੁਣੋ ਗੇ ਜੀ ?	kee <u>t</u>usee<u>n</u> sunho ge jee?	*Will you please listen?*

The tone of the request can be softened with the word ਜ਼ਰਾ **zaraa**, *just a little* used in combination with the infinitive form of the verb. The infinitive specifies the action of what is being requested. The colloquial sense of the earlier request becomes ਜ਼ਰਾ ਸੁਣਨਾ zaraa sunhnaa, *have a listen*. With ਦੇਖਣਾ dekhnhaa, *to look* the request becomes:

| ਜ਼ਰਾ ਦੇਖਣਾ | zaraa <u>d</u>ekhnhaa | *have a look* |

> ## Insight
> It is quite acceptable to use the following imperative forms in an informal manner. Examples: **sunhee<u>n</u>** 'ਸੁਣੀ' (*listen*) and **jaaee<u>n</u>** 'ਜਾਈਂ' (*go*).

Ordinal numbers

In Unit 3 you learned the cardinal numbers from 1 to 20. To expand your knowledge of numbers further here are some ordinal numbers.

ਪਹਿਲਾ	pahilaa	*first*
ਦੂਸਰਾ/ਦੂਜਾ	<u>d</u>oosraa/<u>d</u>oojaa	*second*
ਤੀਸਰਾ/ਤੀਜਾ	<u>t</u>eesraa/<u>t</u>eejaa	*third*
ਚੌਥਾ	chau<u>th</u>aa	*fourth*
ਪੰਜਵਾਂ	pa<u>n</u>jvaa<u>n</u>	*fifth*
ਛੇਵਾਂ	<u>ch</u>evaa<u>n</u>	*sixth*
ਸੱਤਵਾਂ	sattvaa<u>n</u>	*seventh*
ਅੱਠਵਾਂ	aththvaa<u>n</u>	*eighth*

As you can see, from *fifth* onwards ordinal numbers are formed with the ending -ਵਾਂ **vaan**. Since ordinals are adjectives, they follow the same rules of agreement as other adjectives. The endings of ordinals will therefore agree with the nouns that they are describing.

| ਪਹਿਲੀ ਵਾਰੀ | pahilee vaaree | *first time* |
| ਦੂਜਾ ਦਿਨ | <u>d</u>oojaa <u>d</u>in | *second day* |

What time is it?

In English, time is expressed by the use of *o'clock* which refers specifically to the position of the hands on the clock when telling the time. Similarly in Panjabi, time is most commonly expressed through the use of the verb ਵੱਜਣਾ **vajjnhaa** which means *to chime, to strike*. When asking someone the time, the same rules apply as when transforming

statements into interrogative sentences as shown in Unit 5. The word
ਕੀ **kee** is simply placed at the beginning of the sentence. However,
other words for time are also appropriate when asking someone the
time in Panjabi. Here are a few commonly used phrases:

ਕੀ ਵਕਤ ਹੈ?	kee vakaṯ hai?	*What time is it?*
ਕਿੰਨੇ ਵਜੇ ਹਨ?	kinne vaje han?	*What time is it?*
		(lit. how many times
		has the clock struck?)
ਕੀ ਟਾਇਮ ਹੈ?	kee taaim hai?	*What is the time?*

Therefore, when someone says that it is one o'clock, the expression
in Panjabi would be:

| ਇੱਕ ਵਜਿਆ ਹੈ | ikk vajiaa hai | *It is one o'clock.* |

The verb ਵੱਜਣਾ **vajjnhaa** is formed in the present perfect tense here,
literally meaning that *the clock has struck one*. Note that ਵਜਿਆ
vajiaa is the singular form as it agrees with the number one. All
other times which relate to the number one (such as quarter to one,
quarter past one, half past one) also take on the singular form:

ਡੇਢ ਵਜਿਆ ਹੈ	dedh vajiaa hai	*It is half past one.*
ਪੌਣਾ ਇੱਕ ਵਜਿਆ ਹੈ	paunhaa ikk vajiaa hai	*It is a quarter to one.*
ਸਵਾ ਇੱਕ ਵਜਿਆ ਹੈ	savaa ikk vajiaa hai	*It is a quarter past one.*

As you will have noticed in the earlier examples there are terms in
Panjabi for each 15-minute sequence of time on the clock. 1.30 and
2.30, however, have specific names while all other times use ਸਵਾ
savaa, ਸਾਢੇ **saadhe** and ਪੌਣੇ **paunhe**:

half past one = ਡੇਢ **dedh**
half past two = ਢਾਈ **dhaaee**

quarter past the hour = ਸਵਾ savaa
30 minutes past the hour = ਸਾਢੇ saadhe
quarter to the hour = ਪੌਣਾ paunhaa, ਪੌਣੇ paunhe

All times relating to numbers greater than one use the plural form of ਵਜਿਆ. Here are some examples:

ਦੋ ਵਜੇ ਹਨ	<u>d</u>o vaje han	*It is two o'clock.*
ਪੌਣੇ ਦੋ ਵਜੇ ਹਨ	paunhe <u>d</u>o vaje han	*It is a quarter to two.*
ਤਿੰਨ ਵਜੇ ਹਨ	<u>t</u>inn vaje han	*It is three o'clock.*
ਸਾਢੇ ਤਿੰਨ ਵਜੇ ਹਨ	saadhe <u>t</u>inn vaje han	*It is three thirty.*
ਚਾਰ ਵਜੇ ਹਨ	chaar vaje han	*It is four o'clock.*
ਸਵਾ ਚਾਰ ਵਜੇ ਹਨ	savaa chaar vaje han	*It is a quarter past four.*
ਪੰਜ ਵਜੇ ਹਨ	pan<u>j</u> vaje han	*It is five o'clock.*
ਛੇ ਵਜੇ ਹਨ	<u>ch</u>e vaje han	*It is six o'clock.*
ਪੌਣੇ ਛੇ ਵਜੇ ਹਨ	paunhe <u>ch</u>e vaje han	*It is a quarter to six.*
ਸੱਤ ਵਜੇ ਹਨ	satt vaje han	*It is seven o'clock.*
ਅੱਠ ਵਜੇ ਹਨ	athth vaje han	*It is eight o'clock.*
ਨੌਂ ਵਜੇ ਹਨ	naun vaje han	*It is nine o'clock.*
ਦਸ ਵਜੇ ਹਨ	<u>d</u>as vaje han	*It is ten o'clock.*
ਸਾਢੇ ਗਿਆਰਾਂ ਵਜੇ ਹਨ	saadhe giaaraan vaje han	*It is 11.30.*
ਬਾਰਾਂ ਵਜੇ ਹਨ	baar-h-aan vaje han	*It is 12 o'clock.*

When the exact nature of the time is being expressed, it is also possible to use other forms of expression. Here are a few examples:

ਕਲਾਸ ਇੱਕ ਵਜੇ ਸ਼ੁਰੂ ਹੁੰਦੀ ਹੈ	kalaas ikk vaje shuroo hundee hai	*The class starts at one o'clock.*
ਤਿੰਨ ਵੱਜ ਰਹੇ ਹਨ	<u>t</u>inn vaj rahe han	*It is just three o'clock.*
ਨੌਂ ਵਜਣ ਵਾਲੇ ਹਨ	nau<u>n</u> vajanh vaale han	*It is nearly nine o'clock.*

When the time of day needs to be specified, *morning* (ਸਵੇਰ saver), *afternoon* (ਦੁਪਹਿਰ <u>d</u>upahir), *day* (ਦਿਨ <u>d</u>in), *evening* (ਸ਼ਾਮ shaam) and *night* (ਰਾਤ raa<u>t</u>) can also be used:

ਛੇ ਵਜੇ ਸ਼ਾਮ ਨੂੰ	<u>ch</u>e vaje shaam noo<u>n</u>	*at six o'clock in the evening*
ਸਵੇਰ ਦੇ ਅੱਠ ਵਜੇ	saver <u>d</u>e athth vaje	*at eight o'clock in the morning*

ਦੁਪਹਿਰ ਦੇ ਡੇਢ ਵਜੇ	dupahir de dedh vaje	*at 1.30 in the afternoon*
ਦਿਨ ਦੇ ਦੋ ਵਜੇ	din de do vaje	*at two o'clock in the*
		afternoon (day)
ਬਾਰ੍ਹਾਂ ਵਜੇ ਰਾਤ ਨੂੰ	baar-h-aan vaje	*at 12 o'clock at night*
	raat noon	

Further usages and expressions of time will be explained in subsequent units.

Insight

Generally, half past the hour is 'saadhe' 'ਸਾਢੇ' + *number*. For example, 30 minutes past 3 is spoken 'saadhe tinn' 'ਸਾਢੇ ਤਿੰਨ' and so on, but 30 minutes past 1 and 30 minutes past 2 are exceptions which have special terminology i.e. *dedh* ਡੇਢ and *dhaaee* ਢਾਈ respectively.

ਵਿਆਖਿਆ   viaakhiaa   *Commentary*

1 Repetitive and echo/rhyming words

The habitual use of repetitive and echo words is one of the many special characteristics of Panjabi which make it such an expressive language. Many words in Panjabi are repeated in the written and spoken forms to add emphasis. Repetition occurs when the same word is repeated while the echoing and rhyming of words occur through the use of two words which sound similar. Here are some examples:

ਹੋਲੀ ਹੋਲੀ ਚਲੋ	haulee haulee chalo	*walk slowly* (emphasizing slowly)
ਹਟ ਹਟ	hat hat	*get away* (showing intensity)
ਦੇਸ ਦੇਸ ਤੋਂ ਲੋਕ ਆਏ	des des ton lok aae	*people came from different countries* (emphasis on countries to signify the many different countries)
ਚਾਹ ਚੂ	chaah choo	*tea* [here the echo word ਚੂ has no specific meaning other than for emphasis]
ਦੁੱਖ ਸੁੱਖ	dukhkh sukhkh	*miseries and comforts*

ਦਿਨ ਰਾਤ	din raat	day and night (all the time) [these words technically neither rhyme nor are echo words. However, their opposite meanings uttered together gives the idea of continuity.]
ਸੱਚ ਸੱਚ	sachch sachch	*the whole truth*
ਚੁੱਪ ਚਾਪ	chupp chaap	(absolutely) *quiet*

2 Days of the week

There are two words for *day* in Panjabi which are used to designate the days of the week: ਦਿਨ din and ਵਾਰ vaar. If you want to ask someone what the day of the week is today, there are two ways to ask:

ਅੱਜ ਕੀ ਦਿਨ ਹੈ?	ajj kee din hai?	*What day is it today?*
ਅੱਜ ਕੀ ਵਾਰ ਹੈ?	ajj kee vaar hai?	*What day is it today?*

The names of the days of the week are all masculine nouns. Some of the days of the week are different in West Panjab due to the influence of the Islamic calendar in Pakistan. The days of the week in Panjabi are as follows (*shows the Islamic calendar days):

◆) CD 1, TR 8, 02:30

Monday	ਸੋਮਵਾਰ	somvaar
	ਪੀਰ*	peer
Tuesday	ਮੰਗਲਵਾਰ	mangalvaar
Wednesday	ਬੁੱਧਵਾਰ	budhdhvaar
Thursday	ਵੀਰਵਾਰ	veervaar
	ਜੁਮੇਰਾਤ*	jumeraat
Friday	ਸ਼ੁੱਕਰਵਾਰ	shukkarvaar
	ਜੁਮਾ*	jumaa
Saturday	ਸਨਿਚਰਵਾਰ	sanicharvaar
	ਹਫ਼ਤਾ*	haftaa
Sunday	ਐਤਵਾਰ	aitvaar

Other useful calendar terms are:

ਹਫ਼ਤਾ	haftaa	*week* (m.)
ਸਪਤਾਹ	saptaah	*week* (m.)

110

ਮਹੀਨਾ	maheenaa	*month* (m.)
ਦਿਨ	<u>d</u>in	*day* (m.)
ਸਾਲ	saal	*year* (m.)

3 Expressions of friendship

You will have noticed in Dialogue 2 that Mr Ali greets Mr Malik as ਭਾਈ ਸਾਹਿਬ **bhaaee saahib** (*brother*) and Mrs Malik as ਭਾਬੀ ਜੀ **bhaabee jee** (*sister-in-law*). It is not uncommon to address people with whom you wish to express closeness or affection with such terms ordinarily associated with kinship. In this example, it is quite clear that Mr Ali and Mr Malik are not brothers, but their friendship is the basis for Mr Ali referring to Mr Malik as *brother*. Since the relationship is primarily based upon the two men, Mrs Malik is referred to as ਭਾਬੀ ਜੀ **bhaabee jee** (as Mr Malik's wife) and not *sister*.

Insight

Apart from the honorific particles of '*jee*' 'ਜੀ' and '*saahib*', 'ਸਾਹਿਬ' in West Panjab, the word '*janaab*' 'ਜਨਾਬ' (sir) is frequently used both in spoken and written form.

ਅਭਿਆਸ abhiaas *Exercises*

1 The imperative

You are trying to convey to someone that he or she should listen to you. How would you form the imperative of ਸੁਣਨਾ **sunhnaa** *to listen* in the following circumstances?

a to someone who is younger than you (informal)
b to someone who is older than you (formal)
c to someone to whom you wish to show respect (formal, polite)
d to someone with whom you wish to use a mild tone of request

2 What time is it?

Write the answers in Panjabi.

3 The future tense

After reviewing the future tense section in the unit, express the fact that you will have tea in the following gender and number situations:

a singular male
b singular female
c plural male
d plural female

4 Conversation

Suppose you have been asked to go to someone's house. Express the following conversational phrases in Panjabi.

a Yes, thank you.
b Yes, I'll come tomorrow.
c No, I'm in a hurry.
d Fine then. I'll wait.

> **Insight**
>
> There are specific words in Panjabi to represent the words 'thank you' and 'please' but these are not as frequently used as in English. Politeness in Panjabi is expressed in a number of other ways.

Ten important things to remember

1 The meaning of '*jee aaiaan noon*' 'ਜੀ ਆਇਆਂ ਨੂੰ' is 'welcome', which is used in a formal manner to greet guests or visitors.

2 The meaning of '*tashreef rakhkho jee*' 'ਤਸ਼ਰੀਫ਼ ਰੱਖੋ ਜੀ' is – 'Please have a seat'. It is quite a popular phrase used in West Panjab.

3 The future tense is formed by adding the future suffix '*gaa*' 'ਗਾ' (*gee, ge and geeaan*) (ਗੀ, ਗੇ, ਤੇ ਗੀਆਂ") to the subjunctive forms of the verb.

4 The meaning of the future suffix '*gaa*' 'ਗਾ' etc. is 'will', 'shall' or 'would'.

5 In the future tense the root of the main verb varies according to the nature of the verb itself, number and person of the subject.

6 It is quite common to address people with whom you wish to express closeness or affection with such terms ordinarily associated with kinship.

7 In Panjabi there is one word '*kallh*' 'ਕੱਲ੍ਹ' which means both 'yesterday' and 'tomorrow'. The sense in which this word is used can be ascertained from the tense and context of the sentence.

8 The habitual use of repetitive and echo words is one of the many special characteristics of Panjabi which make it such an expressive language.

9 Since ordinal numbers are adjectives, they follow the same rules of agreement as other adjectives.

10 To address someone senior to you by his/her first name is not good social etiquette.

8

ਮੈਨੂੰ ਸਿਤਾਰ ਵਜਾਉਣ ਦਾ ਸ਼ੋਕ ਹੈ
mainoon sitaar vajaaunh daa shauk hai
I enjoy playing the sitar

In this unit you will learn:

- How to express your likes and dislikes
- How to express need, want, should, ought
- How to discuss visas
- How to negotiate a taxi ride

---

1   *I enjoy playing the sitar*
ਗੱਲ ਬਾਤ ੧ ਮੈਨੂੰ ਸਿਤਾਰ ਵਜਾਉਣ ਦਾ ਸ਼ੋਕ ਹੈ
gall baat 1 mainoon sitaar vajaaunh daa shauk hai

◀) **CD 2, TR 1, 00:23**

Jaspreet and Simran are two sisters living in Yuba City, California. They are planning a trip to India and are having a conversation with their father, Mr Sandhu.

ਮਿਸਟਰ ਸੰਧੂ **Mr Sandhu**	ਤੁਹਾਨੂੰ ਭਾਰਤ ਜਾਣ ਲਈ ਕਿੰਨੇ ਪੈਸੇ ਚਾਹੀਦੇ ਹਨ ? tuhaanoon bhaarat jaanh laee kinne paise chaaheede han?

114

ਜਸਪ੍ਰੀਤ ਤੇ ਸਿਮਰਨ	ਸਾਨੂੰ ਘੱਟੋ ਘੱਟ (੨੦੦੦) ਦੋ ਹਜ਼ਾਰ ਡਾਲਰ ਚਾਹੀਦੇ ਹਨ।
Jaspreet and Simran	saanoon ghatto ghatt (2000) <u>d</u>o hazaar daalar chaahee<u>d</u>e han.
ਮਿਸਟਰ ਸੰਧੂ	ਐਨੇ ਸਾਰੇ ਪੈਸੇ? ਤੁਹਾਡਾ ਖ਼ਰਚਾ ਇੰਨਾ ਕਿਵੇਂ ਹੋਵੇ ਗਾ?
Mr Sandhu	aine saare paise? <u>t</u>uhaadaa <u>kh</u>archaa i<u>n</u>naa kiven hove gaa?
ਜਸਪ੍ਰੀਤ	ਪਿਤਾ ਜੀ! ਤੁਹਾਨੂੰ ਪਤਾ ਹੈ ਕਿ ਮੈਨੂੰ ਸਿਤਾਰ ਵਜਾਉਣ ਦਾ ਸ਼ੋਕ ਹੈ। ਮੈਂ ਉੱਥੋਂ ਵਧੀਆ ਸਿਤਾਰ ਲਿਆਵਾਂ ਗੀ।
Jaspreet	pi<u>t</u>aa jee! <u>t</u>uhaanoon pa<u>t</u>aa hai ki mainoo<u>n</u> si<u>t</u>aar vajaaunh <u>d</u>aa shauk hai. main u<u>thth</u>on vadheeaa si<u>t</u>aar liaavaan gee.
ਸਿਮਰਨ	... ਤੇ ਮੈਨੂੰ ਘੁੰਮਣਾ ਫਿਰਨਾ ਪਸੰਦ ਹੈ।
Simran	... <u>t</u>e mainoon ghu<u>n</u>mnhaa phirnaa pasa<u>nd</u> hai.
ਮਿਸਟਰ ਸੰਧੂ	ਮੇਰੀਓ ਧੀਓ, ਮੈਨੂੰ ਅਫ਼ਸੋਸ ਹੈ ਕਿ ਤੁਹਾਨੂੰ ਦੇਣ ਲਈ ਮੇਰੇ ਕੋਲ ਐਨੇ ਪੈਸੇ ਨਹੀਂ ਹਨ।
Mr Sandhu	mereeo <u>dh</u>eeo, mainoon afsos hai ki tuhaanoo<u>n</u> <u>d</u>enh laee mere kol aine paise nahee<u>n</u> han.
ਜਸਪ੍ਰੀਤ ਤੇ ਸਿਮਰਨ	ਤੁਸੀਂ ਫ਼ਿਕਰ ਨਾ ਕਰੋ, ਪਿਤਾ ਜੀ। ਮਾਤਾ ਜੀ ਕੋਲ ਪੈਸੇ ਬਹੁਤ ਹਨ!
Jaspreet and Simran	tusee<u>n</u> fikar naa karo, pi<u>t</u>aa jee. maa<u>t</u>aa jee kol paise bahu<u>t</u> han!

Mr Sandhu	*How much money do you need for going to India?*
Jaspreet and Simran	*We need at least $2000.*
Mr Sandhu	*So much money? Why will your expenses be so high?*
Jaspreet	*Father, you know that I am fond of playing the sitar. I'm going to bring a good quality sitar from there.*
Simran	*... and I like travelling around.*
Mr Sandhu	*My daughters, I am sorry that I don't have that much money to give you.*
Jaspreet and Simran	*Don't worry, Father. Mother has plenty of money!*

ਸ਼ਬਦਾਵਲੀ	shab<u>d</u>aavalee	*Vocabulary*
ਲਈ	laee	*for, in order to*
ਕਿੰਨੇ	ki<u>n</u>ne	*how much, how many*
ਚਾਹੁਣਾ	chaahunhaa	*to need, to want*

ਖ਼ਰਚਾ	kharchaa	expense, expenses (m.)
ਘੱਟੋ ਘੱਟ	ghatto ghatt	at least
ਡਾਲਰ	daalar	dollar (m.)
ਐਨੇ ਸਾਰੇ	aine saare	so much
ਪਤਾ	pataa	to know
ਸਿਤਾਰ	sitaar	sitar (f.) (a stringed classical musical instrument)
ਵਜਾਉਣਾ	vajaaunhaa	to play (music)
ਸ਼ੋਕ	shauk	fondness, enjoyment
ਵਜਾਉਣ ਦਾ ਸ਼ੋਕ	vajaaunh daa shauk	fond of playing, enjoy playing
ਉੱਥੋਂ	uththon	from there
ਵਧੀਆ	vadheeaa	good quality
ਲਿਆਉਣਾ	liaaunhaa	to bring
ਘੁੰਮਣਾ	ghunmnhaa	to go around
ਫਿਰਨਾ	phirnaa	to travel
ਘੁੰਮਣਾ ਫਿਰਨਾ	ghunmnhaa phirnaa	to travel around
ਪਸੰਦ	pasand	like
ਅਫ਼ਸੋਸ	afsos	regret, sorry
ਕੋਲ	kol	with, next to, in possession
ਮੇਰੇ ਕੋਲ ਨਹੀਂ	mere kol naheen	not with me, not in my possession
ਫ਼ਿਕਰ	fikar	worry (m.)
ਧੀਓ	dheeo	daughters (f.) (vocative case: see Language points)

ਅਭਿਆਸ abhiaas *Exercises*

After reading the dialogue and/or listening to the recording, try to do the following exercises.

1 Crossword

Complete the crossword in Gurmukhi script using the clues given.

1 a stringed classical instrument   3 expense
2 US currency   4 to travel

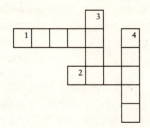

2 Match the statements

a ਫ਼ਿਕਰ ਨਾ ਕਰੋ।   i *I will bring a good quality sitar.*

b ਐਨੇ ਸਾਰੇ ਪੈਸੇ?   ii *Don't worry.*

c ਮੈਂ ਵਧੀਆ ਸਿਤਾਰ ਲਿਆਵਾਂ ਗੀ।   iii *So much money?*

---

2 *We want to go to Connaught Place*
ਗੱਲ ਬਾਤ ੨ ਅਸੀਂ ਕਨਾਟ ਪਲੇਸ ਜਾਣਾ ਚਾਹੁੰਦੀਆਂ ਹਾਂ
gall baat 2 aseen kanaat pales jaanhaa chaahundeeaan haan

◆) CD 2, TR 1, 02:00

Simran and Jaspreet have just arrived at the airport in Delhi. They have approached the immigration counter where they show their passports to the officer with whom they are having a conversation.

ਇਮੀਗ੍ਰੇਸ਼ਨ ਅਫ਼ਸਰ **Immigration officer**	ਤੁਸੀਂ ਅਮਰੀਕਾ ਕਿੰਨਾ ਚਿਰ ਤੋਂ ਰਹਿ ਰਹੀਆਂ ਹੋ? tuseen amreekaa kinnaa chir ton rahi raheeaan ho?
ਸਿਮਰਨ **Simran**	ਅਸੀਂ ਅਮਰੀਕਾ ਵਿਚ ਜੰਮੀਆਂ ਸੀ। aseen amreekaa vich janmeeaan see.
ਇਮੀਗ੍ਰੇਸ਼ਨ ਅਫ਼ਸਰ **Immigration officer**	ਤੁਹਾਨੂੰ ਐਨੀ ਚੰਗੀ ਪੰਜਾਬੀ ਕਿਵੇਂ ਆਉਂਦੀ ਹੈ? tuhaanoon ainee changee panjaabee kiven aaundee hai?

ਜਸਪ੍ਰੀਤ **Jaspreet**	ਸਾਨੂੰ ਸਿਰਫ਼ ਥੋੜੀ ਬਹੁਤੀ ਆਉਂਦੀ ਹੈ। saanoon siraf <u>th</u>orhee bahu<u>t</u>ee aau<u>nd</u>ee hai.
ਸਿਮਰਨ **Simran**	ਇੱਕ ਬੇਨਤੀ ਹੈ, ਅਫ਼ਸਰ ਸਾਹਿਬ ... ikk ben<u>t</u>ee hai, afsar saahib ...
ਇਮੀਗ੍ਰੇਸ਼ਨ ਅਫ਼ਸਰ **Immigration officer**	ਉਹ ਕੀ ਹੈ? uh kee hai?
ਸਿਮਰਨ **Simran**	ਸਾਡੇ ਕੋਲ ਕੇਵਲ ਇੱਕ ਮਹੀਨੇ ਦਾ ਵੀਜ਼ਾ ਹੈ। ਜੀ ਕੀ ਤੁਸੀਂ ਸਾਨੂੰ ਦੋ ਮਹੀਨੇ ਰਹਿਣ ਦੀ ਆਗਿਆ ਦੇਵੋ ਗੇ? saade kol keval ikk maheene <u>d</u>aa veezaa hai. jee kee <u>t</u>usee<u>n</u> saanoon <u>d</u>o maheene rahinh <u>d</u>ee aagiaa <u>d</u>evo ge?
ਇਮੀਗ੍ਰੇਸ਼ਨ ਅਫ਼ਸਰ **Immigration officer**	ਇਹ ਮੇਰੇ ਵੱਸ ਵਿਚ ਨਹੀਂ ਹੈ। ਤੁਹਾਨੂੰ ਵੀਜ਼ਾ ਅਮਰੀਕਾ ਤੋਂ ਲੈਣਾ ਚਾਹੀਦਾ ਸੀ। ih mere vass vich nahee<u>n</u> hai. <u>t</u>uhaanoon veezaa amreekaa <u>t</u>on lainhaa chaaheedaa see.
ਸਿਮਰਨ ਤੇ ਜਸਪ੍ਰੀਤ **Simran and Jaspreet**	ਫਿਰ ਸਾਨੂੰ ਇੱਕ ਮਹੀਨੇ ਵਿਚ ਸਾਰਾ ਕੁਝ ਦੇਖਣਾ ਪੈਣਾ। phir saanoo<u>n</u> ikk maheene vich saaraa kujh <u>d</u>ekhnhaa painhaa.
ਇਮੀਗ੍ਰੇਸ਼ਨ ਅਫ਼ਸਰ **Immigration officer**	ਦਿੱਲੀ ਦੇ ਆਸ ਪਾਸ ਕਾਫ਼ੀ ਕੁਝ ਦੇਖਣ ਵਾਲਾ ਹੈ। ਅਨੰਦ ਮਾਣੋ! <u>d</u>illee <u>d</u>e aas paas kaafee kujh <u>d</u>ekhanh vaalaa hai. ana<u>n</u>d maanho!

Immigration officer	*How long have you been living in America?*
Simran	*We were born in America.*
Immigration officer	*How do you know Panjabi so well?*
Jaspreet	*We only know a little.*
Simran	*Officer, one request ...*
Immigration officer	*What is it?*
Simran	*We only have a one-month visa. Could you please give us permission to stay for two months?*
Immigration officer	*This is not within my authority. You should have obtained the visa from America.*
Simran and Jaspreet	*In that case, we'll have to see everything in a month.*
Immigration officer	*There are plenty of things to see around Delhi. Enjoy yourselves!*

Jaspreet and Simran have cleared customs with their luggage and exit from the airport. They approach a taxi driver about travelling into the centre of Delhi.

ਜਸਪ੍ਰੀਤ	ਅਸੀਂ ਕਨਾਟ ਪਲੇਸ ਜਾਣਾ ਚਾਹੁੰਦੀਆਂ ਹਾਂ। ਤੂੰ ਕਿੰਨੇ ਪੈਸੇ ਲਵੇਂ ਗਾ?
Jaspreet	aseen kanaat pales jaanhaa chaahundeeaan haan. kinne paise laven gaa?
ਟੈਕਸੀਵਾਲਾ	ਸਿਰਫ਼ ਸੌ ਰੁਪਇਆ।
Taxi driver	siraf sau rupaiaa.
ਸਿਮਰਨ	ਕਨਾਟ ਪਲੇਸ ਹਵਾਈ ਅੱਡੇ ਤੋਂ ਕਿੰਨੀ ਦੂਰ ਹੈ?
Simran	kanaat pales havaaee adde ton kinnee door hai?
ਟੈਕਸੀਵਾਲਾ	ਤਕਰੀਬਨ ਵੀਹ ਮੀਲ ਦੂਰ ਹੈ। ਤੁਸੀਂ ਠੀਕ ਕਿਹੜੀ ਜਗ੍ਹਾ ਜਾਣਾ ਹੈ?
Taxi driver	takreeban veeh meel door hai. tuseen theek kihrhee jag-h-aa jaanhaa hai?
ਸਿਮਰਨ	ਅਸੀ ਅੰਤਰ ਰਾਸ਼ਟਰੀ ਯੁਵਕ ਹੋਸਟਲ ਜਾਣਾ ਹੈ ਪਰ ਤੂੰ ਜ਼ਿਆਦਾ ਪੈਸੇ ਮੰਗ ਰਿਹਾ ਹੈਂ।
Simran	aseen antar raashtaree yuvak hostal jaanhaa hai par toon ziaadaa paise mang rihaa hain.
ਟੈਕਸੀਵਾਲਾ	ਨਹੀਂ ਨਹੀਂ। ਮੈਂ ਕਿਰਾਇਆ ਵਾਜਬੀ ਦੱਸਿਆ ਹੈ। ਤੁਸੀਂ ਦੋ ਸਵਾਰੀਆਂ ਹੋ ਤੇ ਸਮਾਨ ਵੀ ਬਹੁਤ ਹੈ। ਤੁਸੀਂ ਜਾਣਾ ਏ ਕਿ ਨਹੀਂ?
Taxi driver	naheen naheen. main kiraaiaa vaajbee dassiaa hai. tuseen do savaareeaan ho te samaan vee bahut hai. tuseen jaanhaa e ki naheen?
ਜਸਪ੍ਰੀਤ	ਅੱਛਾ, ਕਾਹਲਾ ਨ ਪਓ। ਸਮਾਨ ਰੱਖ ਗੱਡੀ ਵਿਚ।
Jaspreet	achchaa, kaahalaa na pao. samaan rakhkh gaddee vich.
Jaspreet	*We want to go to Connaught Place. How much will you charge?**
Taxi driver	*Only 100 rupees.*
Simran	*How far is Connaught Place from the airport?*
Taxi driver	*It's about 20 miles away. Exactly where are you going?*
Simran	*Take us [we want to go] to the International Youth Hostel, but you're asking for too much money.*
Taxi driver	*No, no. I've told you the reasonable fare. There are two of you travelling and there is a lot of luggage. Are you going or not?*
Jaspreet	*OK. Don't be impatient. Put the luggage in the car.*

*The language used in this dialogue with the taxi driver may seem a little informal (or even rude) in the English translation. This is because informal speech is generally used when haggling over the fare with taxi drivers in India and Pakistan (see Unit 2: Language points: Subject pronouns).

ਸ਼ਬਦਾਵਲੀ	shabdaavalee	*Vocabulary*
ਅਮਰੀਕਾ	amreekaa	*America* (m.)
ਚਿਰ	chir	*length of time*
ਕਿੰਨਾ ਚਿਰ ਤੋਂ	kinnaa chir ton	*since when, for how long*
ਜੰਮਣਾ	janmnhaa	*to be born*
ਥੋੜੀ ਬਹੁਤੀ	thorhee bahutee	*more or less, to some extent*
ਬੇਨਤੀ	bentee	*request* (f.)
ਕੇਵਲ	keval	*only*
ਵੀਜ਼ਾ	veezaa	*visa* (m.)
ਆਗਿਆ	aagiaa	*permission* (f.)
ਵੱਸ	vass	*authority, jurisdiction* (m.)
ਪਾਸਪੋਰਟ	paasport	*passport* (m.)
ਅਫ਼ਸਰ	afsar	*officer* (m./f.)
ਸਾਹਿਬ	saahib	*sir* (m.)
ਆਸ ਪਾਸ	aas paas	*around, around and about*
ਕਾਫ਼ੀ ਕੁਝ	kaafee kujh	*quite a lot, plenty*
ਅਨੰਦ ਮਾਣੋ	anand maanho	*enjoy yourselves*
ਚਾਹੁਣਾ	chaahunhaa	*to want, to need*
ਸੌ (੧੦੦)	sau	*100*
ਰੁਪਇਆ	rupaiaa	*rupees* (m.)
ਹਵਾਈ ਅੱਡਾ	havaaee addaa	*airport* (m.)
ਕਿੰਨੀ ਦੂਰ	kinnee door	*how far*
ਦੂਰ	door	*far, distant*

ਵੀਹ (੨੦)	veeh	20
ਮੀਲ	meel	*mile, miles* (m.)
ਜਗ੍ਹਾ	jag-h-aa	*place, location* (f.)
ਅੰਤਰ ਰਾਸ਼ਟਰੀ	<u>an</u>tar raashtaree	*international*
ਯੁਵਕ	yuvak	*youth* (m.)
ਹੋਸਟਲ	hostal	*hostel* (m.)
ਜ਼ਿਆਦਾ	ziaa<u>d</u>aa	*too much*
ਮੰਗਣਾ	ma<u>n</u>gnhaa	*to request, to ask, to charge*
ਕਿਰਾਇਆ	kiraaiaa	*rate, fare, rent* (m.)
ਵਾਜਬੀ	vaajbee	*reasonable, fair, right*
ਸਵਾਰੀਆਂ	savaaree<u>aan</u>	*passengers, travellers* (f.)
ਸਮਾਨ	samaan	*luggage, things* (m.)
ਕਾਹਲਾ	kaahalaa	*impatient, hasty* (v.)
ਪੈਣਾ	painhaa	*to act* (to fall)
ਰੱਖਣਾ	rakhkhnhaa	*to put*
ਗੱਡੀ	gaddee	*car, vehicle* (f.)

ਅਭਿਆਸ abhiaas *Exercises*

After reading the dialogue and/or listening to the recording, try to do the following exercises.

1 Write in the correct word order

a ਹੈ ਪੰਜਾਬੀ ਬਹੁਤੀ ਆਉਂਦੀ ਥੋੜੀ ਸਾਨੂੰ
hai-pa<u>n</u>jaabee-bahu<u>t</u>ee-aau<u>n</u>dee-<u>t</u>horhee-saanoo<u>n</u>
We only know a little Panjabi.

b ਪਲੇਸ ਅਸੀਂ ਹਾਂ ਜਾਣਾ ਚਾਹੁੰਦੀਆਂ ਕਨਾਟ
pales-asee<u>n</u>-haa<u>n</u>-jaanhaa-chaahu<u>n</u>dee<u>aan</u>-kanaat
We want to go to Connaught Place.

c ਤੁਸੀਂ ਜੀ ਦੋ ਦੀ ਦੇਵੋ ਗੇ ਮਹੀਨੇ ਰਹਿਣ ਕੀ ਆਗਿਆ
tusee<u>n</u>-jee-<u>d</u>o-<u>d</u>ee-<u>d</u>evo-ge-maheene-rahinh-kee-aagiaa
Could you please give us permission to stay for two months?

2 Translate into Panjabi

a There are two of you travelling and there is a lot of luggage.

b We only have a one-month visa.

c Enjoy yourselves!

ਬੋਲੀ ਬਾਰੇ bolee baare *Language points*

Pronouns in the oblique

In Unit 2 personal pronouns were introduced representing the English equivalents of *I*, *we*, *you*, *he*, *she* and *they*. As with nouns, personal pronouns also take on the oblique form when followed by postpositions. The most commonly used postposition with pronouns is ਨੂੰ **noon** *to* as is illustrated. Note that interrogative pronouns such as ਕੌਣ **kaunh** *who* and ਕੀ **kee** *what* are also affected by postpositions.

Singular

Direct			Oblique		
I	ਮੈਂ	main	*to me*	ਮੈਨੂੰ	mainoon
you (inf.)	ਤੂੰ	toon	*to you* (inf.)	ਤੈਨੂੰ	tainoon
you (form.)	ਤੁਸੀਂ	tuseen	*to you* (form.)	ਤੁਹਾਨੂੰ	tuhaanoon
he/she/it	ਇਹ	ih	*to him/her/it*	ਇਹ ਨੂੰ,	ih noon
(near)				ਇਸ ਨੂੰ	is noon
he/she/it	ਉਹ	uh	*to him/her/it*	ਉਹ ਨੂੰ,	uh noon
(far)				ਉਸ ਨੂੰ	us noon
Interrogative pronouns					
who	ਕੌਣ	kaunh	*to whom*	ਕਿਸ ਨੂੰ	kis noon
what	ਕੀ	kee	*to what*	ਕਿਹਨੂੰ	kihnoon

Plural

Direct			Oblique		
we	ਅਸੀਂ	aseen	*to us*	ਸਾਨੂੰ	saanoon
you	ਤੁਸੀਂ	tuseen	*to you*	ਤੁਹਾਨੂੰ	tuhaanoon
they (near)	ਇਹ	ih	*to them*	ਇਹਨਾਂ ਨੂੰ	ihnaan noon
they (far)	ਉਹ	uh	*to them*	ਉਹਨਾਂ ਨੂੰ	uhnaan noon
Interrogative pronouns					
who	ਕੌਣ	kaunh	*to whom*	ਕਿਹਨਾਂ ਨੂੰ	kihnaan noon
what	ਕੀ	kee	*to what*	ਕਿਹਨਾਂ ਨੂੰ	kihnaan noon

The postposition ਨੂੰ **noon** is used in a number of ways. Generally, it directs an action, state or object towards the pronoun or noun after which it follows. Here are a few examples of how ਨੂੰ **noon** can be used with pronouns:

ਪੰਜਾਬੀ ਮੈਨੂੰ ਥੋੜੀ ਬਹੁਤੀ ਆਉਂਦੀ ਹੈ	panjaabee mainoon thorhee bahutee aaundee hai	*I know Panjabi to some extent.*
ਸਾਨੂੰ ਮਿਠਿਆਈ ਪਸੰਦ ਹੈ	saanoon mithiaaee pasand hai	*We like sweets.* (lit. sweets are liked by us)
ਤੂੰ ਕਿਹਨਾਂ ਨੂੰ ਦੱਸਿਆ ਸੀ ?	toon kihnaan noon dassiaa see?	*Whom did you tell?*

There are many other postpositions which are also used with pronouns. ਤੋਂ **ton**, ਨਾਲ **naal**, ਵਾਸਤੇ **vaaste**, ਕੋਲ **kol** and ਲਈ **laee** are some commonly used ones which were introduced in Unit 4. The manner in which the oblique is formed with these postpositions is noticeably different from pronouns followed by ਨੂੰ **noon**. The first and second person pronouns are changed to the appropriate possessive adjectives while the third person pronouns follow the same pattern of ਨੂੰ **noon** as already shown. Here are some examples using the postposition ਤੋਂ **ton** (*from*):

1st person

Direct			Oblique		
I	ਮੈਂ	main	*from me*	ਮੇਰੇ ਤੋਂ	mere ton
we	ਅਸੀਂ	aseen	*from us*	ਸਾਡੇ ਤੋਂ	saade ton

2nd person

Direct			Oblique		
you (inf.)	ਤੂੰ	toon	*from you* (inf.)	ਤੇਰੇ ਤੋਂ	tere ton
you (form.)	ਤੁਸੀਂ	tuseen	*from you* (form.)	ਤੁਹਾਡੇ ਤੋਂ	tuhaade ton

3rd person

Direct			Oblique		
he/she/it (singular, near)	ਇਹ	ih	*from him/ her/it*	ਇਸ ਤੋਂ	is <u>ton</u>
he/she/it (singular, far)	ਉਹ	ih	*from him/ her/it*	ਉਸ ਤੋਂ	us <u>ton</u>
they (plural, near)	ਇਹ	ih	*from them*	ਇਹਨਾਂ ਤੋਂ	ihnaan ton
they (plural, far)	ਉਹ	uh	*from them*	ਉਹਨਾਂ ਤੋਂ	uhnaan ton

ਮੇਰੇ ਕੋਲ ਐਨੇ ਪੈਸੇ ਨਹੀਂ ਹਨ	mere kol aine paise naheen han	*I don't have that much money.*
ਉਹਨਾਂ ਵਾਸਤੇ ਵੀ ਚਾਹ ਬਣਾਓ	uhnaan vaaste vee chaah banhaao	*Make tea for them too.*
ਕੀ ਤੁਸੀਂ ਸਾਡੇ ਨਾਲ ਆਵੋ ਗੇ?	kee <u>tuseen</u> saade naal aavo ge?	*Will you come with us?*
ਅਸੀਂ ਕਪੜੇ ਇਹਨਾਂ ਤੋਂ ਖ਼ਰੀਦਾਂ ਗੇ	aseen kaprhe ihnaan ton khareedaan ge	*We will buy the clothes from them.*

Must, have to

In Panjabi, expressions of compulsion come in three forms: an intention to do something, a certainty about doing something and a strong sense of compulsion about doing something. In each of these cases, it is usually the infinitive of the verb which directs the action related to the situation. Often ਹੋਣਾ **honhaa** is used to give a sense of the present or past condition, depending on which tense of *to be* is used. The direct form of the pronoun is used in these cases:

ਮੈਂ ਜਾਣਾ ਹੈ	main jaanhaa hai	*I am to go/I intend to go*
ਮੈਂ ਜਾਣਾ ਸੀ	main jaanhaa see	*I should have gone/ I was to go/I had to go*

Strong compulsion is indicated by the use of the verb ਪੈਣਾ **painhaa** (*to fall*). This gives a sense of habitual compulsion and is positioned after the infinitive. Note that the infinitive behaves as the subject in many of these expressions, and therefore the form of ਪੈਣਾ **painhaa** generally takes the singular masculine form (in agreement with the infinitive). For example:

| ਮੈਨੂੰ ਹਰ ਰੋਜ਼ ਜਾਣਾ | mainoon har roz | *I have to go* |
| ਪੈਂਦਾ ਹ | jaanhaa paindaa hai | *every day.* |

Use of the verb ਚਾਹੁਣਾ 'chaahunhaa'

In Panjabi, expressions such as *should/ought* and *need/want* are generally formed with the verb ਚਾਹੁਣਾ chaahunhaa (*to want, to need*). These expressions use the infinitive followed by ਚਾਹੀਦਾ chaaheedaa, which is the passive form of the verb ਚਾਹੁਣਾ chaahunhaa. (The passive voice will be explained in a later unit.) ਚਾਹੀਦਾ chaaheedaa in the sentence ਮੈਨੂੰ ਚਾਹੀਦਾ ਹੈ mainoon chaaheedaa hai literally means *it is wanted by me*. However, the use of ਚਾਹੀਦਾ chaaheedaa can have two different meanings:

- should/ought
- need/want

Should, ought

ਚਾਹੀਦਾ chaaheedaa, as with all other verb formations, changes according to the subject. In the case of expressions of *should* and *ought*, pronouns followed by postpositions behave like objects (*to me, for me, with them*). Therefore, in the case of someone who has to go somewhere, the form of ਚਾਹੀਦਾ chaaheedaa must be in the singular masculine form in agreement with the infinitive. Similarly, if the object is feminine and/or plural, then the form of ਚਾਹੁਣਾ chaahunhaa, as well as the infinitive would reflect this:

| ਮੈਨੂੰ ਜਾਣਾ ਚਾਹੀਦਾ ਹੈ | mainoon jaanhaa chaaheedaa hai | *I should go* |
| ਮੈਨੂੰ ਜਾਣਾ ਚਾਹੀਦਾ ਸੀ | mainoon jaanhaa chaaheedaa see | *I should have gone* |

Care must be taken to identify the object in expressions of *ought* and *should*. In our earlier example, the pronoun served as the object, however in the following examples the infinitive and the form of ਚਾਹੀਦਾ chaaheedaa follow the gender and numerical nature of the *subject of obligation* which now becomes the object, in the first case 'tea' and in the second 'books':

| ਮੈਨੂੰ ਚਾਹ ਨਹੀਂ ਪੀਣੀ ਚਾਹੀਦੀ | mainoon chaah naheen peenhee chaaheedee | *I should not drink tea.* |
| ਤੁਹਾਨੂੰ ਹੋਰ ਕਿਤਾਬਾਂ ਪੜ੍ਹਨੀਆਂ ਚਾਹੀਦੀਆਂ ਹਨ | tuhaanoon hor kitaabaan parh-h-neeaan chaaheedeeaan han | *You should read more books.* |

To want, to need

Expressions of desire or necessity are also formed with ਚਾਹੁਣਾ chaahunhaa. However, the verb is formed according to the subject of the sentence. For example, in Dialogue 2 Jaspreet and Simran say to the taxi driver, *We want to go to Connaught Place*. This is expressed as:

ਅਸੀਂ ਕਨਾਟ ਪਲੇਸ ਜਾਣਾ ਚਾਹੁੰਦੀਆਂ ਹਾਂ	aseen kanaat pales jaanhaa chaahundeeaan haan	*We want to go to Connaught Place.*

Notice in this example that ਅਸੀਂ aseen and ਚਾਹੁੰਦੀਆਂ ਹਾਂ chaahundeeaan haan are in agreement with each other. Therefore, the subject *we* dictates the form of *to want*. Here are some more examples of expressions of desire and necessity:

ਕੀ ਤੁਸੀਂ ਅਮਰੀਕਾ ਜਾਣਾ ਚਾਹੁੰਦੇ ਹੋ?	kee tuseen amreekaa jaanhaa chaahunde ho?	*Do you want to go to America?*
ਮੇਰਾ ਭਰਾ ਪੜ੍ਹਨਾ ਚਾਹੁੰਦਾ ਹੈ	meraa bharaa parh-h-naa chaahundaa hai	*My brother wants to study.*

As with constructions of *should* and *ought* the oblique form of pronouns with the postposition ਨੂੰ noon are also used in expressing *need* and *want* with the passive of ਚਾਹੁਣਾ chaahunhaa. This may seem confusing but you will be able to tell from the context of the sentence whether the speaker means that they need or want something, or that they should or ought to do something.

ਮੈਨੂੰ ਇੱਕ ਕਮੀਜ਼ ਚਾਹੀਦੀ ਹੈ	mainoon ikk kameez chaaheedee hai	*I need a shirt.*
ਮੈਨੂੰ ਦੋ ਕਮੀਜ਼ਾਂ ਚਾਹੀਦੀਆਂ ਹਨ	mainoon do kameezaan chaaheedeeaan han	*I need two shirts.*
ਉਹਨਾਂ ਨੂੰ ਪੈਸੇ ਚਾਹੀਦੇ ਹਨ	uhnaan noon paise chaaheede han	*They need money.*

Infinitives in the oblique

The presence of postpositions after nouns, adjectives and pronouns has been discussed in previous units. You know by now that the forms of direct nouns, adjectives and pronouns are changed to the oblique when they are followed by a postposition. The same is true for infinitives. In the first dialogue, Mr Sandhu asks his daughters, *How much money do you need to go to India?* In this sentence *to go to India* is a phrase which contains an infinitive followed by a postposition:

ਭਾਰਤ ਜਾਣ ਲਈ   bhaarat jaanh laee   *to go to India*

The infinitive of the verb *to go* ਜਾਣਾ **jaanhaa** precedes the postposition ਲਈ **laee** requiring the infinitive *to be* in the oblique. The oblique of the infinitive is a shortened form which merely omits the vowel ending ਆ **aa**. Therefore, ਜਾਣਾ **jaanhaa** in the oblique becomes ਜਾਣ **jaanh**. The example given of ਜਾਣਾ **jaanhaa** is that of an infinitive with a vowel-ending stem. Other verbs such as ਖਰੀਦਣਾ **khareednhaa**, ਲਿਖਣਾ **likhnhaa** and ਬੋਲਣਾ **bolnhaa** all have stems which end in consonants. These types of infinitives also have shortened forms which omit the ਆ **aa** ending making them ਖਰੀਦਣ **khareedanh**, ਲਿਖਣ **likhanh** and ਬੋਲਣਾ **bolanh**. Here are some examples of infinitives in the oblique and how they are formed:

ਉਹ ਸਾਨੂੰ ਪੈਸੇ ਦੇਣ ਨੂੰ ਤਿਆਰ ਨਹੀਂ	uh saanoon paise denh noon tiaar naheen	*He isn't ready* [willing] *to give us money.*
ਘੁੰਮਣ ਲਈ ਸਮਾਂ ਚਾਹੀਦਾ ਹੈ	ghunmanh laee samaan chaaheedaa hai	*Time is needed for travelling.*
ਮੈਂ ਦੋਸਤ ਨੂੰ ਮਿਲਣ ਲਈ ਆਈ ਹਾਂ	main dost noon milanh laee aaee haan	*I have come to meet a friend.*

Vocative case

The vocative case is used when addressing somebody directly or as an exclamation to someone. It can be used in both formal and informal situations. For example, in Dialogue 1, Mr Sandhu says ਧੀਓ! **dheeo!** which means *daughters!* Another more formal setting might be in a meeting in which you wish to address the audience: ਭੈਣੋ ਤੇ ਭਰਾਵੋ **bhainho te bharaavo** (*brothers and sisters*). The manner in which the vocative case is formed is quite similar to the plural oblique forms of nouns as shown in Unit 4, though the vocative case ends with ਓ **o** and not ਆਂ **aan**. When the vocative case is used in reference to singular people, the noun takes on the ending ਏ **e** for feminine people and the ending ਆ **aa** for masculine people:

ਮੁੰਡਿਆ!	mundiaa!	*boy!*
ਮੁੰਡਿਓ!	mundio!	*boys!*
ਬੱਚਿਓ!	bachchio!	*children!*

ਕੁੜੀਏ!	kurhee-e!	*girl!*
ਕੁੜੀਓ!	kurheeo!	*girls!*
ਦੋਸਤੋ!	doṣto!	*friends!*

The ending -ਵਾਲਾ 'vaalaa'

ਵਾਲਾ vaalaa is added to nouns and verbs to give two main senses: *the one or ones* or *about to*. The use of **-ਵਾਲਾ vaalaa** with nouns expresses a relationship between the noun and the object or person being referred to. You will recall in the commentary in Unit 3 that the vegetable seller was called **ਸਬਜ਼ੀਵਾਲਾ sabzeevaalaa** and that earlier in this unit the taxi driver was referred to as **ਟੈਕਸੀਵਾਲਾ taikseevaalaa**. The ending **-ਵਾਲਾ vaalaa** in these examples has changed the role of the noun through the following pattern:

ਸਬਜ਼ੀ	+	-ਵਾਲਾ	=	ਸਬਜ਼ੀਵਾਲਾ
sabzee		-vaalaa		sabzeevaalaa
vegetable		*the one*		*vegetable seller*
ਟੈਕਸੀ	+	-ਵਾਲਾ	=	ਟੈਕਸੀਵਾਲਾ
taiksee		-vaalaa		taikseevaalaa
taxi		*the one*		*taxi driver*

Here are some more examples of this type of use of the ending **-ਵਾਲਾ vaalaa** with nouns:

ਲਾਹੌਰਵਾਲੀ ਔਰਤ	laahaurvaalee aurat	*the woman from Lahore*
ਪਿੰਡਵਾਲਾ	pindvaalaa	*villager*
ਪੈਸੇਵਾਲੇ	paisevaale	*wealthy people*
ਸਾੜੀਵਾਲੀ	saarhheevaalee	*the one wearing the sari*
ਘਰਵਾਲਾ	gharvaalaa	*husband*

Note that like other endings or adjectives, the ending **-ਵਾਲਾ vaalaa** changes according to the gender and number of the persons or objects being referred to.

128

The second meaning produced by the ending -ਵਾਲਾ vaalaa is *about to* or *on the point of doing*. This is created when -ਵਾਲਾ vaalaa is used with the oblique of the infinitive. The form resembles that of the oblique infinitive (or shortened form) used with postpositions presented earlier in this unit. Here are some examples of how this meaning is constructed:

ਉਹ ਭਾਰਤ ਜਾਣ ਵਾਲੇ ਹਨ	uh bhaarat jaanh vaale han	*They are about to go to India.*
ਮੈਂ ਤੁਹਾਨੂੰ ਚਿੱਠੀ ਲਿਖਣ ਵਾਲੀ ਸੀ	main tuhaanoon chiththee likhanh vaalee see	*I was about to write you a letter.*
ਕੁੜੀਆਂ ਆਉਣ ਵਾਲੀਆਂ ਸਨ	kurheeaan aaunh vaaleeaan san	*The girls were about to come.*
ਮੈਂ ਕਿਤਾਬ ਪੜ੍ਹਨ ਵਾਲਾ ਹਾਂ	main kitaab parh-h-anh vaalaa haan	*I am about to read the book.*

The ending -ਵਾਲਾ vaalaa used with oblique infinitives can also have the same meaning as that when used with nouns, such as ਇੱਥੇ ਰਹਿਣ ਵਾਲਾ iththe rahinh vaalaa *the one who lives here* or ਕੰਮ ਕਰਨ ਵਾਲੇ kanm karan vaale *the ones who work* or *working people*. Once you understand how to use the ending -ਵਾਲਾ vaalaa, you will find it a very useful tool when referring to people and objects as well as to actions that are about to happen.

Insight

It is quite a fashion among the Sikh religious musicians (*Raagi*) (ਰਾਗੀ) to use the words '**waale**' 'ਵਾਲੇ' (*belonging* to) after their names.

Example: **Bhaaee Harjinder Singh Srinagar waale** (*of/from Srinagar*).

ਵਿਆਖਿਆ viaakhiaa *Commentary*

1 I like it!

Fondness is shown in Panjabi in a number of ways. Depending upon the degree of liking and context, fondness can be expressed through:

ਪਸੰਦ **pasand** means *pleasing* or *like*
ਸ਼ੋਕ **shauk** means *fondness* or *enjoyment*
ਲੱਗਣਾ **laggnhaa** means *seems* (e.g. *it seems nice/bad*)

Therefore, expressions of fondness generally require the use of
ਨੂੰ **noon** in order to direct the feelings or emotions towards the
person. A sentence such as *I like bananas* would translate directly
into Panjabi as *Bananas are liked by me*: ਮੈਨੂੰ ਕੇਲੇ ਪਸੰਦ ਹਨ **mainoon
kele pasand han,** thereby making *bananas* the subject and *me*
the object. Another way of using ਪਸੰਦ **pasand** is in combination
with ਕਰਨਾ **karnaa**. The use of ਕਰਨਾ **karnaa** gives an added sense
of habituality, such as *I generally like bananas* or *I always like
bananas* in ਮੈਂ ਕੇਲਿਆਂ ਨੂੰ ਪਸੰਦ ਕਰਦਾ ਹਾਂ **main keliaan noon pasand
kardaa haan.** ਲੱਗਣਾ **laggnhaa** (*to seem*) is a less specific word
which requires the use of a qualifying adjective such as good,
bad, tasty or ugly in order to express how something seems. If
you were to say *this food is good* one way in Panjabi to express
this would be ਇਹ ਖਾਣਾ ਮੈਨੂੰ ਚੰਗਾ ਲੱਗਦਾ ਹੈ **ih khaanhaa mainoon
changaa laggdaa hai** (lit. *this food seems good to me*). Here are a
few more examples:

ਮੈਨੂੰ ਸਿਤਾਰ ਵਜਾਉਣ ਦਾ ਸ਼ੋਕ ਹੈ	mainoon sitaar vajaaunh daa shauk hai	*I enjoy playing the sitar.*
ਅਸੀਂ ਮਿਠਿਆਈ (ਨੂੰ) ਪਸੰਦ ਕਰਦੇ ਹਾਂ	aseen mithiaaee (noon) pasand karde haan	*We like sweets.*
ਉਹਨਾਂ ਨੂੰ ਕਿਤਾਬਾਂ ਚੰਗੀਆਂ ਲੱਗਦੀਆਂ ਹਨ	uhnaan noon kitaabaan changeeaan laggdeeaan han	*They like books.*

Insight

'I like bananas' can be translated into Panjabi in four different
ways:

a *main kele pasand kardaa haan* - ਮੈਂ ਕੇਲੇ ਪਸੰਦ ਕਰਦਾ ਹਾਂ
b *main keliaan noon pasand kardaa haan* - ਮੈਂ ਕੇਲਿਆਂ ਨੂੰ ਪਸੰਦ ਕਰਦਾ ਹਾਂ
c *mainoon kele pasand han* - ਮੈਨੂੰ ਕੇਲੇ ਪਸੰਦ ਹਨ
d *mainoon kele change laggde han* - ਮੈਨੂੰ ਕੇਲੇ ਚੰਗੇ ਲੱਗਦੇ ਹਨ

2 Usefulness of Panjabi in South Asia

Despite the fact that Hindi and Urdu are the national languages of India and Pakistan respectively, in practice once you leave the urban centres regional languages come to the fore. Panjabi has a unique position in the languages of North India and Pakistan, in that it has a large usage in the urban centres. In Lahore and throughout much of Pakistan, Panjabi is the language of the people and is spoken widely and understood almost universally. Furthermore, in Delhi many taxi drivers, rickshaw **vaalaas** and bus drivers tend to speak Panjabi (sometimes a few words may save the passenger from being overcharged!).

Taxi drivers are notorious in the sub-continent for overcharging and haggling with customers. Even though many main tourist resorts and public transport centres such as railway stations and airports now operate a prepayment system, there are still many occasions where unsuspecting travellers will be caught unaware. This has to be accepted as one of the many facets of travel to the sub-continent and should not cause frustration or anguish. On a more positive front, the fun of haggling, as you will see in the next unit, is a must when shopping.

3 Music in Panjab

Panjab is well known for folk music (as we shall see in Unit 16), however, there is a long tradition of classical music in Panjab. The world-renowned tabla player, Zakheer Hussain, comes from the tradition of the Panjabi gharana, which reflects a particular type of musical style and a particular rhythmic form known as ਕੈਰਵਾ **kairvaa**, which is an eight-beat cycle. One other musical form which crosses over the classical and popular is the **Qawaali**, made popular internationally by the late Nusrat Fateh Ali Khan. The Panjabi **Qawaals** sung by Khan are some of the most popular tunes throughout Panjab, and the elegant, poetic language is quite easy to understand.

ਅਭਿਆਸ abhiaas *Exercises*

1 Fill in the blanks

a ਮੈਨੂੰ ਕਿਤਾਬ _____ ਹੈ।   mainoon kitaab _____ hai. *I want a book.*

b ਮੈਨੂੰ ਜਾਣਾ _____ ਹੈ।   mainoon jaanhaa _____ hai. *I should go.*

c ਮੈਨੂੰ ਸਿਤਾਰ _____ ਦਾ ਸ਼ੋਕ ਹੈ।   mainoon sitaar _____ daa shauk hai. *I like playing the sitar.*

2 Translation

Say the following English sentences in Panjabi.

a What does he want?
b Daughters! What do you want?
c Whom did you tell?
d Should we go?

3 Use of 'vaalaa'

From the following equations work out what the Panjabi words using the ending -ਵਾਲਾ are.

a [house] + ਵਾਲਾ = [husband]

b [taxi] + ਵਾਲਾ = [taxi driver]

c [vegetables] + ਵਾਲਾ = [vegetable vendor]

4 Listening comprehension

🔊 **CD 2, TR 1, 04:10**

You are having a conversation with a taxi driver. Listen to the recording and then answer the following questions.

a How many passengers?
b Where are you travelling to?
c How much is the fare?
d How far is the hotel?
e How much luggage?
f Do you accept the taxi ride?

Ten important things to remember

1 As with nouns, personal pronouns also take on the oblique form when followed by postpositions.

2 There are neither capital letters nor articles (ie. 'the', 'a' 'an', 'some', etc.) in Panjabi.

3 In Panjabi, expressions of compulsion come in three different forms. It is usually the infinitive of the verb which directs the action related to the situation.

4 The expressions such as 'should/ought' and 'need/want' are generally formed with the verb *'chaahunhaa'* 'ਚਾਹੁਣਾ' (to want, to need).

5 There are no silent or soft spoken consonants in Panjabi, but there are some silent vowels.

6 When *'vaalaa'* 'ਵਾਲਾ' is added to nouns, it expresses a relationship between the noun and the object.

7 When *'vaalaa'* 'ਵਾਲਾ' (or its different forms) is added to verbs , it means 'about to'.

8 Fondness or likeness for something is shown in Panjabi in a number of ways.

9 There are words in Panjabi like *'miharbaanee'* 'ਮਿਹਰਬਾਨੀ' and *'kirpaa'* 'ਕਿਰਪਾ' to represent 'please', but they are not used as frequently as in English. In the structure of a Panjabi formal sentence, the sense of 'please' is built in.

10 The mode of address in Panjabi has a lot of variety, ranging from super-politeness to rudeness.

9

ਸਾਡਾ ਕਪੜਾ ਸਭ ਤੋਂ ਵਧੀਆ ਹੈ!
Saadaa kaprhaa sabh <u>ton</u> va<u>dh</u>eeaa hai!
Our cloth is the best!

In this unit you will learn:

- How to compare things
- How to talk about your health
- How to express actions which you can and cannot do
- How to express actions which have already occurred

---

1 *Our cloth is the best!*
ਗੱਲ ਬਾਤ ੧ ਸਾਡਾ ਕਪੜਾ ਸਭ ਤੋਂ ਵਧੀਆ ਹੈ!
gall baa<u>t</u> 1 saadaa kaprhaa sabh <u>ton</u> va<u>dh</u>eeaa hai!

🔊 **CD 2, TR 2, 00:21**

Jaspreet and Simran have arrived in Delhi and are shopping in Karol Bagh, a popular place in Delhi to buy ready-made clothing as well as unstitched cloth. They are just entering a material shop where the shopkeeper greets them.

ਦੁਕਾਨਦਾਰ	ਅੰਦਰ ਆਓ, ਭੈਣ ਜੀ। ਸਾਰੀ ਦਿੱਲੀ ਵਿਚ ਸਾਡਾ ਕਪੜਾ ਸਭ ਤੋਂ ਵਧੀਆ ਹੈ!
Shopkeeper	an<u>d</u>ar aao, bhainh jee. saaree <u>d</u>illee vich saadaa kaprhaa sabh <u>ton</u> va<u>dh</u>eeaa hai!

ਜਸਪ੍ਰੀਤ	ਸਾਨੂੰ ਛਪਾਈਵਾਲਾ ਕਪੜਾ ਚਾਹੀਦਾ ਹੈ ਜਿਸ ਦਾ ਅੱਜ ਕੱਲ੍ਹ ਰਵਾਜ ਹੈ।
Jaspreet	saanoon chapaaeevaalaa kaprhaa chaaheedaa hai jis daa ajj kallh ravaaj hai.
ਦੁਕਾਨਦਾਰ	ਫਿਕਰ ਨਾ ਕਰੋ। ਮੈਂ ਤੁਹਾਨੂੰ ਉਹ ਕਪੜਾ ਦਿਖਾ ਰਿਹਾ ਹਾਂ ਜਿਹੜਾ ਵਧੇਰੇ ਹੰਢਣਸਾਰ ਹੈ ਅਤੇ ਸਭ ਤੋਂ ਵੱਧ ਵਿਕਦਾ ਹੈ।
Shopkeeper	fikar naa karo! main tuhaanoon uh kaprhaa dikhaa rihaa haan jihrhaa vadhere handhanhsaar hai ate sabh ton vadhdh vikdaa hai.

(The shopkeeper shows the girls some cloth pieces.)

ਸਿਮਰਨ	ਮੈਨੂੰ ਇਸ ਕਪੜੇ ਦਾ ਰੰਗ ਪਸੰਦ ਹੈ ਪਰ ਕਪੜਾ ਇਸ ਤੋਂ ਮੋਟਾ ਹੋਣਾ ਚਾਹੀਦਾ ਹੈ।
Simran	mainoon is kaprhe daa rang pasand hai par kaprhaa is ton motaa honhaa chaaheedaa hai.
ਦੁਕਾਨਦਾਰ	ਸਾਡੇ ਕੋਲ ਇਸ ਤੋਂ ਪਤਲਾ ਵੀ ਹੈ ਤੇ ਮੋਟਾ ਵੀ। ਤੁਸੀਂ ਛਾਪੇ ਦੀ ਚੋਣ ਕਰੋ।
Shopkeeper	saade kol is ton patlaa vee hai te motaa vee. tuseen chaape dee chonh karo.
ਸਿਮਰਨ	ਜਸਪ੍ਰੀਤ, ਤੈਨੂੰ ਕਿਹੜਾ, ਵਧੇਰੇ ਚੰਗਾ ਲੱਗਦਾ ਹੈ, ਲਾਲ ਜਾਂ ਨੀਲਾ ?
Simran	jaspreet, tainoon kihrhaa vadhere changaa laggdaa hai, laal jaan neelaa?
ਜਸਪ੍ਰੀਤ	ਨੀਲਾ ਕਪੜਾ ਲਾਲ ਕਪੜੇ ਤੋਂ ਪਤਲਾ ਹੈ, ਪਰ ਫਿੱਕੇ ਰੰਗ ਵਾਲਾ ਸਭ ਤੋਂ ਸੁਹਣਾ ਹੈ।
Jaspreet	neelaa kaprhaa laal kaprhe ton patlaa hai, par phikke rang vaalaa sabh ton suhnhaa hai.
ਸਿਮਰਨ	ਇਹ ਕਪੜਾ ਕਿੰਨੇ ਦਾ ਮੀਟਰ ਹੈ ?
Simran	ih kaprhaa kinne daa meetar hai?
ਦੁਕਾਨਦਾਰ	ਇੱਕ ਸੌ ਵੀਹ ਰੁਪਏ ਦਾ ਮੀਟਰ।
Shopkeeper	ikk sau veeh rupae daa meetar.
ਸਿਮਰਨ	ਇਹ ਕੀਮਤ ਬਹੁਤ ਜ਼ਿਆਦਾ ਹੈ। ਅਸੀਂ ਹੋਰ ਵੀ ਕਈ ਦੁਕਾਨਾਂ ਤੇ ਜਾ ਚੁਕੀਆਂ ਹਾਂ ਅਤੇ ਉਹਨਾਂ ਦੇ ਮੁਕਾਬਲੇ ਵਿਚ ਤੁਹਾਡੀਆਂ ਕੀਮਤਾਂ ਬਹੁਤ ਜ਼ਿਆਦਾ ਹਨ।
Simran	ih keemat bahut ziaadaa hai. aseen hor vee kaee dukaanaan te jaa chukeeaan haan ate uhnaan de mukaable vich tuhaadeeaan keemataan bahut ziaadaa han.

ਦੁਕਾਨਦਾਰ **Shopkeeper**	ਮੈਨੂੰ ਅਫਸੋਸ ਹੈ ਕਿ ਮੈਂ ਕੀਮਤ ਹੋਰ ਘੱਟ ਨਹੀਂ ਕਰ ਸਕਦਾ। mainoo<u>n</u> afsos hai ki mai<u>n</u> keema<u>t</u> hor ghatt nahee<u>n</u> kar sak<u>d</u>aa.
Shopkeeper	*Come in, sisters! Our cloth is the best in all of Delhi!*
Jaspreet	*We want printed cloth that's in fashion these days.*
Shopkeeper	*Don't worry. What I'm showing you is cloth that is durable and sells a lot.*
Simran	*I like the colour, but the material should be thicker than this.*
Shopkeeper	*We have thinner and also thicker than this. Choose whatever print you like.*
Simran	*Jaspreet, which do you like better, red or blue?*
Jaspreet	*The blue is thinner than the red, but the light-coloured one is the nicest.*
Simran	*How much is this cloth per metre?*
Shopkeeper	*120 rupees per metre.*
Simran	*The price is too high. We've been to several other shops and in comparison with them, your prices are very high.*
Shopkeeper	*I'm sorry but (that) I can't lower the price any more.*

ਸ਼ਬਦਾਵਲੀ	**shab<u>d</u>aavalee**	*Vocabulary*
ਦੁਕਾਨਦਾਰ	<u>d</u>ukaan<u>d</u>aar	*shopkeeper* (m.)
ਕਪੜਾ	kaprhaa	*cloth* (m.)
ਸਭ ਤੋਂ ਵਧੀਆ	sabh <u>t</u>on vadheeaa	*the best*
ਛਪਾਈਵਾਲਾ	<u>ch</u>apaaeevaalaa	*the printed one* (m.)
ਜਿਸ	jis	*which* (oblique)
ਰਵਾਜ	ravaaj	*fashion* (m.)
ਅੱਜ ਕੱਲ੍ਹ	ajj kallh	*these days*
ਦਿਖਾਉਣਾ	<u>d</u>ikhaaunhaa	*to show*
ਜਿਹੜਾ	jihrhaa	*that, which*
ਹੰਢਣਸਾਰ	ha<u>n</u>dhanhsaar	*durable, hardwearing*
ਚਲਣਾ	chalnhaa	*to go*
ਵਿਕਣਾ	viknhaa	*to be sold*
ਰੰਗ	ra<u>n</u>g	*colour* (m.)
ਮੋਟਾ	motaa	*fat, thick* (v.)
ਪਤਲਾ	pa<u>t</u>laa	*thin* (v.)
ਛਾਪੇ	<u>ch</u>aape	*print* (m.)
ਚੋਣ	chonh	*choice, selection* (f.)
ਕਿਹੜਾ	kihrhaa	*which*
ਵਧੇਰੇ	vadhere	*more*
ਲਾਲ	laal	*red*

ਨੀਲਾ	neelaa	*blue* (v.)
ਜਾਂ	jaan	*or*
ਫਿੱਕਾ	phikkaa	*light, pale* (v.)
ਸੁਹਣਾ	suhnhaa	*nice, pretty* (v.)
ਕਿੰਨੇ ਦਾ ਮੀਟਰ ?	kinne daa meetar?	*how much per metre?*
ਇੱਕ ਸੋ ਵੀਹ	ikk sau veeh	*120*
ਕੀਮਤ	keemat	*price* (f.)
ਬਹੁਤ ਜ਼ਿਆਦਾ	bahut ziaadaa	*far too much*
ਕਈ	kaee	*several*
ਚੁਕਣਾ	chuknhaa	*to be settled, finished*
ਜਾ ਚੁਕਣਾ	jaa chuknhaa	*have (already) been*
ਮੁਕਾਬਲਾ	mukaablaa	*competition*
ਵੱਧ	vadhdh	*high*
ਘੱਟ	ghatt	*less, lower*
ਸਕਣਾ	saknhaa	*can, to be able to*

ਅਭਿਆਸ abhiaas *Exercises*

After reading the dialogue and/or listening to the recording, try to do the following exercises.

1 In the cloth shop

You are in a cloth shop telling the sales person exactly what you are looking for. Express the following in Panjabi:

a I want light-coloured cloth.
b I want material that is thick and also durable.
c The print should be in fashion.
d The price should not be too high.

2 Complete the table

ਵਧੀਆ		
		better
	keemat	
ਮੁਕਾਬਲਾ		
	sabh ton vadheeaa	

2 What's the problem?
ਗੱਲ ਬਾਤ ੨ ਕੀ ਤਕਲੀਫ਼ ਹੈ?
gall baat 2 kee takleef hai?

🔊 CD 2, TR 2, 02:26

On their way back from the market place in Delhi, Simran and Jaspreet had some snacks at a roadside restaurant, commonly known as a **dhaba**. On their way back to their hotel Simran begins to feel ill and has gone to visit the doctor.

ਡਾਕਟਰ	ਬੇਟੀ, ਕੀ ਤਕਲੀਫ਼ ਹੈ?
Doctor	betee, kee takleef hai?
ਸਿਮਰਨ	ਮੇਰੀ ਤਬੀਅਤ ਖ਼ਰਾਬ ਹੈ।
Simran	meree tabeeat kharaab hai.
ਡਾਕਟਰ	ਕੀ ਤੈਨੂੰ ਬੁਖ਼ਾਰ ਹੈ?
Doctor	kee tainoon bukhaar hai?
ਸਿਮਰਨ	ਹਾਂ ਜੀ। ਮੈਨੂੰ ਠੰਢ ਲੱਗ ਰਹੀ ਹੈ, ਪੇਟ ਵਿਚ ਦਰਦ ਹੈ ਅਤੇ ਮੈਨੂੰ ਕਮਜ਼ੋਰੀ ਵੀ ਹੈ।
Simran	haan jee. mainoon thand lagg rahee hai, pet vich dard hai ate mainoon kamzoree vee hai.
ਡਾਕਟਰ	ਬਿਮਾਰ ਹੋਣ ਤੋਂ ਪਹਿਲੇ ਤੂੰ ਕੀ ਕੁਝ ਖਾਧਾ ਸੀ?
Doctor	bimaar honh ton pahile toon kee kujh khaadhaa see?
ਸਿਮਰਨ	ਮੈਨੂੰ ਯਾਦ ਨਹੀਂ ਪਰ ਮੈਨੂੰ ਇੱਥੋਂ ਦੀਆਂ ਛੱਲੀਆਂ ਬਹੁਤ ਪਸੰਦ ਹਨ।
Simran	mainoon yaad naheen par mainoon iththon deeaan challeeaan bahut pasand han.
ਡਾਕਟਰ	ਹੁਣ ਮੈਂ ਸਮਝਿਆ। ਜਿਹੜੇ ਲੋਕ ਬਾਹਰੋਂ ਆਉਂਦੇ ਹਨ, ਉਹਨਾਂ ਨੂੰ ਦੇਸੀ ਖਾਣਾ ਹਜ਼ਮ ਨਹੀਂ ਹੁੰਦਾ। ਇਹ ਲਵੋ ਦਵਾਈ, ਅਰਾਮ ਕਰੋ ਤੇ ਛੱਲੀਆਂ ਤੋਂ ਦੂਰ ਰਵੋ!
Doctor	hunh main samajhiaa. jihrhe lok baahron aaunde han, uhnaan noon desee khaanhaa hazam naheen hundaa. ih lavo davaaee, araam karo, te challeeaan ton door ravo!
ਸਿਮਰਨ	ਧੰਨਵਾਦ।
Simran	dhannvaad.
Doctor	*Dear (daughter), what's the problem?*
Simran	*I'm not feeling well (lit. my health is bad).*

Doctor	Do you have a fever?
Simran	Yes. I feel cold, I have a stomach ache and I'm also weak.
Doctor	Before falling ill, what did you eat?
Simran	I don't remember, but I like the corn on the cob here a lot.
Doctor	Now I understand. People who come from abroad can't digest the food here. Take this medicine, rest, and stay away from corn on the cob!
Simran	Thank you.

Insight

It is quite common to address people with whom you wish to express closeness or affection with such terms associated with kinship as 'bhainh ji' 'ਭੈਣ ਜਿ' (sister) and 'betee' 'ਬੇਟੀ' (daughter).

ਸ਼ਬਦਾਵਲੀ	shabdaavalee	*Vocabulary*
ਤਕਲੀਫ਼	takleef	*trouble, irritation, bother* (f.)
ਤਬੀਅਤ	tabeeat	*state of health, condition* (f.)
ਬੁਖ਼ਾਰ	bukhaar	*fever/temperature* (m.)
ਠੰਡ	thand	*cold* (f.)
ਲੱਗਣਾ	laggnhaa	*to feel*
ਪੇਟ	pet	*stomach, belly* (m.)
ਦਰਦ	dard	*pain, hurt* (f.)
ਕਮਜ਼ੋਰੀ	kamzoree	*weakness* (f.)
ਬਿਮਾਰ	bimaar	*ill, sick*
ਬਿਮਾਰ ਹੋਣ ਤੋਂ ਪਹਿਲੇ	bimaar honh ton pahile	*before falling ill*
ਯਾਦ	yaad	*memory, remember* (f.)
ਛੱਲੀ	challee	*corn on the cob* (f.)
ਸਮਝਣਾ	samajhnhaa	*to understand/comprehend*
ਬਾਹਰੋਂ	baahron	*from outside/from abroad*
ਦੇਸੀ	desi	*Indian, Panjabi, home*
ਹਜ਼ਮ	hazam	*digest*
ਦੂਰ	door	*far/away*
ਅਰਾਮ	araam	*rest* (m.)
ਦਵਾਈ	davaaee	*medicine* (f.)

ਅਭਿਆਸ abhiaas *Exercises*

After reading the dialogue and/or listening to the recording, try to do the following exercises.

1 Write in the correct word order

a ਹੈ ਤਕਲੀਫ਼ ਕੀ ?   hai <u>t</u>akleef kee?
b ਹੈ ਤੈਨੂੰ ਕੀ ਬੁਖ਼ਾਰ ?   hai <u>t</u>ainoo<u>n</u> kee bu<u>kh</u>aar?
c ਸਮਝਿਆ ਹੁਣ ਮੈਂ   samajhiaa hunh mai<u>n</u>

2 Fill in the blanks

Fill in the blanks with the correct terms from the dialogue. The English has been given in brackets, although not necessarily in the correct order.

You	ਮੇਰੀ _____ ਖ਼ਰਾਬ ਹੈ । (*health*)
	meree _____ <u>kh</u>arab hai.
Dr	ਕੀ _____ ਹੈ ? (*problem*)
	kee _____ hai?
You	ਮੇਰੇ _____ਵਿਚ _____ ਹੈ ਤੇ ਮੈਨੂੰ _____ ਵੀ ਹੈ । (*pain, fever, stomach*)
	mere _____ vich _____ hai <u>t</u>e mainoo<u>n</u> _____ vee hai.
Dr	ਤੈਨੂੰ _____ ਹੈ ਤੇ _____ ਲੱਗ ਰਹੀ ਹੈ ? (*fever, cold*)
	<u>t</u>ainoo<u>n</u> _____ hai <u>t</u>e _____ lagg rahee hai?
You	ਹਾਂ ਜੀ _____ haa<u>n</u> jee.
Dr	ਇਹ _____ ਲਵੋ ਤੇ _____ ਕਰੋ । (*rest, medicine*)
	ih _____ lavo <u>t</u>e _____ karo.

ਬੋਲੀ ਬਾਰੇ bolee baare *Language points*

Comparison of adjectives

When people or things are compared in Panjabi in terms of quality, size, number and price, there are no direct translations of the English expressions *good*, *better*, *best* or *big*, *bigger*, *biggest*. Instead the postpositions ਨਾਲੋਂ naalon (*than*) and ਤੋਂ ton (*from*) are commonly used to express comparison such as *more _____* or *_____ than*. For example:

ਇਸ ਤੋਂ/ਨਾਲੋਂ ਮੋਟਾ	is ton/naalon motaa	*thicker than this*
ਉਸ ਤੋਂ/ਨਾਲੋਂ ਪਤਲਾ	us ton/naalon patlaa	*thinner that that*
ਰਾਮ ਸ਼ਾਮ ਤੋਂ ਲੰਬਾ ਹੈ	raam shaam ton lanbaa hai	*Ram is taller than Sham.*

ਵਧੇਰੇ vadhere and ਜ਼ਿਆਦਾ ziaadaa, which mean *much* or *more* are also used when making comparisons, especially when the object or objects being referred to are absent. The literal translations in Panjabi of *better* ਚੰਗੇਰਾ changeraa and *taller/longer* ਲੰਬੇਰਾ lanberaa are also occasionally used in a similar manner. Note in the following examples how adjectives such as *tall* are changed to comparisons such as *taller*:

ਰਾਮ ਲੰਬਾ ਹੈ	raam lanbaa hai	*Ram is tall.*
ਰਾਮ ਜ਼ਿਆਦਾ ਲੰਬਾ ਹੈ	raam ziaadaa lanbaa hai	*Ram is taller.*
ਰਾਮ ਵਧੇਰੇ ਲੰਬਾ ਹੈ	raam vadhere lanbaa hai	*Ram is taller.*
ਇਹ ਕਪੜਾ ਚੰਗਾ ਹੈ	ih kaprhaa changaa hai	*this cloth is good*
ਇਹ ਕਪੜਾ ਚੰਗੇਰਾ ਹੈ	ih kaprhaa changeraa hai	*this cloth is better*
ਉਹ ਕਮਰਾ ਲੰਬਾ ਹੈ	uh kamraa lanbaa hai	*that room is long*
ਉਹ ਕਮਰਾ ਲੰਬੇਰਾ ਹੈ	uh kamraa lanberaa hai	*that room is longer*

In English the superlative degree is generally expressed with the ending *–est*, such as *tallest*, *biggest* and *nicest*. In Panjabi the superlative degree uses the words ਸਭ sabh, ਸਭਨਾਂ sabhnaan, and ਸਾਰੇ saare which mean *all* or *whole* with the postpositions ਨਾਲੋਂ naalon and ਤੋਂ ton, to give the overall sense *out of all* or *of all*.

The superlative *the best* in Panjabi would literally translate as *out of all the best* in English:

| ਸਭ ਤੋਂ ਚੰਗਾ ਕਪੜਾ | sabh ton changaa kaprhaa | *the best cloth* |

To say that something is even better or even taller, ਹੋਰ ਵੀ hor vee, meaning *more* and *also*, is used. Here are some examples of a variety of different uses of comparison and superlative degrees:

| ਉਹ ਕੁੜੀ ਸਭ ਨਾਲੋਂ ਛੋਟੀ ਹੈ | uh kurhee sabh naalon chotee hai | *This girl is the smallest.* |

ਰਮੇਸ਼ ਸਾਰੇ ਭਰਾਵਾਂ ਨਾਲੋਂ ਲੰਬਾ ਹੈ	ramesh saare bharaavaan naalon lanbaa hai	*Ramesh is the tallest of the brothers.*
ਉਹਨਾਂ ਦਾ ਖਾਣਾ ਸਭ ਤੋਂ ਸੁਆਦ ਹੁੰਦਾ ਹੈ	uhnaan daa khaanhaa sabh ton suaad hundaa hai	*Their food is the tastiest.*
ਉਹਨਾਂ ਦਾ ਖਾਣਾ ਹੋਰ ਵੀ ਸੁਆਦ ਹੁੰਦਾ ਹੈ	uhnaan daa khaanhaa hor vee suaad hundaa hai	*Their food is even tastier.*

ਸਕਣਾ 'saknhaa' *can* and *can't*

You will recall in the first dialogue that during the bargaining over the price of the cloth, the shopkeeper said to Simran and Jaspreet:

| ਮੈਂ ਕੀਮਤ ਹੋਰ ਘੱਟ ਨਹੀਂ ਕਰ ਸਕਦਾ | main keemat hor ghatt naheen kar sakdaa | *I can't lower the price any further.* |

He expressed his inability (or unwillingness!) to lower the price by saying *I can't*. In Panjabi ਸਕਣਾ **saknhaa** is used in combination with the stem of the verb portraying the action which can or cannot be done. In this example, the shopkeeper is saying that he can't (i.e. is not able to) lower the price. Therefore, the stem of ਘਟਣਾ **ghatnhaa** (*to decrease, to lower*) is used with the negative ਨਹੀਂ **naheen** to give the expression *can't lower*. Alternatively, if he had wanted to say *I can lower the price*, the negative ਨਹੀਂ **naheen** would simply have been omitted. The form of ਸਕਣਾ **saknhaa** is always in agreement with the subject. Here are some more examples to illustrate how this construction is formed:

ਅਸੀਂ ਪੰਜਾਬੀ ਬੋਲ ਸਕਦੀਆਂ ਹਾਂ	aseen panjaabee bol sakdeeaan haan	*We can speak Panjabi.*
ਕੀ ਤੁਸੀਂ ਕੱਲ੍ਹ ਨੂੰ ਆ ਸਕੋ ਗੇ ?	kee tuseen kallh noon aa sako ge?	*Will you be able to come tomorrow?*
ਮੈਂ ਗਾ ਨਹੀਂ ਸਕਦੀ	main gaa naheen sakdee	*I cannot sing.*

You should remember that ਸਕਣਾ **saknhaa** rarely stands on its own except in colloquial speech, and therefore always requires the stem, even when giving a reply to a question:

Question	ਕੀ ਤੁਸੀਂ ਕੱਲ੍ਹ ਨੂੰ	kee tuseen kallh	Can you come
	ਆ ਸਕਦੇ ਹੋ?	noon aa sak<u>d</u>e ho?	tomorrow?
Reply	ਹਾਂ ਜੀ, ਮੈਂ ਆ ਸਕਦੀ/	haa<u>n</u> jee, mai<u>n</u> aa	Yes, I can
	ਸਕਦਾ ਹਾਂ	sakdee/sakdaa haa<u>n</u>	(come).

Insight

Sometimes the word **'saknhaa' 'ਸਕਣਾ'** is used in the colloquial form as follows:

Mai<u>n</u> tuhaade laee kee kar saknhaa? **'ਮੈਂ ਤੁਹਾਡੇ ਲਈ ਕੀ ਕਰ ਸਕਣਾ'** (*What can I do for you?*)

ਚੁਕਣਾ 'chuknhaa' *already completed*

The stem of a verb followed by **ਚੁਕਣਾ chuknhaa** means *to have already done* or *to have finished doing*. This type of construction with **ਚੁਕਣਾ chuknhaa** is formed in a fashion similar to that of **ਸਕਣਾ saknhaa** as just described. **ਚੁਕਣਾ chuknhaa** also cannot stand alone and requires a preceding stem to indicate the action that has already occurred.

ਮੈਂ ਖਾ ਚੁਕਾ ਹਾਂ	mai<u>n</u> khaa chukaa haa<u>n</u>	I have (already) eaten.
ਜਸਬੀਰ ਜਾ ਚੁਕਾ ਸੀ	jasbeer jaa chukaa see	Jasbir had (already) gone.
ਕੁੜੀਆਂ ਸਾਰੀਆਂ ਕਿਤਾਬਾਂ ਪੜ੍ਹ ਚੁਕੀਆਂ ਹਨ	kurheeaa<u>n</u> saareeaa<u>n</u> ki<u>t</u>aabaa<u>n</u> parhh chukeeaa<u>n</u> han	The girls have (already) read all of the books.
ਅਸੀਂ ਉੱਥੇ ਜਾ ਚੁਕੇ ਹਾਂ	asee<u>n</u> u<u>thth</u>e jaa chuke haa<u>n</u>	We have (already) been there.

Insight

Please note that in colloquial Panjabi, the expression **'chuk lai' 'ਚੁਕ ਲੈ'** is used to encourage someone to go ahead, to take something, to accept the offer or to have another drink.

The relative pronouns ਜਿਹੜਾ 'jihrhaa' and ਜੋ 'jo'

The English relative pronouns *that* and *which* are used to form relative clauses following a pattern which relates the relative pronouns back to the subject, such as *The woman who came today teaches Urdu.* In Panjabi this sentence would be constructed in a rather different manner: *That woman who came today, she teaches Urdu.* In this example, *that* is the relative pronoun and *she* is the correlative pronoun. Another example of an English relative clause translated into Panjabi would be: *Go to the shop which (that) is closest.* In Panjabi this sentence would be expressed as: *Which shop is closest, go to that one.* In this example, *which* is the relative pronoun and *that one* is the correlative pronoun.

In Panjabi, the relative pronoun and adjective ਜਿਹੜਾ **jihrhaa** is used to represent words such as *that, which, those, he, she* and *who* and changes according to the gender and number of the objects being referred to. The relative pronoun ਜੋ **jo** means *whatever* or *whoever* and is used when referring to more abstract people and things. Often, the presence of the relative pronoun in the English translation is simply understood. Here are some examples of the ways in which relative clauses are formed with ਜਿਹੜਾ **jihrhaa** and ਜੋ **jo**:

ਜੋ ਕੁਝ ਤੁਸੀਂ ਕੀਤਾ ਹੈ ਉਹ ਮੈਨੂੰ ਠੀਕ ਲੱਗਦਾ ਹੈ	jo kujh tuseen keetaa hai, uh mainoon theek laggdaa hai	*Whatever you've done looks fine to me.*
ਜਿਹੜੇ ਲੋਕ ਬਾਹਰੋਂ ਆਉਂਦੇ ਹਨ, ਉਹਨਾਂ ਨੂੰ ਖਾਣਾ ਹਜ਼ਮ ਨਹੀਂ ਹੁੰਦਾ	jihrhe lok baahron aaunde han, uhnaan noon khaanhaa hazam naheen hundaa	*[Those] people who come from abroad can't digest the food.*
ਜਿਹੜਾ ਆਦਮੀ ਅੱਜ ਆਇਆ ਸੀ, ਉਹ ਕੱਲ੍ਹ ਨਹੀਂ ਆ ਸਕੇਗਾ	jihrhaa aadmee ajj aaiaa see, uh kallh naheen aa sakegaa	*That man who came today will not be able to come tomorrow.*

Like other adjectives and pronouns in Panjabi, relative pronouns change their form in the oblique. In the singular ਜਿਹੜਾ **jihrhaa** takes the oblique form ਜਿਸ **jis** and in the plural it becomes ਜਿਹਨਾਂ **jihnaan** followed by the appropriate postposition. Here are some examples of the oblique forms of the relative pronoun ਜਿਹੜਾ **jihrhaa**:

ਅਸੀਂ ਜਿਹਨਾਂ ਦੇ ਘਰ ਗਏ ਸੀ, ਉਹ ਰਾਵਲਪਿੰਡੀ ਦੇ ਹਨ	aseen jinnaan de ghar ge see, uh raavalpindee de han	*(The people) whose house we went to are from Rawalpindi.*

| ਜਿਸ ਜਨਾਨੀ ਨੂੰ ਪੰਜਾਬੀ ਆਉਂਦੀ ਹੈ, ਉਹ ਨੂੰ ਪੁੱਛੋ | jis janaanee noon panjaabee aaundee hai, uh noon puchcho | *Ask the lady who knows Panjabi.* |
| ਜਿਸ ਨੂੰ ਪਤਾ ਸੀ ਉਹ ਦਾ ਕਸੂਰ ਹੈ | jis noon pataa see uh daa kasoor hai | *He [who knew] was aware; it's his fault.* |

More uses of ਨੂੰ 'noon'

By now you should be beginning to feel acquainted with the significance of postpositions in Panjabi. In Unit 4 simple postpositions were introduced as they affect nouns and adjectives in the oblique. In Unit 8 the two sisters Simran and Jaspreet illustrated in the dialogues some further uses of the postposition ਨੂੰ **noon** in expressing likes and dislikes, want, need, should and ought. In this unit more uses of ਨੂੰ **noon** have already been exemplified in the second dialogue, in which Simran and the doctor discuss health conditions. ਨੂੰ **noon** literally means *to* and directs the condition or state towards the person or pronoun it governs. It is used in a number of different senses ranging from awareness and health to feelings. Therefore, when the doctor asks Simran ਕੀ ਤੈਨੂੰ ਬੁਖ਼ਾਰ ਹੈ? **kee tainoon bukhaar hai?** he is literally asking *Is there a fever to you?* Here are some more examples of how ਨੂੰ **noon** can be used in this sense:

ਮੈਨੂੰ ਬੁਖ਼ਾਰ ਹੈ	mainoon bukhaar hai	*I have a fever.*
ਸਾਨੂੰ ਠੰਡ ਲੱਗ ਰਹੀ ਹੈ	saanoon thand lagg rahee hai	*We are feeling cold.*
ਮੈਨੂੰ ਅਫਸੋਸ ਹੈ	mainoon afsos hai	*I am sorry.*
ਉਹ ਨੂੰ ਉਮੀਦ ਹੈ	uh noon umeed hai	*He/she hopes.*
ਉਹਨਾਂ ਨੂੰ ਪਤਾ ਨਹੀਂ	uhnaan noon pataa naheen	*They do not know.*
ਮੈਨੂੰ ਜ਼ੁਕਾਮ ਹੈ	mainoon zukaam hai	*I have a cold.*
ਤੁਹਾਨੂੰ ਕੋਈ ਪਤਾ ਹੈ ਕਿ ਇਕਬਾਲ ਕਿੱਥੇ ਹੈ?	tuhaanoon koee pataa hai ki ikbaal kiththe hai?	*Do you have any idea where Iqbal is?*
ਸਾਨੂੰ ਬਹੁਤ ਖ਼ੁਸ਼ੀ ਹੈ	saanoon bahut khushee hai	*We are very happy.*

Insight

There are numerous English words which have been adopted by the Panjabi language but English has also been infiltrated by some Panjabi/South Asian words like 'khaki ਖ਼ਾਕੀ' and 'guru' guru.

ਵਿਆਖਿਆ viaakhiaa *Commentary*

1 Parts of the body

a	- ਅੱਖ
b	- ਨੱਕ
c	- ਮੂੰਹ
d	- ਕੰਨ
e	- ਸਿਰ
f	- ਹੱਥ
g	- ਗਰਦਨ
h	- ਉੱਂਗਲ
i	- ਬਾਂਹ
j	- ਛਾਤੀ
k	- ਪੇਟ
l	- ਲੱਤ
m	- ਗੋਡਾ
n	- ਪੈਰ
o	- ਪੱਬ

2 Clothes people wear

There are various forms of dress worn by Panjabis. Perhaps the most popular form is the **salwaar kameez** (**shalwaar kameez** in West Panjab). This form of dress is now ubiquitous in almost all of South Asia, but it is most popular in Pakistan Panjab, where both men and women wear it. Traditionally, women in rural Panjab would wear a flowing skirt – **ghagra** – and a blouse, although this is a rare sight in contemporary Panjab. Women may wear a **sari** for special occasions and Christian women often wear dresses as a way of distinguishing themselves. Male dress was traditionally a turban with a flowing top shirt and a wrap called a **lungi** or **dhoti** around the legs. However, Western dress is increasingly popular. The following pictures illustrate the various forms of dress.

ਅਭਿਆਸ abhiaas *Exercises*

1 Word search

The following words are hidden in the word search boxes below. In the first box they are hidden horizontally and in the second they are hidden vertically.

ਬੁਖ਼ਾਰ, ਭੈਣਜੀ, ਕਪੜਾ, ਦੁਕਾਨਦਾਰ, ਬਿਮਾਰ, ਛਾਪੇ, ਦਰਦ, ਕਮਜ਼ੋਰੀ, ਕੀਮਤ, ਹੰਢਣਸਾਰ

ਭੈ	ਣ	ਜੀ	ਜਾ	ਭ
ਜੇ	ਕ	ਪ	ਜ਼ਾ	ਕੀ
ਦੁ	ਕਾ	ਨ	ਦਾ	ਰ
ਉ	ਊ	ਛਾ	ਪੇ	ਸ਼
ਤਾ	ਕੀ	ਮ	ਤ	ਭ
ਨ	ਮੇ	ਰ	ਕ	ਹੰ
ਮਾ	ਬਿ	ਬੁ	ਮ	ਢ

ਦ	ਮਾ	ਖ਼ਾ	ਜੇ	ਣ
ਰ	ਰ	ਰ	ਰੀ	ਸਾ
ਦ	ਦ	ਰੀ	ਗੋ	ਰ

2 Talking to the doctor

Look at the pictures and tell how each person would respond in Panjabi to the doctor's question: ਕੀ ਤਕਲੀਫ਼ ਹੈ? What's the problem?

a *I feel cold.*

b *I have a headache.*

c *I have a stomach ache.*

d *I have a fever.*

3 Write sentences in Panjabi

Express the following sentences in Panjabi using either ਚੁਕਣਾ chuknhaa or ਸਕਣਾ saknhaa:

a I can't come tomorrow.
b Can you speak Panjabi?
c We've already been there.
d They have already eaten.

4 Relative pronouns

Insert the correct forms of the relative pronouns ਜੋ jo, ਜਿਹੜਾ jihrhaa and ਜਿਸ jis:

a _____ ਆਦਮੀ ਅੱਜ ਪਾਕਿਸਤਾਨ ਗਿਆ ਹੈ, ਉਹ ਮੇਰਾ ਚਾਚਾ ਹੈ।
   _____ aadmee ajj paakistaan giaa hai, uh meraa chaachaa hai.
   The man who went to Pakistan today is my uncle.

148

b _____ ਨੂੰ ਪਤਾ ਹੈ, ਉਹ ਨੂੰ ਪੁੱਛੋ ।

_____ noon paṯaa hai, uh noon pu<u>chch</u>o.

Ask the person who knows.

c _____ ਲੋਕ ਪਿੰਡ ਵਿਚ ਰਹਿੰਦੇ ਹਨ ਉਹਨਾਂ ਨੂੰ ਸ਼ਹਿਰ ਪਸੰਦ ਨਹੀਂ ।

_____ lok pi<u>n</u>d vich rahi<u>nde</u> han uhnaa<u>n</u> noo<u>n</u> shahir pasa<u>nd</u> nahee<u>n</u>.

People who live in the village don't like the city.

d _____ ਕੁਝ ਤੁਸੀਂ ਚਾਹੁੰਦੇ ਹੋ ਉਹ ਮੇਰੇ ਲਈ ਠੀਕ ਹੈ ।

_____ kujh ṯusee<u>n</u> chaahu<u>nde</u> ho uh mere laee theek hai.

Whatever you want is fine with me.

Ten important things to remember

1 When people or things are compared in Panjabi, there are no direct translations of the English expressions like good, better, best or big, bigger, biggest.

2 Haggling in Panjab is a style of life while shopping, hiring a taxi or striking any bargain.

3 '*Saknhaa*' 'ਸਕਣਾ' (can/to be able to) is like any other verb, and it is conjugated in different tenses.

4 The word '*saknhaa*' 'ਸਕਣਾ' rarely stands on its own except in the colloquial form.

5 The stem of the verb '*chuknhaa*' 'ਚੁਕਣਾ' means to have already done or to have finished doing.

6 English is popularly understood in India, which is reflected in the inclusion of many English words in day-to-day conversation even when people are speaking in Panjabi.

7 '*Jihrhaa*' is a relative pronoun because it relates one part of the sentence to another and changes according to the gender and number of the objects being referred to.

8 There are two types of simple adjectives in Panjabi: variable adjectives change their form and invariable adjectives never change their form.

9 Suffixed postpositional phrases are available in Panjabi.

10 The postposition '*noon*' 'ਨੂੰ' is frequently used, carrying different idiomatic meanings and senses.

10

ਇੱਕ ਦਿਨ ਪਿੰਡ ਵਿਚ
ikk din pind vich
A day in the village

In this unit you will learn:

- About Panjabi village life
- How to talk about things you've done and seen

What else did you buy?
ਗੱਲ ਬਾਤ ਤੂੰ ਹੋਰ ਕੀ ਕੁਝ ਖ਼ਰੀਦਿਆ ?
gall baat toon hor kee kujh khareediaa?

◀) CD 2, TR 3, 00:20

Jaspreet and Simran have arrived at their relatives' house in Jalandhar after their tour of Delhi. Their aunt is asking them about their stay in Delhi.

ਚਾਚੀ	ਤੁਹਾਡੀ ਦਿੱਲੀ ਦੀ ਸੈਰ ਕਿਵੇਂ ਰਹੀ ?
Aunt (chaachee)	tuhaadee dillee dee sair kiven rahee?
ਜਸਪ੍ਰੀਤ	ਬਹੁਤ ਸੁਹਣੀ ਰਹੀ। ਇੱਕ ਦਿਨ ਮੈਂ ਪੁਰਾਣੀ ਦਿੱਲੀ ਵਿਚ ਘੁੰਮੀ। ਲਾਲ ਕਿਲ੍ਹਾ ਅਤੇ ਸੀਸ ਗੰਜ ਗੁਰਦਵਾਰਾ ਦੇਖਿਆ। ਉਹ ਦਿਨ ਸਭ ਤੋਂ ਚੰਗਾ ਗੁਜ਼ਰਿਆ। ਮੈਂ ਚਾਂਦਨੀ ਚੌਕ ਬਜ਼ਾਰ ਤੋਂ ਸਿਤਾਰ ਵੀ ਖ਼ਰੀਦੀ।

Jaspreet	bahut suhnhee rahee. ikk din main puraanhee dillee vich ghunmee. laal kilhaa ate sees ganj gurdavaaraa dekhiaa. uh din sabh ton changaa guzriaa. main chaandnee chaunk bazaar ton sitaar vee khareedee.
ਚਾਚੀ	ਤੂੰ ਹੋਰ ਕੀ ਕੁਝ ਖ਼ਰੀਦਿਆ ?
Aunt	toon hor kee kujh khareediaa?
ਜਸਪ੍ਰੀਤ	ਚਾਚੀ ਜੀ, ਮੈਂ ਕਪੜੇ ਖ਼ਰੀਦੇ ਤੇ ਜੁੱਤੀ ਵੀ ਖ਼ਰੀਦੀ ।
Jaspreet	chaachee jee, main kaprhe khareede te juttee vee khareedee.
ਚਾਚੀ	ਸਿਮਰਨ, ਤੂੰ ਕੀ ਕੀਤਾ ?
Aunt	simran, toon kee keetaa?
ਸਿਮਰਨ	ਮੈਂ ਹਰ ਕਿਸਮ ਦੇ ਖਾਣੇ ਖਾਧੇ, ਪਰ ਮੈਂ ਬਿਮਾਰ ਹੋ ਗਈ ਸੀ । ਫਿਰ ਮੈਂ ਡਾਕਟਰ ਕੋਲ ਗਈ ਅਤੇ ਉਸ ਨੇ ਮੈਨੂੰ ਦਵਾਈ ਦਿੱਤੀ ।
Simran	main har kisam de khaanhe khaadhe par main bimaar ho gaee see. phir main daaktar kol gaee ate us ne mainoon davaaee dittee.
ਚਾਚੀ	ਉਮੀਦ ਹੈ ਕਿ ਹੁਣ ਤੂੰ ਠੀਕ ਹੈਂ ਕਿਉਂ ਕਿ ਅਸੀਂ ਅੱਜ ਸਰ੍ਹੋਂ ਦਾ ਸਾਗ ਤੇ ਮੱਕੀ ਦੀ ਰੋਟੀ ਬਣਾਈ ਹੈ । ਇਹ ਪੰਜਾਬ ਦੀ ਖ਼ਾਸ ਸੁਗਾਤ ਹੈ।
Aunt	umeed hai ki hunh toon theek hain kion ki aseen ajj sar-h-on daa saag te makkee dee rotee banhaaee hai. ih panjaab dee khaas sugaat hai!
Aunt	*How was your tour of Delhi?*
Jaspreet	*It was very nice. One day I went around Old Delhi. I saw the Red Fort and Sees Ganj Gurdwara. That was the best day I had. I also bought a sitar from Chandni Chowk market.*
Aunt	*What else did you buy?*
Jaspreet	*Aunty Ji, I bought clothes and shoes too!*
Aunt	*Simran, what did you do?*
Simran	*I ate every type of food, but I fell ill. Then I went to the doctor and he gave me some medicine.*
Aunt	*I hope you're fine now since today we've made* sarhon daa saag *and* makkee dee rotee. *This is a speciality of Panjab!*

ਸ਼ਬਦਾਵਲੀ	shabdaavalee	Vocabulary
ਸੈਰ	sair	*tour, trip* (f.)
ਸੁਹਣੀ	suhnhee	*nice, pretty* (v.)
ਪੁਰਾਣੀ	puraanhee	*old* (v.)
ਪੁਰਾਣੀ ਦਿੱਲੀ	puraanhee dillee	*Old Delhi* (f.)
ਕਿਲ੍ਹਾ	kilhaa	*fort* (m.)
ਚੰਗਾ	changaa	*good* (v.)
ਗੁਜ਼ਰਨਾ	guzarnhaa	*to be spent, to go by*
ਚਾਂਦਨੀ	chaandanee	*moonlight*
ਚੌਂਕ	chaunk	*roundabout, circle, centre* (m.)
ਬਜ਼ਾਰ	bazaar	*bazaar* (m.)
ਖ਼ਰੀਦਨਾ	khareednhaa	*to buy*
ਕੀ ਕੁਝ	kee kujh	*what else*
ਕਪੜੇ	kaprhe	*clothes* (m.)
ਜੁੱਤੀ	juttee	*shoes* (f.)
ਹਰ	har	*each, every*
ਕਿਸਮ	kisam	*type*
ਹਰ ਕਿਸਮ ਦੇ ਖਾਣੇ	har kisam de khaanhe	*every type of food*
ਪਰ	par	*but*
ਉਮੀਦ	umeed	*hope, wish* (f.)
ਕਿਉਂ ਕਿ	kion ki	*because, since*
ਸਰ੍ਹੋਂ ਦਾ ਸਾਗ	sarhon daa saag	*mustard leaves* (m.)
ਮੱਕੀ ਦੀ ਰੋਟੀ	makkee dee rotee	*unleavened corn bread* (f.)
ਬਣਾਉਣਾ	banhaaunhaa	*to make*
ਖ਼ਾਸ	khaas	*special*
ਸੁਗਾਤ	sugaat	*gift* (f.)
ਖ਼ਾਸ ਸੁਗਾਤ	khaas sugaat	*speciality* (f.)

ਅਭਿਆਸ abhiaas *Exercises*

After reading the dialogue and/or listening to the recording, try to do the following exercises.

1 True or false?

a ਚਾਚੀ ਜਸਪ੍ਰੀਤ ਤੇ ਸਿਮਰਨ ਨੂੰ ਦਿੱਲੀ ਦੀ ਸੈਰ ਬਾਰੇ   True/False
ਪੁੱਛ ਰਹੀ ਸੀ ।

chaachee jaspreet <u>t</u>e simran noo<u>n</u> <u>d</u>illee
<u>d</u>ee sair baare pu<u>chch</u> rahee see.

b ਚਾਚੀ ਨੇ ਕੁੜੀਆਂ ਨੂੰ ਕਿਹਾ ਕਿ ਜ਼ਿਆਦਾ ਪੈਸਾ ਨਹੀਂ   True/False
ਖ਼ਰਚਣਾ ਚਾਹੀਦਾ ।

chaachee ne kurheeaa<u>n</u> noo<u>n</u> kihaa ki ziaa<u>d</u>aa
paisaa nahee<u>n</u> <u>kh</u>archnhaa chaaheedaa.

c ਸਿਮਰਨ ਮੌਸਮ ਕਰ ਕੇ ਬਿਮਾਰ ਹੋ ਗਈ ਸੀ ।   True/False

simran mausam kar ke bimaar ho gaee see.

2 Match the responses appropriate to the questions

a ਤੂੰ ਹੋਰ ਕੀ ਕੁਝ ਖ਼ਰੀਦਿਆ ?   **i** ਬਹੁਤ ਸੁਹਣੀ ਰਹੀ ।

<u>t</u>oo<u>n</u> hor kee kujh <u>kh</u>areediaa?   bahu<u>t</u> suhnhee rahee.

b ਤੂੰ ਬਿਮਾਰ ਕਿਉਂ ਹੋ ਗਈ ਸੀ ?   **ii** ਮੈਂ ਹਰ ਕਿਸਮ ਦੇ ਖਾਣੇ ਖਾਧੇ ।

<u>t</u>oo<u>n</u> bimaar kiun ho gaee see?   mai<u>n</u> har kisam <u>d</u>e khaanhe
kha<u>dh</u>e.

c ਦਿੱਲੀ ਦੀ ਸੈਰ ਕਿਵੇਂ ਰਹੀ ?   **iii** ਮੈਂ ਕਪੜੇ ਖ਼ਰੀਦੇ ਤੇ ਜੁੱਤੀ ਵੀ
ਖ਼ਰੀਦੀ ।

<u>d</u>illee <u>d</u>ee sair kive<u>n</u> rahee?   mai<u>n</u> kaprhe <u>kh</u>aree<u>d</u>e <u>t</u>e
ju<u>tt</u>ee vee <u>kh</u>areedee.

d ਦਿੱਲੀ ਵਿਚ ਤੁਸੀਂ ਕੀ ਕੁਝ ਦੇਖਿਆ ?   **iv** ਮੈਂ ਲਾਲ ਕਿਲ੍ਹਾ ਅਤੇ ਸੀਸ
ਗੰਜ ਗੁਰਦਵਾਰਾ ਦੇਖਿਆ ।

<u>d</u>illee vich <u>t</u>usee<u>n</u> kee kujh
<u>d</u>ekhiaa?   mai<u>n</u> laal kilhaa a<u>t</u>e sees
gan<u>j</u> gur<u>d</u>avaaraa <u>d</u>ekhiaa.

Passage: A day in the village
ਪੈਰਾ: ਇੱਕ ਦਿਨ ਪਿੰਡ ਵਿਚ
pairaa: ikk <u>d</u>in pi<u>nd</u> vich

Jaspreet and Simran have gone to their mother's family's village
after having seen their father's relatives in Jalandhar. The following
passage is a page from Jaspreet's diary. She has written about the day
that she and her sister spent in the village.

17 Janvaree

aseen ajj jala<u>n</u><u>dh</u>ar ho ke naanke pi<u>n</u>d gaeeaa<u>n</u>. saare saanoon
piaar naal mile. saade maamaa jee naanaa jee <u>t</u>e naanee jee <u>d</u>e
kol rahi<u>n</u>de han. uhnaa<u>n</u> ne saanoo<u>n</u> saaraa pi<u>n</u>d <u>d</u>ikhaaiaa. aseen
taraik<u>t</u>ar <u>t</u>e charh-h-eeaa<u>n</u> a<u>t</u>e khe<u>t</u>aa<u>n</u> vich ghu<u>n</u>meeaa<u>n</u>. aseen
khooh <u>t</u>e ruke. main khooh pahilee vaaree vekhiaa see. simran
majhjh noo<u>n</u> <u>d</u>ekh ke dar gaee <u>t</u>e ikk <u>d</u>am <u>d</u>aurh gaee. khooh <u>d</u>e
naal ikk ba<u>n</u>daa ga<u>nn</u>e <u>d</u>e ras <u>t</u>on gurh banhaa rihaa see. shaam
noo<u>n</u> ja<u>d</u>o<u>n</u> aseen vaapas aae <u>t</u>aa<u>n</u> maamee jee ne saanoo<u>n</u>

154

rotee khuaaee. us <u>t</u>on baa-a-<u>d</u> vihrhe vich asee<u>n</u> naanee jee kolo<u>n</u> puraanheeaa<u>n</u> kahaanheeaa<u>n</u> sunheeaa<u>n</u>. raa<u>t</u> noo<u>n</u> saariaa<u>n</u> ne garam <u>d</u>u<u>dh</u>dh pee<u>t</u>aa a<u>t</u>e phir sau<u>n</u> gae. pi<u>n</u>d <u>d</u>aa maahaul mainoo<u>n</u> bahu<u>t</u> pasa<u>n</u>d hai.

17 January

Today, after having been to Jalandhar, we went to our mother's family's village. Everyone met us with affection. Our mother's brother lives with grandfather and grandmother. He showed us the entire village. We rode on a tractor and went around the fields. We stopped at the well. It was the first time that I had seen a well. Simran saw buffalo, got scared and immediately ran away. Next to the well there was a man who was making Gurh (a sweet delicacy) from the juice of the sugarcane. In the evening when we arrived, mami ji fed us. After that we all sat in the courtyard and heard old stories from grandmother. At night everyone drank hot milk and then went to sleep. I like the atmosphere of the village a lot.

ਸ਼ਬਦਾਵਲੀ	shab<u>d</u>aavalee	*Vocabulary*
ਨਾਨਕੇ ਪਿੰਡ	naanke pi<u>n</u>d	*mother's family's village*
ਪਿਆਰ	piaar	*love, affection* (m.)
ਮਿਲਣਾ	milnhaa	*to meet*
ਟਰੈਕਟਰ	taraiktar	*tractor* (m.)
ਚੜੂਣਾ	charh-h-nhaa	*to climb, to ride*
ਖੇਤ	khe<u>t</u>	*land, field* (m.)
ਖੂਹ	khooh	*water well* (m.)
ਪਹਿਲੀ ਵਾਰੀ	pahilee vaaree	*first time*
ਮੱਝ	majhjh	*buffalo* (f.)
ਡਰਨਾ	darnaa	*to be scared*
ਇੱਕ ਦਮ	ikk <u>d</u>am	*immediately, at once*
ਦੌੜ	<u>d</u>aurh	*to run*
ਬੰਦਾ	ba<u>n</u>daa	*man* (m.)
ਗੰਨਾ	<u>g</u>annaa	*sugarcane* (m.)
ਗੁੜ	gurh	*brown sugar cake* (m.)
ਵਾਪਸ	vaapas	*return, back to*
ਤਾਂ	<u>t</u>aa<u>n</u>	*then*

ਰੋਟੀ	rotee	*food* (lit. unleavened bread which is part of the staple diet of Panjab) (f.)
ਖੁਆਈ	khuaaee	*to feed*
ਉਸ ਤੋਂ ਬਾਅਦ	us <u>t</u>on baa-a-<u>d</u>	*after that*
ਵਿਹੜਾ	vihrhaa	*courtyard* (m.)
ਕਹਾਣੀ	kahaanhee	*story* (f.)
ਗਰਮ	garam	*warm, hot*
ਦੁੱਧ	<u>dudhdh</u>	*milk* (m.)
ਸੌਣਾ	saunhaa	*to sleep*
ਮਾਹੌਲ	maahaul	*atmosphere, environment* (m.)

ਅਭਿਆਸ abhiaas *Exercises*

After reading the passage and/or listening to the recording, try to do the following exercises.

1 Answer the following questions about the passage

a ਜਸਪ੍ਰੀਤ ਤੇ ਸਿਮਰਨ ਦੇ ਮਾਮਾ ਜੀ ਕਿਹਨਾਂ ਕੋਲ ਰਹਿੰਦੇ ਹਨ?
jaspree<u>t</u> <u>t</u>e simran <u>d</u>e maamaa jee kihnaa<u>n</u> kol rahin<u>d</u>e han?

b ਜਿਹੜਾ ਬੰਦਾ ਖੂਹ ਦੇ ਕੋਲ ਸੀ, ਉਹ ਕੀ ਬਣਾ ਰਿਹਾ ਸੀ?
jihrhaa ban<u>d</u>aa khooh <u>d</u>e kol see, uh kee banhaa rihaa see?

c ਰੋਟੀ ਖਾਣ ਤੋਂ ਬਾਅਦ ਕੁੜੀਆਂ ਨੇ ਕੀ ਕੀਤਾ?
rotee khaanh <u>t</u>on baa-a-<u>d</u> kurheeaa<u>n</u> ne kee kee<u>t</u>aa?

d ਸੌਣ ਤੋਂ ਪਹਿਲੇ ਸਾਰਿਆਂ ਨੇ ਕੀ ਪੀਤਾ?
saunh <u>t</u>on pahile saariaa<u>n</u> ne kee pee<u>t</u>aa?

2 Complete the table

ਪਿੰਡ		
	khooh	
ਵਿਹੜਾ		
		fields
	ga<u>n</u>naa	

ਬੋਲੀ ਬਾਰੇ bolee baare *Language points*

The past tense

You have already been introduced to the simple past tense in Unit 6. Verbs in the simple past tense were shown to agree with the number and gender of the subject. To help you remember, here are examples of the verbs ਆਉਣਾ aaunhaa (*to come*), ਰੋਣਾ ronhaa (*to cry*), ਬੋਲਣਾ bolnhaa (*to speak*), ਹੋਣਾ honhaa (*to be*) and ਦੱਸਣਾ dassnhaa (*to tell*) in their simple past forms:

Masculine singular	Masculine plural	Feminine singular	Feminine plural	
ਆਇਆ aaiaa	ਆਏ aae	ਆਈ aaee	ਆਈਆਂ aaeeaan	*came*
ਰੋਇਆ roiaa	ਰੋਏ roe	ਰੋਈ roee	ਰੋਈਆਂ roeeaan	*cried*
ਬੋਲਿਆ boliaa	ਬੋਲੇ bole	ਬੋਲੀ bolee	ਬੋਲੀਆਂ boleeaan	*spoke*
ਦੱਸਿਆ dassiaa	ਦੱਸੇ dasse	ਦੱਸੀ dassee	ਦੱਸੀਆਂ dasseeaan	*told*
ਹੋਇਆ hoiaa	ਹੋਏ hoe	ਹੋਈ hoee	ਹੋਈਆਂ hoeeaan	*happened*

In the past tenses in Panjabi, all verbs can be categorized into two groups: intransitive and transitive. Intransitive verbs do not rely upon an object to dictate the form of the verb. This literally means that the form of the verb is unchanging except, of course, in relation to the subject of the sentence. Intransitive verbs generally do not take a direct object. Transitive verbs are those verbs which do take a direct object and are more flexible. In such cases where an object is present, the ending of the verb will agree with the object. In the examples given above, *cried* and *spoke* are both intransitive verbs, meaning that the act of crying and speaking can stand alone without the requirement of an object. *Told*, on the other hand, can require the presence of an object such as *he told me a story* with *story* being the direct object. The following examples illustrate how the transitive verb is affected by the presence of a direct object:

ਮੈਂ ਕੇਲਾ ਖਾਧਾ	main kelaa khaadhaa	*I ate a banana.*
ਮੈਂ ਕੇਲੇ ਖਾਧੇ	main kele khaadhe	*I ate bananas.*
ਮੈਂ ਨਾਸ਼ਪਾਤੀ ਖਾਧੀ	main naashpaatee khaadhee	*I ate a pear.*
ਮੈਂ ਨਾਸ਼ਪਾਤੀਆਂ ਖਾਧੀਆਂ	main naashpaateeaan khaadheeaan	*I ate pears.*

You will notice that the first two examples both have the same object, except that the first is singular and the second is plural. Therefore, **ਖਾਧਾ khaadhaa** in the first example reflects the singular masculine nature of *banana* and **ਖਾਧੇ khaadhe** refers to the plural masculine nature of *bananas*. The third and fourth examples show a similar pattern for the feminine object *pear* with **ਖਾਧੀ khaadhee** and **ਖਾਧੀਆਂ khaadheeaan** corresponding to the respective singular and plural forms.

The main point to remember when using verbs in the past tense is that some verbs are subject-inflected (meaning that they change according to the subject), while others are object-inflected (i.e. change according to the object of the sentence). However, some verbs can be in either category. There are transitive verbs which behave like intransitive verbs when there is no direct object present, such as **ਸਮਝਣਾ samajhnhaa** (*to understand*) and **ਪੜ੍ਹਨਾ par-h-hnaa** (*to read*). There are also intransitive verbs which can behave as transitive verbs, such as **ਕਹਿਣਾ kahinhaa** (*to say*), **ਪੁੱਛਣਾ puchchnhaa** (*to ask*), and **ਥੁੱਕਣਾ thukknhaa** (*to spit*). However, there is no convention for knowing when a verb is intransitive or transitive apart from the nature of the verb and the presence of an object.

Insight
Generally, a verb agrees with the subject but in the case of the transitive verb in the past tense it agrees with the direct object.

The agentive postposition ਨੇ 'ne'

Nearly all transitive verbs in the past tenses are affected by the postposition **ne ਨੇ** which directs the action of the verb towards the subject. In usual circumstances ਨੇ follows the subject of the sentence. However, in the example ਮੈਂ ਨਾਸ਼ਪਾਤੀ ਖਾਧੀ main naashpaatee khaadhee, ਨੇ ne is implicit and does not appear. The use of ਨੇ ne is illustrated in the table. Note that for some pronouns in the third person, the use of ਨੇ ne is optional as is indicated in parentheses.

Pronouns in the ਨੇ construction

Direct pronouns			In the ਨੇ (ne) construction	
1st person	ਮੈਂ ਅਸੀਂ	main aseen	ਮੈਂ ਅਸੀਂ	no change no change
2nd person	ਤੁਸੀਂ ਤੂੰ	tuseen toon	ਤੁਸੀਂ ਤੂੰ	no change no change
3rd person	ਇਹ (sing.) ਇਸ (sing.) ਉਹ (sing.) ਉਸ (sing.) ਇਹ (formal, plural) ਉਹ (formal, plural) ਕੌਣ (sing.) ਕੌਣ (formal, plural)	ih is uh us ih uh kaunh kaunh	ਇਹ ਨੇ ਇਸ (ਨੇ) ਉਹ ਨੇ ਉਸ (ਨੇ) ਇਹਨਾਂ ihnaan (ਨੇ) ਉਹਨਾਂ uhnaan (ਨੇ) ਕਿਸ kis (ਨੇ) ਕਿਹਨਾਂ kihnaan (ਨੇ)	ਨੇ ne required ਨੇ ne optional ਨੇ ne required ਨੇ ne optional ਨੇ ne optional ਨੇ ne optional ਨੇ ne optional ਨੇ ne optional

Insight

The particle 'ne' 'ਨੇ' is never used with 1st and 2nd person. It only appears with the 3rd person and that is also in a very flexible way.

In cases where no direct object is present or the direct object is already followed by a postposition, the verb is made 'neutral'. The neutral verb is always in the singular masculine form. Most commonly, the postposition ਨੂੰ noon follows the object of the sentence, thus making the verb neutral. Here are some examples of transitive verbs in the ਨੇ ne construction as well as with the postposition ਨੂੰ noon:

ਮੈਂ ਦਰਖ਼ਤ* ਨੂੰ ਕਟਿਆ	main darakhat noon katiaa	*I cut the tree.*
ਮੈਂ ਟਾਹਣੀ* ਨੂੰ ਕਟਿਆ	main taahanhee noon katiaa	*I cut the branch.*
ਮੈਂ ਦਰਖ਼ਤਾਂ* ਨੂੰ ਕਟਿਆ	main darakhataan noon katiaa	*I cut the trees.*
ਮੈਂ ਟਾਹਣੀਆਂ* ਨੂੰ ਕਟਿਆ	main taahanheeaan noon katiaa	*I cut the branches.*

*ਦਰਖ਼ਤ is grammatically masculine
*ਟਾਹਣੀ is grammatically feminine

ਅਸੀਂ ਕਿਰਨ ਨੂੰ ਅੰਮ੍ਰਿਤਸਰ ਵੇਖਿਆ	aseen kiran (f.) noon amritsar vekhiaa	*We saw Kiran in Amritsar.*
ਅਸੀਂ ਤਾਰਿਕ ਨੂੰ ਲੰਡਨ ਵੇਖਿਆ	aseen taarik (m.) noon landan vekhiaa	*We saw Tariq in London*

Note that the verb did not change in these examples even though the gender of the object does because of the presence of ਨੂੰ **noon**.

Here are more examples of the use of transitive verbs:

ਅਮਰ ਨੇ ਕਹਾਣੀ ਸੁਣੀ	amar ne kahaanhee sunhee	*Amar heard the story.*
ਅਮਰ ਨੇ ਤਿੰਨ ਕਹਾਣੀਆਂ ਸੁਣੀਆਂ	amar ne tinn kahaanheeaan sunheeaan	*Amar heard three stories.*
ਅਮਰ ਨੇ ਸੁਣਿਆ	amar ne sunhiaa	*Amar heard.*
ਅਮਰ ਨੇ ਇਸ ਕਹਾਣੀ ਨੂੰ ਸੁਣਿਆ	amar ne is kahaanhee noon sunhiaa	*Amar heard this story.*
ਅਮਰ ਨੇ ਇਹਨਾਂ ਕਹਾਣੀਆਂ ਨੂੰ ਸੁਣਿਆ	amar ne ihnaan kahaanheeaan noon sunhiaa	*Amar heard these stories.*

You will recall from Unit 8 that pronouns and nouns change to their oblique forms when followed by postpositions. Taking the same examples: ਇਹ ਕਹਾਣੀ **ih kahaanhee** *this story* changes to ਇਸ ਕਹਾਣੀ **is kahaanhee** in the sentence:

ਅਮਰ ਨੇ ਇਹ ਕਹਾਣੀ ਸੁਣੀ	amar ne ih kahaanhee sunhee	*Amar heard this story.*
ਅਮਰ ਨੇ ਇਸ ਕਹਾਣੀ ਨੂੰ ਸੁਣਿਆ	amar ne is kahaanhee noon sunhiaa	*Amar heard this story.*

This story in the English is identical in both examples. In Panjabi, however, *this story* in the first example is in the direct form while *this story* in the second example is in the oblique form.

Many verbs can fall within either category of transitive or intransitive making the past tense in Panjabi less straightforward than, say, the present or future tenses which are not reliant upon the object's relationship with the verb. For instance, the verb ਕਰਨਾ **karnaa** *to do* and ਸਮਝਣਾ **samjhnhaa** *to understand* can act as intransitive verbs when not followed by an object or can behave as transitive verbs when an object is present. The same is true for ਪੜ੍ਹਨਾ **parh-h-naa** which can take the ਨੇ **ne** construction when used in the sense *to read* or can stand alone when meaning *to study*. Often, ਨੇ **ne** can be invisible, meaning that the sentence may be dictated by the ਨੇ **ne** construction but that it is simply understood. This, however, occurs with only a few verbs, so you should be cautious when applying these rules. The best way of illustrating transitive verbs with ਨੇ **ne** is through examples.

In the following examples you will see how the ending of the verb in the past tense corresponds with the gender and number of the objects:

ਉਹਨਾਂ (ਨੇ) ਬਹੁਤ ਕੇਲੇ ਖਾਧੇ	uhnaa̲n (ne) bahut kele khaa̲dhe	*They ate many bananas.*
ਉਸ ਨੇ ਇਹ ਕਮੀਜ਼ਾਂ ਕਿਉਂ ਖ਼ਰੀਦੀਆਂ ?	us ne ih kameezaa̲n kiun kha̲reedeeaa̲n?	*Why did he buy these shirts?*
ਕਿਸ ਨੇ ਗੱਡੀ ਨੂੰ ਸਾਫ਼ ਕੀਤਾ ਸੀ ?	kis ne gaddee noon saaf keeṯaa see?	*Who cleaned the car?*
ਰਾਮ ਨੇ ਮੇਰੀ ਗੱਲ ਨਹੀਂ ਸਮਝੀ	raam ne meree gall naheen̲ samajhee	*Ram did not understand what I said.*

Insight

The 'noon' 'ਨੂੰ' postposition can be omitted from the following words but the original words would be slightly modified:

a raa̲t noo̲n ਸਵੇਰ ਨੂੰ - savere ਸਵੇਰੇ - *in the morning*
b raa̲t noo̲n ਰਾਤ ਨੂੰ - raa̲teen ਰਾਤੇ - *at night*

Compound verbs

Compound verbs are formed when the stem of a main verb is followed by an auxiliary verb. These constructions are very common in Panjabi and are the equivalent of two verbs coming together in English such as in the expression *to go to sleep*. In Unit 9 you learned how to express *can* and *already* through the uses of ਸਕਣਾ **saknhaa** and ਚੁਕਣਾ **chuknhaa** which, when combined with other verb stems, form compound verb constructions. In a similar way, other verbs are used as auxiliary verbs to emphasize or give an added meaning to the verb stem. Whereas ਸਕਣਾ **saknhaa** and ਚੁਕਣਾ **chuknhaa** have very specific meanings, this is not the case for most other compound constructions which are less simple to define. A helpful hint regarding compound verbs, however, is that the auxiliary verb loses its own meaning when it accompanies the stem of another verb. Often it is the context of the sentence and the meaning of the main verb that will tell you about the emphasis that the auxiliary verb has added.

The most common auxiliary verbs are ਜਾਣਾ **jaanhaa** (*to go*), ਦੇਣਾ **denhaa** (*to give*) and ਲੈਣਾ **lainhaa** (*to take*). When an intransitive verb is the main verb, ਜਾਣਾ **janhaa** (*to go*) is generally used to give the sense of completeness or change. To show how the meaning of the main verb is affected by the auxiliary ending, here are a few examples:

ਆਉਣਾ	aaunhaa	*to come*	ਆ ਜਾਣਾ	aa jaanhaa	*to arrive*
ਸੋਣਾ	saunhaa	*to sleep*	ਸੋਣ ਜਾਣਾ	saunh jaanhaa	*to go to sleep*
ਖਾਣਾ	khaanhaa	*to eat*	ਖਾ ਜਾਣਾ	khaa jaanhaa	*to eat up*
ਪੀਣਾ	peenhaa	*to drink*	ਪੀ ਜਾਣਾ	pee jaanhaa	*to drink up*

The following sentences illustrate how these compound verbs with **jaanhaa** (*to go*) can be used:

ਚਾਚੀ ਪਿੰਡ ਤੋਂ ਆ ਗਈ ਸੀ	chaachee pin̲d ton̲ aa gaee see	*Aunt had come from the village.*
ਮੈਂ ਬਾਰਾਂ ਵਜੇ ਸੋਣ ਜਾਵਾਂ ਗੀ	main̲ baar-h-aan̲ vaje saunh jaavaan̲ gee	*I will go to sleep at 12 o'clock.*
ਉਹ ਐਨਾ ਭੁੱਖਾ ਸੀ ਕਿ ਉਹ ਸਭ ਕੁਝ ਖਾ ਗਿਆ!	uh ainaa bhukhkhaa see ki uh sabh kujh khaa giaa!	*He was so hungry that he ate everything up!*
ਬਿੱਲੀ ਸਾਰਾ ਦੁੱਧ ਪੀ ਗਈ	billee saaraa d̲udhdh pee gaee	*The cat drank (up) all the milk.*

162

Of the transitive verbs, the auxiliaries of **ਲੈਣਾ lainhaa** (*to take*) and **ਦੇਣਾ denhaa** (*to give*) are the most common. The effects of each upon the main verb can be best described in terms of the direction of the action. **ਲੈਣਾ lainhaa** tends to give the sense that the action is being done towards or for the benefit of the performer while **ਦੇਣਾ denhaa** indicates that the action is being directed away from the performer. The difference between the two can often be quite subtle:

ਇਹ ਕਿਤਾਬ ਰੱਖ ਲੈ	ih kitaab rakhkh lai	*Keep this book (with you).*
ਇਹ ਕਿਤਾਬ ਮੇਜ਼ ਤੇ ਰੱਖ ਦੇ	ih kitaab mez te rakhkh de	*Put this book on the table.*
ਉਹ ਪੰਜਾਬੀ ਪੜ੍ਹ ਲੈਂਦੀ ਹੈ	uh panjaabee parhh laindee hai	*She reads Panjabi.*
ਉਹ ਚਿੱਠੀ ਪੜ੍ਹ ਦੇਂਦੀ ਹੈ	uh chiththee parhh dendee hai	*She reads out the letter.*

ਲੈਣਾ lainhaa and **ਦੇਣਾ denhaa**, in addition to directing the action, also add a feeling of completeness:

ਮੈਂ ਕੰਮ ਜਲਦੀ ਕਰ ਲਿਆ ਸੀ	main kanm jaldee kar liaa see	*I [had] finished the job quickly.*
ਸਿਮਰਨ ਨੇ ਜੁੱਤੀ ਖ਼ਰੀਦ ਲਈ	simran ne juttee khareed laee	*Simran bought shoes.*
ਡਾਕਟਰ ਨੇ ਸਿਮਰਨ ਨੂੰ ਦਵਾਈ ਦੇ ਦਿੱਤੀ	daaktar ne simran noon davaaee de dittee	*The doctor gave Simran medicine.*
ਟੈਕਸੀ ਵਾਲੇ ਨੇ ਸਮਾਨ ਗੱਡੀ ਵਿਚ ਰੱਖ ਦਿੱਤਾ	taiksee vaale ne samaan gaddee vich rakhkh dittaa	*The taxi driver put the luggage in the car.*

The particle -ਕੇ 'ke'

The particle -ਕੇ ke resembles the conjunction *and* in English. In English two verbs can be joined by *and* such as in the case *he came (home) and ate*. In Panjabi the first verb is followed by -ਕੇ ke to denote that the first action occurred first. In this example, the literal meaning would be *having come (home), he ate*. Therefore, the literal meaning of -ਕੇ ke is *having*. In the passage from Jaspreet's diary, you will recall that she says *Simran saw a buffalo and ran away*.

In Panjabi this would be translated as: *Having seen a buffalo, Simran ran away*. Here are a few more examples of how -ਕੇ ke is used:

ਰਾਜਿੰਦਰ ਨੂੰ ਬੁਲਾ ਕੇ ਉਹ ਨੂੰ ਦੱਸੋ	raajindar noon bulaa ke uh noon dasso	*Call Rajinder and tell him.*
ਕੰਮ ਖ਼ਤਮ ਕਰ ਕੇ ਤੂੰ ਘਰ ਨੂੰ ਚਲੇ ਜਾ	kanm khatam kar ke toon ghar noon chale jaa	*After finishing work, go home.*
ਦੁਕਾਨ ਤੇ ਜਾ ਕੇ ਮੱਖਣ ਲਿਆਓ	dukaan te jaa ke makhkhanh liaao	*Go to the shop and bring some butter.*

-ਕੇ ke can be used with more idiomatic expressions as well, which are often not easily translated into English but which are useful ways of expressing what might otherwise be lengthy sentences. Here are some examples of the usage of -ਕੇ ke in idiomatic phrases as well as in adverbial expressions (i.e. expressions which describe actions) which will help you to understand its functions better.

Adverbial phrases

ਅੱਗੇ ਚਲ ਕੇ	agge chal ke	*from now on, in the future*
ਸੋਚ ਕੇ	soch ke	*after thinking*
ਹੱਸ ਕੇ	hass ke	*laughingly*
ਡਰ ਕੇ	dar ke	*being scared*

Idiomatic uses of -ਕੇ

ਚੰਡੀਗੜ੍ਹ ਤੋਂ ਹੋ ਕੇ ਜਾਣਾ	chandeegarh ton hoke jaanhaa	*Go via Chandigarh.*
ਪਿਤਾ ਜੀ ਨੇ ਮੈਨੂੰ ਜਾਣ ਕੇ ਨਹੀਂ ਦੱਸਿਆ	pitaa jee ne mainoon jaanh ke naheen dassiaa	*Father purposely didn't tell me.*
ਇੱਕ ਘਰ ਛੱਡ ਕੇ ਸਾਡਾ ਹੈ	ikk ghar chadd ke saadaa hai	*The house after the next one is ours.*

The particle -ਕੇ ke is also used when expressing the time of the day. You will recall from Unit 7 that the verb ਵੱਜਣਾ vajjnhaa (*to strike, to chime*) is used to tell the time. The times of quarter past, half past, quarter to, and times on the hour which are regularly used were illustrated to you in this unit. When you wish to show that the time is a few minutes before or after the hour, then the particle -ਕੇ ke is combined with ਵੱਜਣਾ vajjnhaa. Therefore, ਵਜ ਕੇ vaj ke means *having struck.* ਵਜਨ ਵਿਚ **vajanh vich** means *before the hour.* The following examples illustrate how **-ਕੇ ke** and **ਵਿਚ vich** are used to express such times:

ਪੰਜ ਵਜਨ ਵਿਚ ਦੋ ਮਿੰਟ ਹਨ	pan̲j vajanh vich d̲o min̲t han	*It is two minutes to five.*
ਪੰਜ ਵਜ ਕੇ ਦੋ ਮਿੰਟ ਹਨ	pan̲j vaj ke d̲o min̲t han	*It is two minutes past five.*
ਬਾਰ੍ਹਾਂ ਵਜਨ ਵਿਚ ਅਠਾਰ੍ਹਾਂ ਮਿੰਟ ਹਨ	baar-haan̲ vajanh vich athaar-haan̲ min̲t han	*It is 18 minutes to 12.*
ਬਾਰ੍ਹਾਂ ਵਜ ਕੇ ਅਠਾਰ੍ਹਾਂ ਮਿੰਟ ਹਨ	baar-haan̲ vaj ke athaar-haan̲ min̲t han	*It is 18 minutes past 12.*

ਵਿਆਖਿਆ viaakhiaa *Commentary*

Rural Panjab

Panjab's predominantly rural society has had a profound impact on the development of the Panjabi language. On the one hand there is a great deal of local diversity, such that dialects and pronunciations can change over small distances. On the other, there is a richness in the language which comes from rural idioms. Conversations in Panjabi are often peppered with these sayings and it is difficult to relate them without some knowledge of village life. As with all rural settings, day-to-day life in a village is dominated by the agricultural economy which is in turn related to the changing seasons.

Panjab is renowned in the whole of India as the 'bread basket' of the country. In the 1970s the region benefited enormously from the introduction of genetically-engineered wheat seeds which resulted in much larger crop returns. This phenomenon has been called the 'Green Revolution' and resulted in Panjab having the greatest per capita income of all the states in the Indian Union.

Insight

Panjabis are stereotypically renowned for their hospitality. They are popularly symbolized as the best farmers during peace, excellent soldiers in war, hearty celebrators on special occasions, and enthusiastic migrants at all times.

ਅਭਿਆਸ abhiaas *Exercises*

1 Use the particle -ਕੇ 'ke' to express the sentences in Panjabi

a Having eaten, we all went to sleep.
b Go to the shop and bring some milk.
c After completing the task, go home.
d Go to Amritsar via Jalandhar.

2 Insert the appropriate past tense forms

Write the appropriate past form of the verbs given to you in parentheses. Remember the rules about transitive and intransitive verbs!

a ਮੈਂ ਦੋ ਕੇਲੇ _____ (ਖਾਣਾ)
main <u>d</u>o kele _____ (khaanhaa)

b ਬੱਚੀ _____ (ਰੋਣਾ)
bachchee _____ (ronhaa)

c ਨਾਨੀ ਜੀ ਨੇ ਸਾਨੂੰ ਕਹਾਣੀ _____ (ਸੁਣਾਉਣਾ)
naanee jee ne saanoo<u>n</u> kahaanhee (sunhaaunhaa)

d ਮੈਂ ਦਰਖ਼ਤ ਨੂੰ _____ (ਕਟਣਾ)
main <u>d</u>ara<u>kh</u>a<u>t</u> noo<u>n</u> _____ (katnhaa)

3 Responses in Panjabi

◄» CD 2, TR 3, 01:55

The following is a conversation between you and your aunt. You are visiting her in London and she is asking you about your trip to central London today. Respond to her questions in Panjabi with the answers given to you in English.

Aunt	ਤੁਹਾਡੀ ਲੰਡਨ ਦੀ ਸੈਰ ਕਿਵੇਂ ਰਹੀ ? <u>t</u>uhaadee la<u>n</u>dan <u>d</u>ee sair kive<u>n</u> rahee?
You	**It was very nice. I went to Trafalgar Square and saw Nelson's Column. I also went to Buckingham Palace.**
Aunt	ਤੁਸੀਂ ਹੋਰ ਕੀ ਕੀਤਾ ? <u>t</u>usee<u>n</u> hor kee kee<u>t</u>aa?
You	**I went to Oxford Circus and bought some clothes.**
Aunt	ਤੁਸੀਂ ਕੀ ਕੁਝ ਖਾਧਾ ? <u>t</u>usee<u>n</u> kee kujh khaa<u>dh</u>aa?

166

You	I only ate some pizza.
Aunt	ਉਮੀਦ ਹੈ ਕਿ ਤੁਹਾਨੂੰ ਭੁੱਖ ਲੱਗੀ ਹੈ ਕਿਉਂ ਕਿ ਅੱਜ ਅਸੀਂ ਮੱਛੀ ਤੇ ਚਿਪਸ ਬਣਾਏ ਹਨ। ਇਹ ਹੈ ਇੰਗਲੈਂਡ ਦੀ ਖ਼ਾਸ ਸੁਗਾਤ!
	umeed hai ki tuhaanoon bhukhkh laggee hai kiun ki ajj aseen machchee te chips banhaae han. ih hai inglaind dee khaas sugaat!

4 Name the numbered objects in Panjabi

1 water well   **2** buffalo   **3** sugarcane   **4** house   **5** fields

---

Ten important things to remember

1 Intransitive verbs generally do not take direct objects.
2 Transitive verbs are those verbs which do take a direct object and are more flexible.
3 Nearly all transitive verbs in the past tense are affected by the postposition '*ne*' 'ਨੇ'.
4 With transitive verbs, '*ne*' 'ਨੇ' never appears with the 1st or 2nd person, whether singular or plural. It only appears with the third person and even then it is optional with some pronouns.
5 The presence of '*noon*' 'ਨੂੰ' with transitive verbs makes the verb neutral in form.

6 Compound verbs are formed when the stem of a main verb is followed by an auxiliary verb. The most common auxiliary verbs are '*jaanhaa*' 'ਜਾਣਾ' (to go), '*denhaa*' 'ਦੇਣਾ' (to give) and '*lainhaa*' 'ਲੈਣਾ' (to take).

7 The particle '*ke*' 'ਕੇ' resembles the conjunction 'and' in English.

8 '*Ke*' 'ਕੇ' can be used with more idiomatic expressions as well. Example: '*main tuhaanoon soch ke dassaan gaa*' 'ਮੈਂ ਤੁਹਾਨੂੰ ਸੋਚ ਕੇ ਦੱਸਾਂ ਗਾ' I will let you know after thinking.

9 The particle '*ke*' 'ਕੇ' is also used when expressing the time of the day. Example: '*panj vaj ke do mint hoe han*' 'ਪੰਜ ਵਜ ਕੇ ਦੋ ਮਿੰਟ ਹੋਏ ਹਨ' It is two minutes past five.

10 We can omit the postposition '*noon*' 'ਨੂੰ' from the following sentence but the oblique form stays. '*main ajj aagre (noon) jaa rihaa haan*' 'ਮੈਂ ਅੱਜ ਆਗਰੇ (ਨੂੰ) ਜਾ ਰਿਹਾ ਹਾਂ' I am going to Agra today.

ਹਰਿਮੰਦਰ ਸਾਹਿਬ
harma<u>n</u>dar saahib
The Golden Temple

In this unit you will learn:

- How to make enquiries and collect information
- How to buy train tickets
- About the Golden Temple

---

1 *Shan-e-Panjab*
ਗੱਲ ਬਾਤ ੧ ਸ਼ਾਨੇ ਪੰਜਾਬ
gall baa<u>t</u> 1 shaane pa<u>n</u>jaab

◄) **CD 2, TR 4, 00:18**

Both sisters are at Jalandhar railway station early in the morning. After visiting their relatives, they are now on their way to pay homage to Harmandar Saahib, the Golden Temple in Amritsar.

ਜਸਪ੍ਰੀਤ	ਅੰਮ੍ਰਿਤਸਰ ਜਾਣ ਲਈ ਸਭ ਤੋਂ ਚੰਗੀ ਗੱਡੀ ਕਿਹੜੀ ਹੈ ?
ਟਿਕਟ ਬਾਬੂ	ਸ਼ਾਨੇ ਪੰਜਾਬ। ਬਹੁਤ ਸਾਰੇ ਸੈਲਾਨੀ ਇਸ ਗੱਡੀ ਵਿਚ ਸਫ਼ਰ ਕਰਦੇ ਹਨ।
ਜਸਪ੍ਰੀਤ	ਅਸੀਂ ਦੋਨੋਂ ਅੱਜ ਜਾਣਾ ਚਾਹੁੰਦੀਆਂ ਹਾਂ। ਕੀ ਸਾਨੂੰ ਫਰਸਟ ਕਲਾਸ ਵਿਚ ਸੀਟ ਮਿਲ ਜਾਏ ਗੀ ?
ਟਿਕਟ ਬਾਬੂ	ਕੀ ਤੁਹਾਨੂੰ ਵਾਪਸੀ ਟਿਕਟ ਚਾਹੀਦੀ ਹੈ ਜਾਂ ਇੱਕ ਪਾਸੇ ਦੀ ?
ਸਿਮਰਨ	ਇੱਕ ਪਾਸੇ ਦੀ। ਗੱਡੀ ਕਿੰਨੇ ਵਜੇ ਚਲਦੀ ਹੈ ?

ਟਿਕਟ ਬਾਬੂ	ਗੱਡੀ ਗਿਆਰਾਂ ਵਜੇ ਸਵੇਰੇ ਚਲਦੀ ਹੈ, ਅਤੇ ਢਾਈ ਵਜੇ ਬਾਅਦ ਦੁਪਹਿਰ ਨੂੰ ਤੁਹਾਨੂੰ ਅੰਮ੍ਰਿਤਸਰ ਪਹੁੰਚਾ ਦੇਂਦੀ ਹੈ।
ਸਿਮਰਨ	ਅੱਛਾ, ਸਾਨੂੰ ਦੋ ਟਿਕਟਾਂ ਦੇ ਦੇਵੋ।
ਟਿਕਟ ਬਾਬੂ	ਨਵੀਆਂ ਥਾਂਵਾਂ ਦੇਖਣਾ ਚੰਗੀ ਗੱਲ ਹੈ। ਇਹ ਹਨ ਤੁਹਾਡੀਆਂ ਦੋ ਟਿਕਟਾਂ।
ਜਸਪ੍ਰੀਤ	ਧੰਨਵਾਦ।
ਟਿਕਟ ਬਾਬੂ	ਸੁਰੱਖਿਅਤ ਸਫ਼ਰ ਲਈ ਸ਼ੁਭ ਇਛਾਵਾਂ।
Jaspreet	*Which is the best train to Amritsar?*
Booking clerk	*The Shan-e-Panjab [the pride of Panjab]. A lot of tourists travel on this train.*
Jaspreet	*The two of us want to go today. Will we be able to get a seat in first class?*
Booking clerk	*Do you want return or single?*
Simran	*Single. What time does the train leave?*
Booking clerk	*The train leaves at 11 in the morning and gets you to Amritsar at 2.30 in the afternoon.*
Simran	*Okay, can we have [lit. give us] two tickets.*
Booking clerk	*It is good to see new places. Here are your two tickets.*
Jaspreet	*Thanks.*
Booking clerk	*Best wishes for a safe journey.*

ਸ਼ਬਦਾਵਲੀ	shabdaavalee	*Vocabulary*
ਗੱਡੀ	gaddee	*automobile, train* (f.)
ਬਹੁਤ ਸਾਰੇ	bahut saare	*a lot, many*
ਸੈਲਾਨੀ	sailaanee	*tourists* (m./f.)
ਸਫ਼ਰ ਕਰਨਾ	safar karnaa	*to travel*
ਮਿਲ ਜਾਣਾ	mil jaanhaa	*to get, to receive*
ਬਾਅਦ ਦੁਪਹਿਰ	baa-a-d dupahir	*afternoon*
ਪਹੁੰਚਾ ਦੇਣਾ	pahunchaa denhaa	*to deliver, to cause to arrive*
ਸੁਰੱਖਿਅਤ ਸਫ਼ਰ	surakhkhiat safar	*safe journey*
ਸ਼ੁਭ ਇਛਾਵਾਂ	shubh ichaavaan	*best wishes*

Insight

'Ticket' is one of the numerous English words which have entered the Panjabi vocabulary. It is used in different expressions as in English but it also can mean 'postage stamp'.

ਅਭਿਆਸ abhiaas *Exercises*

After reading the dialogue and/or listening to the recording, try to do the following exercises.

1 Identify the speaker

The following phrases have been taken from the dialogue. Identify who said each of the phrases.

a ਬਹੁਤ ਸਾਰੇ ਸੈਲਾਨੀ ਇਸ ਗੱਡੀ ਵਿਚ ਸਫ਼ਰ ਕਰਦੇ ਹਨ। _____

b ਅੰਮ੍ਰਿਤਸਰ ਜਾਣ ਲਈ ਸਭ ਤੋਂ ਚੰਗੀ ਗੱਡੀ ਕਿਹੜੀ ਹੈ? _____

c ਨਵੀਆਂ ਥਾਂਵਾਂ ਦੇਖਣਾ ਚੰਗੀ ਗੱਲ ਹੈ। _____

d ਗੱਡੀ ਕਿੰਨੇ ਵਜੇ ਚਲਦੀ ਹੈ? _____

e ਕੀ ਸਾਨੂੰ ਫ਼ਰਸਟ ਕਲਾਸ ਵਿਚ ਸੀਟ ਮਿਲ ਜਾਏ ਗੀ? _____

2 Rewrite in the correct word order

a ਅਸੀਂ ਹਾਂ ਜਾਣਾ ਅੱਜ ਚਾਹੁੰਦੀਆਂ

b ਹੈ ਗੱਲ ਚੰਗੀ ਦੇਖਣਾ ਥਾਂਵਾਂ ਨਵੀਆਂ

c ਇਹ ਟਿਕਟਾਂ ਦੋ ਹਨ ਤੁਹਾਡੀਆਂ

---

2 *The Golden Temple*
ਗੱਲ ਬਾਤ ੨ ਹਰਿਮੰਦਰ ਸਾਹਿਬ
gall baat 2 harmandar saahib

◀) CD 2, TR 4, 01:41

Simran and Jaspreet are visiting the Golden Temple in Amritsar. They are accompanied by a guide provided by the temple management committee.

ਗਾਇਡ	ਸਿੱਖਾਂ ਦੇ ਚੌਥੇ ਗੁਰੂ, ਰਾਮਦਾਸ ਜੀ ਨੇ ਅੰਮ੍ਰਿਤਸਰ ਸ਼ਹਿਰ ਵਸਾਇਆ ਸੀ ਅਤੇ ਪੰਜਵੇਂ ਗੁਰੂ, ਅਰਜਨ ਦੇਵ ਜੀ ਨੇ ਹਰਿਮੰਦਰ ਸਾਹਿਬ ਬਣਵਾਇਆ ਸੀ।
ਸਿਮਰਨ	ਅੰਮ੍ਰਿਤਸਰ ਦਾ ਅਰਥ ਕੀ ਹੈ?
ਗਾਇਡ	ਇਸ ਦਾ ਲਫ਼ਜ਼ੀ ਅਰਥ ਹੈ: ਅੰਮ੍ਰਿਤ ਦਾ ਸਰੋਵਰ।
ਜਸਪ੍ਰੀਤ	ਹਰਿਮੰਦਰ ਸਾਹਿਬ ਨੂੰ ਸੁਨਹਿਰੀ ਮੰਦਰ ਕਿਉਂ ਕਿਹਾ ਜਾਂਦਾ ਹੈ?

ਗਾਇਡ	ਕਿਉਂ ਕਿ ਗੁੰਬਦਾਂ ਤੇ ਬਹੁਤ ਸਾਰਾ ਸੋਨਾ ਲੱਗਾ ਹੋਇਆ ਹੈ। ਇਹ ਮਹਾਰਾਜਾ ਰਣਜੀਤ ਸਿੰਘ ਨੇ ਲੱਗਵਾਇਆ ਸੀ।
ਸਿਮਰਨ	ਲਗਾਤਾਰ ਹੋ ਰਿਹਾ ਕੀਰਤਨ ਮਨ ਨੂੰ ਸ਼ਾਂਤੀ ਦੇਂਦਾ ਹੈ ਅਤੇ ਸਾਰਾ ਮਾਹੌਲ ਸਵਰਗ ਵਰਗਾ ਹੈ।
ਗਾਇਡ	ਇਸ ਕਰ ਕੇ ਦਰਸ਼ਕ ਨਾ ਕੇਵਲ ਭਾਰਤ ਤੋਂ ਇੱਥੇ ਆਉਂਦੇ ਹਨ ਬਲਕਿ ਸਾਰੀ ਦੁਨੀਆਂ ਤੋਂ ਆਉਂਦੇ ਹਨ।
Guide	*The town of Amritsar was founded by the fourth Guru of the Sikhs, Ram Das, and the fifth Guru Arjan Dev had Harmandar Saahib built.*
Simran	*What does the word Amritsar mean?*
Guide	*The literal meaning is 'a pool of nectar'.*
Jaspreet	*Why is the Harmandar Saahib called the Golden Temple?*
Guide	*Because the domes are covered in a lot of gold. This gold was put on by Maharaja Ranjit Singh.*
Simran	*The continuous recitation of religious hymns gives peace of mind and the entire atmosphere is heavenly.*
Guide	*That is why visitors come here not only from India but from all over the world.*

ਸ਼ਬਦਾਵਲੀ	shabdaavalee	*Vocabulary*
ਸਿੱਖਾਂ ਦੇ	sikhkhaan de	*of the Sikhs*
ਚੌਥੇ ਗੁਰੂ	chauthe guroo	*fourth Guru* (m.)
ਸ਼ਹਿਰ	shahir	*city* (m.)
ਵਸਾਉਣਾ	vasaaunhaa	*to establish, to found*
ਪੰਜਵਾਂ	panjvaan	*fifth*
ਬਣਵਾਉਣਾ	banhvaaunhaa	*to get built*
ਅਰਥ	arth	*meaning*
ਲਫ਼ਜ਼ੀ	lafzee	*literal*
ਅੰਮ੍ਰਿਤ	anmrit	*nectar, holy water* (m.)
ਸਰੋਵਰ	sarovar	*pool* (m.)
ਹਰਿਮੰਦਰ ਸਾਹਿਬ	harmandar saahib	*Golden Temple* (m.)
ਸੁਨਹਿਰੀ	sunahiree	*golden*
ਕਿਉਂ	kiun	*why*
ਕਿਹਾ ਜਾਂਦਾ ਹੈ।	kihaa jaandaa hai	*is said, is called*
ਕਿਉਂ ਕਿ	kiun ki	*because*
ਗੁੰਬਦ	gunbad	*dome* (m.)
ਸੋਨਾ	sonaa	*gold* (m.)

ਲੱਗਣਾ	laggnhaa	to be covered, laden
ਲੱਗਵਾਉਣਾ	laggvaaunhaa	to get covered
ਲਗਾਤਾਰ	lagaataar	continuously
ਕੀਰਤਨ	keertan	singing of hymns (m.)
ਮਨ	man	mind (m.)
ਸ਼ਾਂਤੀ	shaantee	peace (f.)
ਦੇਣਾ	denhaa	to give
ਸਾਰਾ ਮਾਹੌਲ	saaraa maahaul	whole atmosphere (m.)
ਸਵਰਗ	savarag	heaven (m.)
ਵਰਗਾ	vargaa	like (v.)
ਇਸ ਕਰ ਕੇ	is kar ke	that's why
ਦਰਸ਼ਕ	darshak	visitors (m./f.)
ਨਾ ਕੇਵਲ	naa keval	not only
ਬਲਕਿ	balki	but also
ਦੁਨੀਆਂ	duneeaan	world (f.)

Insight

Many Sikhs prefer to use the term '_darbaar saahib_' '**ਦਰਬਾਰ ਸਾਹਿਬ**' or '_harmandar saahib_' '**ਹਰਿਮੰਦਰ ਸਾਹਿਬ**' instead of 'Golden Temple' though all three terms are commonly used and are acceptable.

ਅਭਿਆਸ abhiaas _Exercises_

After reading the dialogue and/or listening to the recording, try to do the following exercises.

1 Matching

Match the questions with the appropriate answers.

ਸਵਾਲ savaal _question_

a ਅੰਮ੍ਰਿਤਸਰ ਦਾ ਅਰਥ ਕੀ ਹੈ?

b ਹਰਿਮੰਦਰ ਸਾਹਿਬ ਕਿਸ ਨੇ ਬਣਵਾਇਆ ਸੀ?

c ਅੰਮ੍ਰਿਤਸਰ ਸ਼ਹਿਰ ਕਿਸ ਨੇ ਵਸਾਇਆ ਸੀ?

d ਗੁੰਬਦਾਂ ਤੇ ਕਿਸ ਨੇ ਸੋਨਾ ਲਗਵਾਇਆ ਸੀ?

ਜਵਾਬ javaab _answer_

i ਚੌਥੇ ਗੁਰੂ ਜੀ ਨੇ।

ii ਅੰਮ੍ਰਿਤ ਦਾ ਸਰੋਵਰ।

iii ਮਹਾਰਾਜਾ ਰਣਜੀਤ ਸਿੰਘ ਨੇ।

iv ਪੰਜਵੇਂ ਗੁਰੂ ਜੀ ਨੇ।

2 Crossword

Complete the crossword in English using the clues given in Panjabi. Can you figure out what the 'mystery word' is in the shaded boxes?

੧ ਸੋਨਾ
੨ ਗੁੰਬਦ
੩ ਦਰਸ਼ਕ
੪ ਦੁਨੀਆਂ
੫ ਸ਼ਹਿਰ
੬ ਗੁਰੂ

ਬੋਲੀ ਬਾਰੇ bolee baare *Language points*

Conjunct verbs

Conjunct verbs have meanings which are specified by the nouns or adjectives that they include. Conjunct verbs are formed by combining a noun or adjective with an infinitive (either in its simple form or as a verb tense). For example, *to clean* in English merely requires the infinitive. In Panjabi *to clean* would require two words: ਸਾਫ਼ (*clean*, adjective) and ਕਰਨਾ (*to do*, infinitive). The adjective specifies the type or nature of the action while the infinitive directs the action. The most common infinitives used in conjunct constructions are ਕਰਨਾ (*to do*) and ਹੋਣਾ (*to be*). Here are some examples of common conjunct verbs using both adjectives and nouns.

With nouns

ਪਿਆਰ ਕਰਨਾ	*to love*
ਪਸੰਦ ਕਰਨਾ	*to like, to prefer*
ਕੰਮ ਕਰਨਾ	*to work*
ਸ਼ੁਰੂ ਕਰਨਾ	*to begin, to commence*
ਮੱਦਦ ਕਰਨਾ	*to help*
ਕੋਸ਼ਿਸ਼ ਕਰਨਾ	*to try*

With adjectives

ਸਾਫ਼ ਕਰਨਾ	*to clean*
ਖ਼ਤਮ ਕਰਨਾ	*to finish, to complete*
ਠੀਕ ਕਰਨਾ	*to fix, to correct*
ਬੰਦ ਕਰਨਾ	*to close*
ਘੱਟ ਕਰਨਾ	*to reduce, to lessen*

Here are a few examples to illustrate how conjunct verbs are used:

1 ਕੰਮ ਸਵੇਰੇ ਸ਼ੁਰੂ ਹੁੰਦਾ ਹੈ   *Work begins in the morning.*
   [ਸ਼ੁਰੂ ਹੋਣਾ *to begin* is an intransitive verb formed with the
   noun ਕੰਮ.]
2 ਮੈਂ ਤੁਹਾਡੀ ਉਡੀਕ ਕਰਾਂ ਗੀ   *I will wait for you.*
   [Here ਉਡੀਕ ਕਰਨਾ *to wait* is a transitive verb with ਉਡੀਕ as
   a noun. This is an example of a verbal expression which is
   formed exactly as a conjunct verb. However, the noun retains
   its own meaning and sense.]
3 ਮੇਰਾ ਵਿਆਹ ੧੯੬੪ ਵਿਚ ਹੋਇਆ ਸੀ   *I got married in 1964.*

There are some conjunct verbs in which neither ਕਰਨਾ nor ਹੋਣਾ is
involved.

ਦਿਖਾਈ ਦੇਣਾ	*to be visible*
ਯਾਦ ਆਉਣਾ	*to come to mind*
ਯਾਦ ਰੱਖਣਾ	*to bear in mind to remember*

Causative verbs

Causative verbs are groups of related verbs which share a similar
meaning, but which differ in terms of who is carrying out the action.
You have already come across such related verbs in Unit 10, in the
first dialogue when Simran says to Chaachee:

ਮੈਂ ਹਰ ਕਿਸਮ ਦੇ ਖਾਣੇ ਖਾਧੇ   *I ate every type of food.*

In the diary passage in Unit 10, Jaspreet writes:

ਮਾਮੀ ਜੀ ਨੇ ਸਾਨੂੰ ਰੋਟੀ ਖੁਆਈ   *Aunt fed us.*

As you can see from these examples, ਖੁਆਣਾ *to feed* and ਖਾਣਾ *to eat*
are clearly related to one another. However, the difference lies in who
the agent or 'doer' of the action is. Not all verbs are grouped into
causative pairs. However, there are a large number of verbs which

can be placed into such groups. Causative pairs and groupings are formed by a pattern of adding a suffix (or ending) to the stem of the verb as the action moves further away from the subject:

ਕਰਨਾ	*to do*
ਕਰਾਉਣਾ	*to cause to be done*
ਕਰਵਾਉਣਾ	*to cause to be done by someone else*
ਦੇਖਣਾ	*to see*
ਦਿਖਾਣਾ	*to be shown, to appear*
ਦਿਖਾਉਣਾ	*to show*
ਬਣਨਾ	**to make, to build**
ਬਣਾਉਣਾ	*to be made, to be built*
ਬਣਵਾਉਣਾ	*to have made or built (from/by someone else)*
ਪਕਾਉਣਾ	**to cook**
ਪਕਣਾ	*to be cooked*
ਪਕਵਾਉਣਾ	*to have cooked (by someone else), to cause to be cooked*
ਜਾਗਣਾ	**to wake**
ਜਗਾਉਣਾ	*to awaken*
ਜਗਵਾਉਣਾ	*to cause to wake*

The infinitive as a verbal noun

The simple verb, or infinitive, was explained in Unit 3 as the base of all Panjabi verbs. To refresh your memory, the infinitive of Panjabi verbs is formed by the root of the verb plus the ending -ਣਾ or -ਨਾ. By now you should be familiar with the various tenses of the Panjabi verb. In addition to being the base of all verb tenses, the infinitive can also be used as a noun. You will recall in the first dialogue that the booking clerk says to Jaspreet and Simran:

ਨਵੀਆਂ ਥਾਂਵਾਂ ਦੇਖਣਾ ਚੰਗੀ ਗੱਲ ਹੈ   *It's good seeing [to see] new places.*

Notice that the infinitive ਦੇਖਣਾ is not the verb of the sentence (ਹੋਣਾ is the verb) but that it is a verbal noun indicating an action (which behaves as a noun) within the sentence. Here are a few more examples of the infinitive as a verbal noun:

ਜਲਦੀ ਉਠਣਾ ਜ਼ਰੂਰੀ ਹੈ	*Waking up [to wake up] early is necessary.*
ਜ਼ਿਆਦਾ ਬੋਲਣਾ ਚੰਗਾ ਨਹੀਂ ਲੱਗਦਾ	*Talking [to talk] too much doesn't look good.*

ਪੜ੍ਹਨਾ ਸੌਖਾ ਹੈ, ਲਿਖਣਾ ਮੁਸ਼ਕਲ   *Reading [to read] is easy,*
                                                      writing [to write] is difficult.

When the infinitive has an object, it will correspond to the gender and number of that noun. Since the infinitive already has a masculine/singular appearance with the -ਆ ending, it does not change when the object is masculine and singular. However, when the object is masculine/plural it will take the ending -ਏ and when the object is feminine, then the ending changes to -ਈ, -ਈਆਂ if plural. Note the following examples:

ਨੌਕਰੀ ਕਰਨੀ	*working* (to work, to have a job)
ਕਿਤਾਬਾਂ ਪੜ੍ਹਨੀਆਂ	*reading* (to read) *books*
ਖਾਣਾ ਬਣਾਉਣਾ	*cooking* (to cook, to make food)
ਦਰਵਾਜ਼ੇ ਖੋਲ੍ਹਣੇ	*opening* (to open) *the doors*

Like other nouns, the infinitive is also affected by postpositions. The ending of the infinitive in the oblique, therefore, changes to the shortened form as discussed in Unit 8. Here are some examples of verbal nouns in the oblique:

ਮੈਂ ਹਾਲੇ ਬਾਹਰ ਜਾਣ ਨੂੰ ਤਿਆਰ ਨਹੀਂ ਹਾਂ	*I am not ready to go out yet.*
ਉਹਨਾਂ ਦੇ ਇੱਥੇ ਆਉਣ ਨਾਲ ਮੇਰਾ ਸਮਾਂ ਜ਼ਾਇਆ ਹੋ ਗਿਆ	*Their coming here wasted my time.*
ਚਾਹ ਪੀਣ ਮੌਕਾ ਨਹੀਂ ਮਿਲਿਆ	*There wasn't an opportunity to drink tea.*

The passive voice

In English *I said* is in the active voice (i.e. the subject of the verb is directly carrying out the action) and *it was said* is in the passive voice (i.e. the subject is on the receiving end of the action). The same distinction is also true in Panjabi. The passive voice can be formed in two ways. In the first form the passive verb (the participle [see Unit 12] and the form of ਜਾਣਾ) agrees with the subject:

ਲੁਧਿਆਣੇ ਵਿਚ ਪੰਜਾਬੀ ਬੋਲੀ ਜਾਂਦੀ ਹੈ	*Panjabi is spoken in Ludhiana.*
ਕਿਹਾ ਜਾਂਦਾ ਹੈ ਕਿ ਅੰਮ੍ਰਿਤਸਰ ਸਿੱਖਾਂ ਦਾ ਸ਼ਹਿਰ ਹੈ	*It is said that Amritsar is the city of the Sikhs.*
ਕੱਲ੍ਹ ਤਕ ਸਾਰਾ ਕੰਮ ਕਰ ਲਿਆ ਜਾਏਗਾ	*By tomorrow all of the work will be done.*

The passive voice can also be expressed by using the postpositions ਤੋਂ and ਕੋਲੋਂ to indicate by whom the action was done. In this form the verb of the sentence agrees with the object. Note the following examples:

ਕਪ ਮੇਰੇ ਤੋਂ ਟੁੱਟ ਗਿਆ	*The cup was broken by me.*
ਕੁਰਸੀ ਮੇਰੇ ਤੋਂ ਟੁੱਟ ਗਈ	*The chair was broken by me.*
ਗਲਤੀ ਪਿਤਾ ਜੀ ਕੋਲੋਂ ਹੋਈ	*The mistake was made by father.*

You will recall from earlier in this unit that causative verbs are groups of related verbs. Active intransitive verbs and passive transitive verbs (see Unit 10) can both be used to express the passive voice. For example, the verb ਬਣਨਾ *to be made* and ਬਣਾਉਣਾ *to make* can both be used to give the sense *is/are made*.

ਜੁੱਤੀਆਂ ਇੱਥੇ ਬਣਦੀਆਂ ਹਨ	*Shoes are made here.*
ਜੁੱਤੀਆਂ ਇੱਥੇ ਬਣਾਈਆਂ ਜਾਂਦੀਆਂ ਹਨ	*Shoes are made here.*

ਵਰਗਾ 'vargaa' *like*

The postposition ਵਰਗਾ is used when comparing objects or people with one another in terms of quality, size, colour, etc. You will recall in Dialogue 2 that the guide described the atmosphere of the Golden Temple: ਮਾਹੌਲ ਸਵਰਗ ਵਰਗਾ ਹੈ (*the atmosphere is heavenly* (lit. like heaven)). ਵਰਗਾ is affected by the gender and number of the person or object being likened to, so that the ending of ਵਰਗਾ is masculine, in this example, since *heaven* is a masculine noun. Note in the following examples how the ending of ਵਰਗਾ changes accordingly:

ਇਹ ਕੁੜੀ ਪਰੀ ਵਰਗੀ ਹੈ	*This girl is like a fairy.*
ਇਹ ਕੁੜੀਆਂ ਪਰੀਆਂ ਵਰਗੀਆਂ ਹਨ	*The girls are like fairies.*
ਉਸ ਦਾ ਮਕਾਨ ਮੱਹਲ ਵਰਗਾ ਵੱਡਾ ਹੈ	*His house is big like a palace.*
ਉਹ ਮੁੰਡੇ ਦੈਂਤਾਂ ਵਰਗੇ ਹਨ	*Those boys are like giants.*
ਉਹ ਦਵਾਈ ਖੰਡ ਵਰਗੀ ਮਿੱਠੀ ਹੈ	*That medicine is sweet like sugar.*

There are also other words for describing likeness in Panjabi: ਜਿਹਾ (jihaa), ਵਾਂਗੂੰ (vaa<u>n</u>goo<u>n</u>) and ਤਰ੍ਹਾਂ (<u>t</u>ar-h-aa<u>n</u>). These words all appear in this book.

> ### Insight
> The construction of the sentence '*naa keval . . . bal ki*' 'ਨਾ ਕੇਵਲ . . . ਬਲਕਿ' is an idiomatic one. It resembles the English

178

construction of 'not only . . . but'. There are a number of words in English which convey the meaning of 'bal ki' 'ਬਲਕਿ' such as 'but', 'rather', 'on the contrary,' and 'on the other hand'.

ਵਿਆਖਿਆ viaakhiaa *Commentary*

1 Railways

India has one of the largest railway networks in the world. Trains may be both the most luxurious and most uncomfortable way to travel in India, but they are always entertaining. The fastest trains to Panjab from Delhi are the Shan-e-Panjab and the Shatabdi. However, almost all trains heading north from Delhi will pass through Panjab. There is also a train called the Samjota Express which crosses the India–Pakistan border from East to West Panjab at Attari.

2 The city of Amritsar

The city of Amritsar is one of the central towns in the corridor to India for those travelling by land to and from Central Asia. Amritsar is a cultural and religious centre not only in the state of Panjab but also in South Asia. Founded over 400 years ago, Amritsar has become the political and cultural centre of the region and is the religious centre for the Sikh faith. At the time of the annexation of Panjab by the British in 1849, Amritsar was the largest city in Panjab. However, other larger cities such as Lahore and Ludhiana have now surpassed

Amritsar in terms of size and economic dynamism since the partition in 1947. Today Amritsar is still the most significant religious centre for the Sikhs, being the home of the Golden Temple, and continues to be regarded as one of the main tourist attractions of Panjab.

Insight

Culture and language go together. We cannot appreciate any language without the knowledge of costume, dress, food, rituals, celebrations, history, literature, music and religion of the native speakers.

ਅਭਿਆਸ abhiaas *Exercises*

After reading the dialogue and/or listening to the recording, try to do the following exercises.

1 Fill in the blanks

a ਜਿਹੜੀ ਗੱਡੀ ਜਲੰਧਰ ਤੋਂ ਅੰਮ੍ਰਿਤਸਰ ਜਾਂਦੀ ਹੈ ਉਸ ਦਾ ਨਾਮ _____ ਹੈ।

b ਬਹੁਤ ਸਾਰੇ _____ ਉਸ ਗੱਡੀ ਵਿਚ _____ ਹਨ।

c ਅੰਮ੍ਰਿਤਸਰ ਦਾ _____ ਅਰਥ ਹੈ: '_____'।

d ਲਗਾਤਾਰ _____ ਮਨ ਨੂੰ _____ ਦੇਂਦਾ ਹੈ ਅਤੇ ਸਾਰਾ ਮਾਹੌਲ _____ ਵਰਗਾ ਹੈ।

2 Answer the following questions in Panjabi

🔊 CD 2, TR 4, 02:48

a Who was the founder of the city of Amritsar?

b What is the meaning of Amritsar?

c Why is Harmandar Saahib known as the Golden Temple?

3 Listening

🔊 CD 2, TR 4, 03:24

You are standing at the ticket counter at Amritsar railway station speaking with the booking clerk about your planned journey to Delhi. Listen to the recording and converse with the ticket master by translating the English sentences given to you.

180

You	I want to go to Delhi today. Which is the best train to Delhi?
Ticket master	ਸ਼ੇਤਾਬਦੀ ਐਕਸਪ੍ਰੈਸ ਸਭ ਤੋਂ ਚੰਗੀ ਹੈ। ਬਹੁਤ ਲੋਕ ਉਸ ਵਿਚ ਸਫਰ ਕਰਦੇ ਹਨ।
You	Will I be able to get a seat in second class?
Ticket master	ਹਾਂ ਜੀ ਕੀ ਤੁਹਾਨੂੰ ਸਿਰਫ਼ ਇੱਕ ਪਾਸੇ ਦੀ ਟਿਕਟ ਚਾਹੀਦੀ ਹੈ?
You	No, I want a return ticket. What time does the train leave from Amritsar?
Ticket master	ਗੱਡੀ ਅੰਮ੍ਰਿਤਸਰ ਤੋਂ ਢਾਈ ਵਜੇ ਚਲਦੀ ਹੈ ਅਤੇ ਦਿੱਲੀ ਅੱਠ ਵਜੇ ਰਾਤ ਨੂੰ ਪਹੁੰਚਦੀ ਹੈ।
You	OK, give me one second-class ticket.
Ticket master	ਸੁਰੱਖਿਅਤ ਸਫਰ ਲਈ ਸ਼ੁਭ ਇਛਾਵਾਂ।

Ten important things to remember

1 Conjunct verbs have meanings which are specified by the nouns or adjectives that they include. Example: 'piaar karnaa' **ਪਿਆਰ ਕਰਨਾ** – to love. 'piaar' **ਪਿਆਰ** means 'love' and 'karnaa' **ਕਰਨਾ** means 'to do'. (b) 'saaf karnaa' **ਸਾਫ਼ ਕਰਨਾ** – to clean. 'saaf' **ਸਾਫ਼** means 'clean' and 'karnaa' **ਕਰਨਾ** means 'to do'.

2 Causative verbs are groups of related verbs which share a similar meaning but which differ in terms of who is carrying out the action. Examples: karnaa– to do. 'karaaunhaa' **ਕਰਾਨਾ** – to cause to be done. 'karvaaunhaa' **ਕਰਵਾਨਾ** – to cause to be done by someone else.

3 The infinitive verb is the base of all verb tenses but it can also be used as a noun.

4 The passive voice can be formed in two ways in Panjabi. Examples: a) *ludhiaanhe vich panjaabee bolee jaandee hai* ਲੁਧਿਆਣੇ ਵਿਚ ਪੰਜਾਬੀ ਬੋਲੀ ਜਾਂਦੀ ਹੈ Panjabi is spoken in Ludhiana. b) *kap mere ton tutt giaa see* ਕਪ ਮੇਰੇ ਤੋਂ ਟੁੱਟ ਗਿਆ ਸੀ The cup was broken by me.

5 The postposition '*vargaa*' 'ਵਰਗਾ' is used when comparing objects or people with one another in terms of quality, size, colour, etc. There are also other words for describing likeness in Panjabi, such as: '*jihaa*' 'ਜਿਹਾ', '*vaangoon*' 'ਵਾਂਗੂੰ' and '*tar-h-aan*' 'ਤਰ੍ਹਾਂ'.

6 '*Vargaa*' 'ਵਰਗਾ' is affected by the gender and number of the person or object. Examples: a) *paree vargee kurhee* ਪਰੀ ਵਰਗੀ ਕੁੜੀ Girl like a fairy. b) *daintaan varge munde* ਦੈਂਤਾਂ ਵਰਗੇ ਮੁੰਡੇ Boys like giants.

7 When a verb has more than one object, the verb usually agrees with the last one.

8 Since ordinals are adjectives they follow the same rules of agreement as other adjectives.

9 The word '*gaddee*' 'ਗੱਡੀ' in Panjabi can mean either a car or a train.

10 The Sikhs have a special relationship with the Panjabi language for two reasons a) the majority of Sikhs are originally from Panjab; b) their sacred religious book is written in the '*gurmukhi*'.

12

ਘਰ ਨੂੰ ਚਿੱਠੀ
ghar noo̱n chiththee
A letter home

In this unit you will learn:

- How to write a letter
- How to express *how did it go?*
- How to talk about where you've visited
- How to construct sentences beginning with *if*

---

1 *Changing money*
ਗੱਲ ਬਾਤ ੧ ਪੈਸੇ ਬਦਲਣਾ
gall baa̱t 1 paise ba̱dalnhaa

◀) CD 2, TR 5, 00:17

Simran and Jaspreet are in the Air India office in Chandigarh waiting to get their tickets confirmed. While they are there a German tourist, Paul, strikes up a conversation with them.

ਪੋਲ	ਮੇਰਾ ਨਾਮ ਪੋਲ ਹੈ। ਮੈਂ ਜਰਮਨ ਹਾਂ। ਮੈਨੂੰ ਅੰਗਰੇਜ਼ੀ ਨਹੀਂ ਆਉਂਦੀ ਪਰ ਮੈਂ ਪੰਜਾਬੀ ਬੋਲ ਸਕਦਾ ਹਾਂ।
ਸਿਮਰਨ	ਅਸੀਂ ਅਮਰੀਕਨ ਹਾਂ। ਅਸੀਂ ਵੀ ਪੰਜਾਬੀ ਬੋਲ ਸਕਦੀਆਂ ਹਾਂ। ਅਸੀਂ ਤਿੰਨ ਹਫ਼ਤਿਆਂ ਲਈ ਭਾਰਤ ਆਈਆਂ ਹਾਂ। ਸਾਨੂੰ ਬਹੁਤ ਹੀ ਚੰਗਾ ਲੱਗਾ ਹੈ।
ਪੋਲ	ਮੈਂ ਅੱਜ ਹੀ ਅੰਮ੍ਰਿਤਸਰ ਤੋਂ ਵਾਪਸ ਆਇਆ ਹਾਂ। ਜੇ ਅਸੀਂ ਪਹਿਲੇ ਮਿਲਦੇ ਤਾਂ ਅਸੀਂ ਇਕੱਠੇ ਘੁੰਮਦੇ। ਤੁਸੀਂ ਕਿੱਥੇ ਕਿੱਥੇ ਗਈਆਂ ?

ਜਸਪ੍ਰੀਤ	ਅਸੀਂ ਬਹੁਤ ਜਗ੍ਹਾ ਦੇਖੀਆਂ ਹਨ। ਤੁਹਾਨੂੰ ਕਿਹੜੀ ਜਗ੍ਹਾ ਸਭ ਤੋਂ ਚੰਗੀ ਲੱਗੀ ?
ਪੋਲ	ਤਾਜ ਮੱਹਲ ਮੈਂ ਪਹਿਲੇ ਦੇਖ ਚੁਕਾ ਸੀ। ਹੁਣ ਮੈਂ ਹਰਿਮੰਦਰ ਸਾਹਿਬ ਦੇਖਿਆ ਹੈ। ਹਰਿਮੰਦਰ ਸਾਹਿਬ ਦਾ ਕੋਈ ਮੁਕਾਬਲਾ ਨਹੀਂ।
ਜਸਪ੍ਰੀਤ ਤੇ ਸਿਮਰਨ	ਅਸੀਂ ਤੁਹਾਡੇ ਨਾਲ ਸਹਿਮਤ ਹਾਂ।
ਪੋਲ	ਮੈਂ ਪੈਸੇ ਬਦਲਣਾ ਚਾਹੁੰਦਾ ਹਾਂ। ਮੇਰੇ ਕੋਲ ਯੂ.ਐਸ. ਡਾਲਰ ਹਨ। ਮੈਨੂੰ ਕੀ ਕਰਨਾ ਚਾਹੀਦਾ ਹੈ ?
ਸਿਮਰਨ	ਤੁਸੀਂ ਕਿਸੇ ਬੈਂਕ ਜਾਓ। ਡਾਲਰ ਦੇ ਕੇ ਰੁਪਏ ਲੈ ਲਵੋ। ਇਹ ਕੰਮ ਸੌਖਾ ਹੈ।
ਪੋਲ	ਜੇ ਮੈਂ ਬੈਂਕ ਦੇ ਰੇਟ ਤੋਂ ਜ਼ਿਆਦਾ ਲੈਣਾ ਚਾਵਾਂ ?
ਜਸਪ੍ਰੀਤ	. . . ਤਾਂ ਤੁਹਾਨੂੰ ਕਿਸੇ ਦੁਕਾਨਦਾਰ ਨੂੰ ਪੁੱਛਣਾ ਚਾਹੀਦਾ ਹੈ।
ਪੋਲ	ਧੰਨਵਾਦ। ਮੇਰੀ ਵਾਰੀ ਆ ਗਈ ਹੈ। ਉਮੀਦ ਹੈ ਕਿ ਫਿਰ ਮਿਲਾਂ ਗੇ।

Paul	*My name is Paul. I'm German. I don't know any English but I can speak Panjabi.*
Simran	*We are American. We can also speak Panjabi. We've come to India for three weeks. We like it very much.*
Paul	*I have just come from Amritsar today. Had we met before, we could have travelled together. Where have you been?*
Jaspreet	*We have seen many places. Which one did you like the most?*
Paul	*I had already seen the Taj Mahal. Now I have seen Harmandar Saahib. There is no comparison with Harmandar Saahib.*
Jaspreet and Simran	*We agree with you.*
Paul	*I want to change some money. I have US dollars. What should I do?*
Simran	*Go to any bank. Get rupees by giving dollars. This is not difficult to do [lit. an easy task].*
Paul	*And if I want a higher rate than the bank?*
Jaspreet	*. . . then you should ask any shopkeeper.*
Paul	*Thanks. My turn has come now. Hope we'll meet again.*

ਸ਼ਬਦਾਵਲੀ	shab<u>d</u>aavalee	*Vocabulary*
ਵਾਪਸ	vaapas	*return, back*
ਜੇ	je	*if*
ਮਿਲਣਾ	milnhaa	*to meet*
ਪਹਿਲੇ	pahile	*before*
ਇਕੱਠੇ	ikaththe	*together* (v.)
ਤਾਂ	<u>taan</u>	*then*

ਜਗ੍ਹਾ	jag-h-aa	*place* (f.)
ਦੇਖਣਾ	<u>d</u>ekhnhaa	*to see*
ਮੁਕਾਬਲਾ	mukaablaa	*comparison, competition* (m.)
ਸਹਿਮਤ	sahima<u>t</u>	*agree*
ਬਦਲਣਾ	ba<u>d</u>alnhaa	*to change, exchange*
ਕੰਮ	ka<u>n</u>m	*job, work, task* (m.)
ਸੌਖਾ	saukhaa	*easy, simple* (v.)
ਉਮੀਦ	umee<u>d</u>	*hope* (f.)
ਫਿਰ	phir	*again*

Insight

The ordinal number 'first', can be translated into Panjabi as either *'pahilaa'* ਪਹਿਲਾ or *'pahilee'* ਪਹਿਲੀ. The oblique form of *'pahilaa'* ਪਹਿਲਾ is *'pahile'* ਪਹਿਲੇ but here *'pahile'* ਪਹਿਲੀ means 'before'.

ਅਭਿਆਸ abhiaas *Exercises*

After reading the dialogue and/or listening to the recording, try to do the following exercises.

1 True or false?

a ਜਸਪ੍ਰੀਤ ਤੇ ਸਿਮਰਨ ਅਮਰੀਕਨ ਹਨ ਪਰ ਉਹਨਾਂ ਨੂੰ ਪੰਜਾਬੀ ਨਹੀਂ ਆਉਂਦੀ ।   True/False

b ਪੌਲ ਨੇ ਕਿਹਾ ਕਿ ਜੇ ਉਹ ਪਹਿਲੇ ਮਿਲਦੇ ਤਾਂ ਉਹ ਇਕੱਠੇ ਘੁੰਮਦੇ ।   True/False

c ਜਦੋਂ ਪੌਲ ਨੇ ਦੋਨਾਂ ਭੈਣਾਂ ਨੂੰ ਪੈਸੇ ਬਦਲਣ ਬਾਰੇ ਪੁੱਛਿਆ ਤਾਂ ਉਹਨਾਂ ਨੇ ਜਵਾਬ ਦਿੱਤਾ ਕਿ ਇਹ ਕੰਮ ਬਹੁਤ ਮੁਸ਼ਕਲ ਹੈ ।   True/False

d ਜਸਪ੍ਰੀਤ ਤੇ ਸਿਮਰਨ ਨੇ ਪੌਲ ਨੂੰ ਕਿਹਾ ਕਿ ਜੇ ਉਹ ਬੈਂਕ ਦੇ ਰੇਟ ਤੋਂ ਜ਼ਿਆਦਾ ਲੈਣਾ ਚਾਹੁੰਦਾ ਹੈ ਤਾਂ ਫਿਰ ਕਿਸੇ ਦੁਕਾਨਦਾਰ ਨੂੰ ਪੁੱਛਣਾ ਚਾਹੀਦਾ ਹੈ ।   True/False

2 Fill in the blanks

a ਪੌਲ _____ ਹੈ ਤੇ ਉਸ ਨੂੰ _____ ਨਹੀਂ ਆਉਂਦੀ ਪਰ ਉਹ _____ ਬੋਲ ਸਕਦਾ ਹੈ ।

b ਪੌਲ _____ ਪਹਿਲੇ ਦੇਖ ਚੁਕਾ ਸੀ ।

c ਜਸਪ੍ਰੀਤ, ਸਿਮਰਨ ਤੇ ਪੌਲ _____ ਹਨ ਕਿ ਹਰਿਮੰਦਰ ਸਾਹਿਬ ਦਾ ਕੋਈ _____ ਨਹੀਂ ।

d ਪੌਲ ਅੱਜ ਹੀ _____ ਤੋਂ ਵਾਪਸ ਆਇਆ ਹੈ ।

A letter home ਘਰ ਨੂੰ ਚਿੱਠੀ **ghar noo<u>n</u> chiththee**

ਪਿਆਰੇ ਪਿਤਾ ਤੇ ਮਾਤਾ ਜੀ,   ੪ ਜੁਲਾਈ

ਸਤਿ ਸ੍ਰੀ ਅਕਾਲ

ਸਾਨੂੰ ਉਮੀਦ ਹੈ ਕਿ ਤੁਸੀਂ ਠੀਕ ਠਾਕ ਹੋ। ਅਸੀਂ ਇੱਥੇ ਖ਼ੁਸ਼ ਹਾਂ। ਅਸੀਂ ਪਿੰਡ ਗਈਆਂ
ਸੀ ਤੇ ਉਹ ਮਕਾਨ ਦੇਖਿਆ ਜਿੱਥੇ ਤੁਸੀਂ ਰਹਿੰਦੇ ਹੁੰਦੇ ਸੀ। ਪਿੰਡ ਦੇ ਲੋਕਾਂ ਨੇ ਸਾਨੂੰ ਬਹੁਤ
ਪਿਆਰ ਦਿਖਾਇਆ, ਪਰ ਗਰਮੀ ਬਹੁਤ ਸੀ। ਇੱਕ ਵਾਰੀ ਤਿੰਨ ਦਿਨ ਲਗਾਤਾਰ ਬਾਰਸ਼
ਹੁੰਦੀ ਰਹੀ ਸੀ। ਇੱਥੇ ਆ ਕੇ ਸਾਡੀ ਪੰਜਾਬੀ ਦੀ ਸ਼ਬਦਾਵਲੀ ਬਹੁਤ ਵੱਧ ਗਈ ਹੈ। ਅਸੀਂ
ਹੈਰਾਨ ਹੋਈਆਂ ਹਾਂ ਕਿ ਇੱਥੇ ਐਨੀ ਅਬਾਦੀ ਤੇ ਟੈਰਿਫ਼ਿਕ ਹੈ। ਅਸੀਂ ਤੁਹਾਡੇ ਲਈ ਬਹੁਤ
ਸੁਗਾਤਾਂ ਖ਼ਰੀਦੀਆਂ ਹਨ। ਅਸੀਂ ਚਾਹੁੰਦੀਆਂ ਸੀ ਕਿ ਤੁਸੀਂ ਸਾਡੇ ਨਾਲ ਹੁੰਦੇ।

ਸ਼ੁਭ ਇੱਛਾਵਾਂ ਨਾਲ
ਤੁਹਾਡੀਆਂ ਪਿਆਰੀਆਂ ਬੇਟੀਆਂ
ਜਸਪ੍ਰੀਤ ਤੇ ਸਿਮਰਨ

Dear Dad and Mum,   4 July

Sat sri akal.

*We hope that you are fine. We are happy here. We went to the
village and saw the house where you used to live. The people of
the village have shown us tremendous affection but it was very
hot. Once, it rained for three days without stopping. Our Panjabi
vocabulary has increased a lot by coming here. We are astonished
to see so many people and so much traffic. We have bought many
presents for you. We wish you were here with us.*

With best wishes,
Your loving daughters,
Jaspreet and Simran

ਸ਼ਬਦਾਵਲੀ	**shab<u>d</u>aavalee**	*Vocabulary*
ਪਿਆਰੇ	piaare	*dear, beloved* (v.)
ਕਿ	ki	*that*
ਖ਼ੁਸ਼	<u>kh</u>ush	*happy*

ਮਕਾਨ	makaan	*house* (m.)
ਜਿੱਥੇ	ji<u>thth</u>e	*where*
ਲੋਕ	lok	*people* (m.)
ਪਿਆਰ	piaar	*love, affection* (m.)
ਦਿਖਾਉਣਾ	<u>d</u>ikhaaunhaa	*to show*
ਗਰਮੀ	garmee	*heat, warmth (hot, warm)* (f.)
ਵਾਰੀ	vaaree	*turn, instance* (f.)
ਅਬਾਦੀ	abaa<u>d</u>ee	*population* (f.)
ਲਗਾਤਾਰ	lagaa<u>t</u>aar	*continuously, on-going*
ਬਾਰਸ਼	baarash	*rain* (f.)

Insight

The use of greetings is a social and cultural obligation. That is why greetings are frequently exchanged when meeting someone, speaking on the telephone and in the form of salutation in letters.

ਅਭਿਆਸ abhiaas *Exercises*

After reading the letter and/or listening to the recording, try to do the following exercises.

1 Complete the box

ਲਗਾਤਾਰ		
	piaare	
ਖ਼ੁਸ਼		
		warmth
	vaaree	

2 Answer the questions about Jaspreet and Simran's letter home

a ਜਸਪ੍ਰੀਤ ਤੇ ਸਿਮਰਨ ਨੇ ਪਿੰਡ ਵਿਚ ਕੀ ਦੇਖਿਆ ?
b ਇੱਕ ਵਾਰੀ ਤਿੰਨ ਦਿਨ ਲਗਾਤਾਰ ਕੀ ਹੁੰਦੀ ਰਹੀ ਸੀ ?

c ਜਸਪ੍ਰੀਤ ਤੇ ਸਿਮਰਨ ਕਿਉਂ ਹੈਰਾਨ ਹੋਈਆਂ ਹਨ?

d ਜਸਪ੍ਰੀਤ ਤੇ ਸਿਮਰਨ ਨੇ ਆਪਣੇ ਮਾਤਾ ਜੀ ਤੇ ਪਿਤਾ ਜੀ ਲਈ ਕੀ ਖ਼ਰੀਦਿਆ?

---

2 Simran at the post office
ਗੱਲ ਬਾਤ ੨ ਸਿਮਰਨ ਡਾਕਖ਼ਾਨੇ ਤੇ
gall baat 2 simran daakkhaane te

◀ CD 2, TR 5, 02:54

ਸਿਮਰਨ	ਮੈਂ ਇਹ ਚਿੱਠੀ ਅਮਰੀਕਾ ਭੇਜਣੀ ਹੈ।
ਡਾਕਬਾਬੂ	ਕੀ ਤੁਸੀਂ ਸਮੁੰਦਰੀ ਡਾਕ ਰਾਹੀਂ ਭੇਜਣੀ ਹੈ ਜਾਂ ਹਵਾਈ ਡਾਕ ਰਾਹੀਂ?
ਸਿਮਰਨ	ਹਵਾਈ ਡਾਕ ਰਾਹੀਂ।
ਡਾਕਬਾਬੂ	ਇਸ ਤੇ ੧੨ ਰੁਪਏ ਦੀਆਂ ਟਿਕਟਾਂ ਲਾਓ।
ਸਿਮਰਨ	ਅੱਛਾ ਜੀ। ਧੰਨਵਾਦ।

Simran	*I want to send this letter to America.*
Postal worker	*Do you want to send the letter by sea or by air mail?*
Simran	*By air mail.*
Postal worker	*Put 12 rupees' worth of stamps on it [the letter].*
Simran	*OK. Thanks.*

ਸ਼ਬਦਾਵਲੀ	shabdaavalee	*Vocabulary*
ਚਿੱਠੀ	chiththee	*letter* (f.)
ਭੇਜਣਾ	bhejnhaa	*to send, to post*
ਸਮੁੰਦਰ	samundar	*sea* (m.)

ਡਾਕ	daak	*mail, post* (f.)
ਸਮੁੰਦਰੀ ਡਾਕ	sam<u>u</u>ndaree daak	*sea mail* (f.)
ਰਾਹੀਂ	raahee<u>n</u>	*via, by*
ਹਵਾਈ	havaaee	*by air*
ਹਵਾਈ ਡਾਕ	havaaee daak	*air mail* (f.)
ਟਿਕਟ	tikat	*stamp* (f.)

ਬੋਲੀ ਬਾਰੇ   bolee baare   *Language points*

The perfect tenses

The perfect tenses describe actions which have been completed.

Present perfect

The present perfect tense in Panjabi refers to those actions which have just occurred, such as *I have eaten*. It is generally used when one is concerned with the present effects of something which happened in the recent past. You will recall from Unit 9 that the verb ਚੁਕਣਾ is used to express *to have already done* or *to have finished doing*. The stem that is used with ਚੁਕਣਾ represents the action in the present perfect tense that has already occurred. The present perfect of ਖਾਣਾ *to eat* is as follows:

Masculine singular	ਮੈਂ ਖਾ ਚੁਕਾ/ਚੁਕਿਆ ਹਾਂ	*I have eaten*
Feminine singular	ਮੈਂ ਖਾ ਚੁਕੀ ਹਾਂ	*I have eaten*
Masculine plural	ਅਸੀਂ ਖਾ ਚੁਕੇ ਹਾਂ	*we have eaten*
Feminine plural	ਅਸੀਂ ਖਾ ਚੁਕੀਆਂ ਹਾਂ	*we have eaten*
Masculine informal singular	ਤੂੰ ਖਾ ਚੁਕਾ/ਚੁਕਿਆ ਹੈਂ	*you have eaten*
Feminine informal singular	ਤੂੰ ਖਾ ਚੁਕੀ ਹੈਂ	*you have eaten*
Formal/masculine plural	ਤੁਸੀਂ ਖਾ ਚੁਕੇ ਹੋ	*you have eaten*
Masculine singular	ਇਹ/ਉਹ ਖਾ ਚੁਕਾ/ਚੁਕਿਆ ਹੈ	*he has eaten*
Feminine singular	ਇਹ/ਉਹ ਖਾ ਚੁਕੀ ਹੈ	*she has eaten*
Formal/masculine plural	ਇਹ/ਉਹ ਖਾ ਚੁਕੇ ਹਨ	*(he has)/they have eaten*
Feminine plural	ਇਹ/ਉਹ ਖਾ ਚੁਕੀਆਂ ਹਨ	*they have eaten*

Past perfect

The past perfect tense is used when the effects of an action in the remote past are being referred to in the more recent past. In English *to eat* in the past perfect would be expressed as *had eaten*. The past perfect tense in Panjabi is formed similarly to the present perfect tense as just shown, except that the present auxiliary verbs are used in the present perfect while the past perfect tense is formed with the past form of the auxiliary verbs. The following examples show *to eat* ਖਾਣਾ in the past perfect tense:

Masculine singular	ਮੈਂ ਖਾ ਚੁਕਾ/ਚੁਕਿਆ ਸੀ	*I had eaten*
Feminine singular	ਮੈਂ ਖਾ ਚੁਕੀ ਸੀ	*I had eaten*
Masculine plural	ਅਸੀਂ ਖਾ ਚੁਕੇ ਸੀ	*we had eaten*
Feminine plural	ਅਸੀਂ ਖਾ ਚੁਕੀਆਂ ਸੀ	*we had eaten*
Masculine informal singular	ਤੂੰ ਖਾ ਚੁਕਾ/ਚੁਕਿਆ ਸੀ	*you had eaten*
Feminine informal singular	ਤੂੰ ਖਾ ਚੁਕੀ ਸੀ	*you had eaten*
Formal/masculine plural	ਤੁਸੀਂ ਖਾ ਚੁਕੇ ਸੀ	*you had eaten*
Masculine singular	ਇਹ/ਉਹ ਖਾ ਚੁਕਾ/ ਚੁਕਿਆ ਸੀ	*he had eaten*
Feminine singular	ਇਹ/ਉਹ ਖਾ ਚੁਕੀ ਸੀ	*she had eaten*
Formal/masculine plural	ਇਹ/ਉਹ ਖਾ ਚੁਕੇ ਸਨ	*he/they had eaten*
Feminine plural	ਇਹ/ਉਹ ਖਾ ਚੁਕੀਆਂ ਸਨ	*they had eaten*

Compound constructions with ਲੈਣਾ, ਦੇਣਾ and ਜਾਣਾ can also be used to express the present and past perfect, most commonly when there is an object present. Notice the following examples:

ਮੈਂ ਖਾਣਾ ਖਾ ਲਿਆ ਹੈ	*I have eaten food.*
ਉਸ ਨੇ ਸਾਨੂੰ ਸੁਗਾਤ ਦੇ ਦਿੱਤੀ ਹੈ	*He has given us a gift.*

The present perfect continuous and the past perfect continuous are expressed in the same manner as the present and past continuous tenses except that an indication of time is used to denote whether or not the action is in the perfect tense:

present continuous	ਬਾਰਸ਼ ਹੋ ਰਹੀ ਹੈ	*It is raining.*
present perfect continuous	ਬਾਰਸ਼ ਦੋ ਦਿਨ ਤੋਂ ਹੋ ਰਹੀ ਹੈ	*It has been raining for two days.*

past continuous	ਬਾਰਸ਼ ਹੋ ਰਹੀ ਸੀ	*It was raining.*
past perfect	ਬਾਰਸ਼ ਦੇ ਦਿਨ ਤੋਂ	*It had been raining*
continuous	ਹੋ ਰਹੀ ਸੀ	*for two days.*

How did it go?

In Panjabi, *how did it go?* is expressed through the use of the continuous form of **ਰਹਿਣਾ**. You have already been introduced to **ਰਹੀ/ਰਿਹਾ** as the continuous tense form of **ਰਹਿਣਾ** *to stay, to live* equivalent to the English -*ing*. In Unit 5 Geeta asks Sita: **ਤੂੰ ਕੀ ਕਰ ਰਹੀ ਹੈਂ ?** literally meaning *What are you doing?* The continuous form of **ਰਹਿਣਾ** can have another quite different sense as *how did it go?*. Although the form of **ਰਹਿਣਾ** is in the continuous, the sense of the sentence refers to the past:

| ਤੁਹਾਡੀ ਇੰਡੀਆ ਦੀ ਫੇਰੀ ਕਿਵੇਂ ਰਹੀ ? | *How was your tour of India?* |
| ਤੁਹਾਡਾ ਦਿਨ ਕਿਵੇਂ ਰਿਹਾ ?| *How was your day?* |

ਰਹੀ/ਰਿਹਾ in these examples means outcome or conclusion. Therefore, this sentence has the sense *How did your trip to India go?* and *How did your day go?* Notice that the form of **ਰਹਿਣਾ** corresponds with the gender/number character of the object being described, in this case **ਫੇਰੀ** (*trip*, *tour*) which is feminine. *How did it go?* is a colloquial phrase which you will find useful when informally asking someone about their day or trip.

The subjunctive

The subjunctive mood (set of verb tenses) is commonly used when there is a sense of possibility, vagueness or indefiniteness. When the exact time or state of an action is uncertain, the subjunctive is used. The present subjunctive is formed in a way similar to the future tense, except that the -ਗਾ/-ਗੀ/-ਗੇ/-ਗੀਆਂ endings are left out. In English we rarely use the subjunctive mood, but learners of other European languages will be aware of this system of verbal constructions:

ਮੈਂ ਕਰਾਂ
ਅਸੀਂ ਬੋਲੀਏ
ਤੂੰ ਕਰੇਂ
ਤੁਸੀਂ ਬੋਲੋ
ਇਹ/ਉਹ ਬੋਲੇ
ਇਹ/ਉਹ ਬੋਲਣ

The range of situations in which the present subjunctive is used can be best compared with the future tense, as in the following examples:

Future

ਉਹ ਕਿੱਥੇ ਜਾਏਗੀ?	*Where will she go?*
ਮੈਂ ਕੁਝ ਕਵਾਂਗੀ	*I will say something.*
ਅਸੀਂ ਕੀ ਕਰਾਂਗੇ?	*What will we do?*

Present subjunctive

ਉਹ ਕਿੱਥੇ ਜਾਏ?	*Where shall he/she go?*
ਮੈਂ ਕੁਝ ਕਵਾਂ?	*Shall/may I say something?*
ਅਸੀਂ ਕੀ ਕਰੀਏ?	*What might we do?*

The examples of the future tense show that an action is to occur sometime in the future while the present subjunctive gives a sense that an action *may* happen.

Past subjunctive

The past subjunctive expresses that an action might have happened in the past, but that it did not occur. It is formed in exactly the same way as the present imperfect tense which you learned in Unit 4, and, unlike the present subjunctive, is affected by gender:

ਮੈਂ ਕਰਦਾ/ਕਰਦੀ
ਅਸੀਂ ਕਰਦੇ/ਕਰਦੀਆਂ
ਤੂੰ ਕਰਦਾ/ਕਰਦੀ
ਤੁਸੀਂ ਕਰਦੇ
ਇਹ/ਉਹ ਕਰਦਾ/ਕਰਦੀ
ਇਹ/ਉਹ ਕਰਦੇ/ਕਰਦੀਆਂ

The past subjunctive will be illustrated in the following section where conditional sentences will be introduced. The subjunctive is also used when there is a feeling of possibility, commonly expressed through *perhaps* ਸ਼ਾਇਦ or *it is possible* ਹੋ ਸਕਦਾ ਹੈ:

| ਸ਼ਾਇਦ ਉਹ ਆਵੇ, ਸ਼ਾਇਦ ਨਾ ਆਵੇ | *Perhaps he'll come, perhaps he won't come.* |
| ਹੋ ਸਕਦਾ ਹੈ ਕਿ ਬੱਚੇ ਬਾਹਰ ਹੋਣ | *It is possible that the children are outside.* |

More complex sentences can be constructed by combining the present tense or present continuous tense to express the nature of the action in question, such as *perhaps he might be coming,* in which *coming* is in the continuous tense while the sense of possibility is expressed through the subjunctive form of ਹੋਣਾ, which is ਹੋਣ:

ਸ਼ਾਇਦ ਮੁੰਡੇ ਗੁਜਰਾਤੀ ਸਿੱਖ ਰਹੇ ਹੋਣ	*Perhaps the boys are learning Gujarati.*
ਸ਼ਾਇਦ ਪਿਤਾ ਜੀ ਆਉਂਦੇ ਹੋਣ	*Perhaps father might be coming.*

The subjunctive is also used in a number of other situations in which necessity, command or obligation are being expressed. Notice such instances in the following examples:

ਜ਼ਰੂਰੀ ਹੈ ਕਿ ਅਸੀਂ ਠੀਕ ਸਮੇਂ ਤੇ ਨਿਕਲੀਏ	*It is necessary that we leave on time.*
ਉਹ ਨੂੰ ਦੱਸ ਕਿ ਚੁੱਪ ਰਵੇ!	*Tell him to be quiet!*

Conditional sentences

Conditional sentences (i.e. where an action is dependent on a *condition*) in Panjabi are formed by using a sequence of ਜੇ *if* and ਤਾਂ *then*. In English, conditional sentences also follow a similar pattern: *if he comes, then I won't go.* In Panjabi this sentence would be ਜੇ ਉਹ ਆਏ ਗਾ ਤਾਂ ਮੈਂ ਨਹੀਂ ਜਾਵਾਂ ਗਾ । If the conditional action being referred to is in the future, such as in this example, the verb tense of the *if* clause will be in the future. However, when the action in an *if* clause is not definite or certain, it must be expressed in the subjunctive mood. In the following examples both the future tense and the subjunctive mood are used:

Future

ਜੇ ਉਹ ਆਏ ਗਾ ਤਾਂ ਮੈਂ ਸੌਵਾਂ ਗਾ	*If he comes (will come), then I'll sleep.*

Subjunctive

ਜੇ ਅਸੀਂ ਸੱਤ ਵਜੇ ਨਿਕਲੀਏ ਤਾਂ ਕਿੰਨੇ ਵਜੇ ਘਰ ਪਹੁੰਚਾਂ ਗੇ ?	*If we leave at 7 o'clock, (then) what time will we reach home?*
ਜੇ ਟੈਕਸੀ ਨਾ ਮਿਲੇ ਤਾਂ ਬਸ ਫੜੋ	*If you don't get a taxi, then catch a bus.*

The present tense can be used in the *if* clause when the action being referred to is in the past. In the first dialogue in this unit, Paul says to Jaspreet and Simran: ਜੇ ਅਸੀਂ ਪਹਿਲੇ ਮਿਲਦੇ ਤਾਂ ਅਸੀਂ ਇਕੱਠੇ ਘੁੰਮਦੇ meaning *If we had met before, then we would have travelled together:*

ਜੇ ਉਹ ਆਉਂਦਾ ਤਾਂ ਮੈਂ ਸੌਂਦਾ	*If he had come, I would have slept.*
ਜੇ ਤੁਸੀਂ ਸਾਡੇ ਨਾਲ ਹੁੰਦੇ ਤਾਂ ਜ਼ਿਆਦਾ ਮਜ਼ਾ ਆਉਂਦਾ	*If you had been with us, we would have enjoyed it more.*

ਵਿਆਖਿਆ viaakhiaa *Commentary*

Letter-writing

Letter-writing in Panjabi is similar to English. As *Dear* in English is used, in Panjabi ਪਿਆਰੇ (which translates literally as *dear* or *beloved*) is generally used to address people who are relatively familiar to the writer. For more formal letters ਪਿਆਰੇ is often too intimate an address, so ਮਾਨਯੋਗ (*respected*) followed by the name of the person or ਸ੍ਰੀਮਾਨ ਜੀ (*Dear Sir*) are often more appropriate when writing to someone not known to you.

Greetings (see Unit 1) such as ਸਤਿ ਸ੍ਰੀ ਅਕਾਲ, ਨਮਸਕਾਰ and ਅੱਸਲਾਮ ਅਲੈਕਮ are commonly placed after the initial address on the line below, according to the religion of the addressee. The body of the letter follows no specific rules. However, a letter is generally concluded with the equivalent of the appropriate endings such as ਪਿਆਰ ਨਾਲ *with affection,* ਤੁਹਾਡਾ ਦੋਸਤ *your friend,* ਤੁਹਾਡੀਆਂ ਬੇਟੀਆਂ *your daughters* (as Jaspreet and Simran finish their letter to their parents), or whichever ending is fitting.

Doaba

Jaspreet and Simrans's trip to Jalandhar is no surprise when considering the pattern of migration from Panjab. The Doaba region, of which Jalandhar is a central town, is the main area in India from which migration has taken place. People from this region can be found in the four corners of the world. In fact the 'Doaba' dialect is what you are most likely to encounter if you are learning and using Panjabi in the West. It is often said that there is no family in the Doaba without a relative in the USA, UK, Far East or the Gulf.

Insight

Most Panjabi parents living abroad are very keen that their children should learn Panjabi, no matter where they live in the world. The main purpose of the two sisters Simran and Jaspreet visiting Panjab is to fulfil this aim.

ਅਭਿਆਸ abhiaas *Exercises*

1 Write the following in Panjabi

Make the following statements in Panjabi according to the directions in parentheses:

a I have eaten. (singular/male)
b I have eaten. (singular/female)
c They had spoken. (plural/male)
d He had been speaking for ten minutes. (singular/masculine)

2 Listening

◆) **CD 2, TR 5, 03:25**

Paul is at the bank changing some money. Listen to the dialogue between Paul and the bank teller on the recording. Answer the following questions about the dialogue:

ਪੌਲ ਕੋਲ ਕਿਹੜੇ ਦੇਸ਼ ਦੇ ਪੈਸੇ ਹਨ ?
ਪੌਲ ਕਿੰਨੇ ਪੈਸੇ ਬਦਲਣਾ ਚਾਹੁੰਦਾ ਹੈ ?
ਅੱਜ ਦਾ ਰੇਟ ਕੀ ਹੈ ?
ਕੀ ਰੁਪਇਆਂ ਦਾ ਰੇਟ ਕੱਲ੍ਹ ਤੋਂ ਘੱਟ ਹੈ ਜਾਂ ਵੱਧ ?
ਪੌਲ ਕੋਲ ਕਿਹੜਾ ਪਾਸਪੋਰਟ ਹੈ ?

3 Writing a postcard

You are writing a postcard to your friend Sonia about your stay in Panjab. Some words are missing. Select the appropriate words from the list to complete the postcard.

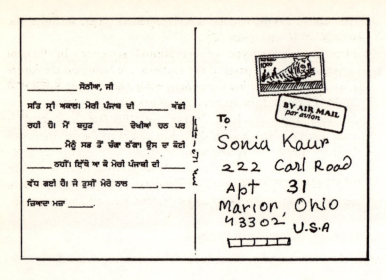

_____ ਸੋਨੀਆ, ਜੀ

ਸਤਿ ਸ੍ਰੀ ਅਕਾਲ। ਮੇਰੀ ਪੰਜਾਬ ਦੀ _____ ਸੋਹੀ

ਰਹੀ ਹੈ। ਮੈਂ ਬਹੁਤ _____ ਦੇਖੀਆਂ ਹਨ ਪਰ

_____ ਮੈਨੂੰ ਸਭ ਤੋਂ ਚੰਗਾ ਲੱਗਾ। ਉਸ ਦਾ ਕੋਈ

_____ ਨਹੀਂ। ਇੱਥੇ ਆ ਕੇ ਮੇਰੀ ਪੰਜਾਬੀ ਦੀ _____

ਵੱਧ ਗਈ ਹੈ। ਜੇ ਤੁਸੀਂ ਮੇਰੇ ਨਾਲ _____, _____

ਜ਼ਿਆਦਾ ਮਜ਼ਾ _____.

To
Sonia Kaur
222 Carl Road
Apt 31
Marion, Ohio
43302 U.S.A

- ਤਾਂ • ਜਗ੍ਹਾ • ਪਿਆਰ • ਹੁੰਦੇ • ਫੇਰੀ • ਮੁਕਾਬਲਾ
- ਸ਼ਬਦਾਵਲੀ • ਆਉਂਦਾ • ਹਰਿਮੰਦਰ ਸਾਹਿਬ

Ten important things to remember

1 The present perfect tense describes actions which have been completed. The stem of the verb that is used with '_chuknhaa_' 'ਚੁਕਣਾ' represents the action in the present perfect tense.

2 The past perfect tense is used when the effects of an action in the remote past are being referred to in the more recent past.

3 The present perfect continuous tense describes an action which occurred in the past and is still carrying on in the present.

4 The past perfect continuous tense describes an action which occurred in the remote past in a continuous manner during a specified time.

5 '_Kiven rihaa_' 'ਕਿਵੇਂ ਰਿਹਾ' (how did it go?) is a colloquial phrase used informally asking someone about his/her feelings and experiences regarding a specific occasion.

6 The English language circulates widely in South Asia, so much so that the daily use of common words like bus, station, computer, etc. have no equivalent words in the vernacular.

7 The construction of conditional sentences often includes the words '*je*' 'ਜੇ' and '*taan*' 'ਤਾਂ'.

8 Here is another type of conditional sentence. In Panjabi construction, both parts of the sentence are based on the future tense. Example: *je uh aae gaa taan main sauvaan gaa* ਜੇ ਉਹ ਆਏ ਗਾ ਤਾਂ ਮੈਂ ਸੌਵਾਂ ਗਾ. If he comes (will come) then I'll sleep.

9 In formal correspondence, '*maan yog*' 'ਮਾਨ ਯੋਗ' (respected) is used instead of '*piaare*' 'ਪਿਆਰੇ' (dear). In West Panjab the word '*janaab*' 'ਜਨਾਬ' (sir) is frequently used.

10 The subjunctive mood is commonly used when there is a sense of possibility, vagueness or indefiniteness. A range of subjunctive sentences can be expressed under present, past and future tenses.

13

......

ਵਿਆਹ ਦੀਆਂ ਰਸਮਾਂ
viaah deeaan rasmaan
Marriage customs

In this unit you will learn:

- More about Panjabi marriage customs
- How to tell the date and month of year
- How to express *sort of*, *rather*

Matrimonial advertisement
ਵਿਆਹ ਸਬੰਧੀ
viaah sabandhee

The following paragraph is a matrimonial advertisement taken from a widely read Panjabi newspaper in Britain called *Des Pardes* (*Home and Abroad*). The parents of a young man have placed the advertisement in order to find a partner for their son.

ਲੁਧਿਆਣੇ ਤੋਂ ਪਤਵੰਤੇ ਹਿੰਦੂ ਖਤਰੀ ਮਾਪਿਆਂ ਦੇ ਲੜਕੇ ਲਈ ਯੋਗ ਰਿਸ਼ਤੇ ਦੀ ਲੋੜ ਹੈ। ਲੜਕਾ ਪੜ੍ਹਿਆ ਲਿਖਿਆ, ਪੇਸ਼ਾਵਾਰ, ਸੱਚੀ ਮੁੱਚੀ ਸੁਹਣਾ ਤੇ ਨਰਮ ਸੁਭਾ ਦਾ ਹੈ। ਲੜਕੇ ਦਾ ਕੱਦ ੫ ਫੁੱਟ ੮ ਇੰਚ ਤੇ ਉਮਰ ੨੮ ਸਾਲ ਹੈ। ਲੜਕੀ ਪਤਲੀ, ਗੋਰੀ, ਸੁਹਣੀ, ਬ੍ਰਿਟਿਸ਼ ਸ਼ਹਿਰੀਅਤ ਵਾਲੀ, ਪੜ੍ਹੀ ਲਿਖੀ, ਵਿਹਾਰੀ ਨੌਕਰੀ ਤੇ ਲੱਗੀ ਹੋਣੀ ਚਾਹੀਦੀ ਹੈ। ਪੂਰਬ ਤੇ ਪੱਛਮ ਦੀਆਂ ਕਦਰਾਂ ਨੂੰ ਸਮਝਣ ਵਾਲੀ ਹੋਣੀ ਚਾਹੀਦੀ ਹੈ। ਲੜਕੀ ਦੀ ਉਮਰ ੨੫ ਸਾਲ ਤੋਂ ਵੱਧ ਨਾ ਹੋਵੇ। ਫੋਟੋ ਵਾਪਸ ਭੇਜ ਦਿੱਤੀ ਜਾਏ ਗੀ। ਤਲਾਕ ਸ਼ੁਦਾ ਕੁੜੀਆਂ ਨੂੰ ਲਿਖਣ ਦੀ ਲੋੜ ਨਹੀਂ। ਸੰਪਰਕ ਕਰੋ: Box number 2961 c/o ਦੇਸ ਪਰਦੇਸ।

Respectable Hindu Khatri parents from Ludhiana seek suitable match for their son. The boy is educated, a professional, genuinely handsome and kind natured. The boy is 5 ft 8 inches tall and he is 28 years old. The girl should be slim, fair, beautiful, a British citizen, educated and professionally employed. Should understand Eastern and Western values and be not more than 25 years of age. Photo returnable. Divorcees need not apply. Contact: Box number 2961 c/o Des Pardes.

ਸ਼ਬਦਾਵਲੀ	shabdaavalee	Vocabulary
ਪਤਵੰਤੇ	patvante	*respectable* (v.)
ਖਤਰੀ	khatree	*Khatri* (m./f.) *(caste)*
ਮਾਪਿਆਂ	maapiaan	*parents* (m.)
ਰਿਸ਼ਤਾ	rishtaa	*(marriage) relation* (m.)
ਯੋਗ	yog	*suitable*
ਲੋੜ	lorh	*require, necessity, wanted*
ਪੜ੍ਹਿਆ ਲਿਖਿਆ	parh-h-iaa likhiaa	*educated* (v.)
ਪੇਸ਼ਾਵਾਰ	peshaavar	*professional* (m./f.)
ਸੱਚੀ ਮੁੱਚੀ	sachchee muchchee	*genuinely*
ਸੁਹਣਾ	suhnhaa	*handsome* (v.)
ਨਰਮ ਸੁਭਾ	naram subhaa	*kind natured* (m.)
ਕੱਦ	kadd	*height* (m.)
ਉਮਰ	umar	*age* (f.)
ਪਤਲੀ	patlee	*thin, slim* (v.)
ਗੋਰੀ	goree	*fair, white* (v.)
ਸ਼ਹਿਰੀਅਤ	shahireeat	*citizen* (f.)
ਵਿਹਾਰੀ ਨੌਕਰੀ	vihaaree naukaree	*professionally employed* (f.)
ਨੌਕਰੀ	naukaree	*job, employment* (f.)
ਪੂਰਬ	poorab	*east* (m.)
ਪੱਛਮ	pachcham	*west* (m.)
ਕਦਰਾਂ	kadraan	*values* (f.)
ਵਾਪਸ	vaapas	*return*
ਭੇਜਣਾ	bhejnhaa	*to send*

| ਤਲਾਕ | ṯalaak | *divorce* (m.) |
| ਸੰਪਰਕ | sanparak | *contact* (m.) |

Insight

The whole marriage process is changing among the Panjabi diaspora but parents still tend to play their role in finding matches for their grown-up children.

ਅਭਿਆਸ abhiaas *Exercises*

After reading the passage and/or listening to the recording, try to do the following exercises.

1 Answer the questions about the passage

a ਕੀ ਲੜਕੇ ਦੇ ਮਾਪੇ ਹਿੰਦੂ ਹਨ?

b ਕੀ ਲੜਕਾ ਪੜ੍ਹਿਆ ਲਿਖਿਆ ਹੈ?

c ਕੀ ਲੜਕੀ ੨੦ ਸਾਲ ਤੋਂ ਘੱਟ ਹੋਵੇ?

2 Reply to matrimonial advertisement

The following is a reply to the matrimonial advertisement. From the personal information given, decide whether or not the couple are a suitable match (i.e. they have at least five of the qualities that were specified in the advertisement). It's up to you to decide!

Box number 2961 c/o ਦੇਸ ਪਰਦੇਸ:

ਦਿੱਲੀ ਤੋਂ ਮਾਪੇ ਆਪਣੀ ਲੜਕੀ ਲਈ ਰਿਸ਼ਤਾ ਲੱਭ ਰਹੇ ਹਨ। ਲੜਕੀ ਸੁਹਣੀ ਤੇ ਪਤਲੀ ਹੈ। ਪੜ੍ਹੀ ਲਿਖੀ ਹੈ ਪਰ ਨੌਕਰੀ ਨਹੀਂ ਕਰਦੀ ਹੈ। ਭਾਰਤੀ ਸ਼ਹਿਰੀਅਤ ਵਾਲੀ ਹੈ। ਪੂਰਬ ਤੇ ਪੱਛਮ ਦੀਆਂ ਕਦਰਾਂ ਸਮਝਣ ਵਾਲੀ ਹੈ ਅਤੇ ਉਸ ਦੀ ਉਮਰ ੨੮ ਸਾਲਾਂ ਦੀ ਹੈ। ਵਿਆਹ ਇੱਕ ਵਾਰੀ ਹੋ ਚੁਕਾ ਹੈ।

---

3 Say or write in the correct word order

a ਵਿਹਾਰੀ ਨੌਕਰੀ ਹੈ ਲੜਕੀ ਚਾਹੀਦੀ ਤੇ ਹੋਣੀ ਲੱਗੀ

b ਤਲਾਕ ਸ਼ੁਦਾ ਲਿਖਣ ਨੂੰ ਲੜਕੀਆਂ ਲੋੜ ਦੀ ਨਹੀਂ

c ਉਮਰ ਦੀ ਲੜਕੀ ੨੫ ਸਾਲ ਹੋਵੇ ਵੱਧ ਨਾ ਤੋਂ

d ਲੜਕਾ ਸੁਹਣਾ ਸੱਚੀ ਮੁੱਚੀ ਹੈ

A wedding invitation
ਗੱਲ ਬਾਤ ਸੱਦਾ ਪੱਤਰ
gall baat saddaa pattar

🔊 CD 2, TR 6, 00:18

Debra has received an invitation to attend a Panjabi wedding. Since she has never been to a Panjabi wedding, she has gone to her friend Darshana to ask her what the ceremonies will be like.

ਡੇਬਰਾ	ਮੇਰੀ ਸਹੇਲੀ ਜੀਤੀ ਦੇ ਵਿਆਹ ਦਾ ਸੱਦਾ ਪੱਤਰ ਆਇਆ ਹੈ। ਵਿਆਹ ੨੮ ਜਨਵਰੀ ਨੂੰ ਹੈ। ਮੈਨੂੰ ਮਹਿੰਦੀ ਬਾਰੇ ਕੁਝ ਦੱਸ।
ਦਰਸ਼ਨਾ	ਮਹਿੰਦੀ ਪਰਵਾਰਕ ਰਸਮ ਹੈ। ਕੁੜੀਆਂ ਆਪਣੇ ਹੱਥਾਂ ਤੇ ਮਹਿੰਦੀ ਲਗਾਉਂਦੀਆਂ ਹਨ। ਕਈ ਤਰ੍ਹਾਂ ਦੇ ਨਮੂਨੇ ਬਣਾਂਦੀਆਂ ਹਨ ਅਤੇ ਵਿਆਹ ਦੇ ਗੀਤ ਵੀ ਗਾਏ ਜਾਂਦੇ ਹਨ।
ਡੇਬਰਾ	ਕੀ ਆਦਮੀ ਇਸ ਰਸਮ ਵਿਚ ਸ਼ਾਮਲ ਹੁੰਦੇ ਹਨ?
ਦਰਸ਼ਨਾ	ਨਹੀਂ, ਇਹ ਕੇਵਲ ਔਰਤਾਂ ਲਈ ਹੈ। ਆਦਮੀ ਬਰਾਤ ਵਿਚ ਸ਼ਾਮਲ ਹੁੰਦੇ ਹਨ।
ਡੇਬਰਾ	ਬਰਾਤ ਦਾ ਕੀ ਮਤਲਬ ਹੈ?
ਦਰਸ਼ਨਾ	ਬਰਾਤ ਵਿਚ ਲਾੜੇ ਦੇ ਰਿਸ਼ਤੇਦਾਰ ਅਤੇ ਦੋਸਤ ਸ਼ਾਮਲ ਹੁੰਦੇ ਹਨ। ਇਹ ਛੋਟਾ ਜੇਹਾ ਜਲੂਸ ਹੁੰਦਾ ਹੈ। ਮੁੰਡਾ ਘੋੜੀ ਤੇ ਚੜ੍ਹਿਆ ਹੁੰਦਾ ਹੈ ਅਤੇ ਅੱਗੇ ਅੱਗੇ ਵਾਜੇ ਵਾਲੇ ਹੁੰਦੇ ਹਨ। ਜਾਂਵੀ ਭੰਗੜਾ ਪਾਉਂਦੇ ਹਨ।
ਡੇਬਰਾ	ਸੱਦਾ ਪੱਤਰ ਤੇ ਲਿਖਿਆ ਹੋਇਆ ਹੈ ਕਿ ਡੋਲੀ ਚਾਰ ਵਜੇ ਤੁਰੇਗੀ। ਇਹ ਕੀ ਰਸਮ ਹੈ?
ਦਰਸ਼ਨਾ	ਡੋਲੀ ਦਾ ਮਤਲਬ ਹੈ ਕਿ ਕੁੜੀ ਦਾ ਪੇਕੇ ਛੱਡ ਕੇ ਸਹੁਰੇ ਜਾਣਾ। ਇਹ ਮੌਕਾ ਖੁਸ਼ੀ ਤੇ ਗਮੀ ਦਾ ਮੇਲ ਹੈ।
ਡੇਬਰਾ	ਇਹ ਗੱਲ ਬੜੀ ਦਿਲਚਸਪ ਲੱਗਦੀ ਹੈ। ਮੈਂ ਵਿਆਹ ਤੇ ਜਾਣ ਲਈ ਉਤਸੁਕ ਹਾਂ।
Debra	*My friend Jeeti's wedding invitation has come. The wedding is on the 28th of January. Tell me something about* mehndi.
Darshana	*Mehndi is a family custom. Girls put henna on their hands. They draw different designs and wedding songs are sung.*
Debra	*Are men present during this ritual?*
Darshana	*No. This is just for the women. Men are present at the* baraat.
Debra	*What is the meaning of* baraat?

Darshana	*At the* baraat *the groom's relatives and friends are present.*	
	This is a sort of small procession. The boy is on a mare and	
	in front are some musicians. The wedding party performs	
	bhangra *(a folk dance of Panjab).*	
Debra	*It's written on the invitation that the* doli *will leave at 4 o'clock.*	
	What is this custom?	
Darshana	Doli *means that the girl leaves her family's home to go to her*	
	in-laws. This time is a happy and sad occasion.	
Debra	*This seems interesting. I look forward to going to*	
	the wedding!	

ਸ਼ਬਦਾਵਲੀ	**shabdaavalee**	*Vocabulary*
ਸਹੇਲੀ	sahelee	*friend* (f.)
ਸੱਦਾ ਪੱਤਰ	sad̲d̲aa pat̲t̲ar	*invitation* (m.)
ਮਹਿੰਦੀ	mahin̲dee	*henna* (f.)
ਜਾਣਨਾ	jaanhnaa	*to know*
ਆਪਣਾ	aapnhaa	*one's own*
ਪਰਵਾਰਕ	parvaarak	*family (relating to family)*
ਰਸਮ	rasam	*custom, ritual* (f.)
ਕਈ ਤਰ੍ਹਾਂ	kaee t̲ar-h-aan̲	*different types*
ਨਮੂਨਾ	namoonaa	*pattern, design* (m.)
ਗੀਤ	geet̲	*song* (m.)
ਗਾਣਾ	gaanhaa	*to sing*
ਸ਼ਾਮਲ	shaamal	*to be present, to join or participate*
ਬਰਾਤ	baraat̲	*procession of the groom's relatives and friends* (f.)
ਮਤਲਬ	mat̲lab	*meaning, definition* (m.)
ਲਾੜਾ	laarhaa	*groom* (m.)
ਰਿਸ਼ਤੇਦਾਰ	risht̲edaar	*relatives* (m./f.)
ਜਿਹਾ	jihaa	*sort of, rather*
ਜਲੂਸ	jaloos	*procession, parade* (m.)
ਘੋੜੀ	ghorhee	*mare* (f.)
ਚੜੂਨਾ	charh-h-naa	*to be upon, to ride*
ਵਾਜੇ ਵਾਲੇ	vaaje vaale	*band of musicians* (m.)
ਜਾਂਵੀ	jaan̲njee	*members of groom's wedding party* (m./f.)

ਭੰਗੜਾ	bhangrhaa	*bhangra* (m.) (style of Panjabi dance) (see Commentary, Unit 16)
ਡੋਲੀ	dolee	*ceremony* (f.) *bidding farewell to the bride* (see Commentary)
ਤੁਰਨਾ	turnaa	*to walk, to depart, to leave*
ਪੇਕੇ	peke	*bride's family, bride's parents* (m.)
ਛੱਡਨਾ	chaddnaa	*to leave*
ਸਹੁਰੇ	sahure	*in-laws* (m.)
ਮੌਕਾ	maukaa	*opportunity, occasion* (m.)
ਖ਼ੁਸ਼ੀ	khushee	*happiness* (f.)
ਗ਼ਾਮੀ	ghamee	*sadness* (f.)
ਮੇਲ	mel	*meeting, combination* (m.)
ਦਿਲਚਸਪ	dilchasp	*interesting*
ਉਤਸੁਕ	utsuk	*anxious, awaiting*

Insight

Panjabi weddings may vary according to different religious groups but all weddings are celebrated with great pomp and show, often with much money spent lavishly by both the groom's and bride's families.

ਅਭਿਆਸ abhiaas *Exercises*

After reading the dialogue and/or listening to the recording, try to do the following exercises.

1 Match the questions with the correct answer

1 ਮਹਿੰਦੀ ਦੀ ਰਸਮ ਕੀ ਹੈ?

2 ਵਿਆਹ ਕਿਸ ਤਾਰੀਖ਼ ਨੂੰ ਹੈ?

3 ਬਰਾਤ ਵਿਚ ਕੌਣ ਸ਼ਾਮਲ ਹੁੰਦਾ ਹੈ?

4 ਡੋਲੀ ਕੀ ਹੁੰਦੀ ਹੈ?

a ਵਿਆਹ ੨੮ ਜਨਵਰੀ ਨੂੰ ਹੈ।

b ਕੁੜੀਆਂ ਆਪਣੇ ਹੱਥਾਂ ਤੇ ਮਹਿੰਦੀ ਲਗਾਉਂਦੀਆਂ ਹਨ।

c ਕੁੜੀ ਦਾ ਪੇਕੇ ਛੱਡ ਕੇ ਸੁਹਰੇ ਜਾਣ ਨੂੰ ਡੋਲੀ ਕਿਹਾ ਜਾਂਦਾ ਹੈ।

d ਲੜਕੇ ਦੇ ਦੋਸਤ ਅਤੇ ਰਿਸ਼ਤੇਦਾਰ ਸ਼ਾਮਲ ਹੁੰਦੇ ਹਨ।

> Bhupinder Singh and Harjinder Kaur Panesar
> cordially request your company at the wedding of their son
> Manjit Singh to Kanwaljit Kaur
> daughter of Gurbax Singh and Jasvir Kaur Kalsi, Ilford
> on May 23 at the Sikh Gurdwara of North London
> Baraat: 9:30 a.m. Anand Karaj: 10 a.m. Guru ka langar: 12:00
>
> RSVP
> The Panesar Family
> 23 Old Road, Edinburgh, Scotland

2 Answer the questions about the wedding invitation

a ਮੁੰਡੇ ਦੇ ਮਾਪੇ ਕਿੱਥੇ ਰਹਿੰਦੇ ਹਨ?

b ਕੁੜੀ ਦੇ ਮਾਪੇ ਕਿੱਥੋਂ ਦੇ ਹਨ?

c ਮੁੰਡੇ ਦਾ ਨਾਮ ਕੀ ਹੈ?

d ਕੁੜੀ ਦਾ ਨਾਮ ਕੀ ਹੈ?

e ਕੁੜੀ ਦੇ ਮਾਪਿਆਂ ਦੇ ਨਾਮ ਕੀ ਹਨ?

f ਵਿਆਹ ਕਿਹੜੇ ਸ਼ਹਿਰ ਵਿਚ ਹੋ ਰਿਹਾ ਹੈ?

g ਵਿਆਹ ਕਿਹੜੀ ਤਾਰੀਖ਼ ਨੂੰ ਹੈ?

h ਬਰਾਤ ਕਿੰਨੇ ਵਜੇ ਤੁਰੇਗੀ?

i ਅਨੰਦ ਕਾਰਜ ਕਦੋਂ ਸ਼ੁਰੂ ਹੋਣਾ ਹੈ?

j ਗੁਰੂ ਦਾ ਲੰਗਰ ਕਿੰਨੇ ਵਜੇ ਵਰਤੇ ਗਾ?

ਬੋਲੀ ਬਾਰੇ bolee baare *Language points*

Participial uses

A participle is part of a verb which is used to describe an object or an action. Therefore, participle constructions in Panjabi can either be used adjectively to describe nouns or adverbially to describe actions. You will remember from the matrimonial advertisement that the boy is described as *educated*. In Panjabi this was expressed as ਪੜ੍ਹਿਆ ਲਿਖਿਆ. Both verbs ਪੜ੍ਹਨਾ and ਲਿਖਣਾ are combined in their perfect forms in agreement with ਲੜਕਾ. Similarly, the prospective girl was said to be *educated*, expressed as ਪੜ੍ਹੀ ਲਿਖੀ, also showing agreement with the object being described. Often, the perfect forms of ਹੋਣਾ can also be used to strengthen the participial expression. Here are some more examples of how the participle can be used in Panjabi:

Adjective participles

ਮੈਂ ਉਬਲੇ ਹੋਏ ਅੰਡੇ ਨਹੀਂ ਖਾਂਦਾ	*I don't eat boiled eggs.*
ਉਹ ਬੈਠਾ ਹੋਇਆ ਆਦਮੀ ਕੋਣ ਹੈ?	*Who is that man sitting down (i.e. seated)?*
ਮਾਤਾ ਜੀ ਨੇ ਡਰੀ ਹੋਈ ਕੁੜੀ ਨੂੰ ਚੁੱਕ ਲਿਆ	*Mum picked up the scared girl.*

Adverbial participles

ਉਹ ਮੁਸਕਰਾਂਦਾ ਹੋਇਆ ਲਤੀਫ਼ਾ ਸੁਣਾ ਰਿਹਾ ਸੀ	*He was telling a joke smilingly.*

Another use of the participle is in order to emphasize the on-going nature or repetitiveness of the action being described. This can be done in two ways: by repeating the verb in the simple present tense or by using the past participle with a form of ਜਾਣਾ, both forms agreeing with the subject:

ਪੜ੍ਹਦੇ ਪੜ੍ਹਦੇ ਅਸੀਂ ਥੱਕ ਗਏ ਹਾਂ	*We are tired from constantly studying.*
ਰਸਤੇ ਵਿਚ ਜਾਂਦੇ ਜਾਂਦੇ ਮੈਨੂੰ ਮਿਲਣਾ	*As you go (along) the way, come and see me.*
ਛੋਟੀ ਲੜਕੀ ਬੋਲੀ ਜਾਂਦੀ ਹੈ	*The little girl keeps on talking.*

The particle ਜਿਹਾ 'jihaa'

ਜਿਹਾ is a particle which is added after an adjective in order to give it a modest or diluted sense. In English the sense of a description is diluted in a number of different ways, most commonly by using such words as *rather, sort of, quite,* and the suffix *-ish.* The form of ਜਿਹਾ is affected by the gender and number of the noun being described and can therefore also appear in the following forms: ਜਿਹੀ, ਜਿਹੇ and ਜਿਹੀਆਂ:

ਛੋਟਾ ਜਿਹਾ ਘਰ	*rather a small house*
ਥੋੜ੍ਹਾ ਜਿਹਾ	*quite a small (amount)*
ਪੁਰਾਣੀ ਜਿਹੀ ਗੱਡੀ	*an old-ish car*

The opposite of ਜਿਹਾ, in this sense, is ਸਾਰਾ. This is used to exaggerate rather than dilute a description, such as in Unit 11 when the booking clerk is telling the girls how popular the train to Amritsar, Shan-e-Panjab, is: ਬਹੁਤ ਸਾਰੇ ਸੈਲਾਨੀ ਇਸ ਗੱਡੀ ਵਿਚ ਸਫ਼ਰ ਕਰਦੇ ਹਨ *A lot of tourists travel on this train.*

The particle -ਜਿਹਾ can also follow a noun in order to give the sense *like*. Therefore, the noun preceding -ਜਿਹਾ represents what the description is being likened to. For example:

ਪਟਾਕਾ -ਜਿਹਾ	*like a firecracker*

When asking the question *what sort of?* or *what is it like?* then ਕਿਹੋ is combined with ਜਿਹਾ.

ਕਿਹੋ ਜਿਹਾ ਮਕਾਨ ?	*what sort of house?*
ਕਿਹੋ ਜਿਹੇ ਕਪੜੇ ?	*what sort of clothes?*

Reflexive adjectives and pronouns

In English *myself* and *themselves* are reflexive pronouns indicating that the action is directed towards or belongs to the subject of the sentence. In Panjabi the reflexive adjective ਆਪਣਾ means *one's own* and is defined by the noun or pronoun being affected by the reflexive nature of the sentence. Like other adjectives, it also changes according to the gender and number of the object that it is describing as well as in the oblique form.

ਉਹ ਆਪਣੇ ਘਰ ਵਿਚ ਰਹਿੰਦਾ ਹੈ	*He lives in his own house.*
ਉਹ ਆਪਣੇ ਭਰਾ ਨਾਲ ਆਇਆ ਹੈ	*He has come with his (own) brother.*
ਹਰ ਚੀਜ਼ ਆਪਣੀ ਜਗ੍ਹਾ ਤੇ ਹੋਣੀ ਚਾਹੀਦੀ ਹੈ	*Everything should be in its proper place.*
ਆਪਣੀਆਂ ਲੜਕੀਆਂ ਕੀ ਕਰਦੀਆਂ ਹਨ ?	*What do your (own) daughters do?*

Reflexive pronouns, unlike reflexive adjectives, do not rely upon another noun or adjective to be defined. If you recall from Unit 2, pronouns were introduced as naming words. The reflexive pronouns, in a similar way, are also naming words which are used to represent a person. The most common reflexive pronoun is ਆਪ which translates as *by oneself*. ਖ਼ੁਦ, which is borrowed from Persian, can also be used to give the same sense. Note the following examples:

ਮੈਂ ਇਹ ਕੰਮ ਆਪ ਕਰਾਂ ਗਾ	*I will do this work myself.*
ਮੈਂ ਸਾਰਾ ਖਾਣਾ ਖ਼ੁਦ ਬਣਾਇਆ ਹੈ	*I have made all the food myself.*
ਉਹ ਨੇ ਆਪ ਜਾ ਕੇ ਫਲ ਖ਼ਰੀਦਿਆ	*She went and bought fruit herself.*

The reflexive adjective **ਆਪਣਾ** and the reflexive pronoun **ਆਪ** can be combined to give another meaning: *on one's own* or *without anyone's help* **ਆਪਣੇ ਆਪ**.

| ਕਿਰਨ ਆਪਣੇ ਆਪ ਪੰਜਾਬੀ ਪੜ੍ਹਦੀ ਹੈ | *Kiran studies Panjabi on her own (without anyone else's help).* |
| ਸੰਜੀਵ ਆਪਣੇ ਆਪ ਨੂੰ ਬਹੁਤ ਸਮਝਦਾ ਹੈ | *Sanjeev thinks highly of himself.* |

ਆਪਸ, meaning *fraternity*, is used to express situations of mutuality or reciprocity with the postposition **ਵਿਚ** to form *among* or *between*.

| ਅਸੀਂ ਆਪਸ ਵਿਚ ਗੱਲ ਕਰ ਰਹੇ ਸੀ | *We were talking among ourselves.* |
| ਬੱਚੇ ਆਪਸ ਵਿਚ ਖੇਡ ਰਹੇ ਸਨ | *The children were playing among themselves.* |

Finally, **ਆਪਾਂ** is used specifically with a group of people otherwise referred to as **ਅਸੀਂ** *us*. Therefore, the new meaning given by the reflexive pronoun is *let's* or *all of us*:

| ਆਪਾਂ ਚਲੀਏ | *let's go* |

Insight

'*uh aapnhaa bandaa e*' **'ਉਹ ਆਪਣਾ ਬੰਦਾ ਏ'** (He is one of us) are words frequently used by Panjabi people This expression conveys the sense that a certain person belongs to our own village, clan, state, country, religion, caste or other affiliation or background.

ਵਿਆਖਿਆ viaakhiaa *Commentary*

1 What's the date today?

When asking someone today's date in Panjabi, you would say **ਅੱਜ ਕੀ ਤਾਰੀਖ਼ ਹੈ** ? This is different from asking someone the day or day of the week, as explained in Unit 7 with the words **ਦਿਨ** *day* and **ਵਾਰ** *day of the week*. **ਤਾਰੀਖ਼** literally means *date* and the reply to your question would be a numerical figure of the date accompanied by the month of the year: ਅੱਜ ਅਠਾਰ੍ਹਾਂ ਜੂਨ ਹੈ *Today is the 18th of June.* It is also not uncommon to use ordinal numbers for the first three or four days of the month: ਅੱਜ ਮਹੀਨੇ ਦੀ ਤੀਜੀ ਤਾਰੀਖ਼ ਹੈ *It is the third day of the month.*

Months of the year

ਜਨਵਰੀ	janvaree	*January*
ਫ਼ਰਵਰੀ	farvaree	*February*
ਮਾਰਚ	maarch	*March*
ਅਪਰੈਲ	aprail	*April*
ਮਈ	maee	*May*
ਜੂਨ	joon	*June*
ਜੁਲਾਈ	julaaee	*July*
ਅਗਸਤ	agas<u>t</u>	*August*
ਸਤੰਬਰ	sata<u>n</u>bar	*September*
ਅਕਤੂਬਰ	ak<u>t</u>oobar	*October*
ਨਵੰਬਰ	nava<u>n</u>bar	*November*
ਦਸੰਬਰ	<u>d</u>asa<u>n</u>bar	*December*

The four seasons of the year in English are spring, autumn, winter and summer which describe the weather of the period. In Panjabi there are terms less influenced by English (as the months of the year) to denote the seasons which, in Pakistan and North India, are quite distinctive.

ਬਸੰਤ	basa<u>nt</u>	*spring*
ਗਰਮੀ	garmee	*summer*
ਬਰਸਾਤ	barsaa<u>t</u>	*rainy season*
ਪੱਤਝੜ	pattjharh	*autumn*
ਸਰਦੀ	sar<u>d</u>ee	*winter*

Insight

The first day of the Indian month is known as '*sangraa<u>nd</u>*' 'ਸੰਗਰਾਂਦ'. People consider it as a holy day and many would aspire to visit a '*gurdwara*' 'ਗੁਰਦੁਆਰਾ', shrine or '*mandar*' 'ਮੰਦਰ' to mark the start of the new month in an auspicious way.

2 Marriage customs

Panjabi weddings are lavish affairs with numbers of guests usually in the hundreds, sometimes in the thousands, and large amounts of food and decoration. Weddings are seen as social occasions and signify the coming together of two families rather than of two individuals, as is traditionally the case in Western marriages. It is this aspect of Panjabi – and most other South Asian – weddings that leads to them often being labelled as 'arranged'. Usually the families arrange the weddings of their offspring, in that families are present at the meeting of the man and woman. There is huge variety in the process of arranging marriages from one extreme where the man and woman do not meet until the wedding day (which is rare in the diaspora) to a situation where the man and woman see each other and make their own decision about whether they wish to marry or not. It is this latter version that is more usual in the diaspora.

When families are involved in the selection of the partner, they take into account a range of factors, such as those outlined in the advert at the beginning of this unit. Alongside education and other social aspects, the advert specifies a particular caste group, in this case **Khatri**. Caste is a form of social grouping and organization which is based upon occupational traditions as well as kinship ties. Even in the diaspora, caste affiliations are still adhered to and most advertisements of this kind carry some sort of caste affiliation. Some common castes are **Jat, Ramgharia** and **Brahmin**.

The wedding ceremonies that we described in this unit are religion-neutral in the Panjabi context and most Sikh, Hindu and Muslim weddings share these customs. The actual wedding vows, however, are of a religious nature and for Sikhs this is called the **Anand Karaj**, for Hindus it is the **Vivaah** and for Muslims the **Nikah**. For all Panjabis, however, weddings are major social events and involve spectacles of emotion, family participation and financial expenditure.

A common Panjabi wedding will involve a **mehndi** ritual, where the bride is adorned on her hands and feet with exquisite patterns in dye. The groom arrives on horseback with his relatives at the bride's house and the wedding ceremony takes place here. The ceremony is followed by a feast. The saddest occasion is when the bride is seen off at the end of the ceremony. This is called the **doli** and often involves protracted crying and sadness. Each of the events of the Panjabi wedding is accompanied by music.

ਅਭਿਆਸ abhiaas *Exercises*

After reading the dialogue and/or listening to the recording, try to do the following exercises.

1 Write a matrimonial advertisement

Prepare a matrimonial advertisement in Panjabi on behalf of the parents of a girl giving the following information:

a The parents are Sikhs living in London.
b The girl is beautiful, educated and works in a bank.
c The girl is 25 years of age and is 5' 3'' tall.
d The boy should be from a respectable family, be a British citizen and professionally employed.

2 Complete the sentences

Use the appropriate forms of **ਆਪਣਾ** and **ਜਿਹਾ**.

a ਥੋੜਾ _____ ਹੋਰ ਦੁੱਧ ਦੇਵੋ।   *Give me a little more milk.*

b ਮੈਂ _____ ਪਿਤਾ ਜੀ ਨਾਲ ਆਇਆ ਹਾਂ।   *I have come with my father.*

c ਮੇਰੀਆਂ _____ ਭੈਣਾਂ ਵਿਆਹ ਤੇ ਨਹੀਂ ਗਈਆਂ।   *My own sisters didn't go to the wedding.*

d ਉਹ ਕਿਹੋ _____ ਲੋਕ ਸਨ?   *What sort of people were they?*

3 Fill in the blanks

Use the appropriate participle expressions.

a _____ _____ ਅੰਡੇ   *boiled eggs*

b _____ _____ ਮੁੰਡਾ   *scared boy*

c _____ _____ ਲੜਕਾ   *educated boy*

4 Listening

◀ CD 2, TR 6, 01:58

The following passage has been recorded. Listen to it and then answer the questions in Panjabi.

ਡੇਬਰਾ ਨੂੰ ਜੀਤੀ ਦੇ ਵਿਆਹ ਦਾ ਸੱਦਾ ਪੱਤਰ ਆਇਆ ਹੈ। ਵਿਆਹ ੨੮ ਜਨਵਰੀ ਨੂੰ ਹੈ। ਡੇਬਰਾ ਪਹਿਲੇ ਕਦੇ ਕਿਸੇ ਪੰਜਾਬੀ ਵਿਆਹ ਤੇ ਨਹੀਂ ਗਈ। ਉਹ ਵਿਆਹ ਦੀਆਂ ਰਸਮਾਂ ਬਾਰੇ ਜਾਣਨਾ ਚਾਹੁੰਦੀ ਹੈ। ਇਸ ਲਈ ਉਹ ਆਪਣੀ ਸਹੇਲੀ ਦਰਸ਼ਨਾ ਕੋਲ ਗਈ ਹੈ।

a ਵਿਆਹ ਦਾ ਸੱਦਾ ਪੱਤਰ ਕਿਸ ਨੂੰ ਆਇਆ ਹੈ?

b ਵਿਆਹ ਕਿਸ ਦਾ ਹੈ?

c ਕੀ ਡੇਬਰਾ ਕਦੀ ਪੰਜਾਬੀ ਵਿਆਹ ਤੇ ਗਈ ਹੈ?

d ਵਿਆਹ ਕਿਹੜੀ ਤਾਰੀਖ਼ ਹੈ?

e ਡੇਬਰਾ ਦਰਸ਼ਨਾ ਕੋਲ ਕਿਉਂ ਗਈ ਹੈ?

Ten important things to remember

1 A participle is part of a verb which is used to describe an object or an action. Examples: a) *parh-h-iaa likhiaa* **ਪੜ੍ਹਿਆ ਲਿਖਿਆ** educated b) *uble hoe ande* **ਉਬਲੇ ਹੋਏ ਅੰਡੇ** boiled eggs.

2 *'Jihaa'* 'ਜਿਹਾ' is a particle which is added after an adjective in order to give it a modest or diluted sense. Example: *chotaa jihaa ghar* ਛੋਟਾ ਜਿਹਾ ਘਰ a rather small house.

3 Sometimes Panjabi words like *'saaraa, saaree, saare'* 'ਸਾਰਾ, ਸਾਰੀ, ਸਾਰੇ', etc. (a lot, all) are used to impart the opposite meaning to 'jihaa'. Example: *'bahut saare sailaanee'* 'ਬਹੁਤ ਸਾਰੇ ਸੈਲਾਨੀ' (a lot of tourists).

4 The Indian calendar is based on a lunar system. Each of the twelve months of the year has an equivalent Panjabi name called *'desi maheene'* 'ਦੇਸੀ ਮਹੀਨੇ' (Indian/Panjabi months).

5 These Panjabi names of the months are important reference points for the changing seasons, religious days and festivals. In day-to-day use, English months are commonly referred to, but their pronunciation is not the same as in English. For example: February is pronounced as *'Farvary'* 'ਫ਼ਰਵਰੀ' in Panjabi.

6 In Panjabi the reflexive adjective *'aapnhaa'* 'ਆਪਣਾ' means 'one's own'. Example: *ih meree aapnhee gaddee hai* ਇਹ ਮੇਰੀ ਆਪਣੀ ਗੱਡੀ ਹੈ This is my own car.

7 Sometimes *'aapnhaa'* 'ਆਪਣਾ' is used to show politeness by replacing the word *'tuhaadaa'* 'ਤੁਹਾਡਾ' (your). Example: *aapnhaa kee naam hai?* ਆਪਣਾ ਕੀ ਨਾਮ ਹੈ? (What is your name?)

8 The usage of the reflexive pronoun *'aap'* 'ਆਪ' by oneself. Example: *main ih kanm aap karaan gaa.* ਮੈਂ ਇਹ ਕੰਮ ਆਪ ਕਰਾਨ ਗਾ (I will do this work myself.).

9 The word *'khud'* 'ਖ਼ੁਦ' (self), which is borrowed from Persian, can also be used to give the same sense as *'aap'* ਆਪ.

10 The reflexive adjective *'aapnhaa'* 'ਆਪਣਾ' and the reflexive pronoun *'aap'* 'ਆਪ' can be combined to mean 'on one's own, without anyone else's help'. Example: *kiran aapnhe aap panjaabee parh-h-dee hai* ਕਿਰਨ ਆਪਣੇ ਆਪ ਪੰਜਾਬੀ ਪੜ੍ਹਦੀਅੀ ਹੈ Kiran studies Panjabi on her own.

14

ਉਹਨਾਂ ਨੇ ਮੇਰੇ ਬਾਰੇ ਕੀ ਕਿਹਾ ਸੀ?
uhnaan ne mere baare kee kihaa see?
What did they say about me?

In this unit you will learn:

- How to have a conversation about school
- How to speak with a police officer and a social worker
- How to use purpose clauses with *so that*

---

1   *Did you meet my class teacher?*
ਗੱਲ ਬਾਤ ੧ ਕੀ ਤੁਸੀਂ ਮੇਰੇ ਸ਼੍ਰੇਣੀ ਅਧਿਆਪਕ ਨੂੰ ਮਿਲੇ ਸੀ?
gall baat 1 kee tuseen mere shrenhee adhiaapak noon mile see?

◄) CD 2, TR 7, 00:22

Mr Lall has just attended his son Ramesh's parents' evening at his school. Mr Lall has come home and is talking to Ramesh.

ਰਮੇਸ਼	ਪਾਪਾ ਜੀ! ਕੀ ਤੁਸੀਂ ਮੇਰੇ ਸ਼੍ਰੇਣੀ ਅਧਿਆਪਕ ਨੂੰ ਮਿਲੇ ਸੀ?
ਮਿਸਟਰ ਲਾਲ	ਹਾਂ, ਮੈਂ ਉਸ ਤੋਂ ਇਲਾਵਾ ਤੇਰੇ ਦੂਜੇ ਮਜ਼ਮੂਨਾਂ ਦੇ ਅਧਿਆਪਕਾਂ ਨੂੰ ਵੀ ਮਿਲਿਆ ਸੀ।
ਰਮੇਸ਼	ਉਹਨਾਂ ਨੇ ਮੇਰੇ ਬਾਰੇ ਕੀ ਕਿਹਾ ਸੀ?

ਮਿਸਟਰ ਲਾਲ	ਹਿਸਾਬ ਦੇ ਅਧਿਆਪਕ ਨੇ ਕਿਹਾ ਕਿ ਤੂੰ ਘਰ ਦਾ ਕੰਮ ਕਰਨ ਵਿਚ ਲਾ ਪਰਵਾਹ ਹੈਂ ਅਤੇ ਸ਼੍ਰੇਣੀ ਵਿਚ ਗਾਲੜੀ ਹੈਂ।
ਰਮੇਸ਼	ਉਹ ਮੈਨੂੰ ਪਸੰਦ ਨਹੀ ਕਰਦਾ। ਅੰਗਰੇਜ਼ੀ ਦੇ ਅਧਿਆਪਕ ਨੇ ਕੀ ਕਿਹਾ?
ਮਿਸਟਰ ਲਾਲ	ਉਸ ਨੇ ਕਿਹਾ ਕਿ ਰਮੇਸ਼ ਵਿਚ ਲਿਆਕਤ ਹੈ ਪਰ ਉਹ ਵਰਤਦਾ ਨਹੀਂ।
ਰਮੇਸ਼	ਉਹ ਸਾਨੂੰ ਚੰਗੀ ਤਰ੍ਹਾਂ ਪੜ੍ਹਾਂਦਾ ਨਹੀਂ।
ਮਿਸਟਰ ਲਾਲ	ਖ਼ੈਰ! ਤੈਨੂੰ ਪੜ੍ਹਾਈ ਵਿਚ ਮਿਹਨਤ ਕਰਨੀ ਚਾਹੀਦੀ ਹੈ ਤਾਂ ਕਿ ਤੂੰ ਚੰਗੇ ਗਰੇਡ ਲੈ ਕੇ ਡਾਕਟਰ ਬਣ ਸਕੇਂ।

Ramesh	*Dad! Did you meet my class teacher?*
Mr Lall	*Yes and apart from him I also met your other subject teachers.*
Ramesh	*What did they say about me?*
Mr Lall	*The maths teacher said that you were careless in doing your homework and talkative in class.*
Ramesh	*He doesn't like me. What did the English teacher say?*
Mr Lall	*He said that Ramesh has the ability but does not use it.*
Ramesh	*He does not teach us properly.*
Mr Lall	*Anyway! You should study hard so that you get good grades and can become a doctor.*

ਸ਼ਬਦਾਵਲੀ	shabdaavalee	*Vocabulary*
ਸ਼੍ਰੇਣੀ	shrenhee	*class* (f.)
ਅਧਿਆਪਕ	adhiaapak	*teacher* (m./f.)
ਤੋਂ ਇਲਾਵਾ	ton ilaavaa	*apart from, besides*
ਦੂਜੇ	dooje	*others*
ਮਜ਼ਮੂਨਾਂ	mazmoonaan	*subjects* (m.)
ਹਿਸਾਬ	hisaab	*maths* (m.)
ਘਰ ਦਾ ਕੰਮ	ghar daa kanm	*homework* (m.)
ਲਾ ਪਰਵਾਹ	laa parvaah	*careless*
ਗਾਲੜੀ	gaalrhee	*talkative*
ਲਿਆਕਤ	liaakat	*ability* (f.)
ਵਰਤਣਾ	vartnhaa	*to use*
ਤਰ੍ਹਾਂ	tar-h-aan	*way, style*
ਪੜ੍ਹਾਉਣਾ	parh-h-aaunhaa	*to teach*
ਖ਼ੈਰ	khair	*anyway*
ਪੜ੍ਹਾਈ	parh-h-aaee	*studies* (f.)

214

ਤਾਂ ਕਿ	<u>taan</u> ki	*so that*
ਗਰੇਡ	gared	*grade* (m.)
ਬਣਨਾ	banhnaa	*to become*

Insight

Nouns can be changed into adjectives by making a slight adjustment.

Examples:

gall ਗੱਲ (talk) – *gaalrhee* ਗਾਲੜੀ (talkative)
shahir ਸ਼ਹਿਰ (city*)* – *shairee* ਸ਼ਹਿਰੀ (city dwelling)
sharaab ਸ਼ਰਾਬ (alcohol) – *sharaabee* ਸ਼ਰਾਬੀ (alcoholic)

ਅਭਿਆਸ abhiaas *Exercises*

After reading the dialogue and/or listening to the recording, try to do the following exercises.

1 Insert the missing vowels

The vowel signs in the following sentences are missing. Rewrite them after inserting the vowels and joining the letters.

a ਪ ਪ ਜ ! ਕ/ਤ ਸ/ਮ ਰ/ਸ਼ ਣ/ਅ ਧ ਅ ਪ ਕ/ਨੰ/ਮ ਲ/ਸ ?

b ਓ ਹ/ਸ ਨੰ/ਚੰ ਗ/ਤ ਗੁੰ/ਪੜੰ ਦ/ਨ ਹੰ ।

c ਤ ਨੰ/ਪੜੂ ਇ/ਵ ਚ/ਮ ਹ ਨ ਤ/ਕਰਨ/ਚ ਹ ਦ/ਹ ।

2 Crossword

Complete the crossword in English using the clues given in Panjabi.

੧ ਅਧਿਆਪਕ

੨ ਰਮੇਸ਼

੩ ਘਰ ਦਾ ਕੰਮ

੪ ਹਿਸਾਬ

੫ ਲਾ ਪਰਵਾਹ

Insight

Many Panjabi parents take a zealous interest in their children's education, and as an ideal would prefer that their children, particularly sons, should adopt the medical or engineering professions, though this is not a blanket statement.

2 Yes, officer
ਗੱਲ ਬਾਤ ੨ ਹਾਂ ਜੀ, ਅਫਸਰ ਸਾਹਿਬ
gall baa<u>t</u> 2 haa<u>n</u> jee, afsar saahib

◀) CD 2, TR 7, 02:22

Sheela has been stopped by a police officer for using her mobile phone while driving her car.

ਪੁਲਿਸ ਅਫਸਰ	ਬੀਬੀ ਜੀ, ਕਾਰ ਇੱਕ ਪਾਸੇ ਖੜ੍ਹੀ ਕਰੋ ਅਤੇ ਮੋਬਾਇਲ ਫੋਨ ਬੰਦ ਕਰੋ ਤਾਂ ਕਿ ਤੁਸੀਂ ਮੈਨੂੰ ਸੁਣ ਸਕੋ ।
ਸ਼ੀਲਾ	ਹਾਂ ਜੀ, ਅਫਸਰ ਸਾਹਿਬ ।
ਪੁਲਿਸ ਅਫਸਰ	ਤੁਸੀਂ ਅਪਰਾਧ ਕਰ ਰਹੇ ਹੋ । ਤੁਹਾਡੇ ਤੇ ਕਾਰ ਚਲਾਂਦਿਆਂ ਮੋਬਾਇਲ ਫੋਨ ਦੀ ਵਰਤੋਂ ਕਰਨ ਦਾ ਦੋਸ਼ ਲਗਾਇਆ ਜਾਂਦਾ ਹੈ ।
ਸ਼ੀਲਾ	ਮੈਂ ਕੇਵਲ ਇੱਕ ਮਿੰਟ ਲਈ ਫੋਨ ਵਰਤ ਰਹੀ ਸੀ ।
ਪੁਲਿਸ ਅਫਸਰ	ਤੁਸੀਂ ਪਿਛਲੇ ਦਸ ਮਿੰਟ ਤੋਂ ਗੱਲਾਂ ਕਰ ਰਹੇ ਸੀ । ਤੁਸੀਂ ਕਾਰ ਤੋਂ ਬਾਹਰ ਆਓ ਅਤੇ ਆਪਣਾ ਲਾਇਸੈਂਸ ਦਿਖਾਓ ।
ਸ਼ੀਲਾ	ਅਫਸਰ ਸਾਹਿਬ, ਕਿਰਪਾ ਕਰ ਕੇ ਇਸ ਵਾਰੀ ਮੈਨੂੰ ਮਾਫ ਕਰ ਦੇਵੋ ।
ਪੁਲਿਸ ਅਫਸਰ	ਤੁਸੀਂ ਕਨੂੰਨ ਦੀ ਉਲੰਘਣਾ ਕੀਤੀ ਹੈ । ਇਹ ਤੁਹਾਡੀ ਟਿਕਟ ਹੈ । ਹਫਤੇ ਅੰਦਰ ਆਪਣੇ ਕਾਰ ਦੇ ਕਾਗਜ਼ਾਤ ਪੇਸ਼ ਕਰੋ ।
Police officer	*Madam, please pull the car over to one side and stop using the telephone so that you can listen to me.*
Sheela	*Yes, officer.*
Police officer	*You are committing an offence. I am charging you [lit. you are charged] for using a mobile phone while driving.*
Sheela	*I was only using the phone for one minute.*
Police officer	*You've been talking for the last ten minutes. Please get out of the car and show me your licence.*
Sheela	*Officer, please let me off this time.*
Police officer	*You have broken the law. Here is your ticket. Please produce your car documents within one week.*

ਸ਼ਬਦਾਵਲੀ	shab<u>d</u>aavalee	*Vocabulary*
ਬੀਬੀ	beebee	*madam* (f.)
ਇੱਕ ਪਾਸੇ	ikk paase	*one side*
ਖੜ੍ਹਨਾ	kharh-h-naa	*to stand, to park*
ਬੰਦ	ban<u>d</u>	*closed, off*
ਅਪਰਾਧ	apraa<u>dh</u>	*offence* (m.)
ਦੋਸ਼	<u>d</u>osh	*charge* (m.)
ਗੱਲਾਂ	gallaa<u>n</u>	*speech, conversation* (f.)
ਲਾਇਸੈਂਸ	laaisai<u>n</u>s	*licence* (m.)
ਇਸ ਵਾਰੀ	is vaaree	*this time*
ਮਾਫ਼	maaf	*pardon, excuse*
ਕਾਨੂੰਨ	kaanoo<u>n</u>n	*law* (m.)
ਉਲੰਘਣਾ	ula<u>n</u>ghnhaa	*to disobey, to break*
ਕਾਗ਼ਜ਼ਾਤ	kaa<u>gh</u>zaa<u>t</u>	*papers, documents* (m.)
ਪੇਸ਼ ਕਰਨਾ	pesh karnaa	*to present, to produce*

ਅਭਿਆਸ abhiaas *Exercises*

After reading the dialogue and/or listening to the recording, try to do the following exercises.

1 Complete the table

ਕਾਨੂੰਨ		law
	beebee	
		documents
ਮਾਫ਼		
	ula<u>n</u>ghnhaa	

2 Loan words

Make a list of five words borrowed from English used in Dialogue 2.

3   *I am a social worker*
ਗੱਲ ਬਾਤ 3 ਮੈਂ ਸਮਾਜ ਸੇਵਕ ਹਾਂ
gall baat 3 main samaaj sevak haan

◀) CD 2, TR 7, 04:09

A social worker, Mrs Kaur, visits Kuldeep's house. She is following a complaint that under-aged children have been left unattended for long periods in the house.

ਸਮਾਜ ਸੇਵਕ	ਹੈਲੋ। ਮੈਂ ਸਮਾਜ ਸੇਵਕ ਹਾਂ ਅਤੇ ਮੇਰਾ ਨਾਮ ਮਿਸਜ਼ ਕੌਰ ਹੈ। ਇਹ ਮੇਰਾ ਸ਼ਨਾਖ਼ਤੀ ਕਾਰਡ ਹੈ। ਮੈਂ ਤੁਹਾਡੇ ਨਾਲ ਗੱਲ ਕਰਨ ਆਈ ਹਾਂ।
ਕੁਲਦੀਪ	ਅੰਦਰ ਆ ਜਾਓ। ਕੀ ਗੱਲ ਹੈ?
ਸਮਾਜ ਸੇਵਕ	ਤੁਹਾਡੇ ਖ਼ਿਲਾਫ਼ ਸਾਡੇ ਦਫ਼ਤਰ ਵਿਚ ਇੱਕ ਸ਼ਿਕਾਇਤ ਪਹੁੰਚੀ ਹੈ।
ਕੁਲਦੀਪ	ਕੀ ਹੋ ਗਿਆ ਹੈ? ਕੀ ਮੈਂ ਕੋਈ ਗਲਤ ਕੰਮ ਕਰ ਬੈਠੀ ਹਾਂ?
ਸਮਾਜ ਸੇਵਕ	ਤੁਸੀਂ ਆਪਣੇ ਦੋਨਾਂ ਬੱਚਿਆਂ ਨੂੰ ਇਕੱਲੇ ਘਰ ਦੇ ਅੰਦਰ ਛੱਡ ਕੇ, ਕੰਮ ਤੇ ਚਲੇ ਜਾਂਦੇ ਹੋ। ਇਹ ਇੱਕ ਖ਼ਤਰਨਾਕ ਸਥਿਤੀ ਬਣ ਸਕਦੀ ਹੈ।
ਕੁਲਦੀਪ	ਮੈਂ ੫ ਵਜੇ ਜਾਂਦੀ ਹਾਂ। ਮੇਰੇ ਪਤੀ ੭ ਵਜੇ ਆਉਂਦੇ ਹਨ। ਸਿਰਫ਼ ਦੋ ਘੰਟੇ ਦੀ ਗੱਲ ਹੈ।
ਸਮਾਜ ਸੇਵਕ	ਇਹਨਾਂ ਦੋ ਘੰਟਿਆ ਵਿਚ ਕੁਝ ਵੀ ਹੋ ਸਕਦਾ ਹੈ। ਕੰਮ ਦੇ ਘੰਟੇ ਬਦਲੋ ਜਾਂ ਕੋਈ ਹੋਰ ਇੰਤਜ਼ਾਮ ਕਰੋ।
ਕੁਲਦੀਪ	ਇਹ ਮੇਰੇ ਲਈ ਮੁਸ਼ਕਲ ਹੈ। ਮੈਂ ਕੰਮ ਨਹੀਂ ਛੱਡ ਸਕਦੀ।
ਸਮਾਜ ਸੇਵਕ	ਕੋਈ ਬੇਬੀ ਸਿਟਰ ਲੱਭੋ।
ਕੁਲਦੀਪ	ਮੈਂ ਪੂਰੀ ਕੋਸ਼ਿਸ਼ ਕਰਾਂ ਗੀ।
Social worker	*Hello, I am a social worker and my name is Mrs Kaur. Here is my identity card. I have come to talk to you.*
Kuldeep	*Please come in. What is the matter?*
Social worker	*We have received a complaint in our office against you.*
Kuldeep	*What has happened? Have I done anything wrong?*
Social worker	*You leave both of your children alone in the house and go to work. This is a potentially dangerous situation.*
Kuldeep	*I leave at 5 o'clock. My husband comes home at 7 o'clock. It is only a matter of two hours.*

Social worker	*Anything can happen in those two hours. Either change your hours of work or make alternative arrangements.*	
Kuldeep	*This is difficult for me. I can't leave work.*	
Social worker	*Find a babysitter.*	
Kuldeep	*I will try my best.*	

ਸ਼ਬਦਾਵਲੀ	shab<u>d</u>aavalee	*Vocabulary*
ਸਮਾਜ ਸੇਵਕ	samaaj sevak	*social worker* (m./f.)
ਸ਼ਨਾਖ਼ਤੀ ਕਾਰਡ	shanaa<u>kh</u>tee kaard	*identity card* (m.)
ਖ਼ਿਲਾਫ਼	<u>kh</u>ilaaf	*against*
ਦਫ਼ਤਰ	<u>d</u>af<u>t</u>ar	*office* (m.)
ਸ਼ਿਕਾਇਤ	shikaai<u>t</u>	*complaint* (f.)
ਗ਼ਲਤ	<u>gh</u>ala<u>t</u>	*wrong*
ਖ਼ਤਰਨਾਕ	<u>kh</u>a<u>t</u>arnaak	*dangerous*
ਸਥਿਤੀ	sa<u>th</u>i<u>t</u>ee	*situation* (f.)
ਇੰਤਜ਼ਾਮ	in<u>t</u>zaam	*arrangements* (m.)
ਬੇਬੀ ਸਿਟਰ	bebee sitar	*babysitter* (m./f.)
ਲੱਭਣਾ	labhbhnhaa	*to find*

ਅਭਿਆਸ abhiaas *Exercises*

After reading the dialogue and/or listening to the recording, try to do the following exercises.

1 Write or say in the correct word order

a ਹਾਂ ਸੇਵਕ ਸਮਾਜ ਮੈਂ   **c** ਜਾਓ ਆ ਅੰਦਰ

b ਹੈ ਕੀ ਗੱਲ?   **d** ਹੈ ਲਈ ਮੇਰੇ ਇਹ ਮੁਸ਼ਕਲ

2 Complete the sentences

Choose the correct word from the bracket to complete the sentence according to the specifications of gender and number. Remember that the verb changes according to the subject.

a ਮੈਂ ਤੁਹਾਡੇ ਨਾਲ ਗੱਲ ਕਰਨ   [masculine singular]
(ਆਈ/ਆਇਆ) ਹਾਂ।
I have come to talk to you.

b ਮੈਂ ਕੰਮ ਨਹੀਂ ਛੱਡ (ਸਕਦੀ/ਸਕਦਾ) ।   [feminine singular]
I can't leave work.

c ਤੁਸੀ ਕੰਮ ਤੇ (ਚਲੇ ਜਾਂਦੇ/ਚਲੀ ਜਾਂਦੇ) ਹੋ ।   [formal singular]
You go to work.

d ਮੈਂ ਪੂਰੀ ਕੋਸ਼ਿਸ਼ (ਕਰਾਂ ਗੇ/ਕਰਾਂ ਗੀ) ।   [feminine singular]
I will try my best.

ਬੋਲੀ ਬਾਰੇ   bolee baare   *Language points*

Purpose clauses

In Unit 7 infinitives in the oblique were shown to express purpose such as ਮੈਂ ਦੋਸਤ ਨੂੰ ਮਿਲਣ ਆਇਆ ਹਾਂ, *I have come to meet a friend.* Another way of expressing purpose is through the use of ਤਾਂ ਕਿ, *so that, in order to.* The verb in the purpose clause is normally in the subjunctive (since the action is often indefinite or uncertain):

ਸਿਮਰਨ ਨੇ ਦਵਾਈ ਲੈ ਲਈ ਤਾਂ ਕਿ ਬੁਖ਼ਾਰ ਉਤਰ ਜਾਏ	*Simran took medicine so that her fever would come down.*
ਮੈਂ ਦਰਵਾਜ਼ਾ ਬੰਦ ਕੀਤਾ ਸੀ ਤਾਂ ਕਿ ਬਿੱਲੀ ਅੰਦਰ ਨਾ ਆ ਸਕੇ	*I closed the door so that the cat couldn't come inside.*
ਇਮਰਾਨ ਉਰਦੂ ਪੜ੍ਹ ਰਿਹਾ ਹੈ ਤਾਂ ਕਿ ਉਹ ਪਾਕਿਸਤਾਨ ਵਿਚ ਆਪਣੇ ਰਿਸ਼ਤੇਦਾਰਾਂ ਨਾਲ ਗੱਲ ਕਰ ਸਕੇ	*Imran is studying Urdu so that he can speak with his relatives in Pakistan.*

Insight

'naheen *te*' 'ਨਹੀਂ ਤੇ' (otherwise) or '*taan* ki' 'ਤਾਂ ਕਿ' (so that) convey the same meaning.

Example: *main darvaazaa band keetaa see naheen te kutte ne andar aa jaanhaa see.*
ਮੈਂ ਦਰਵਾਜ਼ਾ ਬੰਦ ਕੀਤਾ ਸੀ ਨਹੀਂ ਤੇ ਕੁੱਤੇ ਨੇ ਅੰਦਰ ਆ ਜਾਣਾ ਸੀ
I closed the door otherwise the dog would have come inside.

Compound postpositions

In Unit 4 simple postpositions such as ਵਿਚ *in*, ਤੋਂ *from* and ਨੂੰ *to* were introduced. Postpositions having more than one word are called compound postpositions, most commonly using the postposition ਦੇ *of*. Compound postpositions behave in the same way as simple postpositions by requiring the words preceding them to be in the oblique case. Here are some commonly used compound postpositions:

ਦੇ ਅੰਦਰ	*inside*	ਦੇ ਵਾਸਤੇ	*for*
ਦੇ ਉੱਪਰ	*above, upon*	ਦੇ ਲਈ	*for*
ਦੇ ਪਿੱਛੇ	*behind*	ਦੀ ਜਗ੍ਹਾ	*in place of*
ਦੇ ਥੱਲੇ	*below*	ਦੇ ਸਾਹਮਣੇ	*opposite, facing*
ਤੋਂ ਪਹਿਲੇ	*before*	ਦੇ ਬਾਹਰ	*outside*
ਤੋਂ ਬਾਅਦ	*after*	ਤੋਂ ਇਲਾਵਾ	*apart from*
ਦੇ ਨੇੜੇ	*near*	ਤੋਂ ਬਿਨਾਂ/ਬ.ਗੈਰ	*without*
ਦੇ ਬਾਰੇ	*about, concerning*	ਦੇ ਬਾਵਜੂਦ	*in spite of*

Indirect speech

So far in this book we have focused on direct speech, when sentences and phrases have been directly spoken or reproduced. Indirect speech occurs when another action or speech is being reported or conveyed, such as in English: *She told me to call him*, ਉਸ ਨੇ ਮੈਨੂੰ ਕਿਹਾ ਕਿ ਉਹ ਨੂੰ ਬੁਲਾਓ. Indirect speech in Panjabi is expressed with the particle ਕਿ *that* to denote what was actually said or done.

Indirect speech is used when the verb of thought or speech occurred before the thought or speech being conveyed:

ਮੈਂ ਆਪਣੇ ਆਪ ਵਿਚ ਸੋਚਿਆ ਕਿ ਮੈਂ ਜ਼ਰੂਰ ਜਿੱਤਾਂ ਗੀ	*I thought to myself that I would definitely win.*
ਜਗਜੀਤ ਨੇ ਕਿਹਾ ਕਿ ਇਹ ਕਿਤਾਬ ਪੜ੍ਹਨ ਵਾਲੀ ਹੈ	*Jagjit said that this book is worth reading.*
ਕਿਸੇ ਨੇ ਮੈਨੂੰ ਦੱਸਿਆ ਕਿ ਮਿਸਜ਼ ਸ਼ਰਮਾ ਭਾਰਤ ਚਲੀ ਗਈ ਹੈ	*Someone told me that Mrs Sharma had gone to India.*

When the speech being conveyed is a command:

ਉਸ ਨੇ ਬੱਚਿਆਂ ਨੂੰ ਕਿਹਾ ਕਿ ਚੁੱਪ ਰਹੋ	*He told the children to be quiet.*
ਮੈਂ ਸਾਰਿਆਂ ਨੂੰ ਕਿਹਾ ਕਿ ਘਰ ਵਾਪਸ ਚਲੇ ਜਾਓ	*I told everyone to go back home.*

ਅਭਿਆਸ abhiaas *Exercises*

1 Fill in the blanks with the appropriate compound postpositions

a ਸਾਡਾ ਘਰ ਸਕੂਲ _____ ਹੈ। *Our house is near the school.*

b ਬਿੱਲੀ ਡੱਬੇ _____ ਹੈ। *The cat is inside the box.*

c ਉਹ ਰੋਟੀ ਖਾਣ _____ ਆਵੇ ਗਾ। *He will come after eating.*

d ਤਸਵੀਰ _____ ਕੁਝ ਹੋਰ ਚਾਹੀਦਾ ਹੈ। *There should be something else in place of the picture.*

2 Match the pairs

The following four sentences need to be joined with ਤਾਂ ਕਿ. Match the correct pairs of sentences with one another.

a ਮੈਂ ਦਰਵਾਜ਼ਾ ਬੰਦ ਕੀਤਾ		**i** . . . ਸਵੇਰੇ ਜਲਦੀ ਉਠ ਸਕੇ	
b ਅਸੀਂ ਪੰਜਾਬੀ ਬੋਲਾਂ ਗੇ	ਤਾਂ ਕਿ	**ii** . . . ਕੁੱਤਾ ਅੰਦਰ ਨਾ ਆ ਸਕੇ	
c ਤੈਨੂੰ ਜਲਦੀ ਆਉਣਾ ਚਾਹੀਦਾ ਹੈ		**iii** . . . ਸਾਰੇ ਸਮਝ ਜਾਣ	
d ਤੁਸੀਂ ਜਲਦੀ ਸੌਂ ਜਾਓ		**iv** . . . ਅਸੀਂ ਬਸ ਫੜ ਸਕੀਏ	

3 Listening

🔊 CD 2, TR 7, 05:40

Sheela is telling her story to her friend Meena about how she was stopped by the police officer for using her mobile phone while driving. Listen to the recording and answer the following questions. You may answer the questions with short or full answers.

a ਸ਼ੀਲਾ ਆਪਣੀ ਕਾਰ ਵਿਚ ਕਿੱਥੇ ਜਾ ਰਹੀ ਸੀ?

b ਉਹ ਕਿੰਨੀ ਦੇਰ ਤੋਂ ਮੋਬਾਈਲ ਤੇ ਗੱਲਾਂ ਕਰ ਰਹੀ ਸੀ?

c ਕੀ ਸ਼ੀਲਾ ਨੇ ਅਫ਼ਸਰ ਅੱਗੇ ਸੱਚ ਬੋਲਿਆ?

d ਇੱਕ ਹਫ਼ਤੇ ਦੇ ਅੰਦਰ ਸ਼ੀਲਾ ਨੂੰ ਕੀ ਕਰਨਾ ਪੈਣਾ ਹੈ?

4 Alphabetical order

Rearrange the following words into alphabetical order, considering only the first letter of each word.

ਪਾਪਾ	ਵਰਤਣਾ	ਡਾਕਟਰ	ਅਧਿਆਪਕ	ਬਾਰੇ
ਪੜੁਊਣਾ	ਮਜ਼ਮੂਨਾਂ	ਦੂਜੇ	ਹਿਸਾਬ	ਕਲਾਸ
ਲਿਆਕਤ	ਕੰਮ	ਮਿਹਨਤ	ਸ਼੍ਰੇਣੀ	ਇਲਾਵਾ

Ten important things to remember

1. Attending a Panjabi wedding can be an enriching experience gaining insights into the Panjabi language, culture and social customs.
2. There are dozens of customs associated with Panjabi weddings, starting with the 'rokaa' 'ਰੋਕਾ' (when the groom is told not to consider other marriage proposals) and ending with the 'doli' 'ਡੋਲੀ' (when the bride leaves her parental home).
3. Postpositions having more than one word are called compound postpositions. Examples: _de andar_ – ਦੇ ਅੰਦਰ –inside.
4. Indirect speech in Panjabi is expressed with the particle 'ki' 'ਕਿ' (that) to denote what was actually said or done. Moreover the construction of the reported sentence in Panjabi is quite flexible compared to English.
5. '_Saahib_' 'ਸਾਹਿਬ' is an honorific particle like '_jee_' 'ਜੀ' which is most commonly used in Panjabi conversation. The literal meaning of '_saahib_' 'ਸਾਹਿਬ' is 'sir'.

6 There are many nouns in Panjabi like '*adhiaapak*' 'ਅਧਿਆਪਕ' (teacher) and '*samaaj sevak*' 'ਸਮਾਜ ਸੇਵਕ' (social worker) which are grammatically masculine and have their feminine counterparts but they represent both males and females.

7 There are many English words which have been adopted into the Panjabi language but there are some words such as 'police' (pronounced 'pulis' 'ਪੁਲਿਸ') and 'officer' (pronounced 'afsar' 'ਅਫਸਰ') which have slightly modified pronunciation in Panjabi.

8 Instead of '*adhiaapak*' 'ਅਧਿਆਪਕ' (teacher), '*maastar*' 'ਮਾਸਟਰ' or '*maastar jee*' 'ਮਾਸਟਰ ਜੀ' is a more colloquial word frequently used by Panjabis. The female teacher is called '*ustaanee*' 'ਉਸਤਾਨੀ' or '*maastaraanee*' 'ਮਾਸਟਰਨੀ'.

9 The literal meaning of '*gall*' 'ਗੱਲ' is 'talk' but it has also many other different meanings and senses.

10 When '*laa*' 'ਲਾ' is used as a prefix, it conveys a negative meaning to the original word. Example: '*laa*' 'ਲਾ' + '*parvaah*' 'ਪਰਵਾਹ' (care) = '*laa parvaah*' 'ਲਾ ਪਰਵਾਹ' (careless).

15

वैसाखी
vaisaakhee
Vaisakhi

In this unit you will learn:

- About the *Vaisakhi* festival
- About Panjabi poetry and music
- How to express *to allow*

The Vaisakhi fair
वैसाखी दा मेला
vaisaakhee ḏaa melaa

◄) **CD 2, TR 8, 00:20**

The following extract is a news report from the BBC Asian Network reporting on the events of the **Vaisakhi** festival in Birmingham, UK.

नीलू	ਮੈਂ ਨੀਲੂ ਹਾਂ ਤੇ ਮੈਂ ਬੀ. ਬੀ. ਸੀ. ਰੇਡੀਓ ਲਈ ਹੈਂਡਜ਼ਵਰਥ ਪਾਰਕ ਤੋਂ ਰਿਪੋਰਟ ਪੇਸ਼ ਕਰ ਰਹੀ ਹਾਂ। ਇਸ ਸਾਲ ਵੈਸਾਖੀ ਦਾ ਤਿਉਹਾਰ ਬੜੀ ਧੂਮ ਧਾਮ ਨਾਲ ਮਨਾਇਆ ਜਾ ਰਿਹਾ ਹੈ। ਅੱਜ ਲੱਗਦਾ ਹੈ ਜਿਵੇਂ ਸਾਰੇ ਸ਼ਹਿਰ ਦੇ ਪੰਜਾਬੀ ਲੋਕ ਪਹੁੰਚੇ ਹੋਏ ਹਨ। ਹੁਣੇ ਮੈਂ ਅੰਕਲ ਜੀ ਨੂੰ ਪੁੱਛਿਆ ਹੈ ਕਿ ਉਹਨਾਂ ਨੂੰ ਮੇਲਾ ਕਿਵੇਂ ਲੱਗ ਰਿਹਾ ਹੈ।
ਅੰਕਲ	ਮੈਨੂੰ ਆਪਣਾ ਪੇਂਡੂ ਜੀਵਨ ਯਾਦ ਆ ਰਿਹਾ ਹੈ। ਸਾਡੇ ਲਈ ਇਹ ਫ਼ਸਲਾਂ ਕਟਣ ਦੀ ਖ਼ੁਸ਼ੀ ਦਾ ਤਿਉਹਾਰ ਹੈ।

ਨੀਲੂ	. . . ਨਾਲੇ ਵੈਸਾਖ ਪੰਜਾਬੀ ਸਾਲ ਦਾ ਪਹਿਲਾ ਮਹੀਨਾ ਵੀ ਹੈ । ਅੱਛਾ ਆਂਟੀ ਜੀ, ਤੁਸੀਂ ਇੱਥੇ ਅੱਜ ਕਿਉਂ ਆਏ ਹੋ ?
ਆਂਟੀ	ਬੇਟੀ, ਵੈਸਾਖੀ ਸਿੱਖ ਕੌਮ ਦਾ ਜਨਮ ਦਿਨ ਹੈ । ਜਿੱਥੇ ਅਸੀਂ ਖਲੋਤੇ ਹਾਂ, ਉੱਥੇ ਨਗਰ ਕੀਰਤਨ ਆਉਣ ਵਾਲਾ ਹੈ । ਅੱਗੇ ਅੱਗੇ ਨੌਜੁਆਨ ਗਤਕਾ ਖੇਡ ਰਹੇ ਹਨ । ਪਿੱਛੇ ਗੁਰੂ ਗਰੰਥ ਸਾਹਿਬ ਦੀ ਸਵਾਰੀ ਹੈ ।
ਨੀਲੂ	ਮੈਂ ਹੁਣ ਲੰਗਰ ਹਾਲ ਵੱਲ ਜਾ ਰਹੀ ਹਾਂ । ਦੇਖੋ! ਜਲੇਬੀਆਂ, ਪਕੌੜੇ ਅਤੇ ਹੋਰ ਕਈ ਚੀਜ਼ਾ ਸੇਵਾਦਾਰ ਮੁਫ਼ਤ ਵਰਤਾ ਰਹੇ ਹਨ । ਬੱਚਿਆਂ ਨੂੰ ਲੰਗਰ ਪਹਿਲੇ ਲੈਣ ਦੇਵੇ ।
ਕਾਕਾ	ਨੀਲੂ ਆਂਟੀ! ਮੈਂ ਲੰਗਰ ਛਕਣ ਤੋ ਬਾਅਦ ਝੂਟੇ ਲਵਾਂ ਗਾ । ਬੱਚਿਆਂ ਦੇ ਮਨਪਰਚਾਵੇ ਲਈ ਬਹੁਤ ਕੁਝ ਹੈ ।
ਨੀਲੂ	ਅੱਛਾ ਬੇਟਾ । ਝੂਟਿਆਂ ਤੋਂ ਇਲਾਵਾ ਨੁਮਾਇਸ਼ ਵੀ ਲੱਗੀ ਹੋਈ ਹੈ । ਭੰਗੜਾ ਸ਼ੁਰੂ ਹੋਣ ਲੱਗਾ ਹੈ । ਹੁਣ ਮੈਨੂੰ ਇਜਾਜ਼ਤ ਦੇਵੋ । ਸਾਰਿਆਂ ਨੂੰ ਬੀ. ਬੀ. ਸੀ. ਵੱਲੋਂ ਵੈਸਾਖੀ ਦੀ ਵਧਾਈ!

Neelu	*I'm Neelu and I'm reporting for BBC Radio from Handsworth Park. The Vaisakhi festival this year is being celebrated with a 'bang'. It seems today that all the Panjabi people of the city have come here. I have just asked Uncle how he feels about the fair.*
Uncle	*I am remembering my village life. For us this is a happy festival of harvest.*
Neelu	*Vaisakh is also the first month of the Panjabi calendar. Well, Auntie, why have you come here?*
Auntie	*Vaisakhi is the birthday of the Sikh nation. The religious procession is due to arrive where we are standing. In front of the procession young people are playing gatka. It is followed by the installation of the Guru Granth Saahib.*
Neelu	*I am going towards the langar hall. Look! Jalebeeaan, pakaurhe and many other things are being served by volunteers free of charge. Please allow the children to have langar first.*
Young boy	*Auntie Neelu! I will go on the rides after I've had langar. There is a lot of entertainment for the children.*
Neelu	*OK, son. Apart from the rides, there is also an exhibition. Bhangra is about to begin. Now, please excuse me. To everyone from BBC Radio, happy Vaisakhi!*

ਸ਼ਬਦਾਵਲੀ	shabdaavalee	Vocabulary
ਪੇਸ਼	pesh	to present
ਵੈਸਾਖੀ	vaisaakhee	Vaisakhi, one of the Sikh festivals (f.)
ਮੇਲਾ	melaa	fair (m.)
ਧੂਮ ਧਾਮ	dhoom dhaam	bang, pomp and show (f.)
ਮਨਾਉਣਾ	manaaunhaa	to celebrate
ਦਰਸ਼ਕ	darshak	participant, visitor (m./f.)
ਪੁੱਛਣਾ	puchchnhaa	to ask
ਪੇਂਡੂ	pendoo	of the village, village-like
ਜੀਵਨ	jeevan	life (m.)
ਫ਼ਸਲਾਂ	fasalaan	crops (f.)
ਕਟਣ	katanh	to cut
ਤਿਉਹਾਰ	tiuhaar	celebration, festival (m.)
ਵੈਸਾਖ	vaisaakh	one of the Indian months (m.)
ਕੌਮ	kaum	nation, community (f.)
ਜਨਮ ਦਿਨ	janam din	birthday (m.)
ਖਲੋਣਾ	khalonhaa	to be stood, to stand
ਨਗਰ ਕੀਰਤਨ	nagar keertan	religious procession (m.)
ਗਤਕਾ	gatkaa	a Sikh martial art like fencing (m.)
ਖੇਡਣਾ	khednhaa	to play
ਗੁਰੂ ਗਰੰਥ	guroo garanth	Guru Granth; holy book of the Sikhs (m.)
ਸਵਾਰੀ	savaaree	installation (f.)
ਲੰਗਰ	langar	community kitchen cuisine (m.)
ਸੇਵਾਦਾਰ	sevaadaar	volunteer (m./f.)
ਮੁਫ਼ਤ	mufat	free
ਵਰਤਾਉਣਾ	vartaaunhaa	to serve
ਛਕਣਾ	chaknhaa	to take, to consume
ਝੂਟੇ	jhoote	rides (m.)
ਮਨਪਰਚਾਵੇ	manparchaave	entertainment, enjoyment (m.)

ਨੁਮਾਇਸ਼	numaaish	*exhibition* (f.)
ਵੱਲੋਂ	vallo<u>n</u>	*on behalf of*
ਵਧਾਈ	va<u>dh</u>aaee	*congratulations* (f.)

> **Insight**
>
> It is not easy or appropriate to translate religious terms from Panjabi into English. Sometimes the real sense and essence are lost in translation from the believer's point of view.

ਅਭਿਆਸ abhiaas *Exercises*

After reading the dialogue and/or listening to the recording, try to do the following exercises.

1 Answer in Panjabi

Answer the questions in Panjabi in either full sentences or in short form answers. The answers to the questions can be found in the dialogue. The first one has been done for you.

a What is the name of the radio presenter?

ਪੇਸ਼ ਕਰਤਾ ਦਾ ਨਾਮ ਨੀਲੂ ਹੈ। (full sentence) or ਨੀਲੂ (short answer)

b What is the report about?

c Name two main things associated with the Vaisakhi festival.

d What is being served in the community kitchen?

e What is the name of the game being played in front of the procession?

f Name two main activities taking place at the Vaisakhi fair.

2 Identify the appropriate answers

The *Vaisakhi* festival is associated with:

- village people
- candles
- harvest season
- the new year
- Sikh religion

228

3 True or false?

Langar means *community kitchen*.	True/False
Guru Granth is the holy book of the Sikhs.	True/False
Gatka is a group dance.	True/False
Nagar kirtan is singing.	True/False

Insight

Vaisakhi is a harvest festival in India but Sikhs celebrate it on a grand scale because it also has a special religious significance for them.

Folk song: My spinning wheel is of many colours
ਲੋਕ ਗੀਤ: ਚਰਖਾ ਮੇਰਾ ਰੰਗਲਾ
lok geet: charkhaa meraa ranglaa

◀ CD 2, TR 8, 02:46

The following is a traditional Panjabi folk song. Listen to the song on the recording while reading the verses of the song:

ਚਰਖਾ ਮੇਰਾ ਰੰਗਲਾ ਵਿਚ ਸੋਨੇ ਦੀਆਂ ਮੇਖਾਂ
ਵੇ ਮੈਂ ਤੈਨੂੰ ਯਾਦ ਕਰਾਂ ਜਦ ਚਰਖੇ ਵੱਲ ਵੇਖਾਂ

ਚਰਖੇ ਦੇ ਸ਼ੀਸ਼ਿਆਂ 'ਚ ਦਿਸੇ ਤੇਰਾ ਮੁੱਖ ਵੇ
ਵੇਖ ਵੇਖ ਮਿਟ ਦੀ ਨਾ ਅੱਖੀਆਂ ਦੀ ਭੁੱਖ ਵੇ
ਸੀਨੇ ਵਿਚ ਨੇ ਰੜਕ ਦੀਆਂ ਇਹ ਚਰਖੇ ਦੀਆਂ ਮੇਖਾਂ

ਦਿਨ ਰਾਤ ਤੇਰੀਆਂ ਰਾਹਾਂ ਵੱਲ ਜਾਵਾਂ ਝਾਕੀ ਵੇ
ਤੇਰੇ ਬਿਨ ਅਸੀਂ ਕੀ ਮਨਾਉਣੀ ਦੇ ਵੈਸਾਖੀ ਵੇ
ਸੌ ਸੌ ਪੀਰ ਮਨਾਵਾਂ ਨਾਲੇ ਥਾਂ ਥਾਂ ਮੱਥੇ ਟੇਕਾਂ
ਵੇ ਮੈਂ ਤੈਨੂੰ ਯਾਦ ਕਰਾਂ ਜਦ ਚਰਖੇ ਵੱਲ ਵੇਖਾਂ

My spinning wheel is of many colours, studded with gold nails
Oh! I remember you, when I look at the spinning wheel

I see your face in the mirror work of the spinning wheel
Continuously looking does not satisfy my eyes' desire
The studded nails of this spinning wheel prick my heart

Day and night I keep watch on the road for your return
Without you, what kind of Vaisakhi am I to celebrate?
For your return I pray to a hundred holy men
and bow my head at many holy places
Oh! I remember you, when I look at the spinning wheel

ਸ਼ਬਦਾਵਲੀ	shabdaavalee	Vocabulary
ਚਰਖਾ	charkhaa	*spinning wheel* (m.)
ਰੰਗਲਾ	ranglaa	*colourful* (v.)
ਸੋਨਾ	sonaa	*gold* (m.)
ਮੇਖ	mekh	*nail* (f.)
ਵੇ	ve	subjunctive particle
ਵੱਲ	vall	*towards*
ਵੇਖਣਾ	vekhnhaa	*to see*
ਸ਼ੀਸ਼ਾ	sheeshaa	*mirror* (m.)
ਦਿਸਣਾ	disnhaa	*to be visible, to be seen*
ਮੁੱਖ	mukhkh	*face* (m.)
ਮਿਟਣਾ	mitnhaa	*to finish, to vanish*
ਭੁੱਖ	bhukhkh	*hunger* (f.)
ਸੀਨਾ	seenaa	*bosom, heart* (m.)
ਰੜਕਣਾ	rarhkanhaa	*to prick, to rub against*
ਰਾਹਾਂ	raahaan	*roads, routes* (f.)
ਝਾਕਣਾ	jhaaknhaa	*to stare, to look at*

ਪੀਰ	peer	*holy man* (m.)
ਮਨਾਉਣਾ	manaaunhaa	*to pray, to believe*
ਟੇਕਣਾ	teknhaa	*to bow down*

ਅਭਿਆਸ abhiaas *Exercises*

After reading the folk song and/or listening to the recording, try to do the following exercise.

Answer the questions (yes or no)

My spinning wheel is many-coloured.
It is studded with nails of gold.
I remember you whenever I look at it.
These nails make me suffer in love.

ਮੇਰਾ ਚਰਖਾ ਕਈ ਰੰਗਾਂ ਵਾਲਾ ਹੈ।
ਇਸ ਵਿਚ ਸੋਨੇ ਦੀਆਂ ਮੇਖਾਂ ਲੱਗੀਆਂ ਹੋਈਆਂ ਹਨ।
ਜਦੋਂ ਮੈਂ ਇਸ ਵੱਲ ਦੇਖਦੀ ਹਾਂ, ਉਦੋਂ ਤੈਨੂੰ ਯਾਦ ਕਰਦੀ ਹਾਂ।
ਇਹ ਮੇਖਾਂ ਮੈਨੂੰ ਪਿਆਰ ਵਿਚ ਤੜਫਾਂਦੀਆਂ ਹਨ।

a ਕੀ ਇਹ ਗੀਤ ਪਿਆਰ ਬਾਰੇ ਕੁਝ ਦੱਸ ਰਿਹਾ ਹੈ?
b ਕੀ ਚਰਖੇ ਵਿਚ ਲੋਹੇ *(iron)* ਦੀਆਂ ਮੇਖਾਂ ਹਨ?
c ਜਦੋਂ ਔਰਤ ਚਰਖੇ ਵੱਲ ਵੇਖਦੀ ਹੈ ਕੀ ਉਦੋਂ ਆਪਣੇ ਪਿਆਰ ਨੂੰ ਭੁੱਲ ਜਾਂਦੀ ਹੈ?
d ਕੀ ਚਰਖੇ ਦਾ ਸਿਰਫ਼ ਇੱਕ ਰੰਗ ਹੈ?

ਬੋਲੀ ਬਾਰੇ bolee baare *Language points*

Relative–correlatives

You have already been introduced to the most common relative pronoun, **ਜਿਹੜਾ**, which means *that* (see Unit 9 for a review of how sentences with relative pronouns are formed). Relative–correlatives are relative pronouns which are paired with their correlating counterparts. The correlating counterpart of the relative pronoun **ਜਿਹੜਾ** can be either **ਇਹ** or **ਉਹ** (*that . . . which*). In English, the sentence *I will go when he comes* contains only one relative pronoun *when*. However, the same sentence would be expressed in Panjabi as *when he comes, then I will go* with the relative pronoun *when* and its correlative *then*. There are a number of such pairings that can be used to indicate place, time, quantity and likeness. For example:

Relative		Correlative	
ਜਿਹੜਾ	who, which	ਉਹ	he, she, it, that
ਜਿਹੜਾ	who, which	ਇਹ	he, she, it, this
ਜਦੋਂ	when	ਉਦੋਂ	then
ਜੱਦ ਤਕ	as long as	ਤੱਦ ਤਕ	until then
ਜਿਵੇਂ	in such a way	ਉਵੇਂ	in that way
ਜਿੰਨਾਂ	as many, however much	ਉਨਾਂ	that much, that many
ਜਿੰਨਾਂ	as many, however much	ਇੰਨਾਂ	this much, this many
ਜਿਥੇ	where	ਉੱਥੇ	there

ਜਿਥੇ ਅਸੀਂ ਰਹਿੰਦੇ ਹਾਂ ਉੱਥੇ ਪੰਜਾਬੀ ਬੋਲੀ ਜਾਂਦੀ ਹੈ

Panjabi is spoken where we live.
(lit. *Where we live, Panjabi is spoken there.*)

ਜਿਵੇਂ ਤੁਸੀਂ ਚਾਹੁੰਦੇ ਹੋ ਉਵੇਂ ਅਸੀਂ ਕਰਾਂ ਗੇ

We'll do as you like.
(lit. *As you like, that is the way we will do.*)

ਜਿਹੜਾ ਬੰਦਾ ਲਾਹੌਰ ਜਾ ਚੁਕਾ ਹੈ ਉਹ ਨੂੰ ਰਸਤਾ ਪੁੱਛੋ

Ask directions from the man who has been to Lahore.
(lit. *The man who has been to Lahore, ask the way from him.*)

ਜੱਦ ਤਕ ਤੂੰ ਪੰਜਾਬ ਨਹੀਂ ਜਾਂਦਾ ਤੱਦ ਤਕ ਤੈਨੂੰ ਚੰਗੀ ਪੰਜਾਬੀ ਨਹੀਂ ਆਏ ਗੀ

You won't learn good Panjabi until you go to Panjab.
(lit. *As long as you don't go to Panjab, until then you won't learn good Panjabi.*)

ਜਿੰਨਾਂ ਜ਼ਿਆਦਾ ਕੰਮ ਕਰੋ ਗੇ ਉਨੇ ਜ਼ਿਆਦਾ ਪੈਸੇ ਕਮਾ ਸਕੋ ਗੇ

The more you work, the more money you can earn.
(lit. *As much work as you will do, that much more money you will earn.*)

The subjunctive particle ਵੇ 've'

You will recall from Unit 12 that the subjunctive mood is used to indicate uncertainty or indefiniteness. The particle ਵੇ is associated with the endings of the subjunctive mood. It is not, however, uncommon to see the particle ਵੇ on its own, particularly in poetic language and songs. It can appear as part of the verb in the subjunctive or on its own in the phrase or sentence. In the passage of the song ਚਰਖਾ ਮੇਰਾ ਰੰਗਲਾ the particle ਵੇ occurs at the beginning of the second line:

| ਵੇ ਮੈਂ ਤੈਨੂੰ ਯਾਦ ਕਰਾਂ | *(Oh!) I remember you.* |

The vocative case, as you learned in Unit 8, is a projection of an address to someone similar to the English *oh!* or *hey!* ਵੇ is a colloquial form of address in friendly and informal situations.

The verb ਲੱਗਣਾ 'laggnhaa'

The verb ਲੱਗਣਾ has occured a number of times throughout the units so far. In Unit 9 Simran asks Jaspreet about the cloth: ਤੈਨੂੰ ਕਿਹੜਾ ਵਧੇਰੇ ਚੰਗਾ ਲੱਗਦਾ ਹੈ?, *Which one do you like better?* In the second dialogue of Unit 9 Simran says to the doctor: ਮੈਨੂੰ ਠੰਡ ਲੱਗ ਰਹੀ ਹੈ, *I am feeling cold*. The basic definition of ਲੱਗਣਾ is *to be applied to*; however, it can also carry slightly different meanings. In the first example it means *to seem* or *to appear* and in the second example it has the sense *to be struck*. In fact ਲੱਗਣਾ is used in a wide range of situations and it is therefore always necessary to take the context of the sentence into account. Here are some examples of these different, yet related, senses of the verb ਲੱਗਣਾ:

ਲੱਗਣਾ meaning *to seem, to like, to be struck*

ਨਿਆਣੇ ਨੂੰ ਠੰਡ ਲੱਗੇ ਗੀ	*The child will feel cold.*
ਅਮਰੀਕਾ ਰਹਿਣਾ ਮੈਨੂੰ ਅੱਛਾ ਲੱਗਦਾ ਹੈ	*I like living in America.* (lit. *Living in America seems good to me.*)
ਘਰ ਨੂੰ ਅੱਗ ਲੱਗੀ ਹੋਈ ਸੀ	*The house was on* (lit. *struck by*) *fire.*

ਲੱਗਣਾ to meaning *time taken* or *to cost*

ਅੰਮ੍ਰਿਤਸਰ ਪਹੁੰਚਣ ਨੂੰ ਕਿੰਨਾ ਚਿਰ ਲੱਗੇ ਗਾ?	*How long will it take to get to Amritsar?*
ਮੈਨੂੰ ਸਿਰਫ਼ ਦਸ ਮਿੰਟ ਲੱਗੇ	*It only took me ten minutes.*
ਇੱਕ ਟਿਕਟ ਲਈ ਕਿੰਨੇ ਪੈਸੇ ਲੱਗਦੇ ਹਨ?	*How much money does one ticket cost?* (lit. *it take*)

ਲੱਗਣਾ following an oblique infinitive

In this case, its meaning changes to give the sense *to begin*:

ਬਾਰਸ਼ ਹੋਣ ਲੱਗੀ	*It began to rain.*
ਮੈਂ ਕੰਮ ਸ਼ੁਰੂ ਕਰਨ ਲੱਗਾ ਸੀ	*I was about to begin work.*
ਉਹ ਸੋਚਣ ਲੱਗਾ ਕਿ ਸਾਰੇ	*He began to think that everyone*
ਚਲੇ ਗਏ ਹਨ	*had left.*

Oblique infinitives with ਦੇਣਾ 'denhaa'

The general use of ਦੇਣਾ in compound constructions was discussed in Unit 9. ਦੇਣਾ can also be used with oblique infinitives to give the meaning of *to allow to* or *to permit*. Similar to the way in which ਲੱਗਣਾ changes its meaning to *to begin* when following oblique infinitives, ਦੇਣਾ with the oblique infinitive also changes its meaning.

ਕੁੱਤੇ ਨੂੰ ਅੰਦਰ ਆਉਣ ਦੇ	*Let the dog come inside.*
ਪਿਤਾ ਜੀ ਨੇ ਮੈਨੂੰ ਗੱਡੀ	*Father did not allow me to drive the car.*
ਚਲਾਉਣ ਨਹੀਂ ਦਿੱਤੀ	
ਉਹ ਆਪਣੇ ਬੱਚੇ ਨੂੰ ਬਾਹਰ	*They allow their child to play outside.*
ਖੇਡਣ ਦੇਂਦੇ ਹਨ	

ਵਿਆਖਿਆ viaakhiaa *Commentary*

1 Media

There are many opportunities, living in the West, to interact with Panjabi speakers and to hear the language being spoken. In particular there has been a growth in media output. In most big towns and cities in England, and the major cities in North America, there are radio stations which either produce programming totally in Panjabi or have specific Panjabi language programmes. In Toronto, Canada, a mainstream cable television channel broadcasts six hours of Panjabi programming every day. Generally, most satellite and cable TV channels catering for a South Asian audience will have some Panjabi programmes in addition to Hindi/Urdu, Gujarati and Bengali programming.

Much of the programming on these TV channels is taken up with films. The Indian sub-continent produces more films every year than Hollywood. Bombay (Mumbai) is the centre of the Indian film industry and to mark this fact it is affectionately called 'Bollywood'. However, regional film makers are also very significant in the overall production and consumption of cinema in South Asia. In fact the Telegu film industry matches – in terms of number of films produced – that of Mumbai. Despite the presence of large numbers of Panjabi actors and directors – in fact the Kapoor family has dominated Indian films over the last 40 years – the Panjabi-language film industry is not well developed in East Panjab. The majority of Panjabi-language films are produced in Lahore (also called 'Lollywood') and are high in action but low in quality, both cinematically and in terms of language use. However, there are a few films to be recommended which are useful to watch in order to pick up the language. These films are available in any South Asian area in England, Canada and beyond. Wherever a South Asian community is settled, there is always an outlet for videos and, more recently, cinema halls showing films from the sub-continent.

2 Poetry

Panjab is renowned for folk poetry, particularly for the tradition of Sufi-inspired poems. Poetry flourished in medieval times with poets such as Bulleh Shah and Waris Shah making indelible implants on the social consciousness of the Panjabi *literati*. In the modern period, Bhai Vir Singh and Amrita Pritam are two poets worthy of mention. Poetry is popular primarily because of its sung form. The folk song given earlier in this unit is a good example of a form of poetic verse. Much of this music has become professionalized and Panjab is the foremost producer of folk music in India and Pakistan.

Insight

The life-style in Panjab villages is in a transitional stage. Urbanization is changing traditions into trends at a great speed.

ਅਭਿਆਸ abhiaas *Exercises*

1 Fill in the blanks

In this unit you have learned about relative–correlatives in the language points section. Fill in the blanks with the appropriate relative–correlative pairs.

a _____ ਦੌੜੇ ਗਾ, _____ ਇਨਾਮ ਜਿਤੇ ਗਾ ।
The person who runs will win the prize.

b _____ ਤੁਸੀਂ ਚਾਹੁੰਦੇ ਹੋ, _____ ਅਸੀਂ ਕਰਾਂ ਗੇ ।
We will do as you like.

c _____ ਤੁਸੀਂ ਰਹਿੰਦੇ ਹੋ, _____ ਪੰਜਾਬੀ ਬੋਲੀ ਜਾਂਦੀ ਹੈ ।
Panjabi is spoken where you live.

d _____ ਮੈਂ ਦਵਾਈ ਖਾਧੀ, _____ ਹੀ ਆਰਾਮ ਆ ਗਿਆ ।
When I took the medicine I felt relief immediately.

2 Complete the sentences

Complete the sentences in Panjabi with the appropriate expressions of *to allow to*. The first one has been done for you.

a ਉਸ ਨੂੰ ਅੰਦਰ (ਆਉਣ ਦੇ) *Let him come inside.*

b ਕੁੱਤੇ ਨੂੰ _____ *Let the dog go out.*

c ਮੈਨੂੰ ਜੂਸ _____ *Let me drink juice.*

d ਬੀਬੀ ਜੀ ਨੂੰ ਟੀ ਵੀ _____ *Allow the lady to watch TV.*

3 Write sentences using the verb ਲੱਗਣਾ

a It takes 15 minutes to get to work.
b How much does one first-class ticket cost?
c I am feeling hot.
d It started to rain.
e We were about to go out.

Ten important things to remember

1 Correlatives are relative pronouns which are paired with their correlating counterparts: '*udon*' 'ਉਦੋਂ' (then), '*uven*' 'ਉਵੇਂ' (in that way) and '*uththe*' 'ਉੱਥੇ' (there) are correlatives of '*jadon*'

'ਜਦੋਂ' (when), 'jiven' 'ਜਿਵੇਂ' (in such a way) and 'jiththe' 'ਜਿੱਥੇ' (where) respectively.

2 'Ve' 'ਵੇ' and 'nee' 'ਨੀ' are colloquial forms of address in friendly and informal situations: 've' 'ਵੇ' is used for men and 'nee' 'ਨੀ' for ladies.

3 Previously in Panjab villages one of the main chores of daily life for women was working with a spinning wheel *(charkhaa)* (ਚਰਖਾ). Now the *'charkhaa'* 'ਚਰਖਾ' is only a cultural icon and a heritage symbol.

4 Broadly speaking the *'gurmukhi'* 'ਗੁਰਮੁਖੀ' letter *'vavvaa'* 'ਵਾਵਾ' is equivalent to 'v' rather than to 'w'. You will find that in many Panjabi words 'w' is used instead of 'v' as in *'diwali'* (festival of lights) and *'gurdwara'* (Sikh temple).

5 If you are interested in learning more about the Sikh religion, it would be a good idea to pay a visit to a *gurdwara* (Sikh place of worship).

6 It is worth paying a visit to a Panjabi sweet shop to have a first-hand experience of tasting a variety of sweets and savouries.

7 The verb *'laggnhaa'* 'ਲੱਗਣਾ' in Panjabi is used in a variety of senses and meanings. a) In Unit 15 Neelu says *'ajj laggdaa hai'* 'ਅੱਜ ਲਹਦਾ ਹੈ' which means 'it seems today'. b) In Unit 9 *Simran* says *'mainoon thand lagg rahee hai'* 'ਮੈਨੂੰ ਠੰਡ ਲੱਗ ਰਹੀ ਹੈ' which conveys 'I am feeling cold.'

8 The basic definition of *'laggnhaa'* 'ਲੱਗਣਾ' is 'to be applied to' such as *'malam lagaao'* 'ਮਲਮ ਲਗਾਓ' apply the ointment.

9 The verb *'laggnhaa'* 'ਲੱਗਣਾ' is used in an idiomatic sense in the following examples:
   a) *'mainoon siraf das mint lagge'* 'ਮੈਨੂੰ ਸਿਰਫ਼ ਦਸ ਮਿੰਟ ਲੱਗੇ' (it only took me ten minutes)
   b) *'baarash honh laggee'* 'ਬਾਰਸ਼ ਹੋਣ ਲੱਗੀ' (it began to rain).

10 Like *'laggnhaa'* 'ਲੱਗਣਾ', *'denhaa'* 'ਦੇਣਾ' is also used in many senses, such as to give, to pay, to offer, to allow and to impart.

16

ਪੰਜਾਬ ਦੇ ਲੋਕ ਨਾਚ
panjaab de lok naach
Folk dances of Panjab

In this unit you will learn:

- About the folk dances of Panjab
- About experiences of the Panjabi diaspora
- Phrases of choice

---

1   *Folk dances of Panjab*
ਗੱਲ ਬਾਤ ੧ ਪੰਜਾਬ ਦੇ ਲੋਕ ਨਾਚ
gall baat 1 panjaab de lok naach

◀) **CD 2, TR 9, 00:21**

It is the end of Mr Singh's Panjabi class. He has taken all the students to a cultural programme in the Southall Community Centre to see a range of folk dances. As they enter the hall they hear the sound of drums and see the dancers.

ਮਿਸਟਰ ਸਿੰਘ	ਉਹ ਮੁੰਡੇ ਸਟੇਜ ਤੇ ਪੰਜਾਬ ਦਾ ਲੋਕ ਨਾਚ ਭੰਗੜਾ ਪਾ ਰਹੇ ਹਨ। ਉਹਨਾਂ ਨੇ ਚਮਕੀਲੇ ਰੰਗਦਾਰ ਕਪੜੇ ਪਾਏ ਹੋਏ ਹਨ। ਉਹਨਾਂ ਦੇ ਹੱਥਾਂ ਵਿਚ ਭਾਂਗਾਂ ਹਨ।
ਡੇਵਿਡ	ਇੱਕ ਬੰਦੇ ਨੇ ਢੋਲ ਚੁੱਕਿਆ ਹੋਇਆ ਹੈ।
ਮਿਸਟਰ ਸਿੰਘ	ਢੋਲ ਦੇ ਵੱਜਣ ਨਾਲ ਸਿਰਫ਼ ਪੈਰ ਨਹੀਂ ਸਗੋਂ ਦਿਲ ਵੀ ਨੱਚਣ ਲੱਗ ਪੈਂਦਾ ਹੈ।

ਜੇਨ	ਭੰਗੜੇ ਵਾਲਿਆਂ ਦੀਆਂ ਬੋਲੀਆਂ ਪੁਰਾਣੀਆਂ ਹਨ। ਮੈਨੂੰ ਨਵੇਂ ਤੇ ਅਜੋਕੇ ਗੀਤ ਚੰਗੇ ਲੱਗਦੇ ਹਨ ਜਿਹੜੇ ਇੱਥੋਂ ਦੇ ਜੰਮਪਲ ਨੌਜੁਆਨਾਂ ਨੇ ਰਚੇ ਹਨ।
ਮਿਸਟਰ ਸਿੰਘ	ਮੰਨੋ ਜਾਂ ਨਾ ਮੰਨੋ, ਭੰਗੜਾ ਅੰਤਰ ਰਾਸ਼ਟਰੀ ਨਾਚ ਬਣ ਗਿਆ ਹੈ। ਭਾਵੇਂ ਤੁਸੀਂ ਪੰਜਾਬ ਜਾਂ ਬਾਹਰ ਹੋ, ਭੰਗੜਾ ਦੇਖ ਸਕਦੇ ਹੋ।
ਜੇਨ	ਕੀ ਸਿਰਫ਼ ਮੁੰਡੇ ਭੰਗੜਾ ਪਾਉਂਦੇ ਹਨ?
ਮਿਸਟਰ ਸਿੰਘ	ਪੁਰਾਣੇ ਜ਼ਮਾਨੇ ਵਿਚ ਭੰਗੜਾ ਮੁੰਡਿਆਂ ਲਈ ਸੀ ਤੇ ਗਿੱਧਾ ਕੁੜੀਆਂ ਲਈ ਸੀ। ਹੁਣ ਸਭ ਕੁਝ ਰਲ ਮਿਲ ਗਿਆ ਹੈ। ਦੇਖੋ! ਗਿੱਧਾ ਸ਼ੁਰੂ ਹੋ ਗਿਆ ਹੈ।
ਡੇਵਿਡ	ਉਹਨਾਂ ਵਿੱਚੋਂ ਇੱਕ ਕੁੜੀ ਢੋਲਕੀ ਵਜਾ ਰਹੀ ਹੈ ਅਤੇ ਦੂਜੀ ਢੋਲਕੀ ਤੇ ਚਮਚਾ ਮਾਰ ਰਹੀ ਹੈ।
ਜੇਨ	ਹਰ ਕੋਈ ਚੜ੍ਹਦੀ ਕਲਾ ਵਿਚ ਹੈ। ਆਓ, ਆਪਾਂ ਨੱਚੀਏ।

Mr Singh	*Those boys on the stage are performing* bhangra, *a folk dance of Panjab. They are wearing sparkling, colourful clothes. They are carrying long wooden poles in their hands.*
David	*One man is carrying a big drum.*
Mr Singh	*With the beat of the drum, it is not only the feet but also the heart that starts dancing.*
Jane	*The verses of* bhangra *are old fashioned. I like the new, modern songs which are composed by young people born and raised here.*

Mr Singh	*Believe it or not,* bhangra *has become an international dance. Whether you are in Panjab or abroad, you can always see* bhangra.
Jane	*Do only boys perform* bhangra?
Mr Singh	*In the old times,* bhangra *was for the boys and* gidha *was for the girls. Now everything is mixed up. Look! The* gidha *has started.*

David	One of the girls is playing a small drum and the other girl is tapping the small drum with a spoon.
Jane	Everyone is in high spirits. Come on, let's dance!

Insight
It is ideal to learn a language through its own native script.

ਸ਼ਬਦਾਵਲੀ	shabdaavalee	Vocabulary
ਲੋਕ ਨਾਚ	lok naach	folk dance (m.)
ਚਮਕੀਲਾ	chamkeelaa	glittering, shining, sparkling (v.)
ਰੰਗਦਾਰ	rangdaar	colourful
ਡਾਂਗ	daang	long wooden pole (f.)
ਢੋਲ	dhol	big drum (m.)
ਵੱਜਣਾ	vajjnhaa	to be played, to be beaten
ਪੈਰ	pair	feet (m.)
ਸਗੋਂ	sagon	but also
ਦਿਲ	dil	heart (m.)
ਨੱਚਣਾ	nachchnhaa	to dance
ਬੋਲੀਆਂ	boleeaan	folk verse couplets (f.)
ਅਜੋਕਾ	ajokaa	modern
ਜੰਮਪਲ	janmpal	raised, born and bred
ਨੌਜੁਆਨ	naujuaan	youth (m.)
ਰਚਨਾ	rachnaa	composition (f.)
ਮੰਨੋ ਜਾਂ ਨਾ ਮੰਨੋ	manno jaan naa manno	believe it or not
ਅੰਤਰ ਰਾਸ਼ਟਰੀ	antar raashtaree	international
ਜ਼ਮਾਨਾ	zamaanaa	times (m.)
ਗਿੱਧਾ	gidhdhaa	women's folk dance (m.)
ਰਲ ਮਿਲਣਾ	ral milnhaa	to be mixed
ਵਿੱਚੋਂ	vichchon	from within
ਢੋਲਕੀ	dholkee	small drum (f.)
ਵਜਾਉਣਾ	vajaaunhaa	to play (music), to beat
ਚਮਚਾ	chamchaa	spoon (m.)

240

| ਮਾਰਨਾ | maarnaa | *to hit, to tap* |
| ਚੜ੍ਹਦੀ ਕਲਾ | charh-h-<u>d</u>ee kalaa | *high spirits* |

Insight

Gurmukhi ਗੁਰਮੁਖੀ is the most suitable and accurate script to convey the sounds of spoken Panjabi, but from its origins Panjabi was written in *Shahmukhi* ਸ਼ਾਹਮੁਖੀ script and continues so today in Pakistan Panjab.

ਅਭਿਆਸ abhiaas *Exercises*

After reading the dialogue and/or listening to the recording, try to do the following exercises.

1 True or false?

a ਪੁਰਾਣੇ ਜ਼ਮਾਨੇ ਵਿਚ ਭੰਗੜਾ ਸਿਰਫ਼ ਮੁੰਡਿਆਂ ਲਈ ਸੀ ।   True/False

b ਜੈਨ ਨੂੰ ਉਹ ਗੀਤ ਚੰਗੇ ਲੱਗਦੇ ਹਨ ਜਿਹੜੇ ਪੁਰਾਣੇ ਤੇ
ਪੰਜਾਬ ਦੇ ਹਨ ।   True/False

c ਢੋਲਕੀ ਤੇ ਕੁੜੀਆਂ ਡਾਂਗਾਂ ਮਾਰਦੀਆਂ ਹਨ ।   True/False

d ਭੰਗੜਾ ਅੰਤਰ ਰਾਸ਼ਟਰੀ ਨਾਚ ਬਣ ਗਿਆ ਹੈ ।   True/False

2 Write or say the sentences in Panjabi

a I like bhangra.

b I like bhangra more than gidha.

c Whether you're in Panjab or abroad, you can see bhangra.

d Come on, let's dance!

3 Try to identify the items from the descriptions given in the dialogue

2 *Avtar's life story*

ਗੱਲ ਬਾਤ ੨ ਅਵਤਾਰ ਦੀ ਜੀਵਨ ਕਹਾਣੀ

gall baat 2 avtaar dee jeevan kahaanhee

🔊 **CD 2, TR 9, 02:05**

Two men, Avtar and Tarlok, are sitting on a park bench in Vancouver enjoying the sunny day. Avtar is reminiscing about his family's history and how he came to settle in Vancouver.

ਅਵਤਾਰ	ਕੀ ਸਾਨੂੰ ਆਪਣੇ ਬਚਪਨ ਵਿਚ ਕਦੀ ਖ਼ਿਆਲ ਸੀ ਕਿ ਅਸੀਂ ਇਸ ਉਮਰ ਵਿਚ ਕੈਨੇਡਾ ਰਹਿ ਰਹੇ ਹੋਵਾਂ ਗੇ? ਮੇਰਾ ਪੜਦਾਦਾ ਅੰਗਰੇਜ਼ਾਂ ਦੇ ਰਾਜ ਵੇਲੇ ਫ਼ੌਜ ਵਿਚ ਭਰਤੀ ਹੋ ਗਿਆ ਤੇ ਉਸ ਨੂੰ ਮਲੇਸ਼ੀਆ ਭੇਜ ਦਿੱਤਾ ਗਿਆ। ਮੇਰੇ ਦਾਦੇ ਦਾ ਜਨਮ ਉੱਥੇ ਹੋਇਆ। ਜਦੋਂ ਉਹ ਵਾਪਸ ਪਰਤਿਆ ਤਾਂ ਆਜ਼ਾਦੀ ਲਈ ਜਦੋ ਜਹਿਦ ਸ਼ੁਰੂ ਹੋ ਗਈ ਸੀ। ਮੇਰਾ ਦਾਦਾ ਗ਼ਦਰ ਪਾਰਟੀ ਵਿਚ ਸ਼ਾਮਲ ਹੋ ਕੇ ਵੈਨਕੂਵਰ ਆ ਗਿਆ।
ਤਰਲੋਕ	ਕੀ ਤੇਰਾ ਜਨਮ ਕੈਨੇਡਾ ਹੋਇਆ ਸੀ?
ਅਵਤਾਰ	ਕਹਾਣੀ ਲੰਬੀ ਹੈ। ਸਾਡੇ ਵਡੱਕਿਆਂ ਨੇ ਥਾਂ ਥਾਂ ਦਾ ਪਾਣੀ ਪੀਤਾ ਹੈ। ਸਮਾਂ ਪਾ ਕੇ ਮੇਰਾ ਦਾਦਾ ਪੰਜਾਬ ਮੁੜ ਗਿਆ। ਫਿਰ ੧੯੪੭ ਵਿਚ ਪੰਜਾਬ ਦਾ ਬਟਵਾਰਾ ਹੋ ਗਿਆ। ਉਦੋਂ ਮੇਰੇ ਪਿਤਾ ਜੀ ਲਾਇਲਪੁਰ ਸਨ ਤੇ ਸਾਰੇ ਪਰਵਾਰ ਨੂੰ ਜਲੰਧਰ ਜਾਣਾ ਪਿਆ। ਮੇਰਾ ਜਨਮ ਜਲੰਧਰ ਹੋਇਆ ਸੀ।
ਤਰਲੋਕ	ਮੇਰੇ ਦਾਦਾ ਜੀ ਈਸਟ ਅਫ਼ਰੀਕਾ ਰੇਲਵੇ ਬਣਾਉਣ ਚਲੇ ਗਏ। ਮੇਰਾ ਜਨਮ ਅਸਥਾਨ ਯੂਗਾਂਡਾ ਹੈ। ੧੯੭੧ ਵਿਚ ਛੱਡ ਛੁਡਾ ਕੇ ਅਸੀਂ ਪਹਿਲੇ ਇੰਗਲੈਂਡ ਗਏ ਤੇ ਫਿਰ ਕੈਨੇਡਾ ਆ ਗਏ।
ਅਵਤਾਰ	ਇਸ ਦਾ ਮਤਲਬ ਇਹ ਹੈ ਕਿ ਤੁਸੀਂ ਪੰਜਾਬ ਤੋਂ ਕਾਫ਼ੀ ਦੇਰ ਤੋਂ ਉਖੜੇ ਹੋਏ ਹੋ।
ਤਰਲੋਕ	ਹਾਂ। ਪਰ ਹੁਣ ਮੇਰਾ ਦਿਲ ਲੱਗ ਗਿਆ ਹੈ, ਭਾਵੇਂ ਅਸੀਂ ਪੰਜਾਬ ਤੋਂ ਦੂਰ ਹਾਂ। ਇੱਥੇ ਆਪਣੀ ਅਬਾਦੀ ਕਾਫ਼ੀ ਹੈ। ਮਾਹੌਲ ਪੰਜਾਬ ਵਾਂਗੂੰ ਹੈ।
ਅਵਤਾਰ	ਦੁਨੀਆਂ ਵਿਚ ਕਿਸੇ ਵੀ ਜਗ੍ਹਾ ਚਲੇ ਜਾਓ, ਭਾਵੇਂ ਕੈਨੇਡਾ ਭਾਵੇਂ ਇੰਗਲੈਂਡ ਜਾਂ ਅਮਰੀਕਾ, ਕੋਈ ਨਾ ਕੋਈ ਆਪਣਾ ਪੰਜਾਬੀ ਬੰਦਾ ਤੈਨੂੰ ਮਿਲ ਜਾਏ ਗਾ।
ਤਰਲੋਕ	ਪਰ ਸਿਆਣੇ ਲੋਕ ਕਹਿੰਦੇ ਹਨ ਕਿ ਧੋਬੀ ਦਾ ਕੁੱਤਾ ਨਾ ਘਰ ਦਾ ਨਾ ਘਾਟ ਦਾ!
ਅਵਤਾਰ	ਇਹ ਅਖਾਣ ਪੁਰਾਣਾ ਹੈ। ਹੁਣ ਸਾਰੀ ਦੁਨੀਆਂ ਤੁਹਾਡੀ ਹੈ। ਵਾਹਿਗੁਰੂ ਭਲਾ ਕਰੇ ਗਾ।

Avtar	Did we ever dream in our childhood that at this age we would be living in Canada? My great grandfather joined the army during the time of British rule and he was sent to Malaysia. My grandfather was born there. When he returned home, the struggle for independence had started. My grandfather joined the Gadar Party and came to Vancouver.
Tarlok	So, were you born in Canada?
Avtar	It's a long story. Our forefathers have been to many places [lit. our forefathers drank water from many different places]. After a while, my grandfather returned to Panjab. Then in 1947 Panjab was partitioned. At that time my father was in Lyallpur and the whole family had to go to Jalandhar. I was born in Jalandhar.
Tarlok	My grandfather went to East Africa to build the railways. My birthplace is Uganda. In 1971 we left everything and went first to England and then came to Canada.
Avtar	This means that you have been uprooted from Panjab for a long time.
Tarlok	Yes. But even though we are far away from Panjab, I am now happily settled [lit. my heart has been applied or fixed]. There are quite a lot of our own people here. The atmosphere is just like Panjab.
Avtar	Go anywhere in the world, whether it's Canada, England or America, and you will meet a Panjabi person.
Tarlok	But wise men say that immigrants belong to no one place. [Proverb: the dog of a washerman belongs neither at home nor at the washing place.]
Avtar	This is an old proverb. Now the whole world belongs to you. God will watch over you.

Insight

In Pakistan Panjabi is written in *Shahmukhi* ਸ਼ਾਹਮੁਖੀ script.

ਸ਼ਬਦਾਵਲੀ	shabdaavalee	*Vocabulary*
ਜੀਵਨ	jeevan	*life* (m.)
ਬਚਪਨ	bachpan	*childhood* (m.)
ਪੜਦਾਦਾ	parhdaadaa	*great grandfather* (m.)
ਰਾਜ	raaj	*rulership, kingdom* (m.)
ਵੇਲੇ	vele	*period, time* (m.)
ਫੋਜ	fauj	*military* (f.)

ਭਰਤੀ	bhartee	*join*
ਜਨਮ	janam	*birth* (m.)
ਪਰਤਣਾ	partnhaa	*to return*
ਅਜ਼ਾਦੀ	azaadee	*freedom, independence* (f.)
ਜਦੋ ਜਹਿਦ	jado jahid	*struggle* (f.)
ਅਜ਼ਾਦੀ ਲਈ ਜਦੋ ਜਹਿਦ	azaadee laee jado jahid	*struggle for independence*
ਗ਼ਦਰ	ghadar	*mutiny* (m.)
ਗ਼ਦਰ ਪਾਰਟੀ	ghadar paartee	*Gadar Party* (f.) (an anti-colonial political movement in Panjab in the early 20th century which had strong connections with Vancouver because of the large number of exiles from Panjab who went there)
ਲੰਬਾ	lanbaa	*long, lengthy* (v.)
ਵਡੱਕਿਆਂ	vadkkiaan	*ancestors, forefathers* (m.)
ਥਾਂ ਥਾਂ	thaan thaan	*each and every place* (m.)
ਸਮਾਂ ਪਾ ਕੇ	samaan paa ke	*after a while, after some time*
ਮੁੜਨਾ	murhnaa	*to turn around, to return*
ਬਟਵਾਰਾ	batvaaraa	*division, partition* (m.)
ਈਸਟ ਅਫ਼ਰੀਕਾ	eest afreekaa	*East Africa* (m.)
ਯੂਗੰਡਾ	yoogandaa	*Uganda* (m.)
ਜਨਮ ਅਸਥਾਨ	janam asthaan	*birthplace* (m.)
ਉਖੜਨਾ	ukharhnaa	*to be displaced, to be uprooted*
ਦਿਲ ਲੱਗਣਾ	dil laggnhaa	*to feel at home, to be settled, to live happily*
ਕੋਈ ਨਾ ਕੋਈ	koee naa koee	*some one or another*
ਸਿਆਣਾ	siaanhaa	*wise, mature* (v.)
ਧੋਬੀ	dhobee	*washerman* (m.)
ਕੁੱਤਾ	kuttaa	*dog* (m.)
ਘਾਟ	ghaat	place where clothes are washed on the bank of the river or canal (m.)

| ਅਖਾਣ | akhaanh | *proverb, saying* (m.) |
| ਭੱਲਾ | bhallaa | *look after, watch over* |

Insight

In Western countries some people have started using the Roman script to represent Panjabi words for the sake of convenience.

ਅਭਿਆਸ abhiaas *Exercises*

After reading the dialogue and/or listening to the recording, try to do the following exercises.

1 Name four countries mentioned in the dialogue

2 Answer the questions

Answer the following questions in Panjabi either in short form or in full sentences. You may lift the answers from the dialogue.

a ਜਿਹੜੇ ਦੋਨੋਂ ਦੋਸਤ ਆਪਸ ਵਿਚ ਗੱਲਾਂ ਕਰ ਰਹੇ ਹਨ, ਉਹਨਾਂ ਦੇ ਨਾਮ ਕੀ ਹਨ?
b ਅਵਤਾਰ ਦੇ ਦਾਦੇ ਦਾ ਜਨਮ ਕਿੱਥੇ ਹੋਇਆ ਸੀ?
c ਜਦੋਂ ਪੰਜਾਬ ਦਾ ਬਟਵਾਰਾ ਹੋ ਗਿਆ, ਅਵਤਾਰ ਦਾ ਪਿਤਾ ਕਿੱਥੇ ਸੀ?
d ਤਰਲੋਕ ਦਾ ਜਨਮ ਅਸਥਾਨ ਕਿੱਥੇ ਹੈ?
e ਸਿਆਣੇ ਬੰਦੇ ਕੀ ਕਹਿੰਦੇ ਹਨ?

3 Give the reasons why Avtar and Tarlok's families migrated to each place

a ਅਵਤਾਰ ਦੇ ਪੜਦਾਦਾ ਜੀ ਮਲੇਸ਼ੀਆ ਕਿਉਂ ਗਏ ਸੀ?
b ਅਵਤਾਰ ਦੇ ਦਾਦਾ ਜੀ ਵੈਨਕੂਵਰ ਕਿਉਂ ਗਏ ਸੀ?
c ੧੯੪੭ ਵਿਚ ਅਵਤਾਰ ਦੇ ਸਾਰੇ ਪਰਵਾਰ ਨੂੰ ਜਲੰਧਰ ਕਿਉਂ ਜਾਣਾ ਪਿਆ?
d ਤਰਲੋਕ ਦੇ ਦਾਦਾ ਜੀ ਈਸਟ ਅਫਰੀਕਾ ਕਿਉਂ ਗਏ ਸੀ?

ਬੋਲੀ ਬਾਰੇ bolee baare *Language points*

Future continuous

The future continuous is used when an on-going action in the future is being described, similar to the usage in the English sentence *I will be going*. This would be expressed in Panjabi as ਮੈਂ ਜਾ ਰਿਹਾ ਹੋਵਾਂ ਗਾ. The future continuous can also be used in situations when the on-going action in the future was not certain at the time of contemplation. For example, at the beginning of the second dialogue, when Avtar says to Tarlok ਕੀ ਸਾਨੂੰ ਕਦੀ ਖ਼ਿਆਲ ਸੀ ਕਿ ਅਸੀਂ ਕੈਨੇਡਾ ਰਹਿ ਰਹੇ ਹੋਵਾਂ ਗੇ ? *Did we ever dream that we would be living in Canada?* In English the uncertainty of the sentence would be expressed through the use of *would* rather than *will*. In Panjabi the future continuous tense can be used for both types of situations.

In previous units you were introduced to both the present continuous tense and the future tense. The future continuous tense can be most simply understood as a combination of the present continuous and the future tenses. Notice in the following examples how the future continuous combines the two tenses:

Future tense	ਮੈਂ ਜਾਵਾਂ ਗਾ	*I will go*
Present continuous	ਮੈਂ ਜਾ ਰਿਹਾ ਹਾਂ	*I am going*
Future continuous	ਮੈਂ ਜਾ ਰਿਹਾ ਹੋਵਾਂ ਗਾ	*I will/would be going*
Future tense	ਅਸੀਂ ਖਾਵਾਂ ਗੇ ।	*We will eat*
Present continuous	ਅਸੀਂ ਖਾ ਰਹੇ ਹਾਂ	*We are eating*
Future continuous	ਅਸੀਂ ਖਾ ਰਹੇ ਹੋਵਾਂ ਗੇ	*We will/would be eating*

The continuous action in the sentence takes the present continuous form, such as in these examples, with *going* represented through the stem ਜਾ and *eating* with the stem ਖਾ and with the appropriate forms of ਰਿਹਾ. You should have noticed that the auxiliary verb that comes at the end of the present continuous tense does not appear in the future continuous. Instead, the verb ਹੋਣਾ is in the future form with the respective -ਗਾ endings.

Phrases of choice

In English, phrases of choice are expressed through such words as *either . . . or, neither . . . nor* and *not only . . . but also*. In Panjabi there are similar types of constructions to express choice most commonly using the following:

ਭਾਵੇਂ . . . ਭਾਵੇਂ	*either . . . or, whether or not*
ਚਾਹੇ . . . ਚਾਹੇ	*either . . . or, whether or not*
ਨਾ . . . ਨਾ	*neither . . . nor*

ਨਾ ਸਿਰਫ਼ . . . ਸਗੋਂ	*not only . . . but*
ਜਾਂ . . . ਨਾ	*may or not*

Some examples of these words in use:

ਭਾਵੇਂ ਤੁਸੀਂ ਜਾਓ ਭਾਵੇਂ ਨਾ ਜਾਓ, ਮੈਂ ਇੱਥੇ ਰਵਾਂਗੀ ।	*Whether you go or not, I will stay here.* (lit. *Whether you go or whether you do not go, I will stay here.*)
ਚਾਹੇ ਸਾਡੇ ਨਾਲ ਆਓ ਚਾਹੇ ਉਹਨਾਂ ਨਾਲ ਜਾਓ, ਤੁਹਾਨੂੰ ਜਲਦੀ ਨਿਕਲਣਾ ਪੈਣਾ	*Whether you come with us or (whether you) go with them, you'll have to get out quickly.*
ਸਾਡੇ ਕੋਲ ਨਾ ਕਿਤਾਬਾਂ ਹਨ ਨਾ ਕਾਗ਼ਜ਼ ਹੈ	*We have neither books nor paper.*
ਲੋਕ ਨਾ ਸਿਰਫ਼ ਭਾਰਤ ਤੋਂ ਆਉਂਦੇ ਹਨ ਸਗੋਂ ਸਾਰੀ ਦੁਨੀਆਂ ਤੋਂ ਆਉਂਦੇ ਹਨ	*People come not only from India, but from all over the world.*
ਮੰਨੋ ਜਾਂ ਨਾਂ ਮੰਨੋ ਇਹ ਜਗ੍ਹਾ ਸਭ ਤੋਂ ਸੁਹਣੀ ਹੈ ।	*You may or may not agree but this is the nicest place.*

ਹੈ ਗਾ 'hai gaa' and ਸੀ ਗਾ 'see gaa'

In colloquial Panjabi, the verb ਹੋਣਾ is often expressed with the ending -ਗਾ when there is an added emphasis. The ending -ਗਾ merely indicates definiteness or confirmation, and must agree with the number and gender of the subject that it is referring to followed by the appropriate present form of ਹੋਣਾ. In Unit 3 Jane and Henry went to the sweet shop with Mr Singh. Jane asked the shopkeeper ਕੀ ਕੋਈ ਨਮਕੀਨ ਚੀਜ਼ ਹੈ? *Is there anything salty?* This question is general in nature. If Jane had wished to put further emphasis on the definite availability of something salty, she could have said: ਕੀ ਕੋਈ ਨਮਕੀਨ ਚੀਜ਼ ਹੈ ਗੀ ਏ? *Is there anything salty (available)?* The shopkeeper could have then replied ਹਾਂ ਜੀ, ਹੈ ਗੀ ਏ *Yes, there (definitely) is.* Note that the feminine singular form is used (-ਗੀ) in agreement with ਚੀਜ਼, although in the shopkeeper's response the subject is omitted as it is simply understood. Since ਹੈ ਗਾ is only used in informal speech, the auxiliary verb ਹੋਣਾ also appears in its informal form, hence ਏ instead of ਹੈ.

When one wants to express the same type of definiteness in the past, then ਸੀ (was) is followed by the ending -ਗਾ. Again, the number and gender of the subject will determine the ending of -ਗਾ. Some examples are as follows:

ਜਸਪ੍ਰੀਤ ਤੇ ਸਿਮਰਨ ਘਰ ਸੀ ਗੀਆਂ	*Jaspreet and Simran were (definitely) at home.*
ਤੁਸੀਂ ਚੁੱਪ ਚਾਪ ਸੀ ਗੇ	*You (certainly) were quiet.*

You will come across ਹੈ ਗਾ and ਸੀ ਗਾ frequently in spoken colloquial conversation, though rarely in the written form.

ਵਿਆਖਿਆ viaakhiaa *Commentary*

Folk music

Folk music is an integral part of cultural expression not only in Panjab but in the three Panjabs: East Panjab in India, West Panjab in Pakistan and the Panjabi diaspora all over the world. In fact, music is one of the main factors that links Panjabis across religious, national and caste divisions. **Bhangra** music, in particular, has come to prominence in the last 20 years in the West. The following illustration shows the traditional costume of **bhangra** dancers. This active and incessant dance music form is a vital part of a global expression of youth culture as well as a particular link between **des** (*home*) and **pardes** (*abroad*) for many Panjabis.

As we saw in the previous unit, there are many other musical forms from Panjab which focus on the relationship between music and poetry that are less related to the robust dance style of **bhangra** and more to the film music and **ghazal** (*ballad*) form. A wide range of Panjabi music from westernized dance music to slow ballads is widely available in the South Asian shopping centres of London, New York, Toronto and Melbourne.

Insight

The Panjabi folk dance *bhangra* ਭੰਗੜਾ has gained international status because of the presence and visibility of the Panjabi diaspora throughout the world. Many current Bollywood/Hindi films contain *bhangra* ਭੰਗੜਾ beats and dance rhythms with storylines of Panjabi families and smatterings of Panjabi dialogue and song lyrics.

ਅਭਿਆਸ abhiaas *Exercises*

1 Complete the sentences

Complete the sentences (verbally or in written form) with the help of the vocabulary given. The first one has been done for you.

a ਸਾਡੇ ਕੋਲ ਨਾ ਕਿਤਾਬਾਂ ਹਨ, ਨਾ ਕਾਗ਼ਜ਼ ਹੈ ।

We have neither books nor paper.

b ਸਾਡੇ ਕੋਲ ਨਾ _____ ਹਨ, ਨਾ _____ ਹੈ ।

c ਸਾਡੇ ਕੋਲ ਨਾ _____ ਹਨ, ਨਾ _____ ਹੈ ।

d ਸਾਡੇ ਕੋਲ ਨਾ _____ ਹਨ, ਨਾ _____ ਹੈ ।

ਪੈਨਸਲਾਂ	*pencils*	ਕਾਪੀ	*exercise book*	ਘੜੀਆਂ	*watches*
ਰੇਡੀਓ	*radio*	ਬੋਤਲਾਂ	*bottles*	ਪਾਣੀ	*water*

2 Say or write the sentences in Panjabi

a ਮੰਨੋ ਜਾਂ ਨਾ ਮੰਨੋ, ਇਹ ਜਗ੍ਹਾ ਸੋਹਣੀ ਹੈ ।

Believe it or not, this place is beautiful.

b Not only is this book long, but it is also difficult.

c Not only do we like **bhangra**, but we also like **gidha**.

d Whether you live in Panjab or abroad, you can see **bhangra**.

e You may or may not agree, but Vancouver's atmosphere is just like Panjab.

3 Tick the boxes which correspond with Tarlok and Avtar's respective life histories

	ਇੰਗਲੈਂਡ	ਮਲੇਸ਼ੀਆ	ਕੈਨੇਡਾ	ਲਾਇਲਪੁਰ	ਯੂਗੰਡਾ	ਜਲੰਧਰ
ਤਰਲੋਕ						
ਅਵਤਾਰ						

Ten important things to remember

1 Usage of 'whether . . . not'. Example: *'bhaaven tuseen jaao, bhaaven naa jaao, main iththe ravaan gee'*- 'ਭਾਵੇਂ ਤੁਸੀ ਜਾਓ ਭਾਵੇਂ ਨਾ ਜਾਓ, ਮੈਂ ਇੱਥੇ ਰਵਾਂਗੀ l' Whether you go or not, I will stay here. You can replace *'bhaaven'* 'ਭਾਵੇ' with *'chaahe'* 'ਚਾਹੇ', if you wish.

2 Usage of 'neither . . . nor.' Example: *'naa saade kol kitaabaan han, naa painslaan'* 'ਨਾ ਸਾਡੇ ਕੋਲ ਕਿਤਾਬਾਂ ਹਨ ਨਾ ਪੈਂਸਲਾਂ'- We have neither books nor pencils.

3 Usage of 'either . . . or'. Example: *'jaan chaah peeo jaan kaufee'* 'ਜਾਂ ਚਾਹ ਪੀਓ ਜਾਂ ਕੋਫ਼ੀ'. Have either tea or coffee.

4 Usage of 'believe it or not'. Example: *'manno jaan naa manno uh kamaal daa bandaa hai'* 'ਮੰਨੋ ਜਾਂ ਨਾ ਮੰਨੋ ਉਹ ਕਮਾਲ ਦਾ ਬੰਦਾ ਹੈ'- Believe it or not he is a wonderful person.

5 Usage of 'though . . . (yet)'. Example: *'be shak uh budhdhaa aadmee hai phir vee uh chust hai'* 'ਬੇ ਸ਼ਕ ਉਹ ਬੁੱਢਾ ਆਦਮੀ ਹੈ ਫਿਰ ਵੀ ਉਹ ਚੁਸਤ ਹੈ' Though he is an old man, (yet) he is active.

6 Usage of 'not only . . . but'. Example: *'lok naa keval bhaarat ton aaunde han balki saaree duneeaan ton aaunde han'* 'ਲੋਕ ਨਾ ਕੇਵਲ ਭਾਰਤ ਤੋਂ ਆਉਂਦੇ ਹਨ ਬਲਕਿ ਸਾਰੀ ਦੁਨੀਆਂ ਤੋਂ ਆਉਂਦੇ ਹਨ' People come not only from India, but from all over the world. You can replace *'balki'* 'ਬਲਕਿ' with *'sagon'* 'ਸਗੋਂ', if you wish.

7 The fate of migrants is summed up in the following proverb that they belong neither at home nor abroad. Proverb: *'dhobee daa kuttaa naa ghar daa naa ghaat daa'* 'ਧੋਬੀ ਦਾ ਕੁੱਤਾ ਨਾ ਘਰ ਦਾ ਨਾ ਘਾਟ ਦਾ' 'A washerman's dog is neither attached to a place of residence nor to a place of work.'

8 The future continuous tense is used when an on-going action in the future is being described. Example: *'main jaa rihaa hovaan gaa'* 'ਮੈਂ ਜਾ ਰਿਹਾ ਹੋਵਾਂ ਗਾ' I will be going.

9 The usage of *'hai gaa'*. The ending *'gaa'* 'ਗਾ' merely indicates definiteness or confirmation and must agree with the number and gender of the subject that it refers to.

10 The usage of *'see gaa'* 'ਸੀ ਗਾ'. When one wants to express the same type of definiteness in the past, then *'see'* 'ਸੀ' (was) is followed by the ending *'gaa'*. Again the number and gender of the subject will determine the ending *'gaa'* 'ਗਾ'.

Appendices

Appendix 1

Consonants			Velar	Palatal	Retroflex	Dental	Labial
Plosives	Voiceless	Unaspirated	ਕ	ਚ	ਟ	ਤ	ਪ
		Aspirated	ਖ	ਛ	ਠ	ਥ	ਫ
	Voiced	Unaspirated	ਗ	ਜ	ਡ	ਦ	ਬ
		Aspirated	ਘ	ਝ	ਢ	ਧ	ਭ
	Nasals		ਙ	ਞ	ਣ	ਨ	ਮ
Fricatives	Voiceless		ਖ਼	ਸ਼		ਸ	ਫ਼
	Voiced		ਗ਼			ਜ਼	
Flapped and tapped sounds					ੜ	ਰ	
Aspirate, semivowel and liquid			ਹ	ਜ		ਲ	ਵ

Appendix 2

Comparison of tongue positions

a   b   c

- **a** Pronunciation of t and d in English. Tongue against the teeth ridge.
- **b** Pronunciation of ਤ t and ਦ d. Tongue against the base of upper incisors.
- **c** Pronunciation of ਟ t and ਡ d. Tongue against the back hard palate.

Key to exercises

Reading and writing

Section 4 Exercise **2 a** ਰਿੱਛ **b** ਕਿੱਲ **c** ਹਿਰਨ Section 5 Exercise **2 a** ਸੀਟੀ **b** ਬਿੱਲੀ **c** ਵਾਲੀ Section 6 Exercise **2 a** ਢੱਕਣ **b** ਜ਼ਬਾਨ **c** ਉੱਨ Section 7 Exercise **2 a** ਊਠ **b** ਸੂਰ **c** ਝਾੜੂ Section 8 Exercise **2 a** ਲੇਲ **b** ਭੇਡ **c** ਸੇਬ Section 9 Exercise **2 a** ਭੈਣ **b** ਐਤਵਾਰ **c** ਐਨਕ Section 10 Exercise **2 a** ਖੋਤਾ **b** ਮੋਟਾ **c** ਘੋੜਾ Section 11 Exercise **2 a** ਚੌਲ **b** ਖਿਡੋਣੇ **c** ਫ਼ੌਜੀ Section 12 Exercise **2 a** ਜੰਵ **b** ਲੰਬਾ **c** ਵਤਾਊਂ

Unit 1

Dialogue 1 exercises
1 a True **b** True **c** False **2 a** ਮੇਰਾ ਨਾਂ ਡੇਵਿਡ ਹੈ। meraa naa<u>n</u> devid hai. **b** ਤੁਹਾਡਾ ਕੀ ਨਾਮ ਹੈ? <u>t</u>uhaadaa kee naam hai? **c** ਤੇਰਾ ਕੀ ਨਾਂ ਏ? <u>t</u>eraa kee naa<u>n</u> e?

Dialogue 2 exercises
1 a ਅੱਸਲਾਮ ਅਲੈਕਮ। asslaam alaikam. **b** ਤੁਹਾਡਾ ਕੀ ਹਾਲ ਹੈ? <u>t</u>uhaadaa kee haal hai? **c** ਕੀ ਪਰਵਾਰ ਠੀਕ ਹੈ? kee parvaar theek hai? **2 a** 2 **b** 3 **c** 1

End exercises
1 1st line, 2nd letter; 3rd line, 1st letter; 5th line, 4th letter **2 a** ਨਮਸਤੇ nama<u>s</u>te **b** ਵਾਲੈਕਮ ਅੱਸਲਾਮ vaalaikam asslaam **c** ਸਤਿ ਸ੍ਰੀ ਅਕਾਲ sa<u>t</u> sree akaal **3 a** ਤੁਹਾਡਾ <u>t</u>uhaadaa **b** ਤੇਰਾ <u>t</u>eraa **c** ਤੇਰਾ <u>t</u>eraa **4** You: ਸਤਿ ਸ੍ਰੀ ਅਕਾਲ। ਮੇਰਾ ਨਾਮ _____ ਹੈ। ਤੁਹਾਡਾ ਕੀ ਨਾਮ ਹੈ? sa<u>t</u> sree akaal. meraa naam _____ hai. <u>t</u>uhaadaa kee naam hai? You: ਮੈਂ ਠੀਕ ਹਾਂ। ਤੁਸੀਂ ਕਿਵੇਂ ਹੋ? mai<u>n</u> theek haa<u>n</u>. <u>t</u>usee<u>n</u> kive<u>n</u> ho? You: ਰੱਬ ਰਾਖਾ। rabb raakhaa.

Unit 2

Dialogue 1 exercises
1 a False **b** False **c** True **2** Jeevan – Panjabi; John – English; Ram – Gujarati

Dialogue 2 exercises

1 Ashok: ਹਾਂ ਜੀ, ਮੈਂ ਅਸ਼ੋਕ ਹਾਂ। haa<u>n</u> jee, mai<u>n</u> ashok haa<u>n</u>. Mrs Sharma: ਮੇਰਾ ਹਾਲ ਠੀਕ ਹੈ। meraa haal theek hai. Kiran: ਨਹੀਂ, ਮੇਰੇ ਮਾਤਾ ਜੀ ਇੱਥੇ ਨਹੀਂ ਹਨ। nahee<u>n</u>, mere maa<u>t</u>aa jee i<u>thth</u>e nahee<u>n</u> han. **2 a** ਮੈਂ ਕਿਰਨ ਹਾਂ। mai<u>n</u> kiran haa<u>n</u>. **b** ਕੀ ਤੁਸੀਂ ਅਸ਼ੋਕ ਹੋ? kee <u>t</u>usee<u>n</u> ashok ho? **c** ਉਹ ਇੱਥੇ ਨਹੀਂ ਹਨ uh i<u>thth</u>e nahee<u>n</u> han. **3 1** Panjabi **2** English **3** Class **4** Mrs Sharma **5** home

End exercises

1 are, hai, ਹੋ **2 a** ਕੀ ਤੁਸੀਂ ਅਸ਼ੋਕ ਹੋ? kee <u>t</u>usee<u>n</u> ashok ho? **b** ਕੀ ਤੁਸੀਂ ਕਿਰਨ ਹੋ? kee <u>t</u>usee<u>n</u> kiran ho? **c** ਮੈਂ ਕਿਰਨ ਹਾਂ mai<u>n</u> kiran haa<u>n</u> **d** ਉਹ ਅਸ਼ੋਕ ਹੈ uh ashok hai **3 a** ਹੈਂ hai<u>n</u> **b** ਹਾਂ haa<u>n</u> **c** ਹਨ han **4** 1st line, 2nd letter; 3rd line, 1st letter; 4th line, 2nd letter

Unit 3

Dialogue 1 exercises

1 a False **b** False **c** True **d** False **e** True **2** ਕਰੇਲਾ karelaa ਸ਼ਲਗਮ shalgam ਭਿੰਡੀ bhi<u>n</u>dee ਗੋਭੀ gobhee ਟਮਾਟਰ tamaatar ਮਟਰ matar

Dialogue 2 exercises

1 mith<u>th</u>aa, bitter, ਸੁਆਦ **2 a** ਇਹ ਦੁਕਾਨ ਹੈ। ih <u>d</u>ukaan hai. **b** ਇਹ ਚੰਗੀ ਦੁਕਾਨ ਹੈ। ih cha<u>n</u>gee <u>d</u>ukaan hai. **c** ਇਹ ਮਿਠਿਆਈ ਦੀ ਦੁਕਾਨ ਹੈ। ih mithiaaee <u>d</u>ee <u>d</u>ukaan hai. **d** ਇਹ ਚੰਗੀ ਮਿਠਿਆਈ ਦੀ ਦੁਕਾਨ ਹੈ। ih cha<u>n</u>gee mithiaaee <u>d</u>ee <u>d</u>ukaan hai.

End exercises

1 a ਛੋਟਾ <u>ch</u>otaa **b** ਵੱਡਾ vaddaa **c** ਛੋਟੀ <u>ch</u>otee **d** ਵੱਡੀ vaddee **e** ਛੋਟਾ <u>ch</u>otaa **f** ਵੱਡਾ vaddaa **2** Mr Singh: samosaa, pakaurhe, bhi<u>n</u>dee; Jane: samosaa, laddoo, pakaurhe; Henry: ras malaaee, bhi<u>n</u>dee, gobhee **3 a** ਗੁਲਾਬ ਜਾਮਣ gulaab jaamanh **b** ਬਰਫੀ barfee **c** ਸਮੋਸਾ samosaa **d** ਪਕੌੜੇ pakaurhe **4 a** ਉਹਨਾਂ ਦੇ uhnaa<u>n</u> <u>d</u>e **b** ਮੇਰੇ mere **c** ਸਾਡੀਆਂ saadeeaa<u>n</u> **d** ਤੁਹਾਡੀਆਂ <u>t</u>uhaadeeaa<u>n</u>

Unit 4

Dialogue 1 exercises

1 b ਕੀ ਇਹ ਸੀਟ ਖ਼ਾਲੀ ਹੈ? kee ih seet <u>kh</u>aalee hai? ਹਾਂ ਜੀ, ਖ਼ਾਲੀ ਹੈ। haa<u>n</u> jee, <u>kh</u>aalee hai. **c** ਮੈਂ ਅਧਿਆਪਕਾ ਹਾਂ। mai<u>n</u> a<u>dh</u>iaapkaa haa<u>n</u>. **d** ਤੁਸੀਂ ਕੀ ਕਰਦੇ ਹੋ? <u>t</u>usee<u>n</u> kee kar<u>d</u>e ho? **2 a** ਮੈਂ ਵੀ ਬਰਮਿੰਘਮ

ਰਹਿੰਦਾ ਹਾਂ main vee barmingham rahindaa haan. **b** ਮੈਂ ਦਿੱਲੀ ਤੋਂ ਹਾਂ main dillee ton haan **c** ਤੁਸੀਂ ਕੀ ਕਰਦੇ ਹੋ? tuseen kee karde ho? **3 1** c **2** a **3** b **4** e **5** d

Dialogue 2 exercises

1 a True **b** True **c** False **2 a** ਮੇਰਾ ਨਾਮ (____) ਹੈ। meraa naam (____) hai. **b** ਮੈਂ (____) ਹਾਂ। main (____) haan. **c** ਮੈਂ (____) ਤੋਂ ਹਾਂ। main (____) ton haan. **d** ਮੈਂ (____) ਰਹਿੰਦਾ/ਰਹਿੰਦੀ ਹਾਂ। main (____) rahindaa/rahindee haan.

End exercises

1 a True **b** False **c** False **d** False **2 a** Mrs Sharma **b** Mrs Khan **c** Dr Singh **3 a** direct **b** oblique **c** direct **d** oblique **e** oblique **4 b** ਮੇਰੀਆਂ ਬੇਟੀਆਂ ਸਕੂਲ ਵਿਚ ਪੜ੍ਹਦੀਆਂ ਹਨ। mereeaan beteeaan sakool vich parhhdeeaan han. *My daughters study in school.* **c** ਤੁਹਾਡੇ ਲੜਕੇ ਕਿੱਥੇ ਰਹਿੰਦੇ ਹਨ? tuhaade larke kiththe rahinde han? *Where do your sons live?* **d** ਕੀ ਉਹ ਮੁੰਡੇ ਪੰਜਾਬੀ ਬੋਲਦੇ ਹਨ? kee uh munde panjaabee bolde han? *Do those boys speak Panjabi?*

Unit 5

Dialogue 1 exercises

1 a ਨਮਸਤੇ, ਤੂੰ ਕੀ ਕਰ ਰਹੀ ਹੈਂ? namaste, toon kee kar rahee hain? **b** ਮੈਂ ਜੇਬਾਂ ਲਗਾ ਰਹੀ ਹਾਂ। main jebaan lagaa rahee haan. **c** ਮੈਨੇਜਰ ਸਾਡੀ ਤਲਖ਼ਾਹ ਨਹੀਂ ਵਧਾ ਰਿਹਾ। mainejar saadee tankhaah naheen vadhaa rihaa. **2 1** machine **2** work **3** salary **4** pockets **5** time **6** needle

Dialogue 2 exercises

1 1st line, 2nd letter; 2nd line, 1st letter; 3rd line, 3rd letter; 4th line, 2nd letter. **2 a** ਸੁਮੀਤ ਫ਼ਿਲਮ ਦੇਖ ਰਹੀ ਸੀ। sumeet filam dekh rahee see. **b** ਬੱਚੇ ਖੇਡ ਰਹੇ ਸਨ। bachche khed rahe san. **c** ਸੁਮੀਤ ਦਾ ਪਤੀ ਕਾਰ ਧੋ ਰਿਹਾ ਸੀ। sumeet daa patee kaar dho rihaa see.

End exercises

1 a ਤੁਸੀਂ ਸਮਾਂ ਜ਼ਾਇਆ ਕਰ ਰਹੇ ਹੋ। tuseen samaan zaaiaa kar rahe ho. **b** ਤੁਸੀਂ ਕੰਮ ਕਿਉਂ ਛੱਡ ਰਹੇ ਹੋ? tuseen kanm kiun chadd rahe ho? **c** ਤੁਸੀਂ ਠੀਕ ਕਹਿ ਰਹੇ ਹੋ। tuseen theek kahi rahe ho. **2** patee, house/home, ਕੱਲ੍ਹ **3 b** ਤੁਸੀਂ ਕੀ ਪੁੱਛ ਰਹੇ ਸੀ? tuseen kee puchch rahe see? *What were you asking?* **c** ਉਹ ਕੀ ਕਰ ਰਹੇ ਸਨ? uh kee kar rahe san? *What were they doing?* **d** ਉਹ ਕਾਰ ਧੋ ਰਿਹਾ ਸੀ। uh kaar dho rihaa see. *He was washing the car.* **4 a** ਗੀਤਾ ਟੈਨਸ ਖੇਡ ਰਹੀ ਹੈ। geetaa tainas khed rahee hai. *Geeta is playing tennis.* **b** ਅਵਤਾਰ ਖਾਣਾ ਖਾ ਰਿਹਾ ਹੈ। avtaar khaanhaa khaa rihaa hai. *Avtar is eating food.* **c** ਸੀਤਾ ਤੇ ਗੀਤਾ ਪੰਜਾਬੀ ਬੋਲ ਰਹੀਆਂ ਹਨ। seetaa te geetaa panjaabee bol raheeaan han. *Sita and Geeta are speaking Panjabi.* **d** ਮੁੰਡਾ ਕਿਤਾਬ ਪੜ੍ਹ ਰਿਹਾ ਹੈ। mundaa kitaab parh-h rihaa hai. *The boy is reading a book.*

Unit 6

Dialogue 1 exercises
1 a ਪਵਨ ਲੰਡਨ ਸੀ। pavan landan see. *Pavan was in London.* **b** ਪਵਨ ਦੀ ਭਤੀਜੀ ਦਾ ਵਿਆਹ ਸੀ। pavan dee bhateejee daa viaah see. *It was Pavan's niece's wedding.* **c** ਮਾਨਚੈਸਟਰ maanchaistar *Manchester* **d** ਤਕਰੀਬਨ ੧੦੦ ਬੰਦੇ takreeban 100 bande *about 100 people* **2 a** ਤੁਸੀਂ ਐਤਵਾਰ ਕਿੱਥੇ ਸੀ? tuseen aitvaar kiththe see? **b** ਤੁਸੀਂ ਕੱਲ ਕਿੱਥੇ ਸੀ? tuseen kallh kiththe see? **c** ਤੁਸੀਂ ਹਫ਼ਤੇ ਦੇ ਅਖ਼ੀਰ ਕਿੱਥੇ ਸੀ? tuseen hafte de akheer kiththe see?

Dialogue 2 exercises
1 ਇਸਤਰੀ, *woman*; ikathth, *gathering*; ਪ੍ਰਾਹੁਣੇ, praahunhe; ਕਾਲਜ, *college*; ਭਾਬੀ, bhaabee **2 a** informal **b** informal **c** formal

End exercises
1

2 a ii b iii c i 3 a True b False c True 4 b ਉਹ ਹਫ਼ਤੇ ਦੇ ਅਖ਼ੀਰ ਲੰਡਨ ਨਹੀਂ ਗਏ ਸਨ। uh hafte de akheer landan naheen gae san. ਕੀ ਉਹ ਹਫ਼ਤੇ ਦੇ ਅਖ਼ੀਰ ਲੰਡਨ ਗਏ ਸਨ? kee uh hafte de akheer landan gae san? c ਅਸੀਂ ਇਕੱਠੇ ਟੈਨਸ ਨਹੀਂ ਖੇਡਦੇ ਸੀ। aseen ikaththe tainas naheen khedde see. ਕੀ ਅਸੀਂ ਇਕੱਠੇ ਟੈਨਸ ਖੇਡਦੇ ਸੀ? kee aseen ikaththe tainas khedde see? d ਉਹ ਪੰਜਾਬੀ ਨਹੀਂ ਬੋਲਦੀ ਹੁੰਦੀ ਸੀ। uh panjaabee naheen boldee hundee see ਕੀ ਉਹ ਪੰਜਾਬੀ ਬੋਲਦੀ ਹੁੰਦੀ ਸੀ? kee uh panjaabee boldee hundee see?

Unit 7

Dialogue 1 exercises
1 a ਜ਼ਰੂਰ zaroor b ਕੱਲ੍ਹ kallh c ਕਿੰਨੇ ਵਜੇ kinne vaje 2 4 2 3 1

Dialogue 2 exercises
1 a ਤੁਸੀਂ ਕੀ ਪੀਓ ਗੇ? tuseen kee peeo ge? b ਕੀ ਤੁਸੀਂ ਟੀ ਵੀ ਦੇਖੋ ਗੇ? kee tuseen tee vee dekho ge? c ਕੀ ਤੁਸੀਂ ਰਸ ਲਵੋ ਗੇ ਜਾਂ ਚਾਹ? kee tuseen ras lavo ge jaan chaah? 2 1st line, 1st letter; 3rd line, 3rd letter; 5th line, 2nd letter

End exercises
1 a ਤੂੰ ਸੁਣ toon sunh b ਤੁਸੀਂ ਸੁਣੋ tuseen sunho c ਤੁਸੀਂ ਸੁਣੋ ਜੀ tuseen sunho jee d ਜ਼ਰਾ ਸੁਣਨਾ ਜੀ zaraa sunhnaa jee 2 1 ਦਸ ਵਜੇ ਹਨ das vaje han 2 ਢਾਈ ਵਜੇ ਹਨ dhaaee vaje han 3 ਪੌਣੇ ਛੇ ਵਜੇ ਹਨ paunhe che vaje han 4 ਸਵਾ ਅੱਠ ਵਜੇ ਹਨ savaa athth vaje han 5 ਬਾਰ੍ਹਾਂ ਵਜੇ ਹਨ baar-h-aan vaje han 6 ਸੱਤ ਵਜੇ ਹਨ satt vaje han 3 a ਮੈਂ ਚਾਹ ਪੀਵਾਂ ਗਾ main chaah peevaan gaa b ਮੈਂ ਚਾਹ ਪੀਵਾਂ ਗੀ main chaah peevaan gee c ਅਸੀਂ ਚਾਹ ਪੀਵਾਂ ਗੇ aseen chaah peevaan ge d ਅਸੀਂ ਚਾਹ ਪੀਵਾਂ ਗੀਆਂ aseen chaah peevaan geeaan 4 a ਹਾਂ ਜੀ, ਧੰਨਵਾਦ haan jee, dhannvaad b ਹਾਂ, ਕੱਲ੍ਹ ਮੈਂ ਆਵਾਂ ਗਾ haan, kallh main aavaan gaa c ਨਹੀਂ ਮੈਂ ਕਾਹਲ ਵਿਚ ਹਾਂ naheen main kaahal vich haan d ਚੰਗਾ ਫਿਰ, ਮੈਂ ਉਡੀਕਾਂ ਗਾ changaa phir, main udeekaan gaa

Unit 8

Dialogue 1 exercises
1 1 ਸਿਤਾਰ sitaar 2 ਡਾਲਰ daalar 3 ਖ਼ਰਚਾ kharchaa 4 ਫਿਰਨਾ phirnaa 2 a ii b iii c i

Dialogue 2 exercises

1 a ਸਾਨੂੰ ਥੋੜੀ ਬਹੁਤੀ ਪੰਜਾਬੀ ਆਉਂਦੀ ਹੈ। saanoon thorhee bahutee panjaabee aaun dee hai. **b** ਅਸੀਂ ਕਨਾਟ ਪਲੇਸ ਜਾਣਾ ਚਾਹੁੰਦੀਆਂ ਹਾਂ। aseen kanaat pales jaanhaa chaahundeeaan haan. **c** ਜੀ ਕੀ ਤੁਸੀਂ ਦੋ ਮਹੀਨੇ ਰਹਿਣ ਦੀ ਆਗਿਆ ਦੇਵੋ ਗੇ। jee kee tuseen do maheene rahinh dee aagiaa devo ge. **2 a** ਤੁਸੀਂ ਦੋ ਸਵਾਰੀਆਂ ਹੋ ਤੇ ਸਮਾਨ ਵੀ ਬਹੁਤ ਹੈ। tuseen do savaareeaan ho te samaan vee bahut hai. **b** ਸਾਡੇ ਕੋਲ ਕੇਵਲ ਇੱਕ ਮਹੀਨੇ ਦਾ ਵੀਜ਼ਾ ਹੈ। saade kol keval ikk maheene daa veezaa hai. **c** ਅਨੰਦ ਮਾਣੋ! anand maanho!

End exercises

1 a ਚਾਹੀਦੀ chaaheedee **b** ਚਾਹੀਦਾ chaaheedaa **c** ਵਜਾਉਣ vajaaunh **2 a** ਉਸਨੂੰ ਕੀ ਚਾਹੀਦਾ ਹੈ? us noon kee chaaheedaa hai? **b** ਧੀਓ, ਤੁਹਾਨੂੰ ਕੀ ਚਾਹੀਦਾ ਹੈ? dheeo, tuhaanoon kee chaaheedaa hai? **c** ਤੂੰ ਕਿਹਨਾਂ ਨੂੰ ਦੱਸਿਆ ਸੀ? toon kihnaan noon dassiaa see? **d** ਕੀ ਸਾਨੂੰ ਜਾਣਾ ਚਾਹੀਦਾ ਹੈ? kee saanoon jaanhaa chaaheedaa hai? **3 a** ਘਰ ਵਾਲਾ ghar vaalaa **b** ਟੈਕਸੀ ਵਾਲਾ taiksee vaalaa **c** ਸਬਜ਼ੀ ਵਾਲਾ sabzee vaalaa **4 a** four **b** Ashoka Hotel **c** Rs50 agreed **d** 10 miles **e** none **f** yes

---

Unit 9

Dialogue 1 exercises

1 a ਮੈਨੂੰ ਫਿੱਕੇ ਰੰਗ ਦਾ ਕਪੜਾ ਚਾਹੀਦਾ ਹੈ। mainoon phikke rang daa kaprhaa chaaheedaa hai. **b** ਮੈਨੂੰ ਮੋਟਾ ਅਤੇ ਹੰਢਣਸਾਰ ਕਪੜਾ ਚਾਹੀਦਾ ਹੈ। mainoon motaa ate handhanhsaar kaprhaa chaaheedaa hai. **c** ਅੱਜ ਕੱਲ੍ਹ ਦੇ ਰਵਾਜ ਦੀ ਛਪਾਈ ਚਾਹੀਦੀ ਹੈ। ajj kallh de ravaaj dee chapaaee chaaheedee hai. **d** ਕੀਮਤ ਬਹੁਤ ਜ਼ਿਆਦਾ ਨਹੀਂ ਹੋਣੀ ਚਾਹੀਦੀ। keemat bahut ziaadaa naheen honhee chaaheedee. **2** vadheeaa, *good*; ਵਧੇਰੇ, vadhere; ਕੀਮਤ, *price*; mukaablaa, *comparison*; ਸਭ ਤੋਂ ਵਧੀਆ, *best*

Dialogue 2 exercises

1 a ਕੀ ਤਕਲੀਫ਼ ਹੈ? kee takleef hai? **b** ਕੀ ਤੈਨੂੰ ਬੁਖ਼ਾਰ ਹੈ? kee tainoon bukhaar hai? **c** ਹੁਣ ਮੈਂ ਸਮਝਿਆ। hunh main samajhiaa. **2** You: ਤਬੀਅਤ tabeeat Doctor: ਤਕਲੀਫ਼ takleef You: ਪੇਟ pet, ਦਰਦ dard, ਬੁਖ਼ਾਰ bukhaar Doctor: ਬੁਖ਼ਾਰ bukhaar, ਠੰਡ thand Doctor: ਦਵਾਈ davaaee, ਅਰਾਮ araam

End exercises

1 Horizontal: 1st line, 1st letter; 2nd line, 2nd letter; 3rd line, 1st letter; 4th line, 3rd letter; 5th line, 2nd letter Vertical: 1st column, 3rd letter; 2nd column, 2nd letter; 3rd column, 2nd letter; 4th column, 1st letter; 5th column, 1st letter **2 a** ਮੈਨੂੰ ਠੰਡ ਲੱਗਦੀ ਹੈ। mainoon thand

laggdee hai. **b** ਮੇਰਾ ਸਿਰ ਦੁੱਖਦਾ ਹੈ। meraa sir dukhkhdaa hai. **c** ਮੇਰੇ
ਪੇਟ ਵਿਚ ਦਰਦ ਹੈ। mere pet vich dard hai. **d** ਮੈਨੂੰ ਬੁਖ਼ਾਰ ਹੈ। mainoon
bukhaar hai. **3 a** ਮੈਂ ਕੱਲ੍ਹ ਨਹੀਂ ਆ ਸਕਦਾ/ਸਕਦੀ। main kallh naheen aa
sakdaa/sakdee. **b** ਕੀ ਤੁਸੀਂ ਪੰਜਾਬੀ ਬੋਲ ਸਕਦੇ ਹੋ? kee tuseen panjaabee
bol sakde ho? **c** ਅਸੀਂ ਪਹਿਲੇ ਉੱਥੇ ਜਾ ਚੁਕੇ ਹਾਂ। aseen pahile uththe jaa
chuke haan. **d** ਉਹ ਪਹਿਲੇ ਖਾ ਚੁਕੇ ਹਨ। uh pahile khaa chuke han.
4 a ਜਿਹੜਾ jihrhaa **b** ਜਿਸ jis **c** ਜਿਹੜੇ jihrhe **d** ਜੋ jo

---

Unit 10

Dialogue exercises

1 a True **b** False **c** False **2 i** c **ii** b **iii** a **iv** d

Passage exercises

1 a ਨਾਨਾ ਜੀ ਤੇ ਨਾਨੀ ਜੀ ਕੋਲ naanaa jee te naanee jee kol **b** ਗੁੜ
gurh **c** ਕਹਾਣੀਆਂ ਸੁਣੀਆਂ kahaanheeaan sunheeaan **d** ਦੁੱਧ dudhdh
2 pind, *village*; ਖੂਹ, *water well*; vihrhaa, *courtyard*; ਖੇਤ, khet; ਗੰਨਾ,
sugarcane

End exercises

1 a ਖਾਣਾ ਖਾ ਕੇ ਅਸੀਂ ਸੌਂ ਗਏ! khaanhaa khaa ke aseen saun ge! **b** ਦੁਕਾਨ
ਤੇ ਜਾ ਕੇ ਦੁੱਧ ਲਿਆ! dukaan te jaa ke dudhdh liaa! **c** ਕੰਮ ਖ਼ਤਮ ਕਰ ਕੇ ਤੂੰ ਘਰ
ਨੂੰ ਚਲੇ ਜਾ! kanm khatam kar ke toon ghar noon chale jaa! **d** ਜਲੰਧਰ
ਹੋ ਕੇ ਅੰਮ੍ਰਿਤਸਰ ਜਾਓ! jalandhar ho ke anmritsar jaao! **2 a** ਖਾਧੇ khaadhe
b ਰੋਈ roee **c** ਸੁਣਾਈ sunhaaee **d** ਕਟਿਆ katiaa **3** You: ਬਹੁਤ ਸੁਹਣੀ
ਰਹੀ। ਮੈਂ ਟਰਾਫ਼ਾਲਗਰ ਸਕੁਅਰ (ਗਈ/ਗਿਆ) ਅਤੇ ਨੈਲਸਨ ਕਾ ਕਾਲਮ ਦੇਖਿਆ। ਮੈਂ
ਬਕਿੰਘਮ ਪੈਲਸ ਵੀ (ਗਈ/ਗਿਆ)। bahut suhnhee rahee. main taraafaalgar
sakuar (gaee/giaa) ate nailsan daa kaalam dekhiaa. main bakingham
pailas vee (gaee/giaa). You: ਮੈਂ ਔਕਸਫ਼ੋਰਡ ਸਰਕਸ (ਗਈ/ਗਿਆ) ਅਤੇ ਕੁਝ
ਕਪੜੇ ਖ਼ਰੀਦੇ। main auksford sarkas (gaee/giaa) ate kujh kaprhe khareede.
You: ਮੈਂ ਕੇਵਲ ਪੀਜ਼ਾ ਖਾਧਾ। main keval peezaa khaadhaa. **4 1** ਖੂਹ
khooh **2** ਮੱਝ majhjh **3** ਗੰਨਾ gannaa **4** ਘਰ ghar **5** ਖੇਤ khet

---

Unit 11

Dialogue 1 exercises

1 a ਟਿਕਟ ਬਾਬੂ **b** ਜਸਪ੍ਰੀਤ **c** ਟਿਕਟ ਬਾਬੂ **d** ਸਿਮਰਨ **e** ਜਸਪ੍ਰੀਤ
2 a ਅਸੀਂ ਅੱਜ ਜਾਣਾ ਚਾਹੁੰਦੀਆਂ ਹਾਂ। **b** ਨਵੀਆਂ ਥਾਂਵਾਂ ਦੇਖਣਾ ਚੰਗੀ ਗੱਲ ਹੈ।
c ਇਹ ਹਨ ਤੁਹਾਡੀਆਂ ਦੋ ਟਿਕਟਾਂ।

Dialogue 2 exercises
1 i c **ii** a **iii** d **iv** b **2 1** gold **2** dome **3** visitors **4** world
5 city **6** guru; Mystery word: Amritsar

End exercises
1 a ਸ਼ਾਨੇ ਪੰਜਾਬ **b** ਸੈਲਾਨੀ, ਜਾਂਦੇ **c** ਲਫ਼ਜ਼ੀ, ਅੰਮ੍ਰਿਤ ਦਾ ਸਰੋਵਰ **d** ਹੋ ਰਿਹਾ
ਕੀਰਤਨ, ਸ਼ਾਂਤੀ, ਸਵਰਗ **2 a** ਗੁਰੂ ਰਾਮ ਦਾਸ **b** ਅੰਮ੍ਰਿਤ ਦਾ ਸਰੋਵਰ **c** ਗੁੰਬਦਾਂ
ਤੇ ਸੋਨਾ ਲੱਗਾ ਹੋਇਆ ਹੈ **3** You: ਮੈਂ ਅੱਜ ਦਿੱਲੀ ਜਾਣਾ (ਚਾਹੁੰਦਾ) ਹਾਂ। ਸਭ ਤੋਂ
ਚੰਗੀ ਦਿੱਲੀ ਜਾਣ ਵਾਲੀ ਗੱਡੀ ਕਿਹੜੀ ਹੈ? You: ਕੀ ਮੈਨੂੰ ਸੈਕੰਡ ਕਲਾਸ ਵਿਚ
ਸੀਟ ਮਿਲ ਜਾਏ ਗੀ। You: ਨਹੀਂ, ਮੈਨੂੰ ਵਾਪਸੀ ਟਿਕਟ ਚਾਹੀਦੀ ਹੈ। ਅੰਮ੍ਰਿਤਸਰ
ਤੋਂ ਗੱਡੀ ਕਿੰਨੇ ਵਜੇ ਚਲਦੀ ਹੈ? You: ਅੱਛਾ, ਮੈਨੂੰ ਇੱਕ ਸੈਕੰਡ ਕਲਾਸ ਦੀ
ਟਿਕਟ ਦੇਵੋ।

Unit 12

Dialogue 1 exercises
1 a False **b** True **c** False **d** True **2 a** ਜਰਮਨ, ਅੰਗਰੇਜ਼ੀ, ਪੰਜਾਬੀ
b ਤਾਜ ਮੱਹਲ **c** ਸਹਿਮਤ, ਮੁਕਾਬਲਾ **d** ਅੰਮ੍ਰਿਤਸਰ

Letter exercises
1 lagaataar, *continuously*; ਪਿਆਰੇ, *dear*; <u>khush</u>, *happy*; ਗਰਮੀ, garmee;
ਵਾਰੀ, *instance*. **2 a** ਉੁਹਨਾਂ ਨੇ ਉਹ ਮਕਾਨ ਦੇਖਿਆ ਜਿੱਥੇ ਉੁਹਨਾਂ ਦੇ ਮਾਤਾ ਪਿਤਾ
ਰਹਿੰਦੇ ਹੁੰਦੇ ਸੀ **b** ਬਾਰਸ਼ **c** ਅਬਾਦੀ ਤੇ ਟਰੈਫ਼ਿਕ ਬਹੁਤ ਹੈ **d** ਬਹੁਤ ਸੁਗਾਤਾਂ

End exercises
1 a ਮੈਂ ਖਾ ਚੁਕਾ ਹਾਂ। **b** ਮੈਂ ਖਾ ਚੁਕੀ ਹਾਂ। **c** ਉਹ ਬੋਲ ਚੁਕੇ ਸਨ। **d** ਉਹ ਦਸ
ਮਿੰਟ ਤੋਂ ਬੋਲ ਰਿਹਾ ਸੀ। **2** ਯੂ. ਐਸ. ਡਾਲਰ ੪੦੦ ਡਾਲਰ ੩੫ ਰੁਪਏ ਵੱਧ ਅਮਰੀਕਨ
3 ਪਿਆਰੇ ਫੇਰੀ ਜਗ੍ਹਾ ਹਰਿਮੰਦਰ ਸਾਹਿਬ ਮੁਕਾਬਲਾ ਸ਼ਬਦਾਵਲੀ ਹੁੰਦੇ ਤਾਂ ਆਉਂਦਾ।

Unit 13

Exercises to matrimonial advertisement
1 a Yes **b** Yes **c** No **2** Not a suitable match! **3 a** ਲੜਕੀ
ਵਿਹਾਰੀ ਨੌਕਰੀ ਤੇ ਲੱਗੀ ਹੋਣੀ ਚਾਹੀਦੀ ਹੈ। **b** ਤਲਾਕ ਸ਼ੁਦਾ ਲੜਕੀਆਂ ਨੂੰ ਲਿਖਣ
ਦੀ ਲੋੜ ਨਹੀਂ। **c** ਲੜਕੀ ਦੀ ਉਮਰ ੨੫ ਸਾਲ ਤੋਂ ਵੱਧ ਨਾ ਹੋਵੇ। **d** ਲੜਕਾ ਸੱਚੀ
ਮੁੱਚੀ ਸੁਹਣਾ ਹੈ।

Dialogue exercises
1 a 2 **b** 1 **c** 4 **d** 3 **2 a** Edinburgh **b** Ilford
c Manjit Singh **d** Kanwaljit Kaur **e** Gurbax Singh and

Jasvir Kaur Kalsi   **f** North London   **g** May 23   **h** 9.30 a.m.
i 10.00 a.m.   **j** 12.00 noon

End exercises

1 Matrimonial advertisement ਲੰਡਨ ਵਿਚ ਰਹਿ ਰਹੇ ਸਿੱਖ ਮਾਪਿਆਂ ਦੀ ਲੜਕੀ ਲਈ ਰਿਸ਼ਤੇ ਦੀ ਲੋੜ ਹੈ। ਲੜਕੀ ਦੀ ਉਮਰ ੨੫ ਸਾਲ ਦੀ ਹੈ ਅਤੇ ਕੱਦ ੫'੩" ਹੈ। ਲੜਕੀ ਸੁਹਣੀ ਤੇ ਪੜ੍ਹੀ ਲਿਖੀ ਹੈ। ਬੈਂਕ ਵਿਚ ਕੰਮ ਕਰਦੀ ਹੈ। ਲੜਕਾ ਪਤਵੰਤੇ ਪਰਵਾਰ ਦਾ, ਬ੍ਰਿਟਿਸ਼ ਸ਼ਹਿਰੀਅਤ ਵਾਲਾ ਅਤੇ ਵਿਹਾਰੀ ਨੌਕਰੀ ਤੇ ਲੱਗਾ ਹੋਵੇ। **2 a** ਜਿਹਾ **b** ਆਪਣੇ **c** ਆਪਣੀਆਂ **d** ਜਿਹੇ **3 a** ਉਬਲੇ ਹੋਏ **b** ਡਰਿਆ ਹੋਇਆ **c** ਪੜ੍ਹਿਆ ਲਿਖਿਆ **4 a** ਡੇਬਰਾ **b** ਜੀਤੀ ਦਾ **c** ਨਹੀਂ **d** ੨੮ ਜਨਵਰੀ **e** ਉਹ ਵਿਆਹ ਦੀਆਂ ਰਸਮਾਂ ਬਾਰੇ ਜਾਣਨਾ ਚਾਹੁੰਦੀ ਹੈ।

Unit 14

Dialogue 1 exercises

1 a ਪਾਪਾ ਜੀ! ਕੀ ਤੁਸੀਂ ਮੇਰੇ ਸ਼੍ਰੇਣੀ ਅਧਿਆਪਕ ਨੂੰ ਮਿਲੇ ਸੀ? **b** ਉਹ ਸਾਨੂੰ ਚੰਗੀ ਤਰ੍ਹਾਂ ਪੜ੍ਹਾਂਦਾ ਨਹੀਂ **c** ਤੈਨੂੰ ਪੜ੍ਹਾਈ ਵਿਚ ਮਿਹਨਤ ਕਰਨੀ ਚਾਹੀਦੀ ਹੈ। **2 1** teacher **2** Ramesh **3** homework **4** maths **5** careless

Dialogue 2 exercises

1 kaanoonn; ਬੀਬੀ, *madam*; ਕਾਗ਼ਜ਼ਾਤ, kaaghzaat; maaf, *pardon*; ਉਲੰਘਣਾ, *to disobey* **2** mobile phone, officer, licence, minute, car

Dialogue 3 exercises

1 a ਮੈਂ ਸਮਾਜ ਸੇਵਕ ਹਾਂ। **b** ਕੀ ਗੱਲ ਹੈ? **c** ਅੰਦਰ ਆ ਜਾਓ **d** ਮੇਰੇ ਲਈ ਇਹ ਮੁਸ਼ਕਲ ਹੈ। **2 a** ਆਇਆ **b** ਸਕਦੀ **c** ਚਲੇ ਜਾਂਦੇ **d** ਕਰਾਂ ਗੀ।

End exercises

1 a ਦੇ ਨੇੜੇ **b** ਦੇ ਅੰਦਰ **c** ਤੋਂ ਬਾਅਦ **d** ਦੀ ਜਗ੍ਹਾ **2 a** ii **b** iii **c** iv **d** i **3 a** ਦਫ਼ਤਰ **b** ੧੦ ਮਿੰਟ **c** ਨਹੀਂ **d** ਕਾਗ਼ਜ਼ਾਤ ਪੇਸ਼ ਕਰਨੇ ਹਨ **4** ਅਧਿਆਪਕ, ਇਲਾਵਾ, ਹਿਸਾਬ, ਕੰਮ, ਕਲਾਸ, ਡਾਕਟਰ, ਦੂਜੇ, ਪੜ੍ਹਾਉਣਾ, ਪਾਪਾ, ਬਾਰੇ, ਮਜ਼ਮੂਨਾਂ, ਮਿਹਨਤ, ਲਿਆਕਤ, ਵਰਤਣਾ, ਸ਼੍ਰੇਣੀ।

Unit 15

Dialogue 1 exercises

1 b ਵੈਸਾਖੀ ਮੇਲਾ **c 1** ਫ਼ਸਲਾਂ ਕਟਣਾ **2** ਸਿੱਖ ਕੌਮ ਦਾ ਜਨਮ ਦਿਨ **d** ਜਲੇਬੀਆਂ ਅਤੇ ਪਕੌੜੇ **e** ਗਤਕਾ **f 1** ਨੁਮਾਇਸ਼ **2** ਭੰਗੜਾ

2 village people harvest season Sikh religion the new year **3** True True False False

Folk song exercise
a Yes **b** No **c** No **d** No

End exercises
1 a ਜਿਹੜਾ, ਉਹ **b** ਜਿਵੇਂ, ਉਂਵੇਂ **c** ਜਿੱਥੇ, ਉੱਥੇ **d** ਜਦੋਂ, ਉਦੋਂ **2 b** ਬਾਹਰ ਜਾਣ ਦੇਵੇ **c** ਪੀਣ ਦੇ **d** ਦੇਖਣ ਦੇਵੇ/ਦਿਉ **3 a** ਕੰਮ ਤੇ ਜਾਣ ਲਈ ੧੫ ਮਿੰਟ ਲੱਗਦੇ ਹਨ। **b** ਇੱਕ ਫ਼ਰਸਟ ਕਲਾਸ ਟਿਕਟ ਲਈ ਕਿੰਨੇ ਪੈਸੇ ਲੱਗਦੇ ਹਨ ? **c** ਮੈਨੂੰ ਗਰਮੀ ਲੱਗਦੀ ਹੈ। **d** ਬਾਰਸ਼ ਹੋਣ ਲੱਗੀ। **e** ਅਸੀਂ ਬਾਹਰ ਜਾਣ ਲੱਗੇ ਸੀ।

Unit 16

Dialogue 1 exercises
1 a True **b** False **c** False **d** True **2 a** ਮੈਨੂੰ ਭੰਗੜਾ ਪਸੰਦ ਹੈ। **b** ਮੈਨੂੰ ਭੰਗੜਾ ਗਿੱਧੇ ਨਾਲੋਂ ਜ਼ਿਆਦਾ ਪਸੰਦ ਹੈ। **c** ਭਾਵੇਂ ਤੁਸੀਂ ਪੰਜਾਬ ਜਾ ਬਾਹਰ ਹੋ, ਭੰਗੜਾ ਦੇਖ ਸਕਦੇ ਹੋ। **d** ਆਓ ਆਪਾਂ, ਨੱਚੀਏ। **3 a** drum **b** long wooden pole **c** spoon

Dialogue 2 exercises
1 Canada Uganda Malaysia England **2 a** ਅਵਤਾਰ ਤੇ ਤਰਲੋਕ **b** ਮਲੇਸ਼ੀਆ **c** ਲਾਇਲਪੁਰ **d** ਜੁਗੰਡਾ **e** ਧੋਬੀ ਦਾ ਕੁੱਤਾ ਨਾ ਘਰ ਦਾ ਨਾ ਘਾਟ ਦਾ **3 a** ਕਿਉਂ ਕਿ ਉਹ ਫ਼ੌਜ ਵਿਚ ਭਰਤੀ ਹੋ ਗਏ ਸਨ। **b** ਕਿਉਂ ਕਿ ਉਹ ਗ਼ਦਰ ਪਾਰਟੀ ਵਿਚ ਸ਼ਾਮਲ ਹੋ ਗਏ ਸਨ। **c** ਕਿਉਂ ਕਿ ਪੰਜਾਬ ਦਾ ਬਟਵਾਰਾ ਹੋ ਗਿਆ ਸੀ। **d** ਕਿਉਂ ਕਿ ਉਹ ਰੇਲਵੇ ਬਣਾਉਣ ਗਏ ਸਨ।

End exercises
1 b ਸਾਡੇ ਕੋਲ ਨਾ ਪੈਸਲਾਂ ਹਨ, ਨਾ ਕਾਪੀ ਹੈ। **c** ਸਾਡੇ ਕੋਲ ਨਾ ਘੜੀਆਂ ਹਨ, ਨਾ ਰੇਡੀਓ ਹੈ। **d** ਸਾਡੇ ਕੋਲ ਨਾ ਬੋਤਲਾਂ ਹਨ, ਨਾ ਪਾਣੀ ਹੈ। **2 b** ਨਾ ਸਿਰਫ਼ ਇਹ ਕਿਤਾਬ ਲੰਬੀ ਹੈ, ਸਗੋਂ ਮੁਸ਼ਕਲ ਵੀ ਹੈ। **c** ਨਾ ਸਿਰਫ਼ ਅਸੀਂ ਭੰਗੜਾ ਪਸੰਦ ਕਰਦੇ ਹਾਂ, ਸਗੋਂ ਗਿੱਧਾ ਵੀ ਪਸੰਦ ਕਰਦੇ ਹਾਂ। **d** ਭਾਵੇਂ ਤੁਸੀਂ ਪੰਜਾਬ ਵਿਚ ਹੋ ਭਾਵੇਂ ਬਾਹਰ, ਤੁਸੀਂ ਭੰਗੜਾ ਦੇਖ ਸਕਦੇ ਹੋ। **e** ਮੰਨੇ ਜਾਂ ਨਾ ਮੰਨੋ, ਵੈਨਕੂਵਰ ਦਾ ਮਾਹੌਲ ਪੰਜਾਬ ਵਾਂਗੂੰ ਹੈ। **3** ਤਰਲੋਕ: ਇੰਗਲੈਂਡ, ਕੈਨੇਡਾ, ਜੁਗੰਡਾ ਅਵਤਾਰ: ਮਲੇਸ਼ੀਆ, ਕੈਨੇਡਾ, ਲਾਇਲਪੁਰ

Topic vocabulary

English	Transliteration	ਪੰਜਾਬੀ
Parts of the body	*sareer de ang*	*ਸਰੀਰ ਦੇ ਅੰਗ*
arm	baanh	ਬਾਂਹ
back	piththh	ਪਿੱਠ
beard	daarh-h-ee	ਦਾੜ੍ਹੀ
body	sareer/jisam	ਸਰੀਰ/ਜਿਸਮ
chest	chaatee	ਛਾਤੀ
ear	kann	ਕੰਨ
eye	akhkh	ਅੱਖ
face	moonh/chihraa	ਮੂੰਹ/ਚਿਹਰਾ
finger	unglee	ਉਂਗਲੀ
foot	pair	ਪੈਰ
hair	vaal	ਵਾਲ
hand	haththh	ਹੱਥ
head	sir	ਸਿਰ
knee	godaa	ਗੋਡਾ
leg	latt	ਲੱਤ
moustache	muchchaan	ਮੁੱਛਾਂ
mouth	moonh	ਮੂੰਹ
neck	gardan	ਗਰਦਨ
nose	nakk	ਨੱਕ
shoulder	modhaa	ਮੋਢਾ
stomach	dhidd/pet	ਢਿੱਡ/ਪੇਟ
throat	gal/galaa	ਗਲ/ਗਲਾ
tongue	jeebh/zabaan	ਜੀਭ/ਜ਼ਬਾਨ
tooth	dand	ਦੰਦ
Vegetables	*sabzeeaan*	*ਸਬਜ਼ੀਆਂ*
bitter gourd	karelaa	ਕਰੇਲਾ
brinjal/egg plant	vataaoon/bainganh	ਵਤਾਊਂ/ਬੈਂਗਣ

cabbage	band gobhee	ਬੰਦ ਗੋਭੀ
capsicum	shimlaa mirach	ਸ਼ਿਮਲਾ ਮਿਰਚ
carrot	gaajar	ਗਾਜਰ
cauliflower	gobhee	ਗੋਭੀ
courgette	raam toree	ਰਾਮ ਤੋਰੀ
mushrooms	khunbaan	ਖੁੰਬਾਂ
mustard leaves	sar-h-on de patte (saag)	ਸਰ੍ਹੋਂ ਦੇ ਪੱਤੇ (ਸਾਗ)
okra	bhindee	ਭਿੰਡੀ
peas	matar	ਮਟਰ
potato	aaloo	ਆਲੂ
spinach	paalak	ਪਾਲਕ
tomatoes	tamaatar	ਟਮਾਟਰ
turnip	shalgam/gongloo	ਸ਼ਲਗਮ/ਗੋਂ ਗਲੂ
Fruit	*phal*	ਫਲ
apple	seb	ਸੇਬ
apricot	khurmaanee	ਖ਼ੁਰਮਾਨੀ
banana	kelaa	ਕੇਲਾ
grapes	angoor	ਅੰਗੂਰ
lemon	ninboo	ਨਿੰਬੂ
mango	anb	ਅੰਬ
orange	santraa	ਸੰਤਰਾ
peach	aarhoo	ਆੜੂ
pear	naakh/naashpaatee	ਨਾਖ/ਨਾਸ਼ਪਾਤੀ
pineapple	anaanaas	ਅਨਾਨਾਸ
plums	alooche/aaloobukhaaraa	ਅਲੂਚੇ/ਆਲੂਬੁਖ਼ਾਰਾ
pomegranate	anaar	ਅਨਾਰ
Places	*thaanvaan*	ਥਾਂਵਾਂ
church	girjaa	ਗਿਰਜਾ
college	mahaan vidiaalaa	ਮਹਾਂ ਵਿਦਿਆਲਾ
community kitchen	langar	ਲੰਗਰ
enquiry office	puchch gichch daa daftar	ਪੁੱਛ ਗਿੱਛ ਦਾ ਦਫ਼ਤਰ
exhibition	numaaish/ pardarshanee	ਨੁਮਾਇਸ਼/ ਪਰਦਰਸ਼ਨੀ

factory	kaarkhaanaa	ਕਾਰਖ਼ਾਨਾ
fort	kilhaa	ਕਿਲ੍ਹਾ
Hindu place of worship (temple)	mandar	ਮੰਦਰ
hospital	haspataal	ਹਸਪਤਾਲ
library	pustakaalaa	ਪੁਸਤਕਾਲਾ
market	mandee	ਮੰਡੀ
museum	ajaaib ghar	ਅਜਾਇਬ ਘਰ
Muslim place of worship (mosque)	masjid/maseet	ਮਸਜਿਦ/ਮਸੀਤ
office	daftar	ਦਫ਼ਤਰ
palace	mahhal	ਮੱਹਲ
park	baagh	ਬਾਗ਼
police station	thaanhaa/pulas chaunkee	ਥਾਣਾ/ਪੁਲਸ ਚੌਂਕੀ
post office	daakkhaanaa	ਡਾਕਖ਼ਾਨਾ
roadside restaurant	dhaabaa	ਢਾਬਾ
school	vidiaalaa/madrasaa	ਵਿਦਿਆਲਾ/ਮਦਰਸਾ
shop	dukaan/hattee	ਦੁਕਾਨ/ਹੱਟੀ
Sikh place of worship	gurdavaaraa/ gurduaaraa	ਗੁਰਦਵਾਰਾ/ ਗੁਰਦੁਆਰਾ
zoo	chirheeaa ghar	ਚਿੜੀਆ ਘਰ

Occupations	*peshe*	*ਪੇਸ਼ੇ*
carpenter	tarkhaanh	ਤਰਖਾਣ
cook/chef	laangree	ਲਾਂਗਰੀ
doctor	daaktar	ਡਾਕਟਰ
farmer	kisaan	ਕਿਸਾਨ
gardener	maalee	ਮਾਲੀ
judge	jajj	ਜੱਜ
lawyer	vakeel	ਵਕੀਲ
mechanic	mistaree	ਮਿਸਤਰੀ
milkman	dudhdh vaalaa	ਦੁੱਧ ਵਾਲਾ
policeman	pulas vaalaa	ਪੁਲਸ ਵਾਲਾ
postman	daakeeaa	ਡਾਕੀਆ
priest (Sikh)	garanthee	ਗਰੰਥੀ
singer	gaaik	ਗਾਇਕ

| teacher | adhiaapak | ਅਧਿਆਪਕ |
| writer | lekhak | ਲੇਖਕ |

Colours	*rang*	*ਰੰਗ*
black	kaalaa	ਕਾਲਾ
blue	neelaa	ਨੀਲਾ
brown	badaamee	ਬਦਾਮੀ
gold/golden	sunahiree	ਸੁਨਹਿਰੀ
green	haraa/sabaz	ਹਰਾ/ਸਬਜ਼
grey	saletee	ਸਲੇਟੀ
khaki	khaakee	ਖ਼ਾਕੀ
maroon	laakhaa	ਲਾਖਾ
orange	santaree	ਸੰਤਰੀ
pink	gulaabee	ਗੁਲਾਬੀ
purple	jaamnee	ਜਾਮਨੀ
red	laal	ਲਾਲ
saffron	kesaree	ਕੇਸਰੀ
white	chittaa/safed	ਚਿੱਟਾ/ਸਫ਼ੇਦ
yellow	peelaa	ਪੀਲਾ

Directions	*dishaavaan*	*ਦਿਸ਼ਾਵਾਂ*
behind	pichche	ਪਿੱਛੇ
down	thalle	ਥੱਲੇ
east	poorab	ਪੂਰਬ
far	door	ਦੂਰ
in front	agge	ਅੱਗੇ
left side	khabbe	ਖੱਬੇ
near	nerhe/nazdeek	ਨੇੜੇ/ਨਜ਼ਦੀਕ
north	uttar	ਉੱਤਰ
right side	sajje	ਸੱਜੇ
south	dakhkhanh	ਦੱਖਣ
straight	sidhdhaa, sidhdhe	ਸਿੱਧਾ/ਸਿੱਧੇ
that side	us paase	ਉਸ ਪਾਸੇ
this side	is paase	ਇਸ ਪਾਸੇ
up	uppar	ਉੱਪਰ
west	pachcham	ਪੱਛਮ

Animals	*jaanvar*	ਜਾਨਵਰ
bear	richch	ਰਿੱਛ
buffalo	majhjh	ਮੱਝ
camel	ooth	ਊਠ
cat	billee	ਬਿੱਲੀ
cow	gaan	ਗਾਂ
deer	hiran	ਹਿਰਨ
dog	kuttaa	ਕੁੱਤਾ
elephant	haathee	ਹਾਥੀ
fox	loonbarh	ਲੂੰਬੜ
horse	ghorhaa	ਘੋੜਾ
monkey	baandar	ਬਾਂਦਰ
mouse	choohaa	ਚੂਹਾ
pig	soor	ਸੂਰ
sheep	bhed	ਭੇਡ
tiger	sher	ਸ਼ੇਰ

Moods	*birteeaan*	ਬਿਰਤੀਆਂ
angry	gussaa	ਗੁੱਸਾ
anxious	pareshaan	ਪਰੇਸ਼ਾਨ
contented	santushat	ਸੰਤੁਸ਼ਟ
curious	utsuk	ਉਤਸੁਕ
depressed	udaas	ਉਦਾਸ
determined	nishchit	ਨਿਸ਼ਚਿਤ
disgusted	upraam	ਉਪਰਾਮ
frightened	dariaa hoiaa	ਡਰਿਆ ਹੋਇਆ
happy	khush	ਖ਼ੁਸ਼
irritated	khijhiaa hoiaa	ਖਿਝਿਆ ਹੋਇਆ
lazy	susat	ਸੁਸਤ
loving	piaaraa	ਪਿਆਰਾ
sad/unhappy	ghamgeen	ਗ਼ਮਗੀਨ
surprised	hairaan janak	ਹੈਰਾਨ ਜਨਕ
thoughtful	vichaarsheel	ਵਿਚਾਰਸ਼ੀਲ

Travel and transport	*safar te aavaajaaee*	ਸਫ਼ਰ ਤੇ ਆਵਾਜਾਈ
aeroplane	havaaee jahaaz	ਹਵਾਈ ਜਹਾਜ਼
airport	havaaee addaa	ਹਵਾਈ ਅੱਡਾ

bicycle	saaikal	ਸਾਇਕਲ
boat	berhee	ਬੇੜੀ
booking clerk	tikat baaboo	ਟਿਕਟ ਬਾਬੂ
bus	bas	ਬਸ
bus station	basaan daa addaa	ਬਸਾਂ ਦਾ ਅੱਡਾ
car	kaar/gaddee	ਕਾਰ/ਗੱਡੀ
fare	kiraaiaa	ਕਿਰਾਇਆ
foot (on)	paidal	ਪੈਦਲ
horse carriage	taangaa/yakkaa	ਟਾਂਗਾ/ਯੱਕਾ
journey	yaatraa/safar	ਯਾਤਰਾ/ਸਫ਼ਰ
passenger	savaaree	ਸਵਾਰੀ
road	sarhak	ਸੜਕ
rickshaw	rikshaa	ਰਿਕਸ਼ਾ
ship	samundaree jahaaz	ਸਮੁੰਦਰੀ ਜਹਾਜ਼
ticket	tikat	ਟਿਕਟ
train	rel gaddee	ਰੇਲ ਗੱਡੀ
(to) travel	safar karnaa	ਸਫ਼ਰ ਕਰਨਾ
traveller	yaatree	ਯਾਤਰੀ
vehicle	vaahanh	ਵਾਹਣ
waiting room	udeek ghar/ musaafar khaanaa	ਉਡੀਕ ਘਰ/ ਮੁਸਾਫ਼ਰ ਖ਼ਾਨਾ

| *Personal identification* | *nijjee shanaakhat* | ਨਿੱਜੀ ਸ਼ਨਾਖ਼ਤ |

age	umar	ਉਮਰ
birthday	janam din	ਜਨਮ ਦਿਨ
(to be) born	janmnhaa	ਜੰਮਣਾ
caste	zaat	ਜਾਤ
family name	got	ਗੋਤ
height	kadd	ਕੱਦ
maiden name	pekaa naan	ਪੇਕਾ ਨਾਂ
man	aadmee	ਆਦਮੀ
(to be) married	viaahiaa honhaa	ਵਿਆਹਿਆ ਹੋਣਾ
name	naam/naan	ਨਾਮ/ਨਾਂ
nation	kaum	ਕੌਮ
nationality	kaumeeat	ਕੌਮੀਅਤ
place of birth	janam asthaan	ਜਨਮ ਅਸਥਾਨ

religion	dharam/mazhab	ਧਰਮ/ਮਜ਼ੂਬ
(to be) unmarried	kanvaaraa honhaa	ਕੰਵਾਰਾ ਹੋਣਾ
young	javaan	ਜਵਾਨ

House and home — *makaan te ghar* — ਮਕਾਨ ਤੇ ਘਰ

bathroom	ghusal khaanaa/ ishnaan ghar	ਗ਼ੁਸਲ ਖ਼ਾਨਾ/ ਇਸ਼ਨਾਨ ਘਰ
bed	manjaa/palangh	ਮੰਜਾ/ਪਲੰਘ
bedroom	saunh vaalaa kamraa	ਸੌਣ ਵਾਲਾ ਕਮਰਾ
building	imaarat	ਇਮਾਰਤ
bungalow	banglaa	ਬੰਗਲਾ
carpet	daree	ਦਰੀ
ceiling	andarlee chatt	ਅੰਦਰਲੀ ਛੱਤ
cooker	chullhaa	ਚੁੱਲ੍ਹਾ
court yard	vihrhaa	ਵਿਹੜਾ
dining room	khaanh vaalaa kamraa	ਖਾਣ ਵਾਲਾ ਕਮਰਾ
door	darvaazaa	ਦਰਵਾਜ਼ਾ
floor	farash	ਫ਼ਰਸ਼
garden	bagheechaa	ਬਗ਼ੀਚਾ
key	taalee, chaabee	ਤਾਲੀ, ਚਾਬੀ
kitchen	rasoee	ਰਸੋਈ
light	roshnee	ਰੋਸ਼ਨੀ
lock	taalaa/jandraa	ਤਾਲਾ/ਜੰਦਰਾ
roof	baaharlee chatt	ਬਾਹਰਲੀ ਛੱਤ
room	kamraa	ਕਮਰਾ
sink	chubachchaa	ਚੁਬੱਚਾ
sitting room	baithak	ਬੈਠਕ
stairs	paurheeaan	ਪੌੜੀਆਂ
storey	manzal	ਮੰਜ਼ਲ
tap	nalkaa	ਨਲਕਾ
utensils	bartan/bhaande	ਬਰਤਨ/ਭਾਂਡੇ
wall	deevar/kandh	ਦੀਵਾਰ/ਕੰਧ
window	baaree/khirhkee	ਬਾਰੀ/ਖਿੜਕੀ

Nature — *kudrat* — ਕੁਦਰਤ

| climate | paunh paanhee | ਪੌਣ ਪਾਣੀ |
| earth | dhartee | ਧਰਤੀ |

flowers	phull	ਫੁੱਲ
forest	jangal	ਜੰਗਲ
grass	ghaah	ਘਾਹ
lake	jheel	ਝੀਲ
land	zameen	ਜ਼ਮੀਨ
lightning	bijlee dee chamak	ਬਿਜਲੀ ਦੀ ਚਮਕ
moon	chann	ਚੰਨ
mountains	parbat/pahaarh	ਪਰਬਤ/ਪਹਾੜ
river	dariaa	ਦਰਿਆ
sea	samundar	ਸਮੁੰਦਰ
seasons	ruttaan	ਰੁੱਤਾਂ
sky	asmaan	ਅਸਮਾਨ
star	taaraa	ਤਾਰਾ
sun	sooraj	ਸੂਰਜ
tree	darakhat	ਦਰਖ਼ਤ
Weather	*mausam*	ਮੌਸਮ
breeze	havaa	ਹਵਾ
cloud	baddal	ਬੱਦਲ
cold	thand	ਠੰਡ
drought	sokaa	ਸੋਕਾ
drizzle	boondaa baandee	ਬੂੰਦਾ ਬਾਂਦੀ
dry	khushak	ਖ਼ੁਸ਼ਕ
flood	harh-h	ਹੜੂ
fog	dhund	ਧੁੰਦ
frost	koraa	ਕੋਰਾ
hailstones	garhe	ਗੜੇ
heatwave	loo	ਲੂ
hot	garmee	ਗਰਮੀ
rain	baarash/meenh	ਬਾਰਸ਼/ਮੀਂਹ
shade	chaan	ਛਾਂ
snow	baraf	ਬਰਫ਼
sunshine	dhupp	ਧੁੱਪ
thunder	garaj	ਗਰਜ
wet	sillaa	ਸਿੱਲਾ

Numerals	*ginhtee*	ਗਿਣਤੀ	
0	sifar	ਸਿਫ਼ਰ	੦
1	ikk	ਇੱਕ	੧
2	do	ਦੋ	੨
3	tinn	ਤਿੰਨ	੩
4	chaar	ਚਾਰ	੪
5	panj	ਪੰਜ	੫
6	che	ਛੇ	੬
7	satt	ਸੱਤ	੭
8	athth	ਅੱਠ	੮
9	naun	ਨੌਂ	੯
10	das	ਦਸ	੧੦
11	giaaraan	ਗਿਆਰਾਂ	੧੧
12	baar-h-aan	ਬਾਰ੍ਹਾਂ	੧੨
13	ter-h-aan	ਤੇਰ੍ਹਾਂ	੧੩
14	chaud-h-aan	ਚੌਦ੍ਹਾਂ	੧੪
15	pandraan	ਪੰਦਰਾਂ	੧੫
16	solhaan	ਸੋਲ੍ਹਾਂ	੧੬
17	sataar-h-aan	ਸਤਾਰ੍ਹਾਂ	੧੭
18	athaar-h-aan	ਅਠਾਰ੍ਹਾਂ	੧੮
19	unnee	ਉੱਨੀ	੧੯
20	veeh	ਵੀਹ	੨੦
21	ikkee	ਇੱਕੀ	੨੧
22	baaee	ਬਾਈ	੨੨
23	te-ee	ਤੇਈ	੨੩
24	chauvee	ਚੌਵੀ	੨੪
25	panjhee	ਪੰਝੀ	੨੫
26	chabbee	ਛੱਬੀ	੨੬
27	sataaee	ਸਤਾਈ	੨੭
28	athaaee	ਅਠਾਈ	੨੮
29	unattee	ਉਨੱਤੀ	੨੯
30	teeh	ਤੀਹ	੩੦
31	ikkatee	ਇੱਕਤੀ	੩੧
32	battee	ਬੱਤੀ	੩੨
33	tetee	ਤੇਤੀ	੩੩

34	chauntee	ਚੌਂਤੀ	੩੪
35	paintee	ਪੈਂਤੀ	੩੫
36	chattee	ਛੱਤੀ	੩੬
37	saintee	ਸੈਂਤੀ	੩੭
38	athattee	ਅਠੱਤੀ	੩੮
39	untaalee	ਉਨਤਾਲੀ	੩੯
40	chaalee	ਚਾਲੀ	੪੦
41	iktaalee	ਇਕਤਾਲੀ	੪੧
42	bataalee	ਬਤਾਲੀ	੪੨
43	tirtaalee	ਤਿਰਤਾਲੀ	੪੩
44	chutaalee	ਚੁਤਾਲੀ	੪੪
45	pantaalee	ਪੰਤਾਲੀ	੪੫
46	chitaalee	ਛਿਤਾਲੀ	੪੬
47	santaalee	ਸੰਤਾਲੀ	੪੭
48	athtaalee	ਅਠਤਾਲੀ	੪੮
49	unhnjaa	ਉਨੰਜਾ	੪੯
50	panjaah	ਪੰਜਾਹ	੫੦
51	ikvanjaa	ਇਕਵੰਜਾ	੫੧
52	bavanjaa	ਬਵੰਜਾ	੫੨
53	tarvanjaa	ਤਰਵੰਜਾ	੫੩
54	churanjaa	ਚੁਰੰਜਾ	੫੪
55	pachvanjaa	ਪਚਵੰਜਾ	੫੫
56	chivanjaa	ਛਿਵੰਜਾ	੫੬
57	satvanjaa	ਸਤਵੰਜਾ	੫੭
58	athvanjaa	ਅਠਵੰਜਾ	੫੮
59	unhaahth	ਉਣਾਹਠ	੫੯
60	saththt	ਸੱਠ	੬੦
61	ikaahth	ਇਕਾਹਠ	੬੧
62	baahth	ਬਾਹਠ	੬੨
63	trehth	ਤ੍ਰੇਹਠ	੬੩
64	chaunhth	ਚੌਹਠ	੬੪
65	painhth	ਪੈਂਹਠ	੬੫
66	chiaahth	ਛਿਆਹਠ	੬੬
67	sataahth	ਸਤਾਹਠ	੬੭
68	athaahth	ਅਠਾਹਠ	੬੮
69	un-hattar	ਉਨਹੱਤਰ	੬੯

70	sattar	ਸੱਤਰ	੭੦
71	ik-hattar	ਇਕਹੱਤਰ	੭੧
72	bahattar	ਬਹੱਤਰ	੭੨
73	tihattar	ਤਿਹੱਤਰ	੭੩
74	chauhattar	ਚੌਹੱਤਰ	੭੪
75	pachattar	ਪਚੱਤਰ	੭੫
76	chihattar	ਛਿਹੱਤਰ	੭੬
77	satattar	ਸਤੱਤਰ	੭੭
78	athattar	ਅਠੱਤਰ	੭੮
79	unaasee	ਉਨਾਸੀ	੭੯
80	assee	ਅੱਸੀ	੮੦
81	ikaasee	ਇਕਾਸੀ	੮੧
82	biaasee	ਬਿਆਸੀ	੮੨
83	triaasee	ਤ੍ਰਿਆਸੀ	੮੩
84	churaasee	ਚੁਰਾਸੀ	੮੪
85	pachaasee	ਪਚਾਸੀ	੮੫
86	chiaasee	ਛਿਆਸੀ	੮੬
87	sataasee	ਸਤਾਸੀ	੮੭
88	athaasee	ਅਠਾਸੀ	੮੮
89	unhaanven	ਉਣਾਨਵੇਂ	੮੯
90	navve	ਨੱਵੇ	੯੦
91	ikaanven	ਇਕਾਨਵੇਂ	੯੧
92	baanven	ਬਾਨਵੇਂ	੯੨
93	triaanven	ਤ੍ਰਿਆਨਵੇਂ	੯੩
94	churaanven	ਚੁਰਾਨਵੇਂ	੯੪
95	pachaanven	ਪਚਾਨਵੇਂ	੯੫
96	chiaanven	ਛਿਆਨਵੇਂ	੯੬
97	sataanven	ਸਤਾਨਵੇਂ	੯੭
98	athaanven	ਅਠਾਨਵੇਂ	੯੮
99	narhinven	ਨਿੜਨਵੇਂ	੯੯
100	sau	ਸੌ	੧੦੦
1,000	ikk hazaar	ਇੱਕ ਹਜ਼ਾਰ	੧,੦੦੦
100,000	lakhkh	ਲੱਖ	੧੦੦,੦੦੦
10,000,000	karorh	ਕਰੋੜ	੧੦,੦੦੦,੦੦੦

Panjabi–English glossary

ਉਸ	us	*that*
ਉਹ	uh	*he, she, that, they*
ਉਖੜਨਾ	ukharhnaa	*to be displaced,*
		to be uprooted
ਉਡੀਕਣਾ	udeeknhaa	*to wait*
ਉਤਸੁਕ	utsuk	*anxious, awaiting*
ਉੱਥੇ	uththon	*from there*
ਉਮਰ	umar	*age* (f.)
ਉਮੀਦ	umeed	*hope* (f.)
ਉਰਦੂ	urdoo	*Urdu* (m./f.)
ਉਲੰਘਣਾ	ulanghnhaa	*to disobey, to break*
ਉਠ	ooth	*male camel* (m.)
ਅੱਸਲਾਮ ਅਲੈਕਮ	asslaam alaikam	Muslim greeting
ਅਸੀਂ	aseen	*we*
ਅਸੀਂ ਸਾਰੇ	aseen saare	*all of us, we all*
ਅਸੀਂ ਦੋਨੇਂ	aseen donon	*both of us*
ਅਖਾਣ	akhaanh	*proverb, saying* (m.)
ਅਖੀਰ	akheer	*end*
ਅਗਲਾ	aglaa	*next* (v.)
ਅੰਗਰੇਜ਼	angrez	*English* (m./f.)
ਅੱਛਾ	achchaa	*OK, all right*
ਅੱਜ	ajj	*today*
ਅੱਜ ਕੱਲ੍ਹ	ajj kallh	*these days*
ਅਜ਼ਾਦੀ	azaadee	*freedom,*
		independence (f.)
ਅੰਤਰ ਰਾਸ਼ਟਰੀ	antar raashtaree	*international*
ਅੰਦਰ	andar	*inside*
ਅਤੇ	ate	*and*
ਅਜ਼ਾਦੀ ਲਈ	azaadee laee	*struggle for*
ਜਦੋ ਜਹਿਦ	jado jahid	*independence* (f.)
ਅਜੋਕਾ	ajokaa	*modern*
ਅਨੰਦ ਮਾਣੇ	anand maanho	*enjoy yourself*
ਅਨਾਰਕਲੀ	anaarkalee	name of classic Urdu film (f.)
ਅਪਰਾਧ	apraadh	*offence* (m.)
ਅਫਸਰ	afsar	*officer* (m./f.)
ਅਫਸੋਸ	afsos	*regret, sorry*

ਅਬਾਦੀ	abaadee	population (f.)
ਅਮਰੀਕਾ	amreekaa	America (m.)
ਅੰਮ੍ਰਿਤ	anmrit	nectar, holy water (m.)
ਅਰਥ	arth	meaning (m.)
ਅਰਾਮ	araam	rest (m.)
ਆ ਜਾ	aa jaa	come (informal request)
ਆਉਣਾ	aaunhaa	to come
ਆਓ	aao	come (formal)
ਆਸ ਪਾਸ	aas paas	around and about
ਆਗਿਆ	aagiaa	permission (f.)
ਆਪਣਾ	aapnhaa	one's own
ਆਲੂ	aaloo	potato(es) (m.)
ਅਧਿਆਪਕ	adhiaapak	teacher (m./f.)
ਅਧਿਆਪਕਾ	adhiaapkaa	teacher (f.)
ਐਨੇ ਸਾਰੇ	aine saare	so much
ਐਤਵਾਰ	aitvaar	Sunday (m.)
ਇਸ	is	it, this
ਇਸ ਕਰ ਕੇ	is kar ke	that is why
ਇਸਤਰੀ	istaree	lady (f.)
ਇਸ ਵਾਰੀ	is vaaree	this time
ਇਹ	ih	he, she, it, this
ਇੱਕ	ikk	one, a
ਇੱਕ ਪਾਸੇ	ikk paase	one side
ਇੱਕ ਸੌ ਵੀਹ	ikk sau veeh	120
ਇਕੱਠ	ikaththh	gathering (m.)
ਇਕੱਠੇ	ikaththe	together
ਇੱਕੋ	ikko	same
ਇੰਤਜ਼ਾਮ	intzaam	arrangements (m.)
ਇੱਥੇ	iththe	here
ਇਨਸ਼ਾ ਅੱਲਾ	inshaa allaa	hopefully (lit: if God wishes)
ਈਸਟ ਅਫ਼ਰੀਕਾ	eest afreekaa	East Africa (m.)
ਏ	e	is (informal)
ਸਹਿਮਤ	sahimat	agree
ਸ਼ਹਿਰ	shahir	city (m.)
ਸ਼ਹਿਰੀਅਤ	shahireeat	citizen (f.)
ਸਹੁਰੇ	sahure	in-laws (m.)
ਸਹੇਲੀ	sahelee	friend (f.)
ਸਕਣਾ	saknhaa	can, to be able to
ਸਕੂਲ	sakool	school (m.)
ਸਗੋਂ	sagon	but also

ਸੱਚ	sachch	*true, truth* (v.)
ਸੱਚੀ ਮੁੱਚੀ	sachchee muchchee	*genuinely*
ਸਤਿ ਸ੍ਰੀ ਅਕਾਲ	sat sree akaal	*Sikh greeting*
ਸਥਿਤੀ	sathitee	*situation* (f.)
ਸੱਦਾ ਪੱਤਰ	saddaa pattar	*invitation* (m.)
ਸਨਿਚਰਵਾਰ	sanicharvaar	*Saturday* (m.)
ਸ਼ਨਾਖ਼ਤੀ ਕਾਰਡ	shanaakhtee kaard	*identity card* (m.)
ਸਪਤਾਹ	saptaah	*week* (m.)
ਸੰਪਰਕ	sanparak	*contact* (m.)
ਸਬਜ਼ੀ	sabzee	*vegetable* (f.)
ਸਫ਼ਰ ਕਰਨਾ	safar karnaa	*to travel*
ਸਭ	sabh	*all, every*
ਸਭ ਕੁਝ	sabh kujh	*everything*
ਸਭ ਪਾਸੇ	sabh paase	*everywhere*
ਸਭ ਤੋਂ ਵਧੀਆ	sabh ton vadheeaa	*the best*
ਸਮਝਣਾ	samjhnhaa	*to understand, to comprehend*
ਸਮਾਂ	samaan	*time* (m.)
ਸਮਾਂ ਪਾ ਕੇ	samaan paa ke	*after a while, after some time*
ਸਮਾਜ ਸੇਵਕ	samaaj sevak	*social worker* (m./f.)
ਸਮਾਨ	samaan	*luggage, things* (m.)
ਸਮੁੰਦਰ	samundar	*sea* (m.)
ਸਮੁੰਦਰੀ ਡਾਕ	samundaree daak	*sea mail* (f.)
ਸਮੋਸਾ	samosaa	*triangular stuffed pastry* (m.)
ਸਰਦਾਰ ਸਾਹਿਬ	sardaar saahib	*Mr* (m.)
ਸਰਦੀ	sardee	*winter* (f.)
ਸ਼੍ਰੇਣੀ	shrenhee	*class* (f.)
ਸਰੋਵਰ	sarovar	*pool* (m.)
ਸ਼ਲਗਮ	shalgam	*turnip* (m.)
ਸਵਰਗ	savarag	*heaven* (m.)
ਸਵਾਰੀ	savaaree	*installation* (f.)
ਸਵਾਰੀਆਂ	savaareeaan	*passengers, travellers* (f.)
ਸਵੇਰੇ	savere	*in the morning*
ਸਾਹਿਬ	saahib	*sir* (m.)
ਸਾਡਾ	saadaa	*our*
ਸ਼ਾਂਤੀ	shaantee	*peace* (f.)
ਸਾਫ਼ ਕਰਨਾ	saaf karnaa	*to clean*
ਸ਼ਾਬਾਸ਼	shaabaash	*well done*
ਸ਼ਾਮਲ	shaamal	*to be present, to join in, participate*
ਸਾਲ	saal	*year* (m.)
ਸਾਰਾ ਮਾਹੌਲ	saaraa maahaul	*whole atmosphere* (m.)

ਸਾਰੇ	saare	*everyone, all* (v.)
ਸਾੜ੍ਹੀ ਵਾਲੀ	saarh-h-ee vaalee	*the one wearing the sari* (f.)
ਸਿਆਣਾ	siaanhaa	*wise, mature* (v.)
ਸਿਹਤ	siha<u>t</u>	*health* (f.)
ਸ਼ਿਕਾਇਤ	shikaai<u>t</u>	*complaint* (f.)
ਸਿੱਖਾਂ ਦੇ	sikhkhaa<u>n</u> <u>d</u>e	*of the Sikhs*
ਸਿਤਾਰ	si<u>t</u>aar	*sitar* (f.) (stringed classical musical instrument)
ਸੀਟ	seet	*seat* (f.)
ਸ਼ੀਸ਼ਾ	sheeshaa	*mirror* (m.)
ਸੀਨਾ	seenaa	*bosom, heart* (m.)
ਸੁਆਦ	suaa<u>d</u>	*taste* (m.)
ਸੁਆਦੀ	suaa<u>d</u>ee	*tasty*
ਸੁਹਣਾ	suhnhaa	*nice, pretty* (v.)
ਸ਼ੁੱਕਰਵਾਰ	shukkarvaar	*Friday* (m.)
ਸ਼ੁਕਰੀਆ	shukreeaa	*thank you* (m.)
ਸੁਨਣਾ	sunnhaa	*to listen*
ਸੁਨਹਿਰੀ	sunahiree	*golden*
ਸ਼ੁਭ ਇਛਾਵਾਂ	shubh i<u>ch</u>aavaa<u>n</u>	*best wishes* (f.)
ਸੁਰੱਖਿਅਤ ਸਫ਼ਰ	surakhkhia<u>t</u> safar	*safe journey*
ਸ਼ੁਰੂ ਹੋਣਾ	shuroo honhaa	*to start, to begin*
ਸ਼ੁਰੂ ਕਰਨਾ	shuroo karnaa	*to begin, to commence*
ਸੁਈ	sooee	*needle* (f.)
ਸੇਵਾਦਾਰ	sevaa<u>d</u>aar	*volunteer* (m./f.)
ਸੈਲਾਨੀ	sailaanee	*tourist* (m./f.)
ਸੋਚਣਾ	sochnhaa	*to think*
ਸੋਨਾ	sonaa	*gold* (m.)
ਸੋਮਵਾਰ	somvaar	*Monday* (m.)
ਸੌ (੧੦੦)	sau	*100*
ਸ਼ੌਕ	shauk	*fondness, enjoyment, like* (m.)
ਸੌਖਾ	saukhaa	*easy, simple* (v.)
ਹਜ਼ਮ	hazam	*digest*
ਹੰਢਣਸਾਰ	ha<u>n</u>dhanhsaar	*durable, hardwearing*
ਹਫ਼ਤਾ	haf<u>t</u>aa	*week* (m.)
ਹਫ਼ਤਾ	haf<u>t</u>aa	*Saturday* (m.)
ਹਫ਼ਤੇ ਦੇ ਅਖ਼ੀਰ	haf<u>t</u>e <u>d</u>e a<u>kh</u>eer	*weekend* (m.)
ਹਰ ਪਾਸੇ	har paase	*everywhere*
ਹਰਿਮੰਦਰ ਸਾਹਿਬ	harma<u>nd</u>ar saahib	*Golden Temple* (m.)
ਹਵਾਈ	havaaee	*by air*
ਹਵਾਈ ਅੱਡਾ	havaaee addaa	*airport* (m.)
ਹਵਾਈ ਡਾਕ	havaaee daak	*air mail* (f.)
ਹਾਲ	haal	*condition* (m.)

ਹਾਂ ਜੀ	haan jee	*yes* (polite)
ਹਿਸਾਬ	hisaab	*maths* (m.)
ਹਿੰਦੂ	hindoo	*Hindu* (m./f.)
ਹੁਣ	hunh	*now*
ਹੋਸਟਲ	hostal	*hostel* (m.)
ਹੋਣਾ	honhaa	*to be*
ਹੈ	hai	*is*
ਕਈ	kaee	*several*
ਕਈ ਤਰ੍ਹਾਂ	kaee tar-h-aan	*different types*
ਕਹਿਣਾ	kahinhaa	*to speak*
ਕਟਣਾ	katnhaa	*to cut*
ਕੱਦ	kadd	*height* (m.)
ਕਦਰਾਂ	kadraan	*values* (f.)
ਕਦੀ	kadee	*sometimes*
ਕਦੋਂ	kadon	*when*
ਕਪੜਾ	kaprhaa	*cloth* (m.)
ਕਮਰਾ	kamraa	*room* (m.)
ਕਮਜ਼ੋਰੀ	kamzoree	*weakness* (f.)
ਕੰਮ	kanm	*job, work task* (m.)
ਕੰਮ ਕਰਨਾ	kanm karnaa	*to work*
ਕਰਨਾ	karnaa	*to do*
ਕਰਾਰਾ	karaaraa	*spicy* (v.)
ਕਰੇਲਾ	karelaa	*bitter gourd* (m.)
ਕੱਲ੍ਹ	kallh	*yesterday, tomorrow*
ਕਲਾਸ	kalaas	*class* (f.)
ਕਾਹਲਾ	kaahlaa	*impatient, hasty* (v.)
ਕਾਹਲ ਵਿਚ	kaahal vich	*in a hurry*
ਕਾਗ਼ਜ਼ਾਤ	kaaghzaat	*papers, documents* (m.)
ਕਾਫ਼ੀ ਕੁਝ	kaafee kujh	*quite a lot, plenty*
ਕਾਨੂੰਨ	kaanoonn	*law* (m.)
ਕਾਰ	kaar	*car* (f.)
ਕਾਲਜ	kaalaj	*college* (m.)
ਕਿ	ki	*that*
ਕਿਉਂ	kiun	*why*
ਕਿਉਂ ਕਿ	kiun ki	*because*
ਕਿਹਾ ਜਾਂਦਾ ਹੈ	kihaa jaandaa hai	*is said, is called*
ਕਿਹੜਾ	kihrhaa	*which*
ਕਿੱਥੇ	kiththe	*where*
ਕਿੰਨਾ	kinnaa	*how much?*
ਕਿੰਨੇ	kinne	*how many?*
ਕਿੰਨਾ ਚਿਰ ਤੋਂ	kinnaa chir ton	*since when, for how long?*
ਕਿੰਨੀ ਦੂਰ	kinnee door	*how far?*

ਕਿੰਨੇ ਦਾ ਮੀਟਰ	ki<u>nn</u>e <u>d</u>aa meetar	*how much per metre?*
ਕਿੰਨੇ ਵਜੇ	ki<u>nn</u>e vaje	*what time*
ਕਿਰਪਾ	kirpaa	*blessings (f.)*
ਕਿਰਾਇਆ	kiraaiaa	*rate, fare, rent (m.)*
ਕਿਵੇਂ	kive<u>n</u>	*how*
ਕਿਵੇਂ ਰਿਹਾ	kive<u>n</u> rihaa	*how did it go?*
ਕੀ	kee	*what*
ਕੀਮਤ	keema<u>t</u>	*price (f.)*
ਕੀਨੀਆ	keeneeaa	*Kenya (m.)*
ਕੀਰਤਨ	keer<u>t</u>an	*singing of hymns (m.)*
ਕੁੱਤਾ	ku<u>tt</u>aa	*dog (m.)*
ਕੋਈ	koee	*any*
ਕੋਈ ਨ ਕੋਈ	koee na koee	*some one or another*
ਕੋਸ਼ਿਸ਼ ਕਰਨਾ	koshish karnaa	*to try*
ਕੋਲ	kol	*with, next to,*
		in possession of
ਕੋਣ	kau<u>nh</u>	*who*
ਕੋਮ	kaum	*nation, community (f.)*
ਕੋੜਾ/ਕਸੈਲਾ	kaurhaa/kasailaa	*bitter (v.)*
ਕੇਵਲ	keval	*only*
ਕੈਮਰਾ	kaimraa	*camera (m.)*
ਖ਼ਤਮ ਕਰਨਾ	<u>kh</u>a<u>t</u>am karnaa	*to finish, to complete*
ਖ਼ਤਰਨਾਕ	<u>kh</u>a<u>t</u>arnaak	*dangerous*
ਖਤਰੀ	<u>kh</u>a<u>t</u>ree	*Khatri (m./f.) (caste)*
ਖ਼ਰਚਾ	<u>kh</u>archaa	*expense, expenses (m.)*
ਖਲੋਣਾ	<u>kh</u>alonhaa	*to be stood, to stand*
ਖੜੂਨਾ	kharhhnaa	*to stand, to park*
ਖ਼ਾਸ	<u>kh</u>aas	*special*
ਖਾਣਾ	khaanhaa	*to eat*
ਖ਼ਾਲੀ	<u>kh</u>aalee	*empty, vacant*
ਖ਼ਿਲਾਫ਼	<u>kh</u>ilaaf	*against*
ਖ਼ੁਸ਼	<u>kh</u>ush	*happy*
ਖ਼ੁਸ਼ੀ	<u>kh</u>ushee	*good (f.) (lit. happiness)*
ਖ਼ੁਦਾ ਹਾਫ਼ਿਜ਼	<u>kh</u>u<u>d</u>aa haafiz	*Muslim departing phrase*
ਖੁੱਲ੍ਹਾ	khullhaa	*open, plenty (v.)*
ਖੇਡਣਾ	khednhaa	*to play*
ਖ਼ੈਰ	<u>kh</u>air	*anyway*
ਗੱਡੀ	gaddee	*car, vehicle (f.)*
ਗੱਡੀ	gaddee	*automobile, train (f.)*
ਗਤਕਾ	ga<u>t</u>kaa	*a Sikh martial art,*
		like fencing (m.)

.ਗਦਰ	ghadar	*mutiny* (m.)
.ਗਦਰ ਪਾਰਟੀ	ghadar paartee	*Gadar Party* (f.)
.ਗਮੀ	ghamee	*sadness* (f.)
ਗਰਮੀ	garmee	*summer, heat* (f.)
ਗਰੇਡ	gared	*grade* (m.)
ਗੱਲ	gall	*matter, news* (f.) (lit. talk)
.ਗਲਤ	ghalat	*wrong*
ਗੱਲਾਂ	gallaan	*conversation* (f.)
ਗਾਜਰ	gaajar	*carrot* (f.)
ਗਾਣਾ	gaanhaa	*to sing*
ਗਾਲੜੀ	gaalrhee	*talkative*
ਗਿੱਧਾ	gidhdhaa	women's folk dance (m.)
ਗੀਤ	geet	*song* (m.)
.ਗੁਸਲ ਖ਼ਾਨਾ	ghusal khaanaa	*bathroom* (m.)
ਗੁਜਰਾਤੀ	gujraatee	a person from Gujarat or of Gujarati origin (m./f.)
ਗੁੰਬਦ	gunbad	*dome* (m.)
ਗੋਭੀ	gobhee	*cauliflower* (f.)
ਗੋਰੀ	goree	*fair, white* (v.)
ਘਰ	ghar	*house, home* (m.)
ਘਰ ਦਾ ਕੰਮ	ghar daa kanm	*homework* (m.)
ਘਰਵਾਲਾ	gharvaalaa	*husband* (m.)
ਘੱਟ	ghatt	*less, lower*
ਘੱਟ ਕਰਨਾ	ghatt karnaa	*to reduce, to lessen*
ਘੱਟੋ ਘੱਟ	ghatto ghatt	*at least*
ਘਾਟ	ghaat	place where clothes are washed on the bay (m.)
ਘੁੰਮਣਾ	ghunmnhaa	*to go around*
ਘੁੰਮਣਾ ਫਿਰਨਾ	ghunmnhaa phirnaa	*to travel around*
ਘੋੜੀ	ghorhee	*mare* (f.)
ਚੰਗੀ	changee	*good* (v.)
ਚਮਕੀਲਾ	chamkeelaa	*glittering, shining* (v.)
ਚਮਚਾ	chamchaa	*spoon* (m.)
ਚਰਖਾ	charkhaa	*spinning wheel* (m.)
ਚਲਣਾ	chalnhaa	*to go*
ਚੜ੍ਹਦੀ ਕਲਾ	charh-h-dee kalaa	*high spirits*
ਚੜ੍ਹਨਾ	charh-h-naa	*to be upon, to ride*
ਚਾਹੁਣਾ	chaahunhaa	*to need, to want*
ਚਾਚਾ ਜੀ	chaachaa jee	*uncle* (m) (father's brother)
ਚਿੱਠੀ	chiththee	*letter* (f.)

ਚਿਰ	chir	*length of time*
ਚੀਜ਼	cheez	*thing* (f.)
ਚੁਕਣਾ	chuknhaa	*to be settled, finished*
ਚੁੱਕਣਾ	chukknhaa	*to lift, to pick*
ਚੋਣ	chonh	*choice, selection* (f.)
ਚੌਥੇ ਗੁਰੂ	chauthe guroo	*fourth Guru* (m.)
ਚੌੜਾ	chaurhaa	*wide* (v.)
ਛਕਣਾ	chaknhaa	*to take, to consume*
ਛੱਡਣਾ	chaddnhaa	*to leave, to quit*
ਛਪਾਈਵਾਲਾ	chapaaeevaalaa	*the printed one* (m.)
ਛੱਲੀ	challee	*corn on the cob* (f.)
ਛਾਪਾ	chaapaa	*print* (m.)
ਛੁੱਟੀਆਂ	chutteeaan	*holidays* (f.)
ਛੋਟਾ	chotaa	*small* (v.)
ਜਗ੍ਹਾ	jag-h-aa	*place, location* (f.)
ਜਦੋਂ ਜਹਿਦ	jado jahid	*struggle* (f.)
ਜਨਮ	janam	*birth* (m.)
ਜਨਮ ਅਸਥਾਨ	janam asthaan	*birthplace* (m.)
ਜਨਮ ਦਿਨ	janam din	*birthday* (m.)
ਜੰਮਪਲ	janmpal	*raised, born and bred*
ਜੰਮਣਾ	janmnhaa	*to be born*
ਜ਼ਮਾਨਾ	zamaanaa	*times* (m.)
ਜਰਮਨ	jarman	*German* (m./f.)
ਜ਼ਰੂਰ	zaroor	*definitely*
ਜਲੂਸ	jaloos	*procession, parade* (m.)
ਜਾਂ	jaan	*or*
ਜ਼ਾਇਆ ਕਰਨਾ	zaaiaa karnaa	*to waste time*
ਜਾ ਚੁਕਣਾ	jaa chuknhaa	*have (already) been*
ਜਾਂਞੀ	jaannjee	members of the groom's wedding party (m./f.)
ਜਾਣਨਾ	jaanhnaa	*to know*
ਜ਼ਿਆਦਾ	ziaadaa	*too much*
ਜਿਸ	jis	*which* (oblique)
ਜਿਹਾ	jihaa	*sort of, rather*
ਜਿਹੜਾ	jihrhaa	*that, which*
ਜਿੱਥੇ	jiththe	*where*
ਜੀ	jee	honorific particle signifying respect
ਜੀ ਆਇਆਂ ਨੂੰ	jee aaiaan noon	*welcome*
ਜੀਵਨ	jeevan	*life* (m.)
ਜੁਮਾ	jumaa	*Friday* (m.)

ਜੁਮੇਰਾਤ	jumeraat	*Thursday* (f.)
ਜੇ	je	*if*
ਜੇਬਾਂ	jebaan	*pockets* (m./f.)
ਝਾਕਣਾ	jhaaknhaa	*to stare, to look at*
ਝੂਟੇ	jhoote	*rides* (m.)
ਟਮਾਟਰ	tamaatar	*tomato(es)* (m.)
ਟਿਕਟ	tikat	*stamp* (f.)
ਟੀ. ਵੀ.	tee vee	*TV (television)* (m.)
ਟੇਕਣਾ	teknhaa	*to bow down*
ਟੈਲੀਫ਼ੋਨ	taileefon	*telephone* (m.)
ਟੈਲੀਫ਼ੋਨ ਕਰਨਾ	taileefon karnaa	*to call by telephone*
ਠੰਡ	thand	*cold* (f.)
ਠਹਿਰਨਾ	thahirnaa	*to stay*
ਠੀਕ	theek	*fine/OK/all right/right*
ਠੀਕ ਕਰਨਾ	theek karnaa	*to fix, to correct*
ਠੀਕ ਠਾਕ	theek thaak	*OK, fine*
ਡਾਕ	daak	*mail, post* (f.)
ਡਾਕਟਰ	daaktar	*doctor* (m./f.)
ਡਾਂਗ	daang	long wooden pole (f.)
ਡਾਲਰ	daalar	*dollar* (m.)
ਡੋਲੀ	dolee	ceremony bidding farewell to the bride (f.)
ਢੋਲ	dhol	*big drum* (m.)
ਢੋਲਕੀ	dholkee	*small drum* (f.)
ਤਸ਼ਰੀਫ਼ ਰੱਖੋ ਜੀ	tashreef rakhkho jee	*please have a seat*
ਤਕਰੀਬਨ	takreeban	*about, approximately*
ਤਕਲੀਫ਼	takleef	*trouble, irritation, bother* (f.)
ਤਨਖ਼ਾਹ	tankhaah	*pay, salary* (f.)
ਤਬੀਅਤ	tabeeat	*state of health, condition* (f.)
ਤਰ੍ਹਾਂ	tar-h-aan	*way, style*
ਤਲਾਕ	talaak	*divorce* (m.)
ਤਾਂ	taan	*then*
ਤਾਂ ਕਿ	taan ki	*so that*
ਤਿਉਹਾਰ	tiuhaar	*celebration, festival* (m.)
ਤੁਸੀਂ	tuseen	*you (formal)*
ਤੁਹਾਡਾ	tuhaadaa	*your (formal)*

ਤੁਹਾਡਾ ਕੀ ਹਾਲ ਹੈ	tuhaadaa kee haal hai	how are you?
ਤੁਹਾਡੀ ਕਿਰਪਾ ਹੈ	tuhaadee kirpaa hai	by your blessings
ਤੁਹਾਡੇ ਬਾਰੇ	tuhaade baare	about you
ਤੁਰਨਾ	turnaa	to walk, to depart, to leave
ਤੂੰ	toon	you (informal)
ਤੇ	te	and, on
ਤੇਰਾ	teraa	your (informal)
ਤੋਂ	ton	from
ਤੋਂ ਇਲਾਵਾ	ton ilaavaa	apart from, besides
ਤੋਂ ਪਹਿਲੇ	ton pahile	before
ਤੋਂ ਬਾਅਦ	ton baa-a-d	after
ਤੋਂ ਬਿਨਾਂ ਬਗੈਰ	ton binaan/baghair	without
ਥਾਂ ਥਾਂ	thaan thaan	each and every place (m.)
ਥੋੜੀ ਬਹੁਤੀ	thorhee bahutee	more or less, to some extent
ਦਫ਼ਤਰ	daftar	office (m.)
ਦਰਸ਼ਕ	darshak	participant, visitor (m./f.)
ਦਰਦ	dard	pain, hurt (f.)
ਦਵਾਈ	davaaee	medicine (f.)
ਦਾ	daa	of
ਦਿਸਣਾ	disnhaa	to be visible, to be seen
ਦਿਖਾਉਣਾ	dikhaaunhaa	to show
ਦਿਨ	din	day (m.)
ਦਿਲ	dil	heart (m.)
ਦਿਲਚਸਪ	dilchasp	interesting
ਦਿਲ ਲੱਗਣਾ	dil laggnhaa	to feel at home, to be settled, to live happily
ਦਿੱਲੀ	dillee	Delhi (f.)
ਦੀ ਜਗ੍ਹਾ	dee jag-h-aa	in place of
ਦੁਕਾਨ	dukaan	shop (f.)
ਦੁਕਾਨਦਾਰ	dukaandaar	shopkeeper (m.)
ਦੁਨੀਆਂ	duneeaan	world (f.)
ਦੂਜਾ ਦਿਨ	doojaa din	second day
ਦੂਜੇ	dooje	others
ਦੂਰ	door	far, distant
ਦੂਰ ਤੋਂ	door ton	far from/away from

ਦੇ ਉੱਪਰ	<u>d</u>e uppar	*above, upon*
ਦੇ ਅੰਦਰ	<u>d</u>e an<u>d</u>ar	*inside*
ਦੇਸ਼	<u>d</u>esh	*country* (m.)
ਦੇਸੀ	<u>d</u>esi	*Indian, Panjabi, home*
ਦੇ ਸਾਹਮਣੇ	<u>d</u>e saahmanhe	*opposite, facing*
ਦੇਖਣਾ	<u>d</u>ekhnhaa	*to see, to watch*
ਦੇਣਾ	<u>d</u>enhaa	*to give*
ਦੇ ਥੱਲੇ	<u>d</u>e <u>th</u>alle	*below*
ਦੇ ਨੇੜੇ	<u>d</u>e nerhe	*near*
ਦੇ ਪਿੱਛੇ	<u>d</u>e pi<u>chch</u>e	*behind*
ਦੇ ਬਾਹਰ	<u>d</u>e baahar	*outside*
ਦੇ ਬਾਵਜੂਦ	<u>d</u>e baavjoo<u>d</u>	*in spite of*
ਦੇ ਬਾਰੇ	<u>d</u>e baare	*about, concerning*
ਦੇ ਲਈ	<u>d</u>e laee	*for*
ਦੇ ਵਾਸਤੇ	<u>d</u>e vaas<u>t</u>e	*for*
ਦੋਸ਼	<u>d</u>osh	*charge* (m.)
ਦੋਨੋਂ	<u>d</u>ono<u>n</u>	*both*
ਧੰਨਵਾਦ	<u>dh</u>annvaad	*thanks* (m.)
ਧੀਆਂ	<u>dh</u>eeaa<u>n</u>	*daughters* (f.)
ਧੂਮ ਧਾਮ	<u>dh</u>oom <u>dh</u>aam	*bang, pomp and show*
ਧੋਣਾ	<u>dh</u>onhaa	*to wash*
ਧੋਬੀ	<u>dh</u>obee	*washerman* (m.)
ਨਹੀਂ	nahee<u>n</u>	*no*
ਨਗਰ ਕੀਰਤਨ	nagar keer<u>t</u>an	*religious procession* (m.)
ਨੱਚਣਾ	nachchnhaa	*to dance*
ਨਮਕੀਨ	namkeen	*salty*
ਨਮੂਨਾ	namoonaa	*pattern, design* (m.)
ਨਰਮ ਸੁਭਾ	naram subhaa	*kind natured*
ਨਾਂ	naa<u>n</u>	*name* (m.) (informal)
ਨਾ ਕੇਵਲ	naa keval	*not only*
ਨਾਮ	naam	*name* (m.) (formal)
ਨੀਲਾ	neelaa	*blue* (v.)
ਨੁਮਾਇਸ਼	numaaish	*exhibition* (f.)
ਨੌਕਰ	naukar	*male servant* (m.)
ਨੌਕਰੀ	naukaree	*job, employment* (f.)
ਨੌਜੁਆਨ	naujuaan	*youth* (m.)
ਪਸੰਦ	pasan<u>d</u>	*like, pleasing*
ਪਕੌੜਾ	pakaurhaa	*a type of deep-fried pastry similar to fritters* (m.)

ਪਹਿਲੀ ਵਾਰੀ	pahilee vaaree	*first time*
ਪਹਿਲੇ	pahile	*before*
ਪਹੁੰਚਾ ਦੇਣਾ	pahunchaa denhaa	*to deliver, to cause to arrive*
ਪੰਜਵਾਂ	panjvaan	*fifth*
ਪੱਛਮ	pachcham	*west* (m.)
ਪੰਜ ਵਜੇ	panj vaje	*five o'clock*
ਪੰਜਾਬ	panjaab	*Panjab* (m.)
ਪੰਜਾਬੀ	panjaabee	a person from Panjab or of Panjabi origin (m./f.)
ਪੱਤਝੜ	pattjharh	*autumn* (f.)
ਪਤਨੀ	patnee	*wife* (f.)
ਪਤਲਾ	patlaa	*thin, slim* (v.)
ਪਤਵੰਤੇ	patvante	*respectable* (v.)
ਪਤਾ	pataa	*to know*
ਪਤੀ	patee	*husband* (m.)
ਪਰ	par	*but*
ਪਰਸੋਂ	parson	*day before yesterday/ day after tomorrow*
ਪਰਤਣਾ	partnhaa	*to return*
ਪਰਵਾਰ	parvaar	*family* (m.)
ਪਰਵਾਰਕ	parvaarak	*family* (relating to family)
ਪ੍ਰਾਹੁਣੇ	praahunhe	*guests* (m.)
ਪਲੇਟ	palet	*plate* (f.)
ਪੜਦਾਦਾ	parhdaadaa	*great grandfather* (m.)
ਪੜ੍ਹਨਾ	parh-h-naa	*to read, to study*
ਪੜ੍ਹਾਉਣਾ	parh-h-aaunhaa	*to teach*
ਪੜ੍ਹਾਈ	parh-h-aaee	*studies* (f.)
ਪੜ੍ਹਿਆ ਲਿਖਿਆ	parh-h-iaa likhiaa	*educated* (v.)
ਪਾਸਪੋਰਟ	paasport	*passport* (m.)
ਪਾਸੇ	paase	*direction, way*
ਪਿਆਰ	piaar	*love, affection* (m.)
ਪਿਆਰ ਕਰਨਾ	piaar karnaa	*to love*
ਪਿਆਰੇ	piaare	*dear, beloved* (v.)
ਪਿੰਡਵਾਲਾ	pindvaalaa	*villager* (m.)
ਪੀਣਾ	peenhaa	*to drink*
ਪੀਰ	peer	*holy man* (m.)
ਪੀਰ	peer	*Monday* (m.)
ਪੁੱਛਣਾ	puchchnhaa	*to ask*
ਪੁੱਤਰ	puttar	*son* (m.)
ਪੁਰਸ਼	purash	*gentleman* (m.)
ਪੂਰਬ	poorab	*east* (m.)

ਪੂਰੀਆਂ	pooreeaan	*fulfilling*
ਪੇਸ਼	pesh	*to present*
ਪੇਸ਼ ਕਰਨਾ	pesh karnaa	*to present, to produce*
ਪੇਸ਼ਾਵਰ	peshaavar	*professional* (m./f.)
ਪੇਕੇ	peke	*bride's family, bride's parents* (m.)
ਪੇਟ	pet	*stomach, belly* (m.)
ਪੇਂਡੂ	pendoo	*of the village, village-like* (m./f.)
ਪੈਂਸਲ	painsal	*pencil* (f.)
ਪੈਸੇਵਾਲੇ	paisevaale	*wealthy people* (m.)
ਪੈਣਾ	painhaa	*to act, to fall*
ਪੌੜੀਆਂ	paurheeaan	*stairs* (f.)
ਫ਼ਸਲਾਂ	fasalaan	*crops* (f.)
ਫ਼ਿਕਰ	fikar	*worry* (m.)
ਫਿੱਕਾ	phikkaa	*light, pale* (v.)
ਫਿਰ	phir	*again*
ਫਿਰਨਾ	phirnaa	*to travel*
ਫ਼ਿਲਮ	filam	*film* (f.)
ਫੋਟੋ	foto	*photograph* (f.)
ਫ਼ੌਜ	fauj	*military* (f.)
ਬਸੰਤ	basant	*spring* (f.)
ਬਹੁਤ	bahut	*very*
ਬਹੁਤ ਅੱਛਾ	bahut achchaa	*very good* (v.)
ਬਹੁਤ ਸਾਰੇ	bahut saare	*a lot, many*
ਬਹੁਤ ਸੁਹਣਾ	bahut suhnhaa	*very nice, excellent* (v.)
ਬਹੁਤ ਜ਼ਿਆਦਾ	bahut ziaadaa	*far too much*
ਬਗੀਚਾ	bagheechaa	*garden* (m.)
ਬਚਪਨ	bachpan	*childhood* (m.)
ਬੱਚੇ	bachche	*children* (m.)
ਬਟਵਾਰਾ	batvaaraa	*division, partition* (m.)
ਬਣਨਾ	banhnaa	*to become*
ਬਣਵਾਉਣਾ	banhvaaunhaa	*to get built*
ਬਦਲਣਾ	badalnhaa	*to change, to exchange*
ਬੰਦ	band	*closed, off*
ਬੰਦ ਕਰਨਾ	band karnaa	*to close*
ਬੰਦੇ	bande	*people* (m.)
ਬਰਸਾਤ	barsaat	*rainy season* (f.)
ਬਰਮਿੰਘਮ	barmingham	*Birmingham* (m.)
ਬਰਾਤ	baraat	*procession of the groom's relatives and friends* (f.)

ਬਲਕਿ	balki	*but also*
ਬੜੀ	barhee	*very* (v.)
ਬਾਅਦ ਦੁਪਹਿਰ	baa-a-<u>d</u> dupahir	*afternoon*
ਬਾਹਰੋਂ	baahro<u>n</u>	*from outside/ from abroad*
ਬਾਰਸ਼	baarash	*rain* (f.)
ਬਾਲ	baal	*male child* (m.)
ਬਿਮਾਰ	bimaar	*ill, sick*
ਬਿਮਾਰ ਹੋਣ ਤੋਂ ਪਹਿਲੇ	bimaar honh <u>ton</u> pahile	*before falling ill*
ਬਿਲਕੁਲ	bilkul	*absolutely, perfectly*
ਬੀਬੀ	beebee	*madam* (f.)
ਬੁਖ਼ਾਰ	bu<u>kh</u>aar	*fever/temperature* (m.)
ਬੁੱਧਵਾਰ	bu<u>dhdh</u>vaar	*Wednesday* (m.)
ਬੇਟਾ	betaa	*son* (m.)
ਬੇਟੀ	betee	*daughter* (f.)
ਬੇਨਤੀ	ben<u>t</u>ee	*request* (f.)
ਬੇਬੀ ਸਿਟਰ	bebee sitar	*babysitter* (m./f.)
ਬੈਠਕ	baithak	*sitting room* (f.)
ਬੈਠਣਾ	baithnhaa	*to sit*
ਬੈਠੋ ਜੀ	baitho jee	*please sit down* (formal)
ਬੋਰ ਹੋਣਾ	bor honhaa	*to be bored, to feel bored*
ਬੋਲਣਾ	bolnhaa	*to speak*
ਬੋਲੀ	bolee	*language* (f.)
ਬੋਲੀਆਂ	boleeaa<u>n</u>	*folk verse couplets* (f.)
ਭੰਗੜਾ	bha<u>n</u>grhaa	*bhangra* (m.) (style of Panjabi dance)
ਭਤੀਜੀ	bha<u>t</u>eejee	*niece* (f.)
ਭਰਤੀ	bhar<u>t</u>ee	*join*
ਭਰਾ	bharaa	*brother* (m.)
ਭਲਕ/ਭਲਕੇ	bhalak/bhalke	*tomorrow*
ਭਲਾ	bhalaa	*look after, watch over*
ਭਾਈ ਸਾਹਿਬ	bhaaee saahib	*brother* (m.)
ਭਾਬੀ	bhaabee	*sister-in-law* (f.) (brother's wife)
ਭਾਰਤ	bhaara<u>t</u>	*India* (m.)
ਭਾਰਤੀ	bhaar<u>t</u>ee	*Indian* (m./f.)
ਭਿੰਡੀ	bhi<u>n</u>dee	*okra (type of vegetable)* (f.)
ਭੁੱਖ	bhukhkh	*hunger* (f.)
ਭੇਜਣਾ	bhejnhaa	*to send, to post*
ਭੈਣ	bhainh	*sister* (f.)

ਮਹਿੰਗਾ	mahingaa	*expensive, costly* (v.)
ਮਸ਼ੀਨ	masheen	*machine* (f.)
ਮਹਿੰਦੀ	mahindee	*henna* (f.)
ਮਹੀਨਾ	maheenaa	*month* (m.)
ਮਕਾਨ	makaan	*house* (m.)
ਮੰਗਣਾ	mangnhaa	*to request, to ask for, to charge*
ਮੰਗਲਵਾਰ	mangalvaar	*Tuesday* (m.)
ਮੰਗਾਂ	mangaan	*demands* (f.)
ਮਜ਼ਮੂਨ	mazmoon	*subject* (m.)
ਮਟਰ	matar	*peas* (m.)
ਮਤਲਬ	matlab	*meaning, definition* (m.)
ਮੱਦਦ ਕਰਨਾ	maddad karnaa	*to help*
ਮਨ	man	*mind* (m.)
ਮਨਪਰਚਾਵੇ	manparchaave	*entertainment, enjoyment* (m.)
ਮਨਾਉਣਾ	manaaunhaa	*to pray, to believe, to celebrate*
ਮੰਨੋ ਜਾਂ ਨਾ ਮੰਨੋ	manno jaan naa manno	*believe it or not*
ਮਾਤਾ ਜੀ	maataa jee	*mother* (f.)
ਮਾਫ਼	maaf	*pardon, excuse*
ਮਾਫ਼ ਕਰਨਾ	maaf karnaa	*sorry, to pardon*
ਮਾਨਚੈਸਟਰ	maanchaistar	*Manchester* (m.)
ਮਾਪੇ	maape	*parents* (m.)
ਮਾਰਨਾ	maarnaa	*to hit*
ਮਿਹਰਬਾਨੀ	miharbaanee	*thanks, please* (f.)
ਮਿਟਣਾ	mitnhaa	*to finish, to vanish*
ਮਿੰਟ	mint	*minute* (m.)
ਮਿੱਠਾ	miththaa	*sweet* (v.)
ਮਿਠਿਆਈ	mithiaaee	*a type of Panjabi sweet* (f.)
ਮਿਲ ਜਾਣਾ	mil jaanhaa	*to get, to receive*
ਮਿਲਣਾ	milnhaa	*to meet*
ਮੁੱਖ	mukhkh	*face* (m.)
ਮੁਕਾਬਲਾ	mukaablaa	*comparison, competition* (m.)
ਮੁਫ਼ਤ	mufat	*free*
ਮੁੜਨਾ	murhnaa	*to turn around, to return*
ਮੇਖ	mekh	*nail* (f.)
ਮੇਰਾ	meraa	*my*
ਮੇਰੇ ਕੋਲ ਨਹੀਂ	mere kol naheen	*not with me, not in my possession*

ਮੇਰੇ ਨਾਲ	mere naal	*with me*
ਮੇਲ	mel	*meeting, combination* (m.)
ਮੇਲਾ	melaa	*fair* (m.)
ਮੈਂ	main	*I*
ਮੈਨੇਜਰ	mainejar	*manager* (m./f.)
ਮੋਚੀ	mochee	*cobbler* (m.)
ਮੋਟਾ	motaa	*fat, thick* (v.)
ਮੌਕਾ	maukaa	*opportunity, occasion* (m.)
ਮੌਜਾਂ ਕਰਨਾ	maujaan karnaa	*to enjoy*
ਯਾਦ	yaad	*memory, remembrance* (f.)
ਯੁਵਕ	yuvak	*youth* (m.)
ਯੂਗੰਡਾ	yoogandaa	*Uganda* (m.)
ਯੋਗ	yog	*suitable*
ਰਸ	ras	*(fruit) juice* (m.)
ਰਸਮ	rasam	*custom, ritual* (f.)
ਰਸੋਈ	rasoee	*kitchen* (f.)
ਰਹਿਣਾ	rahinhaa	*to stay, to live*
ਰੱਖਣਾ	rakhkhnhaa	*to put*
ਰੰਗ	rang	*colour* (m.)
ਰੰਗਦਾਰ	rangdaar	*colourful*
ਰੰਗਲਾ	ranglaa	*colourful* (v.)
ਰਚਨਾ	rachnaa	*composition* (f.)
ਰਲ ਮਿਲਣਾ	ral milnhaa	*to be mixed*
ਰਵਾਜ	ravaaj	*fashion* (m.)
ਰੜਕਣਾ	rarhkanhaa	*to prick, to rub against*
ਰਾਹਾਂ	raahaan	*roads, routes* (f.)
ਰਾਹੀਂ	raaheen	*via, by*
ਰਾਜ	raaj	*rulership, kingdom* (m.)
ਰਾਜਾ	raajaa	*king* (m.)
ਰਿਸ਼ਤਾ	rishtaa	*(marriage) relation* (m.)
ਰਿਸ਼ਤੇਦਾਰ	rishtedaar	*relatives* (m./f.)
ਰੁਪਇਆ	rupaiaa	*rupee* (m.)
ਲਈ	laee	*for, in order to*
ਲੱਗਣਾ	laggnhaa	*to be covered, laden, to feel*
ਲਗਵਾਉਣਾ	lagvaaunhaa	*to get covered*
ਲੰਗਰ	langar	*community kitchen* (m.)
ਲਗਾਉਣਾ	lagaaunhaa	*to stitch, to apply, to put on*

ਲਗਾਤਾਰ	lagaataar	*continuously, on-going*
ਲੰਡਨ	landan	*London* (m.)
ਲੱਡੂ	laddoo	*a type of Panjabi sweet* (m.)
ਲਫ਼ਜ਼ੀ	lafzee	*literal*
ਲੰਬਾ	lanbaa	*long, lengthy* (v.)
ਲੱਭਣਾ	labhbhnhaa	*to find*
ਲਾ ਪਰਵਾਹ	laa parvaah	*careless*
ਲਾਇਸੈਂਸ	laaisains	*licence* (m.)
ਲਾਹੌਰਵਾਲੀ ਔਰਤ	laahaurvaalee aurat	*the woman from Lahore* (f.)
ਲਾਲ	laal	*red*
ਲਾੜਾ	laarhaa	*groom* (m.)
ਲਿਖਣਾ	likhnhaa	*to write*
ਲਿਆਉਣਾ	liaaunhaa	*to bring*
ਲਿਆਕਤ	liaakat	*ability* (f.)
ਲੈਣਾ	lainhaa	*to take, to have*
ਲੋਕ	lok	*people* (m.)
ਲੋਕ ਨਾਚ	lok naach	*folk dance* (m.)
ਲੋੜ	lorh	*require, necessity, want* (f.)
ਵੱਸ	vass	*authority, jurisdiction* (m.)
ਵਸਾਉਣਾ	vasaaunhaa	*to establish, to habilitate*
ਵਕਤ	vakat	*time* (m.)
ਵੱਜਣਾ	vajjnhaa	*to be played, to be beaten*
ਵਜਾਉਣ ਦਾ ਸ਼ੋਕ	vajaaunh daa shauk	*fond of playing, enjoy playing*
ਵਜਾਉਣਾ	vajaaunhaa	*to play (music), to beat*
ਵਡੇਰਿਆਂ	vadkkiaan	*ancestors, forefathers* (m.)
ਵੱਡਾ	vaddaa	*big, large* (v.)
ਵੱਧ	vadhdh	*high, more*
ਵਧਾਉਣਾ	vadhaaunhaa	*to increase*
ਵਧਾਈ	vadhaaee	*congratulations* (f.)
ਵਧੀਆ	vadheeaa	*good quality*
ਵਧੇਰੇ	vadhere	*more*
ਵਰਗਾ	vargaa	*like* (v.)
ਵਰਤਣਾ	varatnhaa	*to use*
ਵਰਤਾਉਣਾ	vartaaunhaa	*to serve*
ਵੱਲ	vall	*towards*

ਵੱਲੋਂ	vallon	*on behalf of*
ਵਾਜਬੀ	vaajbee	*reasonable, fair, right*
ਵਾਜੇ ਵਾਲੇ	vaaje vaale	*band of musicians* (m.)
ਵਾਲੈਕਮ ਅੱਸਲਾਮ	vaalaikam asslaam	response to
		Muslim greeting
ਵਾਪਸ	vaapas	*return, back*
ਵਾਰੀ	vaaree	*turn, instance* (f.)
ਵਿਆਹ	viaah	*wedding* (m.)
ਵਿਹਾਰੀ ਨੌਕਰੀ	vihaaree naukaree	*professionally*
		employed (f.)
ਵਿਕਣਾ	viknhaa	*to be sold*
ਵਿਚ	vich	*in*
ਵਿੱਚੋਂ	vichchon	*from within*
ਵਿਦਿਆਰਥੀ	vidiaarthee	*student* (m./f.)
ਵੀ	vee	*also*
ਵੀਹ (੨੦)	veeh	20
ਵੀਜ਼ਾ	veezaa	*visa* (m.)
ਵੀਰਵਾਰ	veervaar	*Thursday* (m.)
ਵੇ	ve	subjunctive particle
ਵੇਖਣਾ	vekhnhaa	*to see*
ਵੇਲੇ	vele	*period, time* (m.)
ਵੈਸਾਖ	vaisaakh	one of the
		Indian months (m.)
ਵੈਸਾਖੀ	vaisaakhee	a Sikh festival (f.)

English–Panjabi glossary

a	ਇੱਕ	ikk
a lot	ਬਹੁਤ ਸਾਰੇ	bahut saare
ability	ਲਿਆਕਤ	liaakat
able to: to be ~	ਸਕਣਾ	saknhaa
about (approximately)	ਤਕਰੀਬਨ	takreeban
about (concerning)	ਦੇ ਬਾਰੇ	de baare
about you	ਤੁਹਾਡੇ ਬਾਰੇ	tuhaade baare
above	ਦੇ ਉੱਪਰ	de uppar
absolutely	ਬਿਲਕੁਲ	bilkul
act: to ~	ਪੈਣਾ	painhaa
affection	ਪਿਆਰ	piaar
after	ਤੋਂ ਬਾਅਦ	ton baa-a-d
after a while	ਸਮਾਂ ਪਾ ਕੇ	samaan paa ke
afternoon	ਬਾਅਦ ਦੁਪਹਿਰ	baa-a-d dupahir
again	ਫਿਰ	phir
against	ਖ਼ਿਲਾਫ਼	khilaaf
age	ਉਮਰ	umar
agree	ਸਹਿਮਤ	sahimat
air mail	ਹਵਾਈ ਡਾਕ	havaaee daak
airport	ਹਵਾਈ ਅੱਡਾ	havaaee addaa
all	ਸਭ, ਸਾਰੇ	sabh, saare
all of us	ਅਸੀਂ ਸਾਰੇ	aseen saare
also	ਵੀ	vee
America	ਅਮਰੀਕਾ	amreekaa
ancestors	ਵਡੱਕਿਆਂ	vadkkiaan
and, on	ਅਤੇ, ਤੇ	ate, te
anxious	ਉਤਸੁਕ	utsuk
any	ਕੋਈ	koee
anyway	ਖ਼ੈਰ	khair
apart from	ਤੋਂ ਇਲਾਵਾ	ton ilaavaa
apply: to ~	ਲਗਾਉਣਾ	lagaaunhaa
around and about	ਆਸ ਪਾਸ	aas paas
arrangements	ਇੰਤਜ਼ਾਮ	intzaam
ask: to ~	ਪੁੱਛਣਾ	puchchnhaa
at least	ਘੱਟੋ ਘੱਟ	ghatto ghatt
authority	ਵੱਸ	vass
automobile	ਗੱਡੀ	gaddee
autumn	ਪੱਤਝੜ	pattjharh

awaiting	ਉਤਸੁਕ	utsuk
away from	ਦੂਰ ਤੋਂ	<u>d</u>oor <u>t</u>on
babysitter	ਬੇਬੀ ਸਿਟਰ	bebee sitar
back	ਵਾਪਸ	vaapas
band of musicians	ਵਾਜੇ ਵਾਲੇ	vaaje vaale
bang, pomp and show	ਧੂਮ ਧਾਮ	<u>dh</u>oom <u>dh</u>aam
bathroom	ਗੁਸਲ ਖ਼ਾਨਾ	ghusal <u>kh</u>aanaa
be: to ~	ਹੋਣਾ	honhaa
beat: to ~	ਵਜਾਉਣਾ	vajaaunhaa
beaten: to be ~	ਵੱਜਣਾ	vajjnhaa
because	ਕਿਉਂ ਕਿ	kiu<u>n</u> ki
become: to ~	ਬਣਨਾ	banhnaa
before	ਤੋਂ ਪਹਿਲੇ, ਪਹਿਲੇ	<u>t</u>on pahile, pahile
before falling ill	ਬਿਮਾਰ ਹੋਣ ਤੋਂ ਪਹਿਲੇ	bimaar honh <u>t</u>on pahile
begin: to ~	ਸ਼ੁਰੂ ਕਰਨਾ	shuroo karnaa
behind	ਦੇ ਪਿੱਛੇ	<u>d</u>e pi<u>chch</u>e
believe: to ~	ਮਨਾਉਣਾ	manaaunhaa
believe it or not	ਮੰਨੋ ਜਾਂ ਨਾ ਮੰਨੋ	ma<u>nn</u>o jaa<u>n</u> naa ma<u>nn</u>o
belly	ਪੇਟ	pet
beloved	ਪਿਆਰੇ	piaare
below	ਦੇ ਥੱਲੇ	<u>d</u>e <u>th</u>alle
besides	ਤੋਂ ਇਲਾਵਾ	<u>t</u>on ilaavaa
best: the ~	ਸਭ ਤੋਂ ਵਧੀਆ	sabh <u>t</u>on va<u>dh</u>eeaa
best wishes	ਸ਼ੁਭ ਇੱਛਾਵਾਂ	shubh i<u>chch</u>aavaa<u>n</u>
bhangra (style of Panjabi dance)	ਭੰਗੜਾ	bha<u>ng</u>rhaa
big	ਵੱਡਾ	vaddaa
Birmingham	ਬਰਮਿੰਘਮ	barmi<u>ng</u>ham
birth	ਜਨਮ	janam
birthday	ਜਨਮ ਦਿਨ	janam <u>d</u>in
birthplace	ਜਨਮ ਅਸਥਾਨ	janam as<u>th</u>aan
bitter	ਕੌੜਾ/ਕਸੈਲਾ	kaurhaa/kasailaa
bitter gourd	ਕਰੇਲਾ	karelaa
blessings	ਕਿਰਪਾ	kirpaa
blue	ਨੀਲਾ	neelaa
bored: to be ~, to feel bored	ਬੋਰ ਹੋਣਾ	bor honhaa
born: to be ~	ਜੰਮਣਾ	janmnhaa
born and bred	ਜੰਮਪਲ	janmpal
bosom	ਸੀਨਾ	seenaa

English	Panjabi	Transliteration
both	ਦੋਨੋਂ	donon
both of us	ਅਸੀਂ ਦੋਨੋਂ	aseen donon
bother	ਤਕਲੀਫ	takleef
bow down: to ~	ਟੇਕਣਾ	teknhaa
bride's family, bride's parents	ਪੇਕੇ	peke
bring: to ~	ਲਿਆਉਣਾ	liaaunhaa
brother	ਭਰਾ, ਭਾਈ ਸਾਹਿਬ	bharaa, bhaaee saahib
built: to get ~	ਬਣਵਾਉਣਾ	banhvaaunhaa
but	ਪਰ	par
but also	ਸਗੋਂ, ਬਲਕਿ	sagon, balki
by	ਰਾਹੀਂ	raaheen
by air	ਹਵਾਈ	hvaaee
by your blessings	ਤੁਹਾਡੀ ਕਿਰਪਾ ਹੈ	tuhaadee kirpaa hai
camel	ਊਠ	ooth
camera	ਕੈਮਰਾ	kaimraa
can	ਸਕਣਾ	saknhaa
car	ਕਾਰ, ਗੱਡੀ	kaar, gaddee
careless	ਲਾ ਪਰਵਾਹ	laa parvaah
carrot	ਗਾਜਰ	gaajar
cauliflower	ਗੋਭੀ	gobhee
celebrate: to ~	ਮਨਾਉਣਾ	manaaunhaa
celebration	ਤਿਉਹਾਰ	tiuhaar
ceremony bidding farewell to the bride	ਡੋਲੀ	dolee
change: to ~	ਬਦਲਣਾ	badalnhaa
charge	ਦੋਸ਼	dosh
charge: to ~	ਮੰਗਣਾ	mangnhaa
childhood	ਬਚਪਨ	bachpan
children	ਬੱਚੇ	bachche
choice	ਚੋਣ	chonh
citizen	ਸ਼ਹਿਰੀਅਤ	shahireeat
city	ਸ਼ਹਿਰ	shahir
class	ਸ਼੍ਰੇਣੀ, ਕਲਾਸ	shrenhee, kalaas
clean: to ~	ਸਾਫ ਕਰਨਾ	saaf karnaa
close: to ~	ਬੰਦ ਕਰਨਾ	band karnaa
closed off	ਬੰਦ	band
cloth	ਕਪੜਾ	kaprhaa
cobbler	ਮੋਚੀ	mochee
cold	ਠੰਡ	thand
college	ਕਾਲਜ	kaalaj
colour	ਰੰਗ	rang

colourful	ਰੰਗਦਾਰ, ਰੰਗਲਾ	rangdaar, ranglaa
combination	ਮੇਲ	mel
come (formal)	ਆਓ	aao
come (informal request)	ਆ ਜਾ	aa jaa
come: to ~	ਆਉਣਾ	aaunhaa
community	ਕੌਮ	kaum
community kitchen	ਲੰਗਰ	langar
comparison	ਮੁਕਾਬਲਾ	mukaablaa
competition	ਮੁਕਾਬਲਾ	mukaablaa
complaint	ਸ਼ਿਕਾਇਤ	shikaait
complete: to ~	ਖ਼ਤਮ ਕਰਨਾ	khatam karnaa
composition	ਰਚਨਾ	rachnaa
condition	ਹਾਲ, ਤਬੀਅਤ	haal, tabeeat
congratulations	ਵਧਾਈ	vadhaaee
consume: to ~	ਛਕਣਾ	chaknhaa
contact	ਸੰਪਰਕ	sanparak
continuously	ਲਗਾਤਾਰ	lagaataar
conversation	ਗੱਲਾਂ	gallaan
corn on the cob	ਛੱਲੀ	challee
correct: to ~	ਠੀਕ ਕਰਨਾ	theek karnaa
costly	ਮਹਿੰਗਾ	mahingaa
country	ਦੇਸ਼	desh
covered: to be ~	ਲੱਗਣਾ	laggnhaa
covered: to get ~	ਲਗਵਾਉਣਾ	lagvaaunhaa
crops	ਫ਼ਸਲਾਂ	fasalaan
custom	ਰਸਮ	rasam
cut: to ~	ਕਟਣਾ	katnhaa
dance: to ~	ਨੱਚਣਾ	nachchnhaa
dangerous	ਖ਼ਤਰਨਾਕ	khatarnaak
daughter	ਬੇਟੀ	betee
daughters	ਧੀਆਂ	dheeaan
day	ਦਿਨ	din
day after tomorrow/ day before yesterday	ਪਰਸੋਂ	parson
days: these ~	ਅੱਜ ਕੱਲ੍ਹ	ajj kallh
dear	ਪਿਆਰੇ	piaare
deep-fried pastry, similar to fritters	ਪਕੌੜਾ	pakaurhaa
definitely	ਜ਼ਰੂਰ	zaroor
definition	ਮਤਲਬ	matlab
Delhi	ਦਿੱਲੀ	dillee
deliver: to ~	ਪਹੁੰਚਾ ਦੇਣਾ	pahunchaa denhaa

English	Panjabi	Transliteration
demands	ਮੰਗਾਂ	ma<u>ng</u>aa<u>n</u>
depart: to ~	ਤੁਰਨਾ	<u>t</u>urnaa
design	ਨਮੂਨਾ	namoonaa
different types	ਕਈ ਤਰੂੰ	kaee <u>t</u>ar-h-aa<u>n</u>
digest	ਹਜ਼ਮ	hazam
direction	ਪਾਸੇ	paase
disobey: to ~	ਉਲੰਘਣਾ	ula<u>ngh</u>nhaa
displaced: to be ~	ਉਖੜਨਾ	ukhrhnaa
distant	ਦੂਰ	<u>d</u>oor
division	ਬਟਵਾਰਾ	batvaaraa
divorce	ਤਲਾਕ	<u>t</u>alaak
do: to ~	ਕਰਨਾ	karnaa
doctor	ਡਾਕਟਰ	daaktar
documents	ਕਾਗ਼ਜ਼ਾਤ	kaa<u>ghz</u>aat
dog	ਕੁੱਤਾ	ku<u>tt</u>aa
dollar	ਡਾਲਰ	daalar
dome	ਗੁੰਬਦ	gunba<u>d</u>
drink: to ~	ਪੀਣਾ	peenhaa
drum: big ~	ਢੋਲ	dhol
durable	ਹੰਢਣਸਾਰ	ha<u>n</u>dhanhsaar
each and every place	ਥਾਂ ਥਾਂ	<u>th</u>aan <u>th</u>aan
east	ਪੂਰਬ	poorab
East Africa	ਈਸਟ ਅਫ਼ਰੀਕਾ	eest afreekaa
easy	ਸੌਖਾ	saukhaa
eat: to ~	ਖਾਣਾ	khaanhaa
educated	ਪੜ੍ਹਿਆ ਲਿਖਿਆ	parh-h-iaa likhiaa
employment	ਨੌਕਰੀ	naukaree
empty	ਖ਼ਾਲੀ	<u>kh</u>aalee
end	ਅਖ਼ੀਰ	a<u>kh</u>eer
English	ਅੰਗਰੇਜ਼	a<u>ng</u>rez
enjoy: to ~	ਮੋਜਾਂ ਕਰਨਾ	mauja<u>n</u> karnaa
enjoy playing	ਵਜਾਉਣ ਦਾ ਸ਼ੋਕ	vajaaunh <u>d</u>aa shauk
enjoy yourself	ਅਨੰਦ ਮਾਣੋ	ana<u>nd</u> maanho
enjoyment	ਸ਼ੋਕ, ਮਨਪਰਚਾਵੇ	shauk, manparchaave
entertainment	ਮਨਪਰਚਾਵੇ	manparchaave
establish: to ~	ਵਸਾਉਣਾ	vasaaunhaa
every	ਸਭ	sabh
everyone	ਸਾਰੇ	saare
everything	ਸਭ ਕੁਝ	sabh kujh
everywhere	ਸਭ ਪਾਸੇ,	sabh paase,
	ਹਰ ਪਾਸੇ	har paase
excellent	ਬਹੁਤ ਸੁਹਣਾ	bahu<u>t</u> suhnhaa

English	Gurmukhi	Transliteration
exchange: to ~	ਬਦਲਣਾ	badalnhaa
excuse	ਮਾਫ਼	maaf
exhibition	ਨੁਮਾਇਸ਼	numaaish
expense(s)	ਖ਼ਰਚਾ	kharchaa
expensive	ਮਹਿੰਗਾ	mahingaa
extent: to some ~	ਥੋੜੀ ਬਹੁਤੀ	thorhee bahutee
face	ਮੁੱਖ	mukhkh
facing	ਦੇ ਸਾਹਮਣੇ	de saahmanhe
fair	ਗੋਰੀ,	goree,
	ਵਾਜਬੀ	vaajbee
family	ਪਰਵਾਰ	parvaar
family (relating to family)	ਪਰਵਾਰਕ	parvaarak
far	ਦੂਰ	door
far from	ਦੂਰ ਤੋਂ	door ton
far too much	ਬਹੁਤ ਜ਼ਿਆਦਾ	bahut ziaadaa
fare	ਕਿਰਾਇਆ	kiraaiaa
fashion	ਰਵਾਜ	ravaaj
fat	ਮੋਟਾ	motaa
feel: to ~	ਲੱਗਣਾ	laggnhaa
feel at home: to ~	ਦਿਲ ਲੱਗਣਾ	dil laggnhaa
festival	ਤਿਉਹਾਰ	tiuhaar
fever	ਬੁਖ਼ਾਰ	bukhaar
fifth	ਪੰਜਵਾਂ	panjvaan
film	ਫ਼ਿਲਮ	filam
find: to ~	ਲੱਭਣਾ	labhbhnhaa
fine	ਠੀਕ	theek
finish: to ~	ਖ਼ਤਮ ਕਰਨਾ, ਮਿਟਣਾ	khatam karnaa, mitnhaa
finished: to be ~	ਚੁਕਣਾ	chuknhaa
first time	ਪਹਿਲੀ ਵਾਰੀ	pahilee vaaree
five o'clock	ਪੰਜ ਵਜੇ	panj vaje
fix: to ~	ਠੀਕ ਕਰਨਾ	theek karnaa
folk dance	ਲੋਕ ਨਾਚ	lok naach
folk verse couplets	ਬੋਲੀਆਂ	boleeaan
fond of playing	ਵਜਾਉਣ ਦਾ ਸ਼ੌਕ	vajaaunh daa shauk
fondness	ਸ਼ੌਕ	shauk
for	ਦੇ ਲਈ, ਦੇ ਵਾਸਤੇ, ਲਈ	de laee, de vaaste, laee
for how long	ਕਿੰਨਾ ਚਿਰ ਤੋਂ	kinnaa chir ton
forefathers	ਵਡੱਿਕਆਂ	vadkkiaan
fourth Guru	ਚੌਥੇ ਗੁਰੂ	chauthe guroo
free	ਮੁਫ਼ਤ	mufat

freedom	ਅਜ਼ਾਦੀ	azaadee
Friday	ਸ਼ੁੱਕਰਵਾਰ, ਜੁਮਾ	shukkarvaar, jumaa
friend	ਸਹੇਲੀ	sahelee
from	ਤੋਂ	ton
from abroad, from outside	ਬਾਹਰੋਂ	baahron
from there	ਉੱਥੋਂ	uththon
from within	ਵਿੱਚੋਂ	vichchon
fulfilling	ਪੂਰੀਆਂ	pooreeaan
Gadar Party	ਗਦਰ ਪਾਰਟੀ	ghadar paartee
garden	ਬਗੀਚਾ	bagheechaa
gathering	ਇਕੱਠ	ikathth
gentleman	ਪੁਰਸ਼	purash
genuinely	ਸੱਚੀ ਮੁੱਚੀ	sachchee muchchee
German	ਜਰਮਨ	jarman
get: to ~	ਮਿਲ ਜਾਣਾ	mil jaanhaa
give: to ~	ਦੇਣਾ	denhaa
glittering	ਚਮਕੀਲਾ	chamkeelaa
go: to ~	ਚਲਣਾ	chalnhaa
go around: to ~	ਘੁੰਮਣਾ	ghunmnhaa
gold	ਸੋਨਾ	sonaa
golden	ਸੁਨਹਿਰੀ	sunahiree
Golden Temple	ਹਰਿਮੰਦਰ ਸਾਹਿਬ	harmandar saahib
good	ਚੰਗੀ	changee
good (lit. happiness)	ਖੁਸ਼ੀ	khushee
good quality	ਵਧੀਆ	vadheeaa
grade	ਗਰੇਡ	gared
great grandfather	ਪੜਦਾਦਾ	parhdaadaa
groom	ਲਾੜਾ	laarhaa
guests	ਪ੍ਰਾਹੁਣੇ	praahunhe
happy	ਖੁਸ਼	khush
hardwearing	ਹੰਢਣਸਾਰ	handhanhsaar
hasty	ਕਾਹਲਾ	kaahlaa
have: to ~	ਲੈਣਾ	lainhaa
have (already) been	ਜਾ ਚੁਕਣਾ	jaa chuknhaa
he	ਇਹ, ਉਹ	ih, uh
health	ਸਿਹਤ	sihat
heart	ਦਿਲ, ਸੀਨਾ	dil, seenaa
heat	ਗਰਮੀ	garmee
heaven	ਸਵਰਗ	savarag
height	ਕੱਦ	kadd

help: to ~	ਮੱਦਦ ਕਰਨਾ	maddad karnaa
henna	ਮਹਿੰਦੀ	mahindee
here	ਇੱਥੇ	iththe
high spirits	ਚੜ੍ਹਦੀ ਕਲਾ	charh-h-dee kalaa
high	ਵੱਧ	vadhdh
Hindu	ਹਿੰਦੂ	hindoo
hit: to ~	ਮਾਰਨਾ	maarnaa
holidays	ਛੁੱਟੀਆਂ	chutteeaan
holy man	ਪੀਰ	peer
holy water	ਅੰਮ੍ਰਿਤ	anmrit
home	ਘਰ, ਦੇਸੀ	ghar, desi
homework	ਘਰ ਦਾ ਕੰਮ	ghar daa kanm
honorific particle signifying respect	ਜੀ	jee
hope	ਉਮੀਦ	umeed
hopefully (lit. if God wishes)	ਇਨਸ਼ਾ ਅੱਲਾ	inshaa allaa
hostel	ਹੋਸਟਲ	hostal
house	ਮਕਾਨ	makaan
how	ਕਿਵੇਂ	kiven
how are you?	ਤੁਹਾਡਾ ਕੀ ਹਾਲ ਹੈ	tuhaadaa kee haal hai
how did it go?	ਕਿਵੇਂ ਰਿਹਾ	kiven rihaa
how far?	ਕਿੰਨੀ ਦੂਰ	kinnee door
how many?	ਕਿੰਨੇ	kinne
how much?	ਕਿੰਨਾ	kinnaa
how much per metre?	ਕਿੰਨੇ ਦਾ ਮੀਟਰ	kinne daa meetar
hunger	ਭੁੱਖ	bhukhkh
husband	ਘਰਵਾਲਾ, ਪਤੀ	gharvaalaa, patee
I	ਮੈਂ	main
identity card	ਸ਼ਨਾਖ਼ਤੀ ਕਾਰਡ	shanaakhtee kaard
if	ਜੇ	je
ill	ਬਿਮਾਰ	bimaar
impatient	ਕਾਹਲਾ	kaahlaa
in	ਵਿਚ	vich
in a hurry	ਕਾਹਲ ਵਿਚ	kaahal vich
in order to	ਲਈ	laee
in place of	ਦੀ ਜਗ੍ਹਾ	dee jag-h-aa
in spite of	ਦੇ ਬਾਵਜੂਦ	de baavjood
in the morning	ਸਵੇਰੇ	savere
increase: to ~	ਵਧਾਉਣਾ	vadhaaunhaa
independence	ਅਜ਼ਾਦੀ	azaadee

298

English	Panjabi	Transliteration
India	ਭਾਰਤ	bhaarat
Indian	ਭਾਰਤੀ, ਦੇਸੀ	bhaartee, desi
in-laws	ਸਹੁਰੇ	sahure
inside	ਅੰਦਰ, ਦੇ ਅੰਦਰ	andar, de andar
installation	ਸਵਾਰੀ	savaaree
instance	ਵਾਰੀ	vaaree
interesting	ਦਿਲਚਸਪ	dilchasp
international	ਅੰਤਰ ਰਾਸ਼ਟਰੀ	antar raashtaree
invitation	ਸੱਦਾ ਪੱਤਰ	saddaa pattar
irritation	ਤਕਲੀਫ਼	takleef
is	ਏ, ਹੈ	e, hai
is called, is said	ਕਿਹਾ ਜਾਂਦਾ ਹੈ	kihaa jaandaa hai
it	ਇਸ, ਇਹ	is, ih
job	ਨੌਕਰੀ, ਕੰਮ	naukaree, kanm
join	ਭਰਤੀ	bhartee
join in: to ~	ਸ਼ਾਮਲ	shaamal
juice (fruit)	ਰਸ	ras
jurisdiction	ਵੱਸ	vass
Kenya	ਕੀਨੀਆ	keeneeaa
Khatri (caste)	ਖਤਰੀ	khatree
kind natured	ਨਰਮ ਸੁਭਾ	naram subhaa
king	ਰਾਜਾ	raajaa
kingdom	ਰਾਜ	raaj
kitchen	ਰਸੋਈ	rasoee
know: to ~	ਜਾਣਨਾ, ਪਤਾ	jaanhnaa, pataa
laden: to be ~	ਲੱਗਣਾ	laggnhaa
lady	ਇਸਤਰੀ	istaree
lady teacher	ਅਧਿਆਪਕਾ	adhiaapkaa
language	ਬੋਲੀ	bolee
large	ਵੱਡਾ	vaddaa
law	ਕਾਨੂੰਨ	kaanoonn
leave: to ~	ਛੱਡਣਾ, ਤੁਰਨਾ	chaddnhaa, turnaa
length of time	ਚਿਰ	chir
lengthy	ਲੰਬਾ	lanbaa
less	ਘੱਟ	ghatt
lessen: to ~	ਘੱਟ ਕਰਨਾ	ghatt karnaa
letter	ਚਿੱਠੀ	chiththee
licence	ਲਾਇਸੈਂਸ	laaisains
life	ਜੀਵਨ	jeevan
lift: to ~	ਚੁੱਕਣਾ	chukknhaa

light	ਫਿੱਕਾ	phikkaa
like	ਵਰਗਾ	vargaa
like (pleasing)	ਪਸੰਦ, ਸ਼ੋਕ	pasand, shauk
listen: to ~	ਸੁਨਣਾ	sunnhaa
literal	ਲਫ਼ਜ਼ੀ	lafzee
live: to ~	ਰਹਿਣਾ	rahinhaa
live happily: to ~	ਦਿਲ ਲੱਗਣਾ	dil laggnhaa
location	ਜਗੁ	jag-h-aa
London	ਲੰਡਨ	landan
long	ਲੰਬਾ	lanbaa
long wooden pole	ਡਾਂਗ	daang
look after	ਭਲਾ	bhalaa
look at: to ~	ਝਾਕਣਾ	jhaaknhaa
love	ਪਿਆਰ	piaar
love: to ~	ਪਿਆਰ ਕਰਨਾ	piaar karnaa
lower	ਘੱਟ	ghatt
luggage	ਸਮਾਨ	samaan
machine	ਮਸ਼ੀਨ	masheen
madam	ਬੀਬੀ	beebee
mail	ਡਾਕ	daak
male child	ਬਾਲ	baal
male servant	ਨੌਕਰ	naukar
manager	ਮੈਨੇਜਰ	mainejar
Manchester	ਮਾਨਚੈਸਟਰ	maanchaistar
many	ਬਹੁਤ ਸਾਰੇ	bahut saare
mare	ਘੋੜੀ	ghorhee
maths	ਹਿਸਾਬ	hisaab
matter	ਗੱਲ	gall
mature	ਸਿਆਣਾ	siaanhaa
meaning	ਅਰਥ	arth
meaning	ਮਤਲਬ	matlab
medicine	ਦਵਾਈ	davaaee
meet: to ~	ਮਿਲਣਾ	milnhaa
meeting	ਮੇਲ	mel
members of the groom's wedding party	ਜਾਂਞੀ	jaannjee
memory	ਯਾਦ	yaad
military	ਫ਼ੋਜ	fauj
mind	ਮਨ	man
minute	ਮਿੰਟ	mint
mirror	ਸ਼ੀਸ਼ਾ	sheeshaa
mixed: to be ~	ਰਲ ਮਿਲਣਾ	ral milnhaa

English	Panjabi	Transliteration
modern	ਅਜੋਕਾ	ajokaa
Monday	ਸੋਮਵਾਰ, ਪੀਰ	somvaar, peer
month	ਮਹੀਨਾ	maheenaa
more	ਵਧੇਰੇ	vadhere
more or less	ਥੋੜੀ ਬਹੁਤੀ	thorhee bahutee
mother	ਮਾਤਾ ਜੀ	maataa jee
Mr	ਸਰਦਾਰ ਸਾਹਿਬ	sardaar saahib
Muslim departing phrase	ਖ਼ੁਦਾ ਹਾਫ਼ਿਜ਼	khudaa haafiz
Muslim greeting	ਅੱਸਲਾਮ ਅਲੈਕਮ	asslaam alaikam
mutiny	ਗ਼ਦਰ	ghadar
my	ਮੇਰਾ	meraa
nail	ਮੇਖ	mekh
name (formal)	ਨਾਮ	naam
name (informal)	ਨਾਂ	naan
nation	ਕੌਮ	kaum
near	ਦੇ ਨੇੜੇ	de nerhe
necessity	ਲੋੜ	lorh
nectar	ਅੰਮ੍ਰਿਤ	anmrit
need: to ~	ਚਾਹੁਣਾ	chaahunhaa
needle	ਸੂਈ	sooee
news (lit. talk)	ਗੱਲ	gall
next	ਅਗਲਾ	aglaa
next to	ਕੋਲ	kol
nice	ਸੁਹਣਾ	suhnhaa
niece	ਭਤੀਜੀ	bhateejee
no	ਨਹੀਂ	naheen
not in my possession	ਮੇਰੇ ਕੋਲ ਨਹੀਂ	mere kol naheen
not only	ਨਾ ਕੇਵਲ	naa keval
not with me	ਮੇਰੇ ਕੋਲ ਨਹੀਂ	mere kol naheen
now	ਹੁਣ	hunh
occasion	ਮੌਕਾ	maukaa
of	ਦਾ	daa
of the Sikhs	ਸਿੱਖਾਂ ਦੇ	sikhkhaan de
of the village	ਪੇਂਡੂ	pendoo
offence	ਅਪਰਾਧ	apraadh
office	ਦਫ਼ਤਰ	daftar
officer	ਅਫ਼ਸਰ	afsar
OK (all right)	ਅੱਛਾ	achchaa
OK (fine)	ਠੀਕ ਠਾਕ	theek thaak
okra (type of vegetable)	ਭਿੰਡੀ	bhindee
on	ਤੇ	te

on behalf of	ਵੱਲੋਂ	vallon
one	ਇੱਕ	ikk
one hundred	ਸੌ (੧੦੦)	sau
one hundred and twenty	ਇੱਕ ਸੌ ਵੀਹ	ikk sau veeh
one side	ਇੱਕ ਪਾਸੇ	ikk paase
one's own	ਆਪਣਾ	aapnhaa
on-going	ਲਗਾਤਾਰ	lagaataar
only	ਕੇਵਲ	keval
open	ਖੁੱਲ੍ਹਾ	khullhaa
opportunity	ਮੋਕਾ	maukaa
opposite	ਦੇ ਸਾਹਮਣੇ	de saahmanhe
or	ਜਾਂ	jaan
others	ਦੂਜੇ	dooje
our	ਸਾਡਾ	saadaa
outside	ਦੇ ਬਾਹਰ	de baahar
pain, hurt	ਦਰਦ	dard
pale	ਫਿੱਕਾ	phikkaa
Panjab	ਪੰਜਾਬ	panjaab
Panjabi	ਦੇਸੀ	desi
Panjabi sweet	ਮਿਠਿਆਈ	mithiaaee
papers	ਕਾਗ਼ਜ਼ਾਤ	kaaghzaat
parade	ਜਲੂਸ	jaloos
pardon	ਮਾਫ਼	maaf
pardon: to ~	ਮਾਫ਼ ਕਰਨਾ	maaf karnaa
parents	ਮਾਪੇ	maape
park: to ~	ਖੜ੍ਹਨਾ	kharhhnaa
partition	ਬਟਵਾਰਾ	batvaaraa
participant	ਦਰਸ਼ਕ	darshak
passengers	ਸਵਾਰੀਆਂ	savaareeaan
passport	ਪਾਸਪੋਰਟ	paasport
pattern	ਨਮੂਨਾ	namoonaa
pay	ਤਨਖ਼ਾਹ	tankhaah
peace	ਸ਼ਾਂਤੀ	shaantee
peas	ਮਟਰ	matar
pencil	ਪੈਂਸਲ	painsal
people	ਬੰਦੇ, ਲੋਕ	bande, lok
perfectly	ਬਿਲਕੁਲ	bilkul
period, time	ਵੇਲੇ	vele
permission	ਆਗਿਆ	aagiaa
person from Gujarat or of Gujarati origin	ਗੁਜਰਾਤੀ	gujraatee
person from Panjab or of Panjabi origin	ਪੰਜਾਬੀ	panjaabee

photograph	ਫੋਟੋ	foto
pick: to ~	ਚੁੱਕਣਾ	chukknhaa
place	ਜਗ੍ਹਾ	jag-h-aa
place where clothes are washed on the bay	ਘਾਟ	ghaat
plate	ਪਲੇਟ	palet
play: to ~	ਖੇਡਣਾ	khednhaa
play (music): to ~	ਵਜਾਉਣਾ	vajaaunhaa
played: to be ~	ਵੱਜਣਾ	vajjnhaa
please	ਮਿਹਰਬਾਨੀ	miharbaanee
please have a seat	ਤਸ਼ਰੀਫ਼ ਰੱਖੋ ਜੀ	tashreef rakhkho jee
please sit down (formal)	ਬੈਠੋ ਜੀ	baitho jee
plenty	ਖੁੱਲ੍ਹਾ, ਕਾਫ਼ੀ ਕੁਝ	khullhaa, kaafee kujh
pockets	ਜੇਬਾਂ	jebaan
pool	ਸਰੋਵਰ	sarovar
population	ਅਬਾਦੀ	abaadee
possession: in ~ of	ਕੋਲ	kol
post	ਡਾਕ	daak
post: to ~	ਭੇਜਣਾ	bhejnhaa
potato(es)	ਆਲੂ	aaloo
pray: to ~	ਮਨਾਉਣਾ	manaaunhaa
present: to ~	ਪੇਸ਼, ਪੇਸ਼ ਕਰਨਾ	pesh, pesh karnaa
present: to be ~	ਸ਼ਾਮਲ	shaamal
pretty	ਸੁਹਣਾ	suhnhaa
price	ਕੀਮਤ	keemat
prick: to ~	ਰੜਕਣਾ	rarhkanhaa
print	ਛਾਪਾ	chaapaa
printed one: the ~	ਛਪਾਈਵਾਲਾ	chapaaeevaalaa
procession	ਜਲੂਸ	jaloos
procession of the groom's relatives and friends	ਬਰਾਤ	baraat
professional	ਪੇਸ਼ਾਵਰ	peshaavar
produce: to ~	ਪੇਸ਼ ਕਰਨਾ	pesh karnaa
professionally employed	ਵਿਹਾਰੀ ਨੌਕਰੀ	vihaaree naukaree
proverb	ਅਖਾਣ	akhaanh
put: to ~	ਰੱਖਣਾ	rakhkhnhaa
put on: to ~	ਲਗਾਉਣਾ	lagaaunhaa
quite a lot	ਕਾਫ਼ੀ ਕੁਝ	kaafee kujh
rain	ਬਾਰਸ਼	baarash
rainy season	ਬਰਸਾਤ	barsaat
raised	ਜੰਮਪਲ	janmpal

rate	ਕਿਰਾਇਆ	kiraaiaa
rather	ਜਿਹਾ	jihaa
read: to ~	ਪੜ੍ਹਨਾ	parh-h-naa
reasonable right	ਵਾਜਬੀ	vaajbee
receive: to ~	ਮਿਲ ਜਾਣਾ	mil jaanhaa
red	ਲਾਲ	laal
reduce: to ~	ਘੱਟ ਕਰਨਾ	ghatt karnaa
regret	ਅਫ਼ਸੋਸ	afsos
relation (marriage)	ਰਿਸ਼ਤਾ	rishtaa
relatives	ਰਿਸ਼ਤੇਦਾਰ	rishtedaar
religious procession	ਨਗਰ ਕੀਰਤਨ	nagar keertan
remembrance	ਯਾਦ	yad
rent	ਕਿਰਾਇਆ	kiraaiaa
request	ਬੇਨਤੀ	bentee
request: to ~	ਮੰਗਣਾ	mangnhaa
require	ਲੋੜ	lorh
respectable	ਪਤਵੰਤੇ	patvante
response to Muslim greeting	ਵਾਲੈਕਮ ਅੱਸਲਾਮ	vaalaikam asslaam
rest	ਅਰਾਮ	araam
return	ਵਾਪਸ	vaapas
return: to ~	ਪਰਤਣਾ	partnhaa
ride: to ~	ਚੜ੍ਹਨਾ	charh-h-naa
rides	ਝੂਟੇ	jhoote
right	ਵਾਜਬੀ	vaajbee
ritual	ਰਸਮ	rasam
roads	ਰਾਹਾਂ	raahaan
room	ਕਮਰਾ	kamraa
routes	ਰਾਹਾਂ	raahaan
rub against: to ~	ਰਗੜਕਣਾ	rarhkanhaa
rulership	ਰਾਜ	raaj
rupee	ਰੁਪਇਆ	rupaiaa
sadness	ਗ਼ਮੀ	ghamee
safe journey	ਸੁਰੱਖਿਅਤ ਸਫ਼ਰ	surakhkhiat safar
salary	ਤਨਖ਼ਾਹ	tankhaah
salty	ਨਮਕੀਨ	namkeen
same	ਇੱਕੋ	ikko
sari: the one wearing the ~	ਸਾੜ੍ਹੀਵਾਲੀ	saarh-h-eevaalee
Saturday	ਸਨਿਚਰਵਾਰ, ਹਫ਼ਤਾ	sanicharvaar, haftaa
saying	ਅਖਾਣ	akhaanh

304

English	Panjabi	Transliteration
school	ਸਕੂਲ	sakool
sea	ਸਮੁੰਦਰ	samundar
sea mail	ਸਮੁੰਦਰੀ ਡਾਕ	samundaree daak
seat	ਸੀਟ	seet
second day	ਦੂਜਾ ਦਿਨ	doojaa din
send: to ~	ਭੇਜਣਾ	bhejnhaa
see: to ~	ਵੇਖਣਾ, ਦੇਖਣਾ	vekhnhaa, dekhnhaa
selection	ਚੋਣ	chonh
serve: to ~	ਵਰਤਾਉਣਾ	vartaaunhaa
settled: to be ~	ਚੁਕਣਾ	chuknhaa
several	ਕਈ	kaee
she	ਇਹ, ਉਹ	ih, uh
shining	ਚਮਕੀਲਾ	chamkeelaa
shop	ਦੁਕਾਨ	dukaan
shopkeeper	ਦੁਕਾਨਦਾਰ	dukaandaar
show: to ~	ਦਿਖਾਉਣਾ	dikhaaunhaa
sick	ਬਿਮਾਰ	bimaar
Sikh greeting	ਸਤਿ ਸ੍ਰੀ ਅਕਾਲ	sat sree akaal
Sikh festival	ਵੈਸਾਖੀ	vaisaakhee
Sikh martial art, like fencing	ਗਤਕਾ	gatkaa
simple	ਸੌਖਾ	saukhaa
since when	ਕਿੰਨਾ ਚਿਰ ਤੋਂ	kinnaa chir ton
sing: to ~	ਗਾਣਾ	gaanhaa
singing of hymns	ਕੀਰਤਨ	keertan
sir	ਸਾਹਿਬ	saahib
sister	ਭੈਣ	bhainh
sister-in-law (brother's wife)	ਭਾਬੀ	bhaabee
sit: to ~	ਬੈਠਣਾ	baithnhaa
sitting room	ਬੈਠਕ	baithak
situation	ਸਥਿਤੀ	sathitee
slim	ਪਤਲਾ	patlaa
small	ਛੋਟਾ	chotaa
small drum	ਢੋਲਕੀ	dholkee
so much	ਐਨੇ ਸਾਰੇ	aine saare
so that	ਤਾਂ ਕਿ	taan ki
social worker	ਸਮਾਜ ਸੇਵਕ	samaaj sevak
sold: to be ~	ਵਿਕਣਾ	viknhaa
someone or another	ਕੋਈ ਨ ਕੋਈ	koee na koee
sometimes	ਕਦੀ	kadee
son	ਪੁੱਤਰ, ਬੇਟਾ	puttar, betaa
song	ਗੀਤ	geet

sorry	ਮਾਫ਼ ਕਰਨਾ, ਅਫ਼ਸੋਸ	maaf karnaa, afsos
sort of	ਜਿਹਾ	jihaa
speak	ਬੋਲਣਾ	bolnhaa
speak: to ~	ਕਹਿਣਾ	kahinhaa
special	ਖ਼ਾਸ	khaas
spicy	ਕਰਾਰਾ	karaaraa
spinning wheel	ਚਰਖਾ	charkhaa
spoon	ਚਮਚਾ	chamchaa
spring	ਬਸੰਤ	basant
stairs	ਪੌੜੀਆਂ	paurheeaan
stamp	ਟਿਕਟ	tikat
stand: to ~	ਖਲੋਣਾ, ਖੜ੍ਹਨਾ	khalonhaa, kharh-h-naa
stare: to ~	ਝਾਕਣਾ	jhaaknhaa
start: to ~	ਸ਼ੁਰੂ ਹੋਣਾ	shuroo honhaa
state of health	ਤਬੀਅਤ	tabeeat
stay: to ~	ਠਹਿਰਨਾ, ਰਹਿਣਾ	thahirnaa, rahinhaa
stitch: to ~	ਲਗਾਉਣਾ	lagaaunhaa
stomach	ਪੇਟ	pet
stood: to be ~	ਖਲੋਣਾ	khalonhaa
stringed classical musical instrument	ਸਿਤਾਰ	sitaar
struggle	ਜਦੋ ਜਹਿਦ	jado jahid
struggle for independence	ਅਜ਼ਾਦੀ ਲਈ ਜਦੋ ਜਹਿਦ	azaadee laee jado jahid
student	ਵਿਦਿਆਰਥੀ	vidiaarthee
studies	ਪੜ੍ਹਾਈ	parh-h-aaee
study: to ~	ਪੜ੍ਹਨਾ	parh-h-naa
subject	ਮਜ਼ਮੂਨ	mazmoon
subjunctive particle	ਵੇ	ve
suitable	ਯੋਗ	yog
summer	ਗਰਮੀ	garmee
Sunday	ਐਤਵਾਰ	aitvaar
sweet	ਮਿੱਠਾ	miththaa
take: to ~	ਛਕਣਾ, ਲੈਣਾ	chaknhaa, lainhaa
talkative	ਗਾਲੜੀ	gaalrhee
task	ਕੰਮ	kanm
taste	ਸੁਆਦ	suaad
tasty	ਸੁਆਦੀ	suaadee
teach: to ~	ਪੜ੍ਹਾਉਣਾ	parh-h-aaunhaa

teacher	ਅਧਿਆਪਕ	adhiaapak
telephone	ਟੈਲੀਫ਼ੋਨ	taileefon
telephone: to ~	ਟੈਲੀਫ਼ੋਨ ਕਰਨਾ	taileefon karnaa
temperature	ਬੁਖ਼ਾਰ	bukhaar
thank you	ਸ਼ੁਕਰੀਆ	shukreeaa
thanks	ਧੰਨਵਾਦ, ਮਿਹਰਬਾਨੀ	dhannvaad, miharbaanee
that	ਉਸ, ਕਿ, ਉਹ	us, ki, uh
that is why	ਇਸ ਕਰ ਕੇ	is kar ke
that, which	ਜਿਹੜਾ	jihrhaa
then	ਤਾਂ	taan
they	ਉਹ	uh
thick	ਮੋਟਾ	motaa
thin	ਪਤਲਾ	patlaa
thing	ਚੀਜ਼	cheez
things	ਸਮਾਨ	samaan
think: to ~	ਸੋਚਣਾ	sochnhaa
this	ਇਹ, ਇਸ	ih, is
Thursday	ਜੁਮੇਰਾਤ, ਵੀਰਵਾਰ	jumeraat, veervaar
time	ਸਮਾਂ, ਵਕਤ	samaan, vakat
time: this ~	ਇਸ ਵਾਰੀ	is vaaree
times	ਜ਼ਮਾਨਾ	zamaanaa
today	ਅੱਜ	ajj
together	ਇਕੱਠੇ	ikaththe
tomato(es)	ਟਮਾਟਰ	tamaatar
tomorrow	ਭਲਕ/ਭਲਕੇ, ਕੱਲ੍ਹ	bhalak/bhalke, kallh
too much	ਜ਼ਿਆਦਾ	ziaadaa
tourist	ਸੈਲਾਨੀ	sailaanee
towards	ਵੱਲ	vall
train	ਗੱਡੀ	gaddee
travel: to ~	ਸਫ਼ਰ ਕਰਨਾ, ਫਿਰਨਾ	safar karnaa, phirnaa
travel around: to ~	ਘੁੰਮਣਾ ਫਿਰਨਾ	ghunmnhaa phirnaa
travellers	ਸਵਾਰੀਆਂ	savaareeaan
triangular stuffed pastry	ਸਮੋਸਾ	samosaa
trouble	ਤਕਲੀਫ਼	takleef
true, truth	ਸੱਚ	sachch
try: to ~	ਕੋਸ਼ਿਸ਼ ਕਰਨਾ	koshish karnaa
Tuesday	ਮੰਗਲਵਾਰ	mangalvaar
turn	ਵਾਰੀ	vaaree
turn around: to ~	ਮੁੜਨਾ	murhnaa
turnip	ਸ਼ਲਗਮ	shalgam

English	Punjabi	Transliteration
TV	ਟੀ ਵੀ	tee vee
twenty	ਵੀਹ (੨੦)	veeh
Uganda	ਯੂਗੰਡਾ	yoogandaa
uncle (father's brother)	ਚਾਚਾ ਜੀ	chaachaa jee
understand: to ~	ਸਮਝਣਾ	samjhnhaa
upon	ਦੇ ਉੱਪਰ	de uppar
upon: to be ~	ਚੜੂਨਾ	charhhnaa
uprooted: to be ~	ਉਖੜਨਾ	ukhrhnaa
Urdu	ਉਰਦੂ	urdoo
use: to ~	ਵਰਤਣਾ	vartnhaa
vacant	ਖ਼ਾਲੀ	khaalee
values	ਕਦਰਾਂ	kadraan
vanish: to ~	ਮਿਟਣਾ	mitnhaa
vegetable	ਸਬਜ਼ੀ	sabzee
vehicle	ਗੱਡੀ	gaddee
very	ਬਹੁਤ, ਬੜੀ	bahut, barhee
very good	ਬਹੁਤ ਅੱਛਾ	bahut achchaa
very nice	ਬਹੁਤ ਸੁਹਣਾ	bahut suhnhaa
via	ਰਾਹੀਂ	raaheen
village-like	ਪੇਂਡੂ	pendoo
villager	ਪਿੰਡਵਾਲਾ	pindvaalaa
visa	ਵੀਜ਼ਾ	veezaa
visible: to be ~	ਦਿਸਨਾ	disnhaa
visitor	ਦਰਸ਼ਕ	darshak
volunteer	ਸੇਵਾਦਾਰ	sevaadaar
wait: to ~	ਉਡੀਕਣਾ	udeeknhaa
walk: to ~	ਤੁਰਨਾ	turnaa
want	ਲੋੜ	lorh
want: to ~	ਚਾਹੁਣਾ	chaahunhaa
wash: to ~	ਧੋਣਾ	dhonhaa
washerman	ਧੋਬੀ	dhobee
waste time: to ~	ਜ਼ਾਇਆ ਕਰਨਾ	zaaiaa karnaa
watch: to ~	ਦੇਖਣਾ	dekhnhaa
watch over	ਭਲਾ	bhalaa
way (direction)	ਪਾਸੇ	paase
way (style)	ਤਰ੍ਹਾਂ	tar-h-aan
we	ਅਸੀਂ	aseen
we all	ਅਸੀਂ ਸਾਰੇ	aseen saare
weakness	ਕਮਜ਼ੋਰੀ	kamzoree

English	Panjabi	Transliteration
wealthy people	ਪੈਸੇਵਾਲੇ	paisevaale
wedding	ਵਿਆਹ	viaah
Wednesday	ਬੁੱਧਵਾਰ	budhdhvaar
week	ਸਪਤਾਹ, ਹਫ਼ਤਾ	saptaah, haftaa
weekend	ਹਫ਼ਤੇ ਦੇ ਅਖ਼ੀਰ	hafte de akheer
welcome	ਜੀ ਆਇਆਂ ਨੂੰ	jee aaiaan noon
well done	ਸ਼ਾਬਾਸ਼	shaabaash
west	ਪੱਛਮ	pachcham
what?	ਕੀ	kee
what time?	ਕਿੰਨੇ ਵਜੇ	kinne vaje
when?	ਕਦੋਂ	kadon
where?	ਕਿੱਥੇ, ਜਿੱਥੇ	kiththe, jiththe
which?	ਕਿਹੜਾ	kihrhaa
which (oblique)	ਜਿਸ	jis
white	ਗੋਰੀ	goree
who?	ਕੌਣ	kaunh
why?	ਕਿਉਂ	kiun
wide	ਚੌੜਾ	chaurhaa
wife	ਪਤਨੀ	patnee
winter	ਸਰਦੀ	sardee
wise	ਸਿਆਣਾ	siaanhaa
with	ਕੋਲ	kol
with me	ਮੇਰੇ ਨਾਲ	mere naal
without	ਤੋਂ ਬਿਨਾਂ/ਬਗ਼ੈਰ	ton binaan/baghair
woman from Lahore	ਲਾਹੌਰਵਾਲੀ ਔਰਤ	laahaurvaalee aurat
women's folk dance	ਗਿੱਧਾ	gidhdhaa
work	ਕੰਮ	kanm
work: to ~	ਕੰਮ ਕਰਨਾ	kanm karnaa
world	ਦੁਨੀਆਂ	duneeaan
worry	ਫ਼ਿਕਰ	fikar
write: to ~	ਲਿਖਣਾ	likhnhaa
wrong	ਗ਼ਲਤ	ghalat
year	ਸਾਲ	saal
yes (polite)	ਹਾਂ ਜੀ	haan jee
yesterday	ਕੱਲ੍ਹ	kallh
you (formal)	ਤੁਸੀਂ	tuseen
you (informal)	ਤੂੰ	toon
your (formal)	ਤੁਹਾਡਾ	tuhaadaa
your (informal)	ਤੇਰਾ	teraa
youth	ਨੌਜੁਆਨ, ਯੁਵਕ	naujuaan, yuvak

Taking it further

If you have enjoyed working your way through *Complete Panjabi* and are interested in enhancing your listening, speaking and reading skills, there are a number of different ways in which you can build upon your existing knowledge and skills.

There are a range of different sources of information and places where you can look for improving your understanding of Panjabi language and culture without having to venture too far away. Some satellite radio stations offer exclusively Panjabi programming, sometimes 24 hours a day, while others have specific slots given to Panjabi programmes:

- Desi Radio: **www.desiradio.org.uk**
- Panjab Radio: **www.panjabradio.co.uk**
- Akash Radio: **www.akashradio.com**
- BBC Asian network: **www.bbc.co.uk/asiannetwork/**

These radio stations are available on the internet, so if you have access you can listen anywhere in the world. There are also a number of newspapers, both printed as well as on the internet. In the UK, *Des Pardes* and *The Punjab Times* are printed weeklies. The most popular newspaper in Panjab itself is *The Ajit* (**www.ajitjalandhar. com/**). A dual language paper from the UK, the *Sikh Times,* is available at **www.sikhtimes.com**.

If you want to get a greater insight into Panjabi poetry and literary matters more generally, then **www.apnaorg.com** is the best resource available. There is also a feast of literature on **www.likhari.com**. Many of these sites require you to download Panjabi fonts. There are many free fonts available on the internet as well as commercial packages. The most advanced software package in Panjabi, 'Akhar', includes a spellchecker and a converter for the many fonts (**www.akhar.net**).

Music and television are also a good source of exposure to Panjabi culture and language. There are a number of digital/satellite television channels, including Sikh Channel, PTC and Zee Punjab/ Alpha ETC Punjabi, which offer a rich view of Panjabi society, religion and culture. Broadcasts of music concerts, news and current affairs programmes are revealing of some of the current concerns of Panjab and Panjabis. Films, DVDs and music CDs are widely available in South Asian shopping areas too.

There are a growing number of Panjabi teaching and learning aides and books available from select sources. The Panjabi Language Development Board (PLDB) in Birmingham, UK, produces and distributes such materials, including dual-language posters and workbooks for all levels (**www.panjabilang.org**). DTF (also in Birmingham, UK) offers an excellent mail order service (**www. dtfbooks.com**). Panjabi University, Patiala (India) hosts the best online learning materials in Panjabi at **www.advancedcentrepunjabi. org/intro1.asp**. There is also a very well-made song of the Panjabi alphabet at **www.maa.com.au**.

Panjabi is no longer a 'foreign' language where Panjabi communities have settled in large numbers outside India, namely in the UK, Canada, the USA, East Africa, Australia and Singapore. This offers opportunities to brush up on your listening and spoken skills, even outside Panjab. Many people from India and Pakistan living in different parts of the world speak Panjabi. In fact, the largest population of native Panjabi speakers live in Pakistan. Our point is that when we look at the geographical spread of its speakers, inside and outside Panjab, Panjabi is very much a living language.

Visiting 'Indian' or 'Pakistani' restaurants and shopping areas such as the Broadway in Southall (UK), Soho Road in Birmingham (UK), Diwan Street in Chicago (USA) or Jackson Heights, New York (USA) can provide a good opportunity to enjoy food and the experience of being in a Panjabi context, while also hearing and engaging in conversation with Panjabi speakers. Visiting a **gurdwara** (Sikh temple) is another place where you would come across native speakers. Congregations are generally very welcoming to new people and outsiders, Sikh and non-Sikh, who wish to visit the temple where **langar** (free community kitchen cuisine) is served to all, irrespective of religion, caste or creed. Of course, to completely immerse yourself in the language, a trip to Panjab (India or Pakistan) would be the best opportunity to improve your skills.

Grammar and verb index

Numbers refer to units.